Essential
Open Source
Toolset

Essential Open Source Toolset

Programming with Eclipse, JUnit, CVS, Bugzilla, Ant, Tcl/Tk and more

Andreas Zeller, Saarland University, Germany
Jens Krinke, University of Hagen, Germany

John Wiley & Sons, Ltd

Other Wiley Editorial Offices

John Wiley & Sons Inc., 111 River Street, Hoboken, NJ 07030, USA

Jossey-Bass, 989 Market Street, San Francisco, CA 94103-1741, USA

Wiley-VCH Verlag GmbH, Boschstr. 12, D-69469 Weinheim, Germany

John Wiley & Sons Australia Ltd, 33 Park Road, Milton, Queensland 4064, Australia

John Wiley & Sons (Asia) Pte Ltd, 2 Clementi Loop #02-01, Jin Xing Distripark, Singapore 129809

John Wiley & Sons Canada Ltd, 22 Worcester Road, Etobicoke, Ontario, Canada M9W 1L1

Wiley also publishes its books in a variety of electronic formats. Some content that appears in print may not be available in electronic books.

Library of Congress Cataloging-in-Publication Data:

Zeller, Andreas.
  Essential open source toolset : Programming with Eclipse, JUnit, CVS,
Bugzilla, Ant, Tcl/Tk and more / Andreas Zeller, Jens Krinke.
    p. cm.
  Includes bibliographical references and index.
  ISBN 0-470-84445-0 (pbk. : alk. paper)
1. Computer software – Development. 2. Open source software. I. Krinke,
Jens. II. Title.
  QA76.76.D47Z45 2004
  005.1 – dc22
                                        2004026271

British Library Cataloguing in Publication Data

A catalogue record for this book is available from the British Library

ISBN 0-470-84445-0

Partly translated by Cybertechnics Ltd, Sheffield. Typeset by the authors and Laserwords Private Limited, Chennai, India
Printed and bound in Great Britain by Biddles Ltd, King's Lynn
This book is printed on acid-free paper responsibly manufactured from sustainable forestry
in which at least two trees are planted for each one used for paper production.

Contents

Preface .... **xi**

1   Introduction **1**
1.1   Structure of the book 1
1.2   Styles and conventions 2
1.3   Using the tools under Unix and Linux 3
1.4   Using the tools under Windows 3
1.5   Literature 4
1.6   The authors 4
1.7   Acknowledgments 5

I   Version Control   7

2   Managing changes using DIFF and PATCH **9**
2.1   Introduction 9
2.2   Determining differences with DIFF 10
2.3   Applying changes with PATCH 13
2.4   Integrating changes manually 14
2.5   Automatically integrating changes 16
2.6   Syntactical and semantic integration 19
2.7   How DIFF works 21

3   Revision management using RCS **27**
3.1   Introduction 27
3.2   Saving and restoring revisions 28
3.3   Branches and variants 30
3.4   Locks 31
3.5   Making changes 32
3.6   Change log and keywords 33
3.7   How RCS stores revisions 35
3.8   Innovations and further developments 39

4   Parallel program development with CVS............. **43**
4.1   From components to software systems.................... 43
4.2   Versioning file hierarchies with CVS 45
4.3   How CVS works 49
4.4   Parallel program development 51
4.5   Conflicts and arrangements 53
4.6   Extensions and Alternatives 54

Exercises I **61**

II   Processing Input   65

5   Lexical analysis using LEX **67**
5.1   Processing input...................................... 67
5.2   Finite automata 68
5.3   Regular expressions................................... 69
5.4   LEX – a scanner generator 72
5.5   LEX specification 73
5.6   Refinements of rule composition........................ 77
5.7   Generating scanners 81

6   Syntactical analysis with YACC **85**
6.1   Introduction 85
6.2   Describing input using grammars 86
6.3   YACC specification 88
6.4   Binding LEX to YACC................................. 94
6.5   How a YACC parser works 95
6.6   Conflicts and how to resolve them 97
6.7   Explicit precedence declarations 100
6.8   GLR parser 101

7   Lexical and syntactic analysis using ANTLR **107**
7.1   Lexical analysis 107
7.2   Syntactic analysis 112
7.3   How recursive descent works 113

Exercises II... **119**

III   Building Programs   121

8   Building programs with MAKE **123**
8.1   Building programs out of components 123

8.2   Incremental construction 124
8.3   How MAKE works 125
8.4   Makefiles in practice 127
8.5   Determining dependencies 133
8.6   Additions and extensions 135
8.7   ANT: A framework for program construction 137

9   Configuring software automatically with AUTOCONF. 143
9.1   Introduction 143
9.2   Explicit variant management 144
9.3   Creating variants from templates 144
9.4   Determining properties 147
9.5   Using configuration scripts 150
9.6   Creating configuration scripts 152
9.7   Further automation possibilities 154
9.8   Variant management with RCS or CVS? 155

10   Documenting programs with JAVADOC 159
10.1   Program documentation 159
10.2   Documenting with JAVADOC 162
10.3   Documenting with DOXYGEN 166
10.4   Literate Programming 168

Exercises III 173

IV   Prototyping   175

11   Creating prototypes using Tcl/Tk 177
11.1   Prototypes and script languages 177
11.2   Tcl: Commands and scripts 179
11.3   Extending Tcl itself 183
11.4   Tk: Buttons and commands 185
11.5   Tcl/Tk as a prototype language 190
11.6   Other script languages 191

Exercises IV 199

V   Testing and Debugging   203

12   Software tests with DEJAGNU 205
12.1   My program ran yesterday – will it run today? 205
12.2   Programmed dialogs with EXPECT 206

12.3 EXPECT in regression tests 209
12.4 DEJAGNU – a framework for regression tests 212
12.5 Testing programs with graphical user interaction 215

13   Component tests with JUNIT **221**
13.1 From system tests to component tests 221
13.2 Validating program states 221
13.3 Executing component tests 223
13.4 JUNIT test cases 223
13.5 Setting up fixture 227
13.6 Organizing test cases 228
13.7 A test-driven development process 229

14   Tracking problems with BUGZILLA **235**
14.1 Tracking and managing problems 235
14.2 Reporting problems 236
14.3 BUGZILLA – a problem tracking system 238
14.4 Classifying problems 238
14.5 Processing problems 240
14.6 Managing problem tracking 243
14.7 Relating problems and tests 244

15   Debugging with GDB and DDD **249**
15.1 Systematic debugging 249
15.2 Setting up and testing hypotheses 251
15.3 Debugging with DDD: An example 256
15.4 Other debugger functionalities 266
15.5 How GDB and DDD work 268
15.6 Validating memory 272
15.7 Avoiding errors 275

Exercises V **279**

VI   Program Analysis   **281**

16   Profiling using GPROF and GCOV **283**
16.1 Improved performance due to profiling 283
16.2 General runtime measurement using TIME 283
16.3 Program profiles with GPROF 284
16.4 Coverage measurement with GCOV 288
16.5 How GPROF and GCOV work 290
16.6 Testing with GPROF and GCOV 291

17   Checking style with CHECKSTYLE **295**
17.1   Programming guidelines 295
17.2   CHECKSTYLE usage 296
17.3   Creating a new check 297

18   Static program analysis with LINT **301**
18.1   Introduction 301
18.2   Type checking using LINT 301
18.3   Data flow analysis 304
18.4   Specifications 308
18.5   Annotations in practice 314

19   Program slicing using UNRAVEL **317**
19.1   Slices and data flow 317
19.2   Program slicing using UNRAVEL 318
19.3   Program dependence graphs 319
19.4   Set operations using slices 324

Exercises VI **329**

VII   Integrated Environments   **333**

20   Integrated development with ECLIPSE 3.0 . . . . **335**
20.1   Projects in ECLIPSE 336
20.2   The user interface 337
20.3   Working in teams 339
20.4   The JAVA editor of ECLIPSE 342
20.5   Program comprehension with JDT 343
20.6   Refactoring 347
20.7   Debugging with ECLIPSE 348
20.8   The design of ECLIPSE 350
20.9   A sample plug-in: the ASTView 354
20.10   Automation and intuition 358

Exercises VII **363**

Bibliography **371**

Index **383**

Preface

Programming is difficult. But the problems that arise in the *areas associated* with programming are even more difficult – problems such as:

- ❏ How can I structure my program so that several developers can work on it without any interference?

- ❏ What do I have to do in order to automate the building of my program?

- ❏ How should I create a program that can run on various machines?

- ❏ I need to do a prototype for my customers quickly. How do I do this?

- ❏ How can I test my program automatically and overcome errors efficiently?

- ❏ How do I increase the performance of my program?

These topics are all addressed in programming courses or textbooks. This is where this book can be useful: we introduce *programming tools* to provide solutions to problems in the programming environment – tools for version control, for program building and configuration, for automatic testing, and for program analysis – , in short, tools for problems, which occur every day in the professional development of software.

We have predominantly chosen "traditional" tools from the area of UNIX and LINUX. For each tool,

- ❏ we will introduce the *specific problems*,

- ❏ we will show how the tool is *used*, and

- ❏ we will describe the *technical principles*.

The last point, how does the tool actually work?, has played a significant part in our selection: the *source code* of all tools is freely available, so everyone can understand the way it works, and in the *operation via command lines*, the basic functionality is completely transparent. When available, we will also introduce *graphical user interfaces*; ECLIPSE, which is dealt with in Chapter 20, integrates almost all the tools we discuss here into a programming environment. This book is thus suitable

- ❏ for *students of computer science* and would-be programmers who wish to learn how to use typical programming tools,

- ❏ for *UNIX and LINUX programmers* who wish to gain a thorough knowledge of the most important tools of their operating system, as well as

- ❏ for *advanced software developers* who wish to get to know the technical framework of their tools.

We assume that you are currently able to program; you should definitely be able to handle your programming environment. However, after reading this book, we would like you to be able to use other tools – in order to work *more confidently*, *better*, and *more efficiently*.

So, have fun reading!

Hagen/Saarbrücken, Fall 2004

Andreas Zeller
Jens Krinke

1 Introduction

1.1 Structure of the book

The structure of this book follows the order in which the tools are used. The book consists of seven parts, each of them dealing with a particular topic. The sections are independent of each other, so you can choose the one you prefer. Each chapter discusses a specific tool.

❑ We begin with the tools used for *version control*, which is typically required at the beginning of a project. First of all, any developer has to identify and manage *changes*, as described in Chapter 2, Managing changes with DIFF and PATCH. After this, we will show how these changes can be *controlled* – in single files (Chapter 3, Managing revisions with RCS), and in directories (Chapter 4, Parallel program development using CVS).

Version control

❑ In fact, writing programs is also a topic of this book – at least, if the programs are created *automatically*. In Chapter 5, Lexical analysis using LEX; Chapter 6, Syntactical analysis using YACC; and Chapter 7, Lexical and syntactic analysis using ANTLR, we explain how to generate programs for *input processing* from abstract structure descriptions.

Input processing

❑ After the coding comes the *program construction* – a finished product is generated from the manually created source code. Chapter 8, Building programs with MAKE, shows how the construction of a program can be automated and what steps are necessary to achieve this. Chapter 9, Configuring software automatically using AUTO-CONF, supplements this with techniques for automatic *porting* of programs to new environments. Finally, Chapter 10, Documenting programs with JAVADOC, highlights methods and tools to generate the documentation out of the program code – and, thus, keep it always up-to-date.

Program building

❑ One major aim in programming is the construction of *prototypes*. Chapter 11, Creating prototypes using Tcl/Tk, gives an introduction

Prototypes

to *Tcl*, a simple script language, and to *Tk*, a library for creating graphical-interactive programs quickly. The languages PERL and PYTHON are also addressed here.

Testing and debugging

❏ After being written, the program has to be *tested*. Chapter 12, Software tests using DEJAGNU, explains how to *automatically test* entire programs; Chapter 13, Component tests with JUNIT, shows how to test individual program components. If a failure occurs – during testing or at the user's site – , it must be documented and tracked. This process is supported by *problem tracking systems*, discussed in Chapter 14, Tracking problems with BUGZILLA. Finally, the defect must be found and fixed – for instance, using a *debugger* from Chapter 15, Searching bugs using GDB and DDD.

Program analysis

❏ The tools for the *static program analysis* provide the necessary basic knowledge of programs. Chapter 16, Profiling using GPROF and GCOV, explains how to handle *performance problems*. Chapter 17, Checking style with CHECKSTYLE, shows how to check whether programs satisfy specific style requirements. In Chapter 18, Static program analysis using LINT, we describe how to show noninitialized variables using *data flow analysis*. Chapter 19, Program slicing using UNRAVEL, explains how to determine *slices* – statements that influence the value of a variable at a particular place in the code.

Integrated environments

❏ Finally, we want to make the tools available in an *integrated environment*. Chapter 20, Integrated development using ECLIPSE, introduces the universal development environment ECLIPSE, which integrates the program tools into a *graphical interface*.

At the end of each chapter there are:

❏ *concepts* as a summary of the content,

❏ *exercises* that enable you to test your knowledge,

❏ *references* to deepen your knowledge.

Furthermore, at the end of each section there is a separate section, Practical exercises, which lets you try out the tools in practice. You should work through these exercises in sequence.

1.2 Styles and conventions

In this book, we will use the universal notation:

❏ Concepts are highlighted in *italics*.

❏ *Programs* and *system names* are written in CAPITAL LETTERS.

❏ Code pieces and data are in `typewriter` font.

❏ In the examples for user interaction, outputs are written in `type-writer font` and user input are written in **`bold typewriter font`**. The "$" character stands for the UNIX prompt, and the "_" (underline) character stands for the input cursor.

The term *the user* has a general and gender-neutral meaning.

1.3   Using the tools under Unix and Linux

All examples in this book were tested under UNIX and should run on any UNIX variant. The easiest way to run the examples is to install LINUX on your PC – the GNU tools are included in every LINUX distribution. On a system running on UNIX, in addition to the GNU tools, you can also find their UNIX distributions, which differ in functionality and robustness.

You can obtain the source codes of the GNU tools from the *Free Software Foundation* at:

$$\texttt{http://www.gnu.org/}$$

In general, you have to configure, compile, and install these tools manually, which sounds harder than it seems – in general, the single command `./configure; make install` suffices.

1.4   Using the tools under Windows

The tools described in this book are also normally available in the WINDOWS operating system. (Indeed, most graphical programming environments built using the command line tools in this book are based on WINDOWS.) In Chapter 20 on ECLIPSE, we will explain how these tools work independently of the operating system. This integrated environment is based on the programming tools introduced in this book – moreover, some of these frequently used tools such as DIFF, RCS, and MAKE are integral components.

All other tools are also available under WINDOWS. The CYGWIN project offers a POSIX interface on WINDOWS and includes all GNU tools that support this interface.

Many of the tools introduced here are not only available as ported versions but are also actively supported under WINDOWS.

1.5   Literature

At the end of each chapter is a "References" section, which refers to further material on the contents of each section.

If after reading this book you are interested in learning the basic principles of software building, we recommend the following books.

❑ As general textbooks about the context of *programming in the small*, we suggest the books by McConnell (1993) and Kernighan and Pike (1999). Both books describe the general principles in the practice of individual software building.

❑ Among the textbooks on *programming in the large*, we recommend *Lehrbuch der Software-Technik* by Balzert (1996, 1997). Not only is it very comprehensive, it is also instructive and refers to the state of the practical software development. Unfortunately, this book is currently available in German only – an English translation is underway.

❑ We also recommend the book by Sommerville (1996b), which provides a good, informal overview. Finally, the textbook by Ghezzi et al. (1991) deals with the basic principles of software technology.

All these works focus on general principles of software construction; concrete tools are discussed as natural instantiations of these principles. The work by Balzert also includes a CD-ROM with useful tools.

1.6   The authors

Andreas Zeller is a professor for software engineering at Saarland University, Saarbrücken, Germany; his research focuses on program analysis and program comprehension.

Jens Krinke works as an assistant professor at Hagen University, Germany; he is an expert in program analysis and software reengineering. His field of research focuses on the analysis of safety-relevant software.

The ECLIPSE chapter was written by Thomas Zimmermann, a PhD student at Saarland University. His research focuses on the analysis of version histories, integrated in the ECLIPSE development environment.

The authors would be pleased to receive feedback! You can get in touch with both authors via the e-mail address:

toolset@wiley.co.uk

2 Managing changes using DIFF and PATCH

2.1 Introduction

The only constant in software development is change. A number of people are involved in a typical software project; some to create software components, some to alter and replace them, and all of them have the same aim. A large software product consists of thousands of such components that have been developed and maintained by hundreds or even thousands of people, which are usually distributed between several locations. But even if only one person develops a program, whatever has been changed or extended must also be comprehended – in short: *Why did my program work yesterday and not today?*

The organization and control of software changes like these is generally called *Software configuration management* or SCM for short. *Configuration management* is the common task of organizing and controlling the evolution of technical systems. Software configuration management is therefore the use of *configuration management in software development*. At the origin of configuration management, Tichy (1995) wrote:

Software configuration management

> Configuration management (CM) is the discipline of organizing and controlling evolving systems. For hardware systems, CM has been an established field since the 1950s. It was initially developed in the aerospace industry as an approach for guaranteeing reproducibility of spacecraft. The problem was that spacecraft underwent numerous, inadequately documented engineering changes during development. Moreover, the prototypes embodying the changes were usually expended during flight test. Consequently, neither accurate plans nor prototypes were available for replicating successful designs. Configuration management was thus born out of the need to track what designers and engineers developed during the course of a project.

Classical configuration management facilitates a strict *identification* of technical components and demands a *fixed procedure* for the documentation and approval of changes. These procedures are also required in SCM. The special feature of SCM is that all the components (software components) are accessible for examination directly and immediately on the computer, which substantially simplifies an *automation* of SCM. On the other hand, nothing is as easy to change as software, and in contrast to technical systems, in software even the smallest change can make the whole system useless. Therefore, SCM is a precondition for every professional software development.

In this and the following two chapters, we will introduce the basic tools for the automation of SCM. As the central concept of SCM is *changes*, we will start off with the tools that actually identify and apply changes automatically. In the following chapters, we will present the RCS and CVS tools, which organize these changes, in order to enable controlled software development.

2.2   Determining differences with DIFF

Changes

Version

DIFF

Commands

The work of software developers can be described as the creation and distribution of *changes*. However, the changes as such are rarely visible; only in editors with an Undo/Redo function can the effects of changes be undone or redone. Otherwise, the result of a change is a new *version* of the document; the changes as such are only described afterward by comparing different versions of a document.

This is precisely the task of DIFF. The DIFF program determines the difference between two text files *A* and *B* and produces a sequence of *commands*, which applied to *A* produce *B*. As DIFF works line by line, a command can either *insert* or *delete* specific line sequences. An insertion and deletion in the same area is summarized by DIFF as a *change* of a line sequence.

As an example, we will look at the two text files, be and ae, which show a text transformed from British spelling to American spelling. Example 2.1 shows the British variant:

Example 2.1
The be *text file in British spelling*

```
1 The change impact was minimised
2 by localising the most
3 important variables,
4 saving approximately
5 1,500 pounds.
```

Example 2.2 shows the American variant:

```
1 The change impact was minimized
2 by localizing the most
3 important variables,
4 saving approximately
5 1,500 pounds.
6 (1,500 pounds are approximately
7 2,100 US$)
```

Example 2.2
The ae *text file in
American spelling*

Let us use DIFF to determine the differences between be and ae. In its simplest form, DIFF contains the names of the two files to be compared as arguments:

```
$ diff be ae
1,2c1,2
< The change impact was minimised
< by localising the most
---
> The change impact was minimized
> by localizing the most
5a6,7
> (1,500 pounds are approximately
> 2,100 US$)
$ _
```

Calling DIFF

The sequence of commands issued by DIFF here should be applied to be to create ae – in short, the difference between be and ae. Every command can be seen as "a chunk of differences". The sequence of commands is read like this:

❏ The first command "1,2c1,2" means that the first two lines of the first file (be) should be *changed*; the letter "c" here stands for "change".

Changing lines

DIFF outputs the corresponding lines after the command: lines starting with "<" are removed from be and are replaced with the lines from ae, starting with ">".

In general, a command in the form of "$n_1, m_1 c n_2, m_2$" generally means that the lines n_1 to m_1 of the first file are replaced by lines n_2 to m_2 of the second file.

If one of the changed areas is only one line long, m_1 or m_2 can be omitted. In this case, $m_1 = n_1$ or $m_2 = n_2$ is assumed.

Appending lines ❏ The third command "5a6,7" means that after line 5 of the first file, lines 6 and 7 from the second file (ae) should be *appended*; "a" stands for "append". The newly inserted lines are output.

In general, a command in the form of "n_1an_2, m_2" means that after line n_1 of the first file, the lines n_2 to m_2 of the second file should be inserted.

In addition to the change command ("c") and the append command ("a"), there is also the *delete command*, which is shown in the following example. We simply mix up the arguments and thus make DIFF generate commands that change ae into be:

```
$ diff ae be
1,2c1,2
< The change impact was minimized
< by localizing the most
---
> The change impact was minimised
> by localising the most
6,7d5
< (1,500 pounds are approximately
< 2,100 US$)
$ _
```

Deleting lines Here, the last command "6,7d5" means that rows 6 and 7 of the first file (ae) should be deleted to create the second file (be); the letter "d" stands for delete.

In general, a command in the form of "n_1, m_1dn_2" states that lines n_1 to m_1 in the first file should be deleted; n_2 had been their position in the second file, if they had not been deleted. As you can see, the DIFF output is symmetrical: mixing the arguments up causes all "<" lines to be replaced by ">" lines as well as the "d" command being replaced by "a".

DIFF in its simplest form is only used on two files. But DIFF can also determine differences between entire *directories*. The option "-r" (for "recursive") is used for this purpose. The call

```
$ diff -r olddir newdir
```

determines the difference between all files (with the same name) in the directories olddir and newdir,olddir/a.txt and newdir/a.txt, olddir/b.txt and newdir/b.txt and so on. Files that only exist in one of the two directories are indicated with the note Only in *directory*: *file name*.

2.3 Applying changes with PATCH

The DIFF output has to be read and interpreted by humans first in order to make sense. But it may happen that changes must be *committed* on multiple copies of a text file – for instance, because several people work on different copies of the same file and communicate their alterations in the form of DIFF output. This step, the commit or *applying* of changes, can also be automated. To illustrate this automation, we use the software tool PATCH as an example.

Using changes

PATCH takes a DIFF output and applies its commands on a file; inserting, deleting, and changing lines as mandated by the commands. For instance, we can apply the changes between be and ae from Section 2.2 to create a copy of be in American spelling.

PATCH

Here is a small sample session using PATCH that illustrates the usage. First, we create a file called DIFFS, which contains the differences between be and ae as DIFF output.

```
$ diff be ae > DIFFS
$ _
```

This DIFFS file can now be distributed to other developers or customers. If they want to commit the changes from your copy of be, they can enter:

```
$ patch --verbose --backup < DIFFS
Hmm...  Looks like a normal diff to me...
File to patch: be
Patching file old using Plan A...
Hunk #1 succeeded at 1.
Hunk #2 succeeded at 6.
done
$ _
```

PATCH call

Because the DIFF output does not contain the filename, the user has to enter the filename herself. After this step, PATCH applies the changes in DIFFS on be, with the result that be is now identical to ae. The --backup option ensures that PATCH saves the former content of be in the newly established file be.orig. (Old PATCH versions that do not understand the --verbose and --backup options are verbose and make backups by default.)

If a DIFF output contains changes from several files (for instance, because the difference between *directories* had been determined), PATCH also can process and apply them. The PATCH option "-p" ensures that files will be found in the correct subdirectories. (Without "-p", PATCH will search exclusively in the current directory.)

As shown, changes can easily be determined and distributed with DIFF and PATCH. As described so far, the procedure is well suited if changes are created in a central place and then distributed to customers, as shown in Figure 2.1.

Figure 2.1
Distribution of changes. The developer creates new changes and distributes them to his customers who apply them to their code basis.

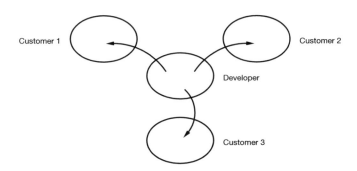

As customers and developers have a common code basis, only changes need to be distributed, which minimizes communication. This method of distribution is particularly suitable for *corrections* on the client side. The changes are then called *corrections* or *patches* and are typically automated and simple to access.

Corrections

Changes in binary file

In the distribution of patches as discussed here, we have assumed that the file to be changed is a text file, and that a PATCH-like program can be distributed to customers. If the customer has only the executable program instead of the source code, the differences between *binary files* must be calculated by special algorithms. These differences are then distributed to customers, along with a program that applies these binary differences. As small differences in the source code lead to huge differences in the converted program, it is often more reasonable to distribute the complete binary files instead of the differences.

2.4 Integrating changes manually

The distribution of changes, as illustrated in Figure 2.1, will only work if the code basis of developers and customers is kept synchronized. This means that customers apply all the changes made by the developers and that they do not have to create changes themselves. This is often the case when fixes are distributed, but is not suitable for exchanging changes between developers.

Integration of changes

In fact, the situation in practice is rather that several developers work on the same code basis and continually exchange changes, with more or less coordination. Therefore, developers, to a certain extent, have to apply changes from other developers in their own code basis, even if they have just made changes to their own code. The problem of applying changes from different sources at the same time is the problem of *change integration*.

Figure 2.2 shows the problem of integration.

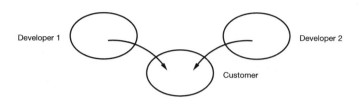

Figure 2.2
Integration of changes. The customer takes on alterations from developer 1 as well as from developer 2.

The customer wants to update her code basis to the most recent version. Developer 1 as well as developer 2 have made some changes. The customer has to *integrate* the changes to check whether the changes are compatible.

Consider the following situation as an example: The be file has been changed to American spelling in the ae variant. In addition, another writer has expanded the content of be to a new file be2. (Example 2.3).

```
1 The change impact was minimised
2 by localising the most
3 important variables,
4 saving approximately
5 1,500 pounds.
6 All the developers
7 were deeply satisfied.
```

Example 2.3
Text file be2 *in British spelling*

We now face the task of integrating the changes from be to ae with the changes from be to be2 in order to create a version containing both alterations – that is, a file in American spelling containing the addition about the developers' satisfaction. There are two ways of doing this:

Two-way integration determines the difference between the two new files (in our case, ae and be2); the user decides interactively what (and from which version) should be present in the integrated version.

Three-way integration also considers the original version (i.e., be). If a piece of text is changed in only *one* of the two files, the changes can automatically be applied. Otherwise, the user must manually integrate the changes.

First of all, we will take a closer look at the (interactive) two-way integration. The software tool SDIFF displays the differences between two files

SDIFF

in two columns. If it is called with the option "-o *file*", the user can create an integrated version *file* and can choose which version to use for every difference, from either file 1 or 2. In Example 2.4, the file ae3 is created on the basis of the integration of ae and be2. Differing sections are marked with a |. Using the "%" prompt, SDIFF queries the user for a decision which side should be taken on in the final version. In our case, the left version is preferred with "1". For the final changes, we call up a text editor with "eb", which contains both versions.

Example 2.4
Two-way integration
with SDIFF

```
$ sdiff -o ae3 ae be2
The change impact was minimized    | The change impact was minimised
by localizing the most             | by localising
the most
%1
important variables,                 important variables,
saving approximately                 saving approximately
1,500 pounds.                        1,500 pounds.
(1,500 pounds are approximately    | All the developers
2,100 US$)                         | were deeply satisfied.
%eb
$ _
```

Using the text editor, we simply place both versions one after the other, so that ae3 is displayed as shown in Example 2.5.

Example 2.5
Integrated text file
ae3

```
1 The change impact was minimized
2 by localizing the most
3 important variables,
4 saving approximately
5 1,500 pounds.
6 (1,500 pounds are approximately
7 2,100 US$)
8 All the developers
9 were deeply satisfied.
```

Although SDIFF is a rather rudimentary tool, its basic mechanisms are used in numerous integration tools. One of the more prominent examples is the EDIFF package of the EMACS editor, where differences are graphically highlighted and numerous options for editing and integrating changes interactively are available.

EDIFF

2.5 Automatically integrating changes

The integration of changes can be considerably simplified if the original version is taken into account as well as the changed files. This *three-way integration* can be done using the PATCH program, which we got to know

Three-way
integration

in Section 2.3 and that applies the changes created by DIFF to the files. The idea for the integration of changes consists of PATCH running on an *already changed* file instead of the original file. In detail: first, the DIFF output from be to ae is applied on be by PATCH, converting be to ae. Then, DIFF applies the difference between be and be2 to ae (even though the second DIFF output actually refers to the original file be).

Here is an example. We will determine the difference between be and be2 and apply it to ae:

```
$ diff be be2
5a6,7
> All the developers
> were deeply satisfied.
$ diff be be2 > DIFFS
$ patch --verbose --backup < DIFFS
Hmm...  Looks like a normal diff to me...
File to patch: ae
Patching file new using Plan A...
Hunk #1 succeeded at 6.
done
$ _
```

Thus, the changes, inserted in line 5 of the clause about the satisfaction of the developers, are applied to the ae file and are integrated.

It is quite obvious that this procedure could go wrong. Let us have a look at the append command of the DIFF-output, which inserts new lines into a specified line number: if the file has already been changed somewhere, the line numbers would no longer be correct and PATCH would insert the new lines at an incorrect position. When processing change and deleting commands, PATCH can at least ensure that the lines to be deleted are just the ones listed in the DIFF output.

The problem can be avoided if the location of the change is not seen as a line number but as a *context* – that is, a number of lines that must appear before and after the change. If PATCH knows the context of a change, it can search for the context lines in the text to determine the location of the change; an exact match of the line number is no longer required.

Context of change

DIFF uses a special *context format* to provide changes with their context. This format is activated with DIFF's "-c" option, optionally followed by the number of context lines. Example 2.6 shows the above DIFF output in context format.

Context-format

```
$ diff -c2 be be2
*** be  Wed Sep 17 09:00:53 2003
```

Example 2.6
DIFF output in
context format

```
--- be2 Wed Sep 17 09:07:13 2003
**************
*** 4,5 ****
--- 4,7 ----
  saving approximately
  1,500 pounds.
+ All the developers
+ were deeply satisfied.
$ _
```

In the context format, some of the differences are separated with a row of "*". Every difference begins with the *line range* of the first file, enclosed in a row of stars – here "*** 4,5 ***". Then the line area of the second file follows, enclosed in dashes – here "--- 4,7 ---". The line range is followed by the changed lines of the specific file:

❑ *Inserted lines* are only listed for the second file; they are labeled with "+" in the first column.

❑ *Deleted rows* are only listed for the first file; they are labeled with "-".

❑ *Changed lines* are listed for both files; they are labeled with "!".

The above changes should read as follows: In the be2 variant, the new clause about the developers is inserted after the line "1,500 pounds.".

Here is another example of a DIFF output in context format. We look into the changes in the C++ file settings.C of the 2.0beta2 version to 2.0beta3 version, displayed in Example 2.7.

These changes should read as follows: two new #include directions are inserted in the new version, and also after the #include directions for <ectype.h> and "Assoc.h". Furthermore, the function body is simplified in the SetOptionCB function. As we now can see the context of every change, we can describe the changes with the surrounding lines; the line number is no longer important.

If PATCH now is "fed" with a DIFF output in context format, it first checks whether the context of a change also appears at the given location (as specified by the line number). If this is not the case, PATCH will search for the context of changes forward and backward, starting with the original line number until it has found a place where the context appears.

If the context is not found, a *conflict* occurs: The changes cannot be carried out. The conflict will be stored in a file with the ending .rej (reject) for further analysis.

It is possible that PATCH can apply a change in the wrong position – for example, if the context lines occur identically in several places in the program. The larger the context, the more probable such a faulty location is – but there is also a higher probability of conflicts, which then have to be removed manually.

If the context is not found, then there is a *conflict*: The change in question cannot be executed. It is put in a file that carried the ending .rej (fromto reject) so that it can be analyzed further.

```
$ diff -c2 ddd-2.0beta2/ddd/settings.C ddd-2.0beta3/ddd/settings.C
*** ddd-2.0beta2/ddd/settings.C Mon Sep  2 21:22:11 1996
--- ddd-2.0beta3/ddd/settings.C Sun Sep 15 11:28:11 1996
***************
*** 48,53 ****
--- 48,55 ----
  #include <Xm/Separator.h>
  #include <ctype.h>
+ #include <string.h>

  #include "Assoc.h"
+ #include "AppData.h"
  #include "Delay.h"
  #include "DestroyCB.h"
***************
*** 81,86 ****
  static void SetOptionCB(Widget w, XtPointer client_data, XtPointer)
  {
!     String set_command = (String)client_data;
!     gdb_command(string(set_command) + " " + XtName(w));
  }

--- 130,134 ----
  static void SetOptionCB(Widget w, XtPointer client_data, XtPointer)
  {
!     gdb_set_command((String)client_data, XtName(w));
  }
$ _
```

Example 2.7
Changes in
settings.C

Of course, we cannot rule out the possibility that PATCH may apply a change in the wrong place – for instance, because the context lines appear identically in several places. The larger the context, the less likely it is that PATCH makes such erroneous decisions – but is also more likely that there will be conflicts that have to be resolved manually. Nevertheless, in practice, these trial-and-error methods work surprisingly well for integrating changes. First, this is due to the fact that the large-scale structure of programs – like function names and function headers – is usually preserved and changes are restricted to function bodies, which makes function headers a usable context. Second, program texts are typically large and the changes are small, which is why there are seldom conflicts.

2.6 Syntactical and semantic integration

The security of automatic integration can be increased further by the fact that we can use syntactical and semantic information from the basic documents. The *syntactical integration* uses the structure of a program to improve the integration. In contrast to the purely text-oriented procedures of DIFF and PATCH, the syntactical integration deals with basic elements of the programming language; its data basis is an *abstract syntax tree* in which each program component is assigned a subtree.

First of all, we will illustrate the syntactical integration with an example. In Figure 2.3, there is an original version V_0 and two versions V_1 and V_2 derived from V_0.

Figure 2.3
Syntactical
integration
(from Westfechtel
(1991))

```
Original V0
MODULE M;
VAR Colour: (White, Grey, Black);
BEGIN
    Colour := White
END M.
```

```
Changed version V1
MODULE M;
VAR Colour: (White, Grey, Black);
BEGIN
    Colour := Grey
END M.
```

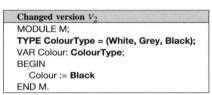

```
Changed version V2
MODULE M;
TYPE ColourType = (White, Grey, Black);
VAR Colour: ColourType;
BEGIN
    Colour := Black
END M.
```

```
Integrated version M
MODULE M;
TYPE ColourType = (White, Grey, Black);
VAR Colour: ColourType;
BEGIN
    Colour := ?
END M.
```

The syntactical integration in the integrated version M can now

❏ determine that the `Colour` is changed in V_2 into `ColourType`;

❏ determine that, in addition, a type definition is inserted in V_2;

❏ identify a conflict between the two assignments of `Colour`.

Furthermore, the integration algorithm can guarantee the *syntactical correctness* of the integrated program in that it recognizes conflicts that would violate syntactical correctness. This syntactical correctness is not guaranteed by text-based tools, but requires an environment where the abstract syntax tree can easily be accessed. In fact, syntactical integration was first realized in programming environments, which work on abstract syntax trees instead of program texts.

The requirements of an integration algorithm can be increased further by requiring *semantic correctness*: the integration of the two changes A and B has to reflect the changed semantics as well as the common unchanged semantics in *A* and *B*. The so-called *semantic integration* procedures are based on *program dependency graphs*, with which, for every statement, the program slice (the so-called *backward slices*) can be calculated, which may influence the program state in this statement. Likewise, one can calculate the program slice that can be affected by this statement (the so-called *forward slice*).

Semantic integration

Let *A* and *B* be changes: if the backward slices of the instructions affected by *A* and *B* are disjoint, and if this also applies to the forward slice, *A* and *B* cannot be in conflict with each other; otherwise, a suitable integration has to be determined. For details on slices, we refer to Chapter 19 as well as to other available literature.

Up until now, in practice, syntactic or semantic integration has not found widespread acceptance; obviously, the danger of a faulty textual integration is too unlikely as to justify additional expenses were for specialized methods.

2.7 How DIFF works

We will end this chapter with a description of how DIFF works. (If you are not interested in these technical details, you can continue reading from page 24.)

The DIFF algorithm is based on the following problem: Let *A* and *B* be two character strings. The edit distance (or in short *distance*) of two character strings is the length of the *shortest sequence* of insert or delete commands that convert *A* into *B*. We will have a look at the character strings as an example:

Edit distance

$$A = abcabba \quad \text{and} \quad B = cbabac$$

There are several possibilities of converting *A* into *B*. For example, we could delete all the characters in *A* and insert the characters from *B*, which would mean using 7 delete and 6 insert commands, or 13 commands altogether. However, there is a need only for 5 commands, as shown in Figure 2.4.

There is no sequence that would use four or less commands to convert *A* into *B*. Therefore, both command sequences from Figure 2.4 are *shortest command sequences*. The aim of the DIFF algorithm is now to determine such a shortest command sequence. However, in the actual DIFF program, the names *a*, *b*, *c*, ... no longer represent characters but *lines* (DIFF implementations typically assign a *hashcode* to every line and can in this way compare lines just as fast as characters.)

Shortest command sequences

Classic algorithms for this problem determine the *longest common subsequence* (LCS) of *A* and *B*; comparing the LCS with *A* and *B* results in

Longest common subsequence

Figure 2.4
Two shortest command sequences. The vertical line | shows where the following command is applied.

Character		Command
A	|abcabba	Insert c
	c|abcabba	Delete a
	cb|cabba	Delete c
	cba|bba	Delete b
	cbaba|	Insert c
B	cbabac	

Character		Command
A	|abcabba	Delete a
	|bcabba	Delete b
	c|abba	Delete a
	cb|ba	Insert a
	cbaba|	Insert c
B	cbabac	

Figure 2.5
A distance matrix

$$
\begin{array}{ccccccc|c}
0 & w & . & . & . & . & . & \\
. & x & . & . & . & . & . & a \\
. & . & y & . & . & . & . & b \\
. & . & . & . & . & . & . & c \\
. & . & . & . & . & . & . & a \\
. & . & . & . & . & . & . & b \\
. & . & . & . & . & . & . & b \\
. & . & . & . & . & . & z & a \\
\hline
 & c & b & a & b & a & c & \\
\end{array}
$$

insert and delete commands. We present an alternative approach here: an algorithm especially designed for DIFF by Miller and Myers.

Distance matrix   The basis for the algorithm is a *distance matrix D*, which entries contain the *distances* – the shortest command sequences for *prefixes* of A and B. The element $D[i,j]$ stands for the distance between the first i characters of A (denoted as $A[1:i]$) and the first j characters of B (denoted as $B[1:j]$).

The distance matrix D can be represented as a matrix, as in Figure 2.5. Here $x = D[1,1]$ is the distance between the prefixes $A[1:1] = a$ and $B[1:1] = c$. In the same way, $y = D[2,2]$ stands for the distance between the prefixes $A[1:2] = ab$ and $B[1:2] = cb$.

In addition, every field $D[i,j]$ is assigned a command sequence. We use two commands to convert $A[1:1] = a$ into $B[1:1] = c$: delete a and insert c. These commands are associated with x; the value of x is the length of the command sequence. This also applies to $x = D[1,1] = 2$. The command sequence of x is also sufficient for y, where $y = D[2,2] = 2$ is valid.

Determining   Our aim is to determine the bottom right field $z = D[7,6]$: It has been
distances   assigned the shortest command sequence, which converts $A[1:7] = A$ into $B[1:6] = B$. We will start from the top left with $D[0,0] = 0$, the distance of both the two empty character strings $A[1:0]$ and $B[1:0]$, and work to the right and downward. An unknown distance $D[i,j]$ can be determined in three different ways, using the three neighbors above and to the left:

Rule 1: "To the right"

If $D[i,j-1]$ is known (the field to the left of $D[i,j]$), then $D[i,j]$ is at most $D[i,j-1]+1$, because it is sufficient to insert the character $B[j]$ behind $A[1:i]$.

Let us consider the field $w = D[0, 1]$ from the example in Figure 2.5. w is the distance between the prefix $A[1:0]$, the empty character string and $B[1:1] = c$. We are now able to determine w from $D[0, 0] = 0$; we have $w = D[0, 1] = D[0, 0] + 1 = 1$. The command sequence associated with w is then to insert after $A[1:0]$ the character $B[1] = c$. $A[1:0]$ is the empty character string (that is, the beginning of A).

Rule 2: "Below"

If $D[i - 1, j]$ is known (the field above $D[i,j]$), $D[i,j]$ is at most $D[i - 1, j] + 1$, because it is sufficient to delete the character $A[i]$.

If we determine the field $x = D[1, 1]$ from the example, then we can determine x from $w = D[0, 1] = 1$ as $x = w + 1 = 2$. The command sequence associated with x is the one from w (namely, to insert c) with an additional command, namely, to delete $A[1] = a$.

Alternatively, we would have been able to establish x from the left field (corresponding to the "To the right" rule). Then, $x = D[1, 0] + 1$ holds and also $x = 2$. In this case, the command sequence would be reversed: to delete a first, then to insert c.

Rule 3: "To the right below"

If $D[i - 1, j - 1]$ is known (the field to the left above $D[i,j]$) and $A[i] = B[j]$ also applies, then $D[i,j] = D[i - 1, j - 1]$ holds. As both characters $A[i]$ and $B[j]$ are equal, no further commands are necessary.

As an example, we look at the field $y = D[2, 2]$. $A[2] = B[2] = b$ holds and, therefore, $y = D[2, 2] = D[1, 1] = x = 2$. The command sequence of x, namely, replacing a with c, therefore, also suffices to change the prefix $A[1:2] = ab$ into $B[1:2] = cb$.

A naive implementation of the DIFF algorithm now determines all the values $D[i,j]$, filling in the fields from the top left to the bottom right. So, when determining a $D[i,j]$, all three neighbors will always be known and DIFF can determine the minimal value in accordance with the above rules.

Figure 2.6 shows an intermediate state and the final state: The matrix is completely filled, and the bottom right field is associated with the shortest command sequence. Under the assumption that the fields that are underlined have led to the determination of the command sequence of its underlined neighbors, we get the first command sequence from Figure 2.4 as a result.

The algorithm from Miller and Myers has the complexity $O(n \times m)$, where n and m stand for the number of lines in A and B. In practice, there are a number of optimizations. In fact, not all values of the distance matrix have to be calculated; first of all, fields can be filled along the diagonals in

Figure 2.6
The distance matrix half full and in its final state

0	1	2	3	4	5	.		0	1	2	3	4	5	6	
1	2	3	2	3	.	.	*a*	1	2	3	2	3	4	5	*a*
2	3	2	3	.	.	.	*b*	2	3	2	3	2	3	4	*b*
3	2	3	.	.	.	.	*c*	3	2	3	4	3	4	3	*c*
4	3	.	.	.	.	.	*a*	4	3	4	3	4	3	4	*a*
5	.	.	.	.	.	.	*b*	5	4	3	4	3	4	5	*b*
.	.	.	.	.	.	.	*b*	6	5	4	5	4	5	6	*b*
.	.	.	.	.	.	.	*a*	7	6	5	4	5	4	5	*a*
	c	*b*	*a*	*b*	*a*	*c*			*c*	*b*	*a*	*b*	*a*	*c*		

accordance with the "To the bottom right" rule. With only few variations between A and B, the bottom right field will very quickly be reached; in extreme cases, $A = B$ therefore only needs n steps. Altogether, the effort is therefore less the less differences there are.

(This is an essential advantage for the approaches of Miller and Myers as compared with LCS-based DIFF implementation. In practice, DIFF is used above all for version management, as explained in Chapter 3, and one starts out from the assumption there that there are only few differences between individual versions. This is where LCS-based implementations show their weaknesses. Even though they have the same complexity, their effort increases with the number of *agreements* and reaches its maximum with n^2 steps, in case $A = B$ holds.)

For a description of other DIFF algorithms as well as details about the algorithm from Miller and Myers, we refer to the literature quoted at the end of this chapter.

Concepts

❑ *Software configuration management* (SCM) organizes and controls the evolution of software systems.

❑ *DIFF* determines the *differences (= changes) between two texts* A and B as a sequence of commands, which converts A to B. The commands are inserting and deleting lines.

❑ For *distribution of changes*, one can apply differences generated by DIFF on other files, using PATCH.

❑ Using *two-way integration*, a new file is created from the two files A and B, in which for each difference, a piece of text is selected interactively from either A or B.

❑ Using *three-way integration*, a common original version is taken into account: If a piece of text is only altered in A or B, the change can automatically take place. If the piece of text is modified in both *A* and *B*, a *conflict* occurs.

❏ The *syntactical integration* and the *semantical integration* take into account syntax or semantics of the document on which the changes are applied.

❏ The *shortest command sequence* for *A* and *B* is determined by DIFF incrementally using the shortest command sequence for *prefixes* of *A* and *B*.

Review exercises

1. Implement the algorithm from Miller and Myers.

2. Look at Figure 2.6. Which other shortest command sequences are possible?

3. Under which conditions is it possible to omit to calculate single fields of the distance matrix? Consider suitable optimizations.

4. Sometimes, code must be changed slightly when porting a program. If the earlier version of the program is to be maintained, both versions are described as *variants*. When correcting errors in a variant, all further variants must also be considered. Can this be carried out automatically?

5. In practice, most changes are determined and propagated over complete file hierarchies. In this way, a change can apply to several files; DIFF and PATCH provide appropriate options. But, what happens if files or directories are added, deleted, or renamed?

6. List further pros and cons for textual, syntactical, and semantical integration. How can disadvantages of textual integration be avoided? (For example, think of comments in source codes or different formatting styles.)

7. Discuss the advantages and disadvantages of the approach of making source code available to the customers.

Further reading

For the topic software configuration management, we recommend the practice-oriented introductions by Babich (1986) and Whitgift (1991); an up-to-date collection of excellent research results was published by Tichy (1994). The formal basics of SCM are to be found in Zeller and

Snelting (1997); the managers' view are represented in SCM norms in IEEE (1988, 1990). The *Symposium on System Configuration Management* presents the present research results, current overview articles and valuable experience reports (previous proceedings: Winkler (1988), Tichy (1989), Feiler (1991), Estublier (1995), Sommerville (1996a), Conradi (1997), Magnusson (1998) and Estublier (1999)).

The DIFF program was first described in Hunt and McIlroy (1976). The underlying LCS algorithms can be found in numerous textbooks, covering basic file structures and algorithms, like for instance Aho et al. (1983). Here, instead of presenting the original algorithm, we have chosen to show the faster version from Miller and Myers (1985), which is implemented in GNU DIFF.

There are several applications in which the DIFF output is interpreted by machines only; the DIFF result thus need not be readable for human beings. Under this prerequisite, algorithms are possible that recognize and store *copied* data blocks effectively. Actually, these algorithms have more in common with compress methods than with original DIFF algorithms; in particular, they are capable of recognizing differences between binary data. Typical approaches are described by Tichy (1984) and Reichenberger (1989). The result of the empirical study from Hunt et al. (1996) shows that the new approaches are clearly superior to the original algorithm in processing text as well as binary data.

Larry Wall (1988) is the original creator of the PATCH program. Our description of PATCH relies on the documentation of MacKenzie et al. (1993); this manual also contains an exact description of GNU DIFF and GNU SDIFF. The EDIFF package from Kifer (1996) is a component of the EMACS editor, described by Stallman (1988a).

The *syntactical* integration of changes is described by Westfechtel (1991) and realized in the IPSEN system (Nagl (1996)). The idea of *semantical* integration has been researched by the group around Horwitz and Reps – see Horwitz et al. (1989), Yang et al. (1992), Binkley et al. (1995), and Berzins (1994) describes alternative approaches.

Other tools for configuration management

On page 59, you will find a list of commercial tools for software configuration management.

3 Revision management using RCS

3.1 Introduction

In Chapter 2, we considered software development in the widest sense as the creation and distribution of *changes* in a software product. In this chapter, we will introduce tools that *organize* and *control* the change process – the subject of software configuration management (SCM) discussed in Section 2.1. These tools cover the following requirements for SCM tools:

Reconstruction: At any point in time, one must be able to restore previous *configurations*; a configuration is a set of software components in particular versions. Reconstruction is important to identify changes between old and new versions and to determine the source code of distributed products for maintenance purposes.

Restoring the previous configurations

Coordination: It has to be guaranteed that changes made by developers do not get inadvertently lost, which means, in particular, that any *conflicts* are resolved, if several developers want to change a component at the same time.

Coordinating changes

Identification: It must always be possible to identify individual versions and components clearly, in order to identify the changes that have been made. This implies accurate tagging of single versions and components.

Identify versions and components

If, in these requirements, we refer to *versions*, we refer to the outcome if we change a software component. Depending on the purpose of the change, we distinguish between *revisions* and *variants*:

Revisions are versions created to *replace* an existing version; the original version should no longer be used. Revisions are usually created during *program maintenance* – for instance, to correct errors. Improvements in the algorithms and data structures that are used or changes in the input environment can also be reasons to create a revision.

Revisions replace versions

Variants are versions that *supplement* an existing version; both versions, the new and the existing one, will be used and developed further.

Variants supplement versions

A typical reason for the existence of variants is the *porting* of a program into another environment, where both variants have to be maintained. Variants are also created during program development, when several developers are working on individual copies.

If the lifetime of a variant is limited from the outset, we call it a *temporary variant*; otherwise, we talk about a *permanent variant*. In this chapter, we will discuss temporary variants, while in Chapter 9, we will describe how to handle *permanent variants*.

"Version" is sometimes also used as a synonym for "revision", so that "version" and "variant" become complements of each other. We will always use the concept "version" as a generic term for revisions and variants.

3.2   Saving and restoring revisions

Version archive   Our first topic is the *reconstruction* of earlier configurations. The basic idea behind reconstruction is to manage a *version archive* (engl. *repository*:), where all versions of all software components are stored. While the software components are usually identified via a unique identifier (such as a filename), revisions typically differ because of *temporal aspects* such as the date of creation. As revisions are ordered along the "replace" relation, simple *numbering* is possible: the higher the number, the more recent the revision. Therefore, for instance, revision 7 is more recent (and hopefully more stable) than revision 5.

In a revision archive, one can file versions using the name, the date of creation, and other attributes – and retrieve these versions using these attributes. This is exactly the task of the *Revision Control System*, or RCS for short.

RCS   The main task of RCS is the management of an *RCS archive*, an archive for file revisions. The RCS archive comes in the form of a single file, so we can call it an *RCS file*. RCS offers two basic functions for accessing the RCS file:

check in: copying a version *into* the version archive

check out: copying a version *from* the version archive.

Work space   Normally, in RCS, each developer has a separate *work space* available, while the RCS files within an *RCS directory* are shared amongst all developers. Using the check out and check in functions, you can also copy files from the RCS directory into the work space, and vice versa (Figure 3.1).

Revision number   To identify the individual versions, RCS assigns a *revision number* to each version. In RCS, a revision number consists of two numbers $n.m$,

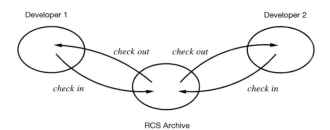

Developer 1 Developer 2

check out *check out*

check in *check in*

RCS Archive

Figure 3.1
*Check in and check
out. The developers
copy the files from
an RCS directory into
their work spaces
(check out), and vice
versa (check in).*

where a higher *n* stands for a major progress and *m* for a minor progress.
Revision numbers are assigned automatically when checking in: the first
revision has the number 1.1, the second 1.2, and so on. The order of the
revision numbers forms a revision tree *revision tree* (also called *revision
history*). In its simplest form, the revision tree appears as a linear *chain* as
shown in Figure 3.2.

Revision tree

| 1.1 | | 1.2 | | 1.3 | | 1.4 | | 1.5 |

Figure 3.2
*A revision chain.
Each new revision is
carried out and
changes the
preceding revision.*

co *command*
*Checking out by
revision*

Individual revisions can be copied from the RCS file by giving the revision
number or by giving the creation date. This is done using the RCS command
co (check out). The co command can be passed a revision number:

```
$ co -r1.1 be
RCS/be,v  -->  be
revision 1.1
done
$ _
```

Here, the revision 1.1 is copied from the RCS file RCS/be,v into the
current directory.

The revision number can be abbreviated, in which case the highest
existing number is used:

```
$ co -r1 be
RCS/be,v  -->  be
revision 1.2
done
$ _
```

Check out of the
Most recent revision

If the revision number is omitted, the *most recent revision* is returned. This is the most frequent application of co.

```
$ co be
RCS/be,v  -->  be
revision 1.2
done
$ _
```

Checking out by date

Instead of a revision number, one can also specify a *date* to be restored. RCS recognizes several date and time representations and returns the revision that has not yet been replaced with a new version.

```
$ co -d'2003/04/21 13:30:30' be
RCS/be,v  -->  be
revision 1.1
done
$ _
```

By specifying a date when checking out, a file can easily be restored to any previous status. To reconstruct a specific configuration of several files, for instance, you just need to know the date of the configuration to reconstruct the suitable file revisions on it.

3.3 Branches and variants

In practice, software is frequently developed in several parallel variants. While one programming team maintains an old variant, which is already adopted by several customers, another programming team is working with a group of beta testers, which will test the next version to be delivered; a third programming team is already engaged in working on the version that will follow.

Using a revision chain, as presented in Figure 3.2, such a situation cannot be modeled in a satisfactory way. The problem is that here we have
Fix
Features
two different kinds of changes: *fixes*, which preserve the existing functionality, and *new features*, which introduce a new functionality – and possibly new errors, too. In a linear revision chain, these kinds of changes cannot be separated from each other clearly: each change requires all previous changes, so that any fix requires all previous new features.

The client, however, is usually more interested in fixes than in untested experimental features. Therefore, the aim must be to *separate fixes from features*. To do so, RCS has the concept of a *branch*. The idea is that fixes
Subpath
Main path
refer to a previous revision – a separate *subpath* in the revision tree. The *main path* is used for further developments.

A typical situation in which branches are used is shown in Figure 3.3. The program has reached revision 1.5 when a client reports an error in revision 1.2 that she uses. Obviously, this error can be corrected in revision 1.5, creating revision 1.6, which is then delivered to the client. The problem is that the client would also receive the untested features of 1.4 and 1.5, which is not desirable. Therefore, by using RCS, a branch is generated originating from revision 1.2 in which new revisions of 1.2, namely 1.2.1.1, 1.2.1.2, and so on, are maintained and delivered to users.

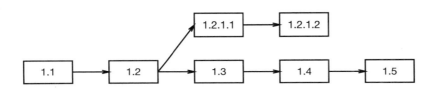

Figure 3.3
A branch in the revision tree. To make changes to an earlier revision, a separate path is set up.

In the case of check in or check out of a revision, RCS automatically determines, on the basis of the revision number, the position in the revision graphs – so, for instance, 1.2.1.1 always indicates revision 1.1 of the revision 1.2. Revision numbers can be arbitrary: a revision number 1.2.1.1.1.1 for instance, would introduce a new secondary path coming from 1.2.1.1. In practice, this kind of branch within a branch occurs only rarely.

The fix made to 1.2, which creates revision 1.2.1.1, eventually has to be merged into the main path with the recent changes. This can occur via one of the *integration procedures* described in Chapter 2.

3.4 Locks

Archiving revisions under arbitrary revision numbers is very useful to *reconstruct* earlier configurations. However, archiving alone is not enough; it must also be ensured that *revisions cannot be changed once they are filed*. This requirement is met easily, as checking in is only possible in the most recent revision of paths. RCS thus prohibits later changes to the revision history.

However, another problem occurs: if two developers want to edit revision 1.5, the first developer adds his revision as revision 1.6 to the revision archive. The second developer would store her changes as revision 1.7. Now, revision 1.7 is a descendant of 1.5; the changes from 1.5 to 1.6 are lost in revision 1.7.

In order to avoid losing these changes, RCS has the concept of *locking*. A developer can only edit a revision if she has set a lock on this revision. A lock on revision *A* prevents all other revisions from replacing a new

Locking

revision *A* with a revision *B* – this right is reserved to the person that has set the lock.

Locks are set in RCS directly when checking out. An ordinary check out copies the file from the version archive as write-protected – so that changes cannot be made. The option "-l" (lock), though, sets a lock and then creates a write-enabled copy.

Check out with lock

For instance, the author Andreas wants to extend the manuscript of a book. He carries out a check out on the file rcs.tex, by entering "-l":

```
andreas$ co -l rcs.tex
RCS/rcs.tex,v  -->  rcs.tex
revision 1.5 (locked)
done
andreas$ _
```

Andreas can edit the file rcs.tex as he likes. If coauthor Jens wants to work on the same manuscript as well, he then has to go through the same procedure, but with a different result:

```
jens$ co -l rcs.tex
RCS/rcs.tex,v  -->  rcs.tex
co: RCS/rcs.tex,v:
    Revision 1.5 has already been locked by Andreas.
jens$ _
```

Jens now has to wait until Andreas has committed his changes; if Andreas introduces a change, his lock is automatically released. In Section 3.5, we will see how the lock can be avoided by creating a *subpath*.

3.5 Making changes

ci command

After carrying out their changes, Andreas and Jens execute a check in. This is done via the ci command, which can be given a revision number, as the co command. If ci is given without any option, the local copy of the file is removed; it can be copied from the version archive again via a renewed co. Normally, ci is used with the "-u" option, which automatically calls a co, or with the option "-l", which has the effect of "co -l".

Let us assume that Andreas has already finished his changes in rcs.tex. He creates a new revision with ci, which contains the following changes:

```
Andreas$ ci -u rcs.tex
RCS/rcs.tex,v  <--  rcs.tex
new revision: 1.6; previous revision: 1.5
enter log message, terminated with a single '.'
```

```
or end of file:
>> _
```

`ci` asks Andreas to type in a *log message* entry for the *change log*. Andreas documents his changes:

```
andreas$ ci -u rcs.tex
RCS/rcs.tex,v  <--  rcs.tex
new revision: 1.6; previous revision: 1.5
enter log message, terminated with single '.'
or end of file:
>> Section about change logs
>> completed
>> .
done.
$ _
```

If one does not specify a revision upon check in, `ci` selects the next free revision in the main path. By explicitly giving a revision number, though, one can set up *secondary paths*. This is the way to go when one wants to *avoid locks*.

Let us assume, for instance, that Andreas has not yet made his changes, so that `rcs.tex` is still locked. Jens, who may just want to correct a few   *Avoiding locks* typos cannot do so. To carry out his changes, Jens can avoid Andreas' lock by setting up a *secondary path* and adding its changes in revision 1.5.1.1:   *Secondary path*

```
jens$ ci -u -r1.5.1.1 rcs.tex
RCS/rcs.tex,v  <--  rcs.tex
new revision: 1.5.1.1; previous revision: 1.5
enter log message, terminated with single '.'
or end of file:
>> Fix: Typos
>> .
done.
$ _
```

Later, when Andreas has concluded his changes, resulting in revision 1.6, Jens can add his changes and create the integrated revision 1.7

3.6 Change log and keywords

The entries given in `ci` for the change log can be listed by means of the RCS command `rlog`. Example 3.1 shows the change log, which results   `rlog` *command* from the previous commands.

A change log is useful whenever a developer wants to be informed about the latest changes. If source code is made available to users, the change logs are frequently included, such that users can trace changes and rationales for these changes.

Keywords

Id

To support change logs, RCS allows for version information to be included in the files using *keywords*. Keywords are identifiers specified in "$...$". They are expanded automatically when the file is checked out. For example, the string $Revision$ is automatically replaced with the current revision number. The keyword Id expands into a standard file header:

$Id: rcs.tex,v 1.6 2003/07/31 19:31:04 andreas Exp $

The header includes the RCS file name, the revision number and the creation date, as well as the name of the developer who checked in this revision.

```
$ rlog rcs.tex
RCS file: RCS/rcs.tex,v
Working file: rcs.tex
head: 1.6
branch:
locks: strict
access list:
symbolic names:
keyword substitution: kv
total revisions: 6;    selected revisions: 6
description:
--------------------------
revision 1.6
date: 2003/07/31 19:31:04; author: andreas; state: Exp; lines: +80
Section about change log completed
--------------------------
revision 1.5
date: 2003/06/23 17:02:51; author: andreas; state: Exp; lines: +30
Section about motivation is completed
--------------------------
...
$ _
```

Example 3.1
RCS change log. For each change, the date, author, and reasons are specified.

You can also integrate change logs into the file via keywords. For this purpose, we use the keyword Log: It acts so that each new entry of the change log is added with each check in. The effect, in the course of time, is that the whole change log becomes a constituent of the file:

```
% $Log: rcs.tex,v $
% Revision 1.6  2003/07/31 19:31:04  andreas
% Section about change log completed
%
```

```
% Revision 1.5  2003/06/23 17:02:51  andreas
% Section about motivation completed
%
```

RCS automatically copies the characters typed in front of the Log key- Log
word in front of the following lines. This is useful to include the change
log as one long comment. In the above example, a LaTeX file, is used "%"
as comment reference.

In practice, the revision identifier is given in a form, which allows the
identification of source files and revisions within executable programs. For
this purpose, the revision identifier is included as a character string in the
source text. In the programming language C, this looks as follows: In the
file dev.C, we add the lines

```
static char version_string[] =
  "$Id$";
```

After the next check out, this expands into

```
static char version_string[] =
  "$Id: dev.C,v 1.9 2003/04/25 06:39:09 joe Exp $";
```

When creating a program from dev.C, the character string
version_string becomes a part of the executable binary file.

To determine the revision number of an executable binary file, we use
the RCS command ident, which reports all character strings in the form ident *command*
$*name*:*text*$ that occur in a file. Let us assume that we have created a
program called myprog, which uses the source code of dev.C. Using
ident, we can determine the names and revision of all included source
files:

```
$ ident myprog
$Id: dev.C,v 1.9 2003/04/25 06:39:09 joe Exp $
$Id: lib.C,v 1.4 2003/04/25 06:37:40 liz Exp $
. . .
$ _
```

3.7 How RCS stores revisions

In the course of time, software components are subject to dozens or even
hundreds of changes, which gives rise to several revisions to be archived. If
each whole revision were always archived, the need for space for the version
archive would soon break any limit; eventually, any developer would have
to weigh up the advantages of archiving against the space requirements for
the archive.

```
┌─────────────────────────────────────┐
│ RCS/be,v                             │
├─────────────────────────────────────┤
│ head 1.2;                            │
│ access;                              │
│ symbols;                             │
│ locks; strict;                       │
│ comment @# @;                        │
│                                      │
│ 1.2                                  │
│ date 2003.09.17.08.19.18;            │
│ author zeller; state Exp;            │
│ branches;                            │
│ next 1.1;                            │
│                                      │
│ 1.1                                  │
│ date 2003.09.17.08.18.58;            │
│ author zeller; state Exp;            │
│ branches;                            │
│ next;                                │
│                                      │
│ desc                                 │
│ @@                                   │
│ 1.2                                  │
│ log                                  │
│ @Added note on developers            │
│ @                                    │
│ text                                 │
│ @The change impact was minimised     │
│ by localising the most               │
│ important variables,                 │
│ saving approximately                 │
│ 1,500 pounds.                        │
│ All the developers                   │
│ were deeply satisfied.               │
│ @                                    │
│                                      │
│ 1.1                                  │
│ log                                  │
│ @Initial revision                    │
│ @                                    │
│ text                                 │
│ @d6 2                                │
│ @                                    │
└─────────────────────────────────────┘
```

```
┌─────────────────────────────────────┐
│ SCCS/s.alt                           │
├─────────────────────────────────────┤
│ ^Ah40901                             │
│ ^As 00002/00000/00005                │
│ ^Ad D 1.2 2003/09/17 09:56:29        │
│     zeller 2 1                       │
│ ^Ac Added note on developers         │
│ ^Ae                                  │
│ ^As 00005/00000/00000                │
│ ^Ad D 1.1 2003/09/17 09:55:57        │
│     zeller 1 0                       │
│ ^Ac date and time created            │
│ ^Ac 2003/09/17 09:55:57 by zeller    │
│ ^Ae                                  │
│ ^Au                                  │
│ ^AU                                  │
│ ^Af e 0                              │
│ ^At                                  │
│ ^AT                                  │
│ The change impact was minimised      │
│ by localising the most               │
│ important variables,                 │
│ saving approximately                 │
│ 1,500 pounds.                        │
│ ^AD 1                                │
│ All the developers                   │
│ were deeply satisfied.               │
│ ^AE 1                                │
└─────────────────────────────────────┘
```

Example 3.2
RCS and SCCS files

Filing revisions into RCS

RCS uses a specific procedure to store a large number of revisions efficiently. Only the *last* revision of the main path is stored completely; for each earlier revision, only the *difference* to the following revision is stored. A revision chain, like the one in Figure 3.2, is stored by RCS as follows:

❏ The last revision 1.5 is stored as a whole.

❏ If necessary, revision 1.4 is created by applying the stored DIFF difference between 1.5 and 1.4 on revision 1.5, as described in Chapter 2.

❏ Revision 1.3 is created by applying the stored difference between 1.4 and 1.3 on revision 1.4 that has just been generated.

❏ Any revision up to revision 1.1 can thus be restored by applying earlier differences.

The basic mechanisms for this procedure have been introduced in Chapter 2: the changes are determined by means of a DIFF algorithm that are applied with a PATCH-like algorithm. In fact, RCS calls the DIFF program to determine the changes; RCS itself handles the application of changes, using the appropriate commands to add and remove lines.

When checking in a new revision, RCS replaces the last revision (stored as a whole in the RCS file) by the new revision; it also stores the difference between the new and the previous revision. For instance, consider Figure 3.2: if some new revision 1.6 has to be stored, the last revision 1.5 stored in the archive is replaced by the new revision 1.6, and in addition, the DIFF difference from 1.6 to 1.5 is stored.

To illustrate the procedure, Example 3.2 shows the RCS archive RCS/be,v, which includes the two revisions of the British English text, taken from Chapter 2.

Following the information such as date, lock, and change log, the RCS archive stores the whole text of the most recent revision 1.2. Revision 1.1 follows, but just as a difference to revision 1.2: the regular DIFF differences are marked with "d" (delete) and "a" (append). In our case, revision 1.1 is created from revision 1.2 by deleting two lines starting at line 6, the last line ("6d2").

Basically, in RCS, changes (named *delta*) are determined and stored *backward* from recent to earlier revisions ("backward delta"). The reason   *Backward delta*
for this is *efficiency*: recent revisions are simply accessed more frequently than older ones. RCS thus minimizes the access time (i.e., the number of changes to be carried out) for recent versions.

In case of *branching* in the revision tree, changes are determined and applied *forward* in the branch from earlier to recent revisions ("forward delta"). For instance, if we want to reconstruct revision 1.2.1.2, represented   *Forward delta*
in Figure 3.4, RCS will execute the following steps:

1. Extract revision 1.5 from the RCS file.

2. Use (backward) changes of 1.5 after 1.4.

Figure 3.4
*Backward and
forward differences.
In the main path,
revisions are set
backward if they are
compared with
recent revisions; in
the secondary paths,
they are set forward
if they are compared
with earlier revisions.*

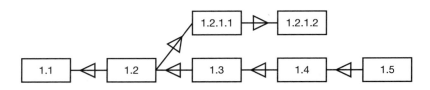

3. Use changes of 1.4 after 1.3.

4. Use changes of 1.3 after 1.2.

5. Use (forward) changes of 1.2 after 1.2.1.1.

6. Use changes of 1.2.1.1 after 1.2.1.2.

The quick access to the most recent revision in RCS therefore comes at the price of slower access to revisions in branches. If several branches are managed, such a weighting of the access speed is not necessarily reasonable.

Interleaved revision representation

Therefore, many SCM tools use an *interleaved* representation of revisions, in which all revisions are restored at the same speed, regardless of the position in the revision tree.

A typical example of interleaved revision representation is the file format of the *Source Code Control Systems* (SCCS), as shown in Example 3.2.

In the SCCS format, individual lines are assigned markers that indicate which revision they belong to. Lines are combined in *blocks*, which begin either with ^AI *n* (insert) or with ^AD *n* (delete) and finish with ^AE (end). Lines contained in a ^AI *n* ... ^AE block belong to revision *n*; lines contained in a ^AD *n* ... ^AE block do *not* belong to revision *n*. Blocks can be arbitrarily nested.

To reconstruct revisions, SCCS simply selects the lines that belong to the required revision in the SCCS file. As an example, let us consider the text line "All the developers". It is contained in ^AD 1...^AE, so it does not belong to revision 1; If revision 1 were to be reconstructed, SCCS would simply omit this line.

According to this pattern, SCCS processes the complete SCCS file until all required lines of the revision have been output. Unlike RCS, the SCCS cost for the reconstruction of the revision is always the same; however, it increases with the length of the SCCS file, that is, the number of changes.

In practice, there is no substantial difference as to whether the underlying representation is uncrossed, as in RCS, or crossed, as in SCCS. Both the tools are very quick in the reconstruction of recent configurations and offer meaningful coordination and identification mechanisms.

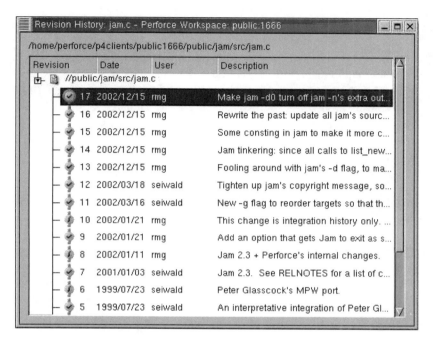

Figure 3.5
Version selection in PERFORCE. The user can view the revision tree and select revisions.

3.8 Innovations and further developments

RCS and SCCS are used as simple tools via a simple command interface. Most users, though, prefer *graphical user interfaces* to access versions. Figure 3.5 shows the version selection in PERFORCE – an SCM tool with a graphical user interface. The revision tree as well as the important SCM functions can be examined and selected by the user.

PERFORCE

The disadvantage of a user interface such as the one in PERFORCE is that programs must be adapted to access versions. New SCM systems avoid this problem by means of *virtual file systems*, in which all versions can be accessed as ordinary files – adapting user programs is therefore superfluous. The CLEARCASE system, for instance, uses *special filenames*, which name *paths in the revision tree* so that the filename zbuf.c@@/color accesses the component zbuf.c in the color variant. The default for the revision path can be set in just one step; it limits the *view* of the file system. If, say, color is set as a revision path, all files are accessible in this variant without the need for further specification.

Virtual file system

CLEARCASE

The *n-DFS system* (*n*-dimensional file system) is a virtual file system, which can be parameterized using any version archives. For example, if a combination of *n*-DFS and RCS is used, the date of the RCS files can be set in by means of environment variables.

Databases   A further trend in SCM is the retrieval from file systems to *databases*. The advantage of a database is that there is a major protection against data loss by means of system error and a better coordination of parallel accesses. However, conventional databases provide only inadequate support for the complex requirements of software development, such as efficient versioning. First trials, though, are quite promising; for instance, the ADELE

ADELE   system uses its own (versioned) database as an archive from which individual views are provided via a virtual file system. Views are specified by

Query languages   special *query languages*; the ADELE query

$$window\text{-}system = x11 \wedge (current \vee status \neq experimental)$$

selects all versions whose user interface is the X Window System and which are either the most recent or experimental versions.

Concepts

❑ Depending on the purpose, versions can either be *revisions* or *variants*. Revisions replace existing versions, variants supplement them.

❑ RCS provides a *version archive* where revisions can be checked in or checked out.

❑ In an RCS archive, revisions are organized in a *revision tree*, in which the end of a path stands for the current revision.

❑ By means of *locks*, RCS guarantees that no more than one developer can work on the same revision at the same time.

❑ Each change is *justified* by the developer; the resulting *change log* documents the history of a software component.

❑ A RCS archive only stores the *differences* between revisions. This saves much space.

Review exercises

1. Why does RCS use an external DIFF, but its own algorithms rather than PATCH?

2. Why are deltas in the branching in the revision tree stored out forward and not backward? What advantages and disadvantages would a backward delta have?

3. RCS works exclusively on individual files; changes in directories, such as adding and removing files, are not included in RCS. Design

a simple scheme in which such information is placed in a central file (and versioned by using RCS), so that the exact set of files can be restored at any time of the program development.

4. Assume that your source files include change logs automatically created using the RCS keyword Log. What happens with the change logs when integrating changes from a branch?

5. Nowadays, software development is frequently distributed across several places. Therefore, one may wonder where and how the data has to be archived. Draw up a procedure for accessing the archive

    (a) using a *central* versions archive

    (b) using several *local* versions archives

Pay particular attention to the *synchronization* of the archives.

6. Your company would like to bring out the system you have run up to now under UNIX in a new WINDOWS variant. Four alternatives are available for organizing the new variant:

    (a) Set up two separate RCS archives for both variants.

    (b) Set up a common RCS archive, where a branch is used for the management of the WINDOWS variant.

    (c) Merge both variants into a common file, controlled by RCS. One of these two variants is selected at compilation time via the C preprocessor (CPP) by "#ifdef ...#endif".

    (d) Encapsulate all system-relevant parts into RCS-controlled subsystems selected for UNIX or WINDOWS when creating the program.

Consider the advantages and disadvantages of both approaches. To what extent can the schemes be extended by further variants? For example, think about the several UNIX variations or a variant for .NET as a further variant of WINDOWS!

Further reading

SCCS by Rochkind (1975) is the first and earliest SCM tool. The original SCCS was developed as batch system for the IBM 370 computer; after that, several SCCS variants for workstations and PCs were added, which were considerably easier to use. In practice, SCCS is no longer developed: RCS, on the other hand, has been continuously maintained since the original version of Tichy (1985). Nowadays, after MAKE (Chapter 8), RCS is one of the most frequently used software tools and is available on practically every development platform.

PERFORCE is described in the section "Other tools for configuration management" in Chapter 4. An extensive view of the CLEARCASE system by Leblang (1994) is provided in the book by Tichy (1994); in the same book, you can find also an article by Fowler et al. (1994), about n-DFS as a representation of database interaction and work spaces in ADELE by Estublier and Casallas (1994). Emmerich et al. (1993) complain about the general insufficiency of actual database systems for software development.

Conradi and Westfechtel (1996) provide a survey of all available SCM systems and versioning concepts.

Other tools for configuration management

On page 59, you can find a list of commercial tools for software configuration management.

4 Parallel program development with CVS

4.1 From components to software systems

In Chapter 3, we showed how changes to individual files can be organized and coordinated using RCS. In practice, however, a software system consists of more than a single component. Instead, it is a basic principle of software design to divide a system into various components, which

❑ offer specifically defined services via their *interface* (declaration) and

❑ whose *implementation* of these services relies on the services of other components.

The aim of this distinction is to reduce the effects of a modification on the implementation of a component. The implementation can change, but, provided the interface remains unchanged, the modification does not affect the rest of the software system.

If a software system consisting of several components is now versioned, there are two objectives to pursue:

Versioning of a software system

Consistency: It must always be ensured that the services of an interface that have been enlisted are also actually available. This means that if an interface is modified and if this leads to further modifications in other components, these modifications have to be *coupled* so that they cannot be applied independently of each other.

Consistency of configurations

Flexibility: As long as the interface remains unchanged, it must be possible to select any version of a component and thus *configure* a system that is suitable for a particular purpose or a certain environment.

Flexibility of configurations

While consistency is an absolute quality requirement for software systems, it is useful to achieve the *greatest possible flexibility*. In an ideal world, interfaces remain unchanged throughout the entire lifetime of a system, so that it is possible for all revisions of any of the components to be combined with each other freely.

Unfortunately, this ideal world does not always exist: the development of a software system calls for regular modifications to be made to established interfaces. Even if all the previous services remain unchanged and only a few new services are added, this still causes an inconsistency. For example, if the component A', as a revision of A, offers extended services, the component B, which uses these extended services, can no longer be combined with A. In practice, this is then said to be "Capable of running on Windows XP Service Pack 1 or later".

SCM systems do not normally have mechanisms for finding evidence as to whether a software system is consistent. However, they can store such evidence and thus, for example, restore the system to a consistent configuration. The prerequisite for this is that configurations can be clearly *identified*. In Figure 4.1 we can see three components, a.c, b.c, and c.c, which appear respectively in various revisions.

Figure 4.1
Threaded representation of configurations. Each thread combines the versions that it touches in a configuration.

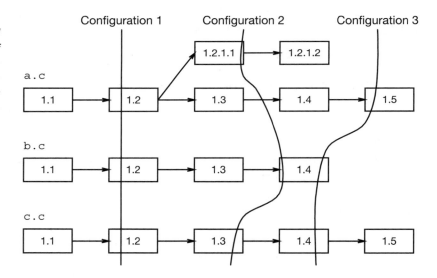

The figure shows three configurations; they are represented by a vertically running *thread*, which traverses the revisions contained in the configuration.
Threads   The configuration 2, therefore, consists of a.c in revision 1.2.1.1, b.c in revision 1.4, as well as c.c in revision 1.3. The issue is to identify these revisions, and, whenever possible, by a simpler means than a simple list of components and revision numbers.

One such simpler means, as provided by RCS and similar SCM systems, is the *tagging of configurations*. A *configuration tag* describes a particular revision of a component. This can be used for several components and therefore indicates a configuration for each revision of these components. Thus, in Figure 4.1, we can give the configuration 2 the tag conf2, and later, if we want to restore the configuration, simply use this tag during the check out instead of a revision number or date.

In RCS, this works as follows: To allocate a configuration name, the service program rcs is used, which using the option -n*name* : *rev* assigns the symbolic tag *name* to the revision *rev*. In order to tag, say, the configuration conf2, the appropriate revision is specified for each file:

Tagging configurations in RCS

```
$ rcs -nconf2:1.2.1.1 a.c
RCS file: RCS/a.c,v
done
$ rcs -nconf2:1.4 b.c
RCS file: RCS/a.c,v
done
$ rcs -nconf2:1.3 c.c
RCS file: RCS/c.c,v
done
$ _
```

To restore this configuration, you just specify the tag conf2 when checking out:

Check out with configuration tag

```
$ co -rconf2 a.c b.c c.c
RCS/a.c,v  -->  a.c
revision 1.2.1.1
done
RCS/b.c,v  -->  b.c
revision 1.4
done
RCS/c.c,v  -->  c.c
revision 1.3
done
$ _
```

The last example also shows the limits of configuration tags: While conf2 is enough to specify the individual revisions, the components still have to be listed individually. The actual set of components is not subject to revision control – if a component is deleted during development, this is not reflected in any of the RCS files. This step from versioned components to versioned software systems, or in other words, from files to file systems is what we want to illustrate in this chapter, using the CVS tool.

4.2   Versioning file hierarchies with CVS

The *Concurrent Versions System*, abbreviated to CVS, is a tool used for versioning file systems. In contrast to RCS, modifications are not only

CVS

incorporated into individual files, the addition and deletion of files in directories is also taken into account. In this way, an entire software product consisting of numerous files in several directories can be versioned as one entity.

Like RCS, CVS also uses a central archive in which all revisions of all source files are stored. (The CVS archive actually consists of a number of RCS archives; see Section 4.3.) And as in the case of RCS, the archive can only be addressed exclusively by means of the SCM tool.

Check out from the CVS archive
`cvs checkout`

Typically, the work on a project begins by copying the source of the project from the *CVS archive* into a work space. This is done using the CVS command `checkout`, which copies an entire directory along with all the files it contains from the CVS archive into the current directory. The commands in CVS have the prefix `cvs`; the entire command, therefore, reads `cvs checkout`, followed by the project directory.

Here is an example: developer Seymour works on a project `plantshop`, which consists of four files. The CVS archive is already set up. Using `checkout`, Seymour copies the entire content of the project into his work directory; as is done with the RCS command `co`, he obtains the most up-to-date revision of the main path.

```
seymour$ cvs checkout plantshop
cvs checkout: Updating plantshop
U plantshop/Makefile
U plantshop/plantshop.h
U plantshop/plants.C
U plantshop/pots.C
seymour$ _
```

The `plantshop` directory now contains the source text from the CVS archive. In addition to this, `plantshop` contains a directory called CVS, which is used internally by CVS. (We will come back to this in Section 4.3.)

```
seymour$ cd plantshop
seymour$ ls
CVS Makefile plantshop.h plants.C pots.C
seymour$ _
```

In contrast to RCS, in CVS, files do not have to be locked before they can be processed; Seymour can start his work straight away.

Submitting modifications to the CVS archive
`cvs commit`

After a final modification, Seymour can copy the new revisions back into the CVS archive and by doing so make them available to others. This is done using the `commit` command . For the time being, Seymour can use `commit` on individual files; it then works in a similar way to the RCS command `ci`. Let us assume that Seymour has made some changes to `plantshop.h` and wants to copy the new version into the CVS archive:

```
seymour$ cvs commit plantshop.h
```

This calls up Seymour's text editor, in which he can enter a comment on the change he has made. Alternatively, Seymour can also enter a comment while commit is being called. In both cases, the outcome is that a new revision is archived within CVS:

```
seymour$ cvs commit -m "New: Plant food" plantshop.h
Checking in plantshop.h;
.../CVS/plantshop/plantshop.h,v  <--  plantshop.h
new revision: 1.2; previous revision: 1.1
done
seymour$ _
```

Using CVS, a modification can also affect several files. During the call of commit without specifying any files, CVS only refers to the files that were modified from the version in the archive. For example, if Seymour has changed plants.C and pots.C, he is presented with:

```
seymour$ cvs commit -m "New: Support larger plants"
cvs commit: Examining .
cvs commit: Committing .
Checking in plants.C;
.../CVS/plantshop/plants.C,v <-- plants.C
new revision: 1.2; previous revision: 1.1
done
Checking in pots.C;
.../CVS/plantshop/pots.C,v <-- pots.C
new revision: 1.4; previous revision: 1.3
done
seymour$ _
```

Let us assume that the resulting configuration is to be delivered to a customer. Seymour gives the configuration a *name* so that it can be restored later. In CVS, this is done by using the tag command, which provides the current revision of every file in the work directory with a name. Seymour chooses the name plantshop1-1 for the current configuration:

cvs tag

```
seymour$ cvs tag plantshop1-1
cvs tag: Tagging .
T Makefile
T plantshop.h
T plants.C
T pots.C
seymour$ _
```

If Seymour later wants to restore the configuration, he can use the option "-r plantshop1-1" with checkout: CVS automatically determines the required files and supplies the appropriate revisions. Should he then also wish to correct an error, he can create a subpath using the additional option "-b". In this subpath, the error in plantshop1-1 can be corrected independently from the main path.

Adding project files

cvs add

At the moment, however, Seymour is still in the main path. Let us assume that Seymour has added a new file audreyII.C. The addition of source files has to be specially declared to CVS. This is done using the add command:

```
seymour$ cvs add audreyII.C
cvs add: scheduling file 'audreyII.C' for addition
cvs add: use 'cvs commit' to add this file
    permanently
seymour$ _
```

With the next commit, audreyII.C is included in the CVS archive.

```
seymour$ cvs commit -m "New: audreyII.C - weird plant"
cvs commit: Examining .
cvs commit: Committing .
RCS file: .../CVS/plantshop/audreyII.C,v
done
Checking in audreyII.C;
.../CVS/plantshop/audreyII.C,v  <--  audreyII.C
initial revision: 1.1
done
seymour$ _
```

Seymour could now give this configuration a new tag; checking out this configuration would automatically include audreyII.C, while in plantshop1-1, the file audreyII.C was not yet available. This illustrates how CVS independently remembers which files belong to a configuration and which do not.

cvs release

To conclude his work, Seymour informs the CVS system that he no longer wants to work on his files. To do this, in the CVS, there is the release command. release checks whether all local modifications have actually been taken on in the CVS archive – if not, a warning is the output. If all of the modifications have been committed, the additional option "-d" deletes the file in the work space.

In principle, the work space could also have been deleted without the use of special CVS commands; CVS would not object to this. However, Seymour uses release because of the added security of doing so.

```
seymour$ cd ..
seymour$ cvs release -d plantshop
```

```
You have [0] altered files in this repository.
Are you sure you want to release
directory 'plantshop': yes
seymour$ _
```

As a result, Seymour's plantshop project is deleted from his work space. He can resume his work at a later date by using checkout plantshop.

4.3   How CVS works

If, in the preceding examples, the messages of CVS are similar to those of RCS, this has a reason: CVS uses the RCS system for the versioning of individual files. As described in Chapter 3, it is only the *differences* between the individual revisions that are saved, and the same mechanisms are used for the management of main and subpaths as well as configuration names.

What distinguishes CVS from RCS is the ability to work on entire *file systems*. In CVS, this is carried out in the following way: For each project, CVS manages an *CVS archive* – its own file systems that contains the same directories and subdirectories as the original project. However, instead of the original files, this contains RCS files, as illustrated in Figure 4.2.

CVS archive

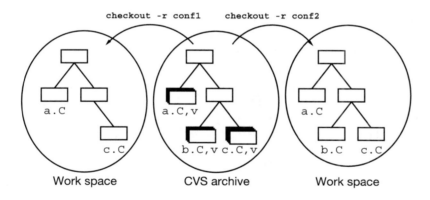

Work space   CVS archive   Work space

Figure 4.2
Check out from a CVS archive. CVS copies the directories of the CVS archive into a work space and determines the appropriate revision for each file.

When checking out, CVS initially lays out the directories in the same structure as in the CVS archive. Following this, the respective revisions are constructed via RCS, using the configuration tag or configuration date and are placed in the work space.

Seymour's plantshop project is, for instance, saved as a plantshop directory by CVS. For each of the files in his work directory, Seymour finds a matching RCS file:

```
seymour$ cd /usr/share/CVS/plantshop
seymour$ ls
```

```
Makefile,v plantshop.h,v    plants.C,v
audreyII.C,v  pots.C,v
seymour$ _
```

Should the plantshop project have subdirectories, these would also appear in the CVS archive; they would then likewise contain an RCS file for each of the project files.

In order to execute a commit correctly, CVS must know which revisions are there in the work space. For this purpose, in the work directory, CVS manages a file called CVS/Entries, in which the numbers and check out times of the revisions are listed:

```
seymour$ cd
seymour$ cd plantshop
seymour$ more CVS/Entries
/Makefile/1.1.1.1/Sat May 10 17:18:00 1986//
/plantshop.h/1.2/Sat May 10 17:34:39 1986//
/plants.C/1.2/Sat May 10 17:42:45 1986//
/pots.C/1.4/Sat May 10 17:42:47 1986//
D
seymour$ _
```

This information is used by CVS to establish which files are present in the work directory of the version control and which are not.

Removing project files

During the course of a project, files are not only added but also deleted, which creates a lot of organizational work for CVS. If Seymour wants to remove the file audreyII.C from the CVS archive again, he has to – like when adding files – explicitly inform CVS of his intention using a command called remove. Like add, remove also only affects the CVS archive

cvs remove

during the next commit.

```
seymour$ rm audreyII.C
seymour$ cvs remove audreyII.C
cvs remove: scheduling 'audreyII.C' for removal
cvs remove: use 'cvs commit'
to remove this file permanently
seymour$ cvs commit -m "audreyII.C deleted"
cvs commit: Examining .
cvs commit: Committing .
Removing audreyII.C;
.../CVS/plantshop/audreyII.C,v  <--  audreyII.C
new revision: delete; previous revision: 1.1
done
seymour$ _
```

Files that have been deleted are dealt with in a special way in the CVS
archive: their RCS file ends up in a special subdirectory called `Attic`.

```
seymour$ cd /usr/share/CVS/plantshop
seymour$ ls
Attic Makefile,v plantshop.h,v
plants.C,v pots.C,v
seymour$ ls Attic
audreyII.C,v
seymour$ _
```

By means of this special positioning in `Attic`, CVS marks the file as
"deleted in the most recent revision". Furthermore, CVS also uses special
configuration names in order to clearly label deleted revisions as such.

4.4 Parallel program development

In our example from Section 4.2, Seymour was able to begin immediately
with the work after the check out – in contrast to RCS, he did not have to
reserve the files he wanted to work on for himself using a lock before every
modification. In fact, CVS does not use locks – the name CVS originates
the fact that CVS explicitly allows parallel work.

CVS is based on the assumption that developers discuss things with each   *Cooperation strategy*
other and apportion work amongst each other so that they do not trespass on
each other's territories – and therefore only rarely come into conflict. The
cooperation strategy from CVS is therefore also said to be *optimistic* – as
opposed to the *pessimistic* cooperation strategy in RCS, which starts out
from the assumption that if there were conflicts, RCS would not prevent
them from using locks.

However, working in parallel requires developers to regularly *synchronize* their work spaces using the CVS archive – that is, take on modifications
from others as well as commit their own modifications to the CVS archive
when necessary. If there is no synchronization, the differences between
the individual work spaces increase – and with these, the probability of a
conflict.

We will explain this *synchronization process* with an example. Let   *Synchronizing*
us assume that developer Audrey is helping Seymour in his work on the   *modifications*
`plantshop` project. As is shown in Figure 4.3, both Audrey and Seymour
have set up a current revision of the project as a work environment, using
`checkout`.

Now Audrey modifies `plantshop.h`. Using `commit`, she copies the
new revision into the CVS archive, as shown in Figure 4.4.

Figure 4.3
*Two work spaces
from one CVS
archive.*

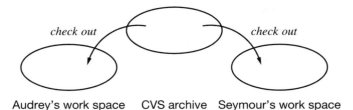

Audrey's work space   CVS archive   Seymour's work space

Figure 4.4
*Transferring
modifications from
a work space.*

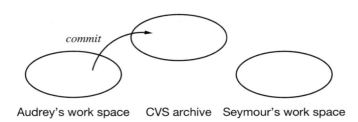

Audrey's work space   CVS archive   Seymour's work space

For his part, Seymour has modified `audreyII.C` and likewise wants to take on the new revision in the CVS archive. During `commit`, however, CVS establishes that Seymour's `plantshop.h` no longer matches the most recent revision: the `commit` command fails.

*Bringing the work
space up-to-date*

`cvs update`

To do justice to the `commit` command, Seymour must first bring his work space up-to-date. To do this, he uses a special CVS command called `update`. The `update` command brings a work space up-to-date by copying out all the files that were modified in the CVS archive since checking out – in our case, the `plantshop.h` file with Audrey's last modifications, as shown in Figure 4.5.

Figure 4.5
*Transferring
modifications into a
work space.*

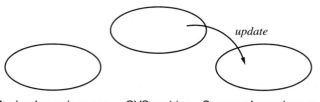

Audrey's work space   CVS archive   Seymour's work space

After Seymour has checked that his local modification to `audreyII.C` and Audrey's modifications in `plantshop.h` are compatible with each other, he can now publicize his modification in the CVS archive by using `commit` after the `update`. Audrey would then take on this modification in her own work space during her next *update*, shown in Figure 4.6.

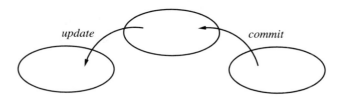

Figure 4.6
The further transfer of modifications.

Audrey's work space   CVS archive   Seymour's work space

But what happens if two developers have changed the same component at the same time? Let us assume that Seymour had also modified `plantshop.h`. The *update* command cannot simply replace Seymour's modified version with the current revision of the CVS archive, since Seymour's modifications are then lost. Instead, the `update` command *integrates* Seymour's modifications and the most recent modifications from the CVS archive, as explained in Section 2.5. The revision from Seymour's last check out or successful *commit* is used as the basis for the original version. Of course, as is also the case with every other *update*, Seymour must also check whether his work space is still consistent – therefore, whether Audrey's and his modifications are compatible.

4.5 Conflicts and arrangements

If Audrey and Seymour modify the same file, as well as the same place within the file, there will be a *conflict*. CVS then inserts *both* modifications into the file and marks the place where the conflict occurs; the conflict then has to be deleted manually. In practice, however, these kinds of conflicts are quite rare. This is because developers typically *coordinate* their work with each other.

Conflict

CVS has another special *preventive measure* to ensure that developers are coordinated. A developer can inform the CVS system that she wishes to *watch* an individual file or a file system. If another developer wants to edit a file, he can declare this explicitly. In doing so, all those who are watching the file are automatically notified of his purpose.

Watching files

Both functions, declaring and watching, are combined in CVS in the `edit` command. `edit` declares that a developer is willing to edit the indicated file; at the same time, the developer is registered as a watcher of the file.

`cvs edit`

Let us assume that Seymour has copied the file `plantshop.h` into his work space using `checkout`. Seymour now explicitly informs the CVS system that he wishes to edit `plantshop.h`:

> seymour$ **cvs edit plantshop.h**

Seymour is now watcher of `plantshop.h`; at the same time, all other watchers are informed. Let us now assume that Audrey also wishes to edit `plantshop.h`:

> audrey$ **cvs edit plantshop.h**

With this action, Seymour is automatically notified that Audrey is also editing the file `plantshop.h`; he can now organize his planned modifications with Audrey.

Regular watching   If Seymour and Audrey have applied their changes using `commit`, they are automatically unregistered as watchers by CVS; therefore, they will not be notified of further modifications to `plantshop.h`. They can, however, also be registered in CVS as *permanent watchers*; they are then also informed about any further modifications.

The mutual notification only makes sense if all users use the `edit` command. This is achieved by using the `watch` command. `watch` marks a file or a file system in CVS as "to be watched": If a file has been marked with `watch`, `checkout` only makes them available as read-only files in the work space. In order to be able to make them writable, the user must first enter the mandatory `edit`.

With the *watching* mechanism, CVS offers a medium between the purely optimistic and the purely pessimistic cooperation strategy: developers are informed about potential conflicts but are not forced to wait until the lock has been removed; instead, they can come to an agreement about how to proceed further.

4.6   Extensions and Alternatives

CVS Adaptation   In addition to specific project directories, the CVS archive also contains a CVS-specific "project" called `CVSROOT`. In this project, CVS events are connected to user actions using special files. A simple example of this is the handling of a *log file*, which with every *commit* is supplemented with a new entry: if the entry

```
^plantshop $CVSROOT/CVSROOT/log.pl
     %s /somewhere/plantshoplog
```

stands in the `loginfo` file, then with every `commit` in the `plantshop` project, the program `log.pl` is called, which appends the *commit* comment (first argument, "%s") to the file `/somewhere/plantshoplog` (second argument). The file `plantshoplog` then contains all the changes that have been made to the `plantshop` project in chronological order.

The files in `CVSROOT` allow far-reaching adaptations of the CVS system. It is not only possible to log changes in a file but also to send them to interested developers by e-mail. During the *commit*, test programs can be called, which make sure that the new revision or the comment conform to certain standards. Specific files (e.g., binary files) can be excluded from the versioning because of name and/or content.

Changes in `CVSROOT` are of course subject to version control; using `cvs checkout CVSROOT`, a copy of `CVSROOT` is created in its own work directory, and using `cvs commit` the modifications are returned to the CVS archive.

As for RCS, there are also numerous graphical user interfaces for CVS; Figure 4.7, for example, shows the `tkcvs` program. All important CVS commands can be selected at a simple touch of a button.

The CVS integration in the EMACS editor under the name `pcl-cvs` is also easy to use; it neatly integrates other EMACS packages for resolving conflicts interactively or for highlighting discrepancies.

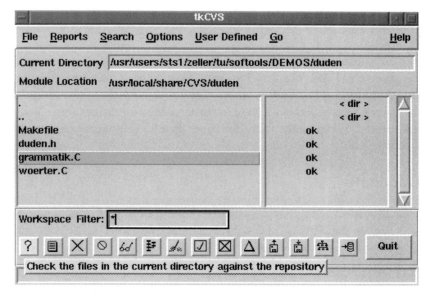

Figure 4.7
A graphical user interface to CVS.

With CVS, every developer has a complete copy of the project. In large projects, this requires a lot of space. Although the cost of the additional disk space is only a fraction of a developer's monthly wage, in practice, it is surprisingly hard to push for this kind of investment. Advanced SCM systems such as CLEARCASE resolve the problem of disk space by using a virtual file system to create the illusion of a separate work space for each user, while in fact, each version of a file is saved only once.

SUBVERSION   Another weak point of CVS is that CVS still relies on the *versioning of individual files:* Each file has its own version history, which makes it difficult to follow the history of the entire system. This is where the SUBVERSION project steps in. SUBVERSION not only places the file contents and the file existence (or nonexistence) under version control but also directories, copies, and renamings.

In CVS, a file can be renamed only by deleting the old file and creating a new file. The new file gets a new version history, but there is no link between new file and old file. In SUBVERSION, the renaming gets versioned as such – the version history is preserved and contains the renaming as a separate entry. Other features include the usage of the *Apache* Web server as a version server using the WebDAV protocol; also, SUBVERSION supports efficient storage and propagation of deltas between versions.

For compatibility, SUBVERSION uses the same commands as CVS; the only difference is that SUBVERSION is invoked using svn instead of cvs. Hence, to check out a system, one enters svn checkout instead of cvs checkout:

```
audrey$ svn checkout \
        http://svn.collab.net/repos subversion
```

The commercial BITKEEPER system goes one step beyond. Not only does it version entire file systems (as SUBVERSION does), it also supports *local version histories.* This feature allows developers to create new versions in their work spaces, without having to synchronize with the central archive. This feature is especially useful for large, distributed projects such as the Linux Kernel.

Concepts

❑ An SCM system must guarantee the *consistency* of configurations and also make sure that there is as much *flexibility* in the selection of configurations as possible.

❑ SCM systems do not usually have any mechanisms for detecting consistency; however, by *tagging configurations*, consistent configurations can be named and restored at a later date.

❑ The CVS system allows for the versioning of entire *file systems* as CVS also considers the *creation* and *deletion* of files.

❑ A *CVS archive* is structured in the same way as the project itself; each versioned file is assigned an RCS archive.

❑ CVS realizes an *optimistic cooperation strategy*, in which several developers integrate changes at the same time.

❑ SUBVERSION and BITKEEPER are reimplementations of CVS that support the full versioning of file systems.

Reviewed exercises

1. Your boss does not wish to buy more disk space nor an expensive SCM system and suggests that several developers share a communal work space. Discuss some less problematic space-saving alternatives.

2. Strictly speaking, CVS only versions single files, including their existence and nonexistence. Changes in the project structure, for instance the addition or deletion of directories, are not versioned; CVS simply deletes directories as soon as they no longer contain any files and creates new ones as soon as they contain at least one. Modifications in the properties of files, like, for example, access rights, are not versioned. What are the practical consequences of this?

3. After nearly having being eaten by a carnivorous plant, Seymour wants to rename the file `plantshop.h` into `horrorshop.h`. There are two ways of doing this:

   ❑ Audrey suggests to add a new file `horrorshop.h` with the latest contents of `plantshop.h` and to delete `plantshop.h`: "This way, we can always recreate any configuration".

   ❑ His friend Arthur suggests to rename the file within the CVS archive from `plantshop.h,v` to `horrorshop.h,v`: "This way, the version history gets preserved".

   What should Seymour do? Why?

4. Check whether SUBVERSION and BITKEEPER solve the problems in Exercises 2 and 3.

5. For certain applications, an integration of changes based purely on text is not that useful: XML or CAD files, for instance, require special integration tools. What must you do if such integration tools are not available? Think back to the cooperation strategy!

6. On the day before he went on a holiday, your colleague made some changes and placed them in the CVS archive. These resulted in you

not being able to compile your project at all. In order to avoid this kind of situation in the future, your boss suggests that a test program should be started automatically with every *commit*, which automatically compiles your project with the proposed changes and carries out several tests. As a result, each *commit* would then take 10 minutes. Discuss the advantages, disadvantages, and alternatives.

Further reading

CVS was introduced for the first time by Berliner (1990); in the original version, CVS was still realized using shell scripts. Since then, CVS has been continually developed and today is a widely distributed system for simple SCM tasks in medium-sized projects. CVS is freely available; advice and support for CVS are offered on a commercial basis by various companies. The work on this book was coordinated using CVS.

The first system to provide a virtual file system for versioning was the SUN Network Software Environment (NSE), described by Courington (1989). In virtual file systems from the NSE, work spaces are realized as *views* to a central archive. Only if a developer changes a file in his work space is a physical copy created. For the developer, this *copy-on-write* is transparent; NSE automatically makes sure that the shared parts are distributed over all work spaces between several developers.

In NSE, the optimistic coordination strategy was introduced under the concept of the *long transaction*. The analogy to the transaction concept in database systems is misleading these days, as there is no equivalent to the comparison of changes in database system.

The interaction of consistency and flexibility when configuring software systems is an old requirement of SCM users. Recent research distinguishes between *intentional* versioning, in which the SCM system arrange the configuration according to the *contents* – that is, in accordance with the user's wishes – and *extensional* versioning dealt with here, in which the versions are listed explicitly. In intentional versioning, changes can be combined freely; systems are configured and constructed using their *properties*. By means of restrictive conditions (e.g., change *A* and change *B* mutually exclude each other), the SCM system can ensure the consistency of the resultant configuration.

EPOS is a prototype intensional SCM system described by Gulla et al. (1991): It makes it possible to combine changes arbitrarily via the selection of options. For the ICE system, in which intentions are expressed using the feature-logic, Zeller and Snelting (1997) prove that the intentional versioning via a skillful selection of restrictive conditions covers all well-known versioning models. The side effect of intensional versioning is that all aspects of the versioning, in particular revisions and variants, are treated the same.

The security of consistency also plays a large part in the *dynamic configuration*, in the case of which the consistency of a configuration is only decided at runtime. Amongst other things, this current topic of research is dealt with by Schmerl and Marlin (1995) as well as Warren and Sommerville (1995).

Other tools for configuration management

In addition to the freely available tools RCS, CVS, SUBVERSION, and BIT-KEEPER that have been described in this book, there are also a number of other, mostly *commercial* tools for software configuration management. We have given a selection of these in the following list.

❑ The company *Open Avenue* (formerly *Cyclic Software*) offers CVS with commercial support.

❑ CLEARCASE from *Rational* (now IBM) is one of the most powerful SCM systems on the market. Its virtual file system allows direct access to arbitrary versions; CLEARCASE also makes it possible to organize the development and modification process by means of individual activities (so-called *unified change management*).

❑ CONTINUUS/CM from *Continuous* also puts particular value on the development and modification process; CONTINUUS organizes these processes like no other tool. In contrast, the actual version control is pushed into the background, but offers everything that is required.

❑ PERFORCE from *Perforce Software* is an extraordinarily quick and easy-to-use system for version control. The procedure of *interfile branching* developed by Seiwald (1996) allows particularly easy access to variants. Like CVS, PERFORCE makes it possible to work on local copies.

❑ PVCS of *Merant* and *Synergex* offer easy version controls that can be integrated well into a number of platforms.

❑ AEGIS is a freely available SCM system, whose development process requires *consistency checks*: a modification can then only be published if the program construction, tests and, if necessary, code inspections have been successfully completed.

❑ RAZOR from Tower Software also offers a highly polished modification and development process based on a standard version control system such as RCS or SCCS.

❑ VISUAL SOURCE SAFE from *Microsoft* has the basic functionality of the version control (e.g., to RCS level) under a WINDOWS interface. In the past, data integrity was said to be a common problem; buyers should look around on Internet forums for advice. The company *Mainsoft* also offers VISUAL SOURCE SAFE for UNIX.

Exercises I

In this exercise, you can carry out some simple program maintenance with CVS. To do so, you must first set up CVS.

Practice

1. In `ftp://ftp.gnu.org/pub/gnu/hello/`, you can find the GNU Hello program – for example, as `hello-1.3.tar.gz`. Copy this into one of your directories and unzip it using:

   ```
   $ gunzip hello-1.3.tar.gz
   $ tar xvf hello-1.3.tar
   $ cd hello-1.3
   ```

2. Now you should put GNU Hello under version control using CVS. Here we will proceed step by step:

   (a) Select a directory in which the CVS archive should be stored (e.g., $HOME/CVS) and set the variable CVSROOT accordingly. Using `sh`, this is done as follows:

   ```
   $ CVSROOT=$HOME/CVS; export CVSROOT
   ```

   If you use `csh` as shell:

   ```
   % setenv CVSROOT $HOME/CVS
   ```

   (b) Set up CVS:

   ```
   $ cvs init
   ```

   (c) Put the packet under CVS control:

   ```
   $ cvs import -m "Import GNU Hello 1.3" \
           hello GNU HELLO_1_3
   ```

   (d) You can now delete the original source.

   ```
   $ cd ..
   $ rm -fr hello-1.3
   ```

   (e) In order to work with the GNU Hello controlled by CVS, you have to first check out GNU Hello:

```
$ cvs checkout hello
```

In the `hello` directory (the work directory), you can now find all GNU Hello sources controlled by CVS.

3. In future CVS sessions with `hello`, you do not have to reset `CVSROOT`. Instead, you can carry on working in your work directory straight away. If, however, you begin a new project, you can proceed in the same way as is shown in point 2.

4. To test for GNU Hello, proceed in the following way:

   (a) Read the instructions in `README` and `INSTALL`, and compile the Hello program for your computer:

   ```
   $ ./configure
   $ make
   ```

   (b) Execute the Hello program:

   ```
   $ ./hello
   ```

Exercises

1. Translate the output of GNU Hello into German (say, "Hallo, Welt"). Look at the file `hello.c` and modify the output accordingly. (You do not need to know any C to carry out this change.) Check the result by compiling and executing GNU Hello.

2. Using `cvs diff`, determine the differences between the original version and your germanized variant. Investigate the effects of the various DIFF options.

3. The changes you have made should now be publicized in the CVS archive. For this, use `cvs commit`.

4. Now create a patch for GNU Hello. For this, you need the differences created by DIFF over several versions. You can also use `cvs diff` for this. Name your patch `hello-de.patch`.

5. Check whether your patch works by using the newly packed out GNU Hello packet. What happens if you use the same patch twice?

6. Create a patch `hello-fr.patch`, which translates the GNU Hello into French ("Bonjour, monde"). What happens if you want to use both patches?

7. Create a patch that renames the file `hello.c` to `hallo.c` in the German version:

(a) Rename `hello.c` as `hallo.c`. Using `cvs add`, you mark the added file and with `cvs remove` the removed file. You can find more details about this under "Moving and renaming files" in the CVS handbook.

(b) When using the patch, you must make sure that empty files are deleted. See "Removing empty files" in the PATCH handbook.

8. Create a file `.cvsignore` so that the system-specific files created by `configure` are ignored by CVS. You can find more notes on this under "Ignoring files via `cvsignore`" in the CVS handbook.

Part II

Processing Input

5 Lexical analysis using LEX

5.1 Processing input

A program receives a text as an input and processes it. A traditional, recurrent task: the program can be a *compiler*, which reads into the program to be compiled; it can be a *search program*, which searches for certain text patterns, or an *application program*, which reads into its configuration files.

As a rule, the input has a certain *structure* that the program that is carrying out the processing must recognize. This structure, the *syntax* of the input, has to be standardized so that it is clear what can and what cannot be processed. At the same time, the syntax acts as a guiding principle during implementation.

Syntax of the input

We consider the following example: there is an application program that at first reads in a *configuration file*. This configuration file consists of individual sections in the following form:

> [*title*]
> *name=value*
> *name=value*
>   ⋮
> [*title*]
> *name=value*
>   ⋮

Title, *name* and *value* are arbitrary strings.

On closer consideration, we establish that *title*, *name*, and *value* cannot be anything you like. *Title* and *name* should not contain " [", "] " nor "=", so that we can identify them clearly. It also makes sense to limit *title*, *name*, and *value* so that they cannot extend over several lines. Obviously, we must fix a precise *syntax description* in order to distinguish between valid and invalid inputs.

Syntax description

5.2   Finite automata

Finite automaton

One of the easiest means of describing the syntax of an input are *finite automata*. A finite automaton reads the input character by character and makes sure that the characters that have been read correspond to the syntax. It consists of the following parts:

State

1. a number of *nodes* that represent the possible *states* of the automata

State transitions

2. a number of possibly marked *edges* that indicate the possible *transitions* between the several states

Start state

3. a labeled *start state*

End state

4. a number of labeled *end states*.

Such an automaton is formally described as *nondeterministic finite automaton* (NFA).

As an example, we will consider the automaton in Figure 5.1, which reads a line of our configuration file.

Figure 5.1
Finite automaton for
configuration files.
During the reading of
a symbol, the
automaton changes
into the next state.

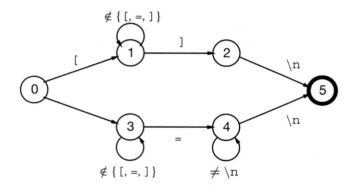

Conditional transitions

Most edges in this automaton carry a *marking* that indicates that the state can only be changed by reading this symbol. Other edges have *no marking* – which means that the state can be changed without having to read a symbol.

In the upper half, for instance, we see that the automaton (beginning with state 0) at first reads in a " [", in order to (state 1) process further symbols (any symbol apart from " [", "=", and "] "), in order to process a "] " (state 2) and a line end symbol ("\n", state 5). Similarly, the *name*, "=", and *value* are read in the lower halves.

Figure 5.2 shows an algorithm according to which an NFA works.

1. Set the current states S to the starting state.

2. **REPEAT**

   (a) Extend S by all states that can be reached without reading a symbol.

   (b) **IF** there are further readable symbols available **THEN**

      i. Read a symbol x

      ii. Replace S with the states that can be reached the states from S by reading x.

      iii. **IF** $S = \emptyset$ **THEN**
         $\frac{1}{7}$ – Stop, character string does not match the expression.

   (c) **ELSE** (no further readable symbols are available)

      i. **IF** S contains at least one end state **THEN**
         $\checkmark$ – Stop, character string and expression match.

      ii. **ELSE**
         $\frac{1}{7}$ – Stop, character string does not match the expression.

Figure 5.2
Algorithms for the processing by NFAs

Table 5.1 shows that the automaton from Figure 5.1 recognizes line "`[abc]`" but not line "`[abc]=d`".

S	input
{0, 3}	[abc]\n
{1}	abc]\n
{1}	bc]\n
{1}	c]\n
{1}	]\n
{2}	\n
{5}	
$\checkmark$	

S	input
{0, 3}	[abc]=d\n
{1}	abc]=d\n
{1}	bc]=d\n
{1}	c]=d\n
{1}	]=d\n
{2}	=d\n
$\emptyset$	
$\frac{1}{7}$	

Table 5.1
Usage of NFA from Figure 5.1

5.3 Regular expressions

How do you get from a finite automaton to a program? We could just duplicate the automaton 1:1 in a program and assign, for instance, a specific position in the program to each state. However, this is highly prone to errors and hard to maintain. It is much easier to implement the algorithm of Figure 5.2 and to feed it with the *description* of the finite automaton as well as the character string that is to be read in.

Regular expressions

In practice, it is far too laborious to describe the infinite automaton in the form of states and transitions. Therefore, we use a simpler representation – *regular expressions*. Regular expressions are simple but effective ways of describing character patterns. They can be automatically converted into an NFA, which can then read in character strings using the algorithm described.

What do regular expressions look like? For a start, a regular expression is a character string in which each character stands for *a character to be matched*. The regular expression "abc" is therefore equivalent to an automaton, which reads in "a", then "b", and finally "c".

Abstract symbols

However, some characters in regular expressions have a special meaning. They are called *abstract symbols*:

dummy ("."): The dummy "." stands for every character possible, apart from the line end symbol "\n".

Character classes ("[...]"): If you want to indicate a number of possible characters, you can use a *character class* – these are characters that are enclosed in brackets by "[" and "]". You can also give lists such as "[abc]" and ranges such as "[a-c]". These can also be mixed, such as in "[abc0-3xz]".

A character class can also be *negated* by being introduced with an initial "^" – the automation will then accept all characters except those that have been specified. The regular expression "[^0-9]" therefore accepts all characters apart from 0–9.

To incorporate a "]" or "-" in the character class, you put a "\" (the *escape* character) in front.

Repetition ("*" and "+"): The "*" operation comes after a character, a character class, or a dummy; it generates a regular expression that matches an arbitrary number of these characters (including the empty character string). For example, "[a-z]*" matches arbitrary long sequences of characters. (This operation is also called *Kleen closure*.) "+" works in a similar way to "*", but expects at least one occurrence – "*r+*" means the same as "*rr*".

Kleen closure

**Line restrictions ("^" and "$")**: there are two operations that generate a regular expression, which only match the beginning or end of the line. These are "^" for the beginning of the line and "$" for the end. For example, "^xyz" only matches lines that begin with "xyz" and "^[\t]*$" only matches lines that are empty or only contain blank spaces.

Grouping(" (...) "): A regular expression can be enclosed with " (" and
") ". By doing so, operations can be used on the enclosed expression
in the same way as they are used on single characters.

Alternative (" | "): The " | " operation describes a regular expression in
which the regular expression has to match either to the left of " | "
or to the right of " | ".

Option ("?"): The "?" operation comes after a character, a character class,
or a dummy; it creates a regular expression that matches one or no
occurrences of these characters – "*r* ?" means the same as " (*r* |) ".

Escape character("\"): in order to insert an abstract symbol as a concrete
character, you must insert a "\". The regular expression "\ ." therefore detects a dot, "\ * \ * \ *" detects three asterisks. "\\" detects a
single escape character.

> Additionally, special characters are introduced with escape charac-
> ters – for example, "\n" for line break or "\t" for tabulator.

Concrete character: All characters not listed above are *concrete characters*, and therefore stand for themselves.

Here are a couple of examples of regular expressions:

- ❏ " [a-zA-Z_] [a-zA-Z0-9_] *" detects identifiers in C.

- ❏ " [1-9] [0-9] *" detects integers.

- ❏ " [^\] = [] *" detects a sequence of characters, apart from "] ", "="
  and " [".

- ❏ "^\ [[^\] = [] *\] $" detects a line " [*title*] ".

- ❏ "^ [^\] = [] *=.*$" detects a line "*name=value*".

- ❏ "^ (\ [[^\] = [] *\] | [^\] = [] *=.*) $" detects a line of the con-
  figuration file (like the automaton in Figure 5.1).

The main use of regular expression is for *searching*: a number of tools
accept regular expressions as search patterns.

*Searching with
regular expressions*

As an example, we can look at GREP and EGREP that extracts all lines
that contain a given regular expression from a file (EGREP implements
all operations specified here; GREP does not recognize "?", "+", " | " and
" (...) ".)

GREP and EGREP use a *function library* for regular expressions, which
converts a regular expression into an NFA at runtime. The tools then process the input line by line with this NFA. If the automaton finds a matching

*Function library for
regular expressions*

character string, the line is output. In Chapter 11 we introduce the script languages Tcl, PERL, and PYTHON; they provide excellent ways of processing character strings by means of the built-in functions for regular expressions.

The actual translation of a regular expression into an NFA is not difficult: Successive characters correspond to successive states; each operation can be represented by an appropriate pattern in the NFA. The details, we leave to you for exercise; you will find the complete descriptions in further reading.

5.4   LEX – a scanner generator

By using a function library when working with regular expressions, you can cope with all kinds of find-and-replace tasks. You must program the *actions* that are to be carried out when certain regular expressions occur, and you also have to take care of the *assignment* of regular expressions to actions.

If you are searching for several different regular expressions in an input, it is useful to systematize the assignment of patterns – for example by using a *table* that assigns an action to every possible regular expression. It is precisely for this purpose that LEX – a lexical *scanner generator* is used. The following tasks can be carried out one by one using LEX:

Lexical analysis: Breaking down the input stream in its lexical elements by means of the specified pattern. This is where the name LEX originates from.

Data transformation: The transformation of patterns or sequences of characters in the input stream into corresponding character strings in the output stream (like the SED text manipulation program from Section 9.3.1).

Data evaluation: Further analyses, statistics, and calculations can be carried out using the pattern identified in the input stream. Examples of this are character and word counts, or the addition of all floating point numbers that occur.

In contrast to a runtime library, LEX converts regular expressions into an NFA at *compilation time*. This makes the programs more efficient:

❏ Regular expressions do not have to be converted with each program that is run.

❏ Some time-consuming *optimizations* are available, which would otherwise make the runtime of the program too long.

5.5 LEX specification

In order to resolve the tasks in hand, LEX uses a *specification file* that describes the regular expressions, which have to be detected, and the actions that have to be carried out. From this specification file, LEX generates a *program text*, which is executed later by an interpreter or is converted into an executable program by a compiler. (Original LEX supports the C programming language; for other programming languages, there are LEX variants that work in a similar way.) The specification consists of three sections separated by "%%":

Specification file

Layout of a specification file

> *Definitions*
> %%
> *Rules*
> %%
> *Functions*

Definition section: Definitions of regular expressions, which will be used later, as well as text of the target language can be entered here, which is then copied into the generated program as global definitions.

Rules section: This is a table of regular expressions with assigned actions. Regular expressions are separated from the actions by means of blank spaces or tabulators. Actions can be specified by means of special keywords(REJECT, ECHO) and instructions of the target language. If the regular expressions are missing at the beginning of the table, actions are copied as local definitions for the generated analysis routine (as text of the target language).

Function section: This section is optional. If this section is available, it is copied in full into the generated program in the global area behind the generated analysis routine.

From this specification, LEX generates a file lex.yy.c as the source code of the generated program, which must then be compiled and combined with the LEX library (via "-ll") (Figure 5.3).

Generated file

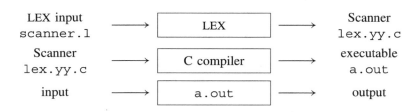

Figure 5.3
Creating an executable program using LEX

5.5.1 Example: Filtering expletives

Example 5.1 shows a simple specification emphasis.l, which is to filter *excessive emphasis*. If the words "very", "quite", or "really" occur in the input stream, they are ignored, as no action is specified (only ";"). However, all other characters are output on the standard output again by means of the ECHO action.

ECHO

Example 5.1
Filter specification
emphasis.l

```
%%
very    |
quite   |
really ;
 .      |
\n      ECHO;
```

It should be noted that the regular expression "." is suitable for all characters *apart from* the line break "\n". Therefore, "\n" must be specified individually. In addition, in this specification, the "|" symbols are not operations of regular expressions (although they are separated by blank spaces) but *special instructions* that adopt the actions of the subsequent rule. The similarity to the "|" operation of regular expressions is intentional.

Here we can see how the generated filter works:

```
$ lex emphasis.l
$ cc -o emphasis lex.yy.c -ll
$ echo "really a very simple example" |
    ./emphasis
 a   simple example
$ _
```

5.5.2 Example: The smallest possible specification

The smallest possible LEX specification consists of the text "%%". This specification leads to a program that copies the standard input onto the standard output (like the cat program). On this occasion, we allow LEX to read its specification from the standard input – the output of the echo command.

```
$ echo '%%' | lex
$ cc -o trivial lex.yy.c -ll
$ ./trivial < lex.yy.c
# include "stdio.h"
# define U(x) x
# define NLSTATE yyprevious=YYNEWLINE
```

```
# define BEGIN yybgin = yysvec + 1 +
# define INITIAL 0
# define YYLERR yysvec
# define YYSTATE (yyestate-yysvec-1)
# define YYOPTIM 1
    ⋮
```

This is based on the characteristic of LEX to automatically append a standard rule at the end of the rules section, which outputs every character that has not yet been processed. Therefore, "`%%`" corresponds to the specification file in Example 5.2.

```
%%
(.|\n)        ECHO;
%%
main() {
  yylex();
};
```

Example 5.2
A simple LEX
specification

In the `main` function, only the `yylex` routine generated by LEX for lexical analysis is started. In the LEX library, this kind of `main` function, which only calls `yylex`, is available by default.

5.5.3 Example: Removing HTML statements

In the previous example, we can also see an important characteristic of LEX-generated programs: *The input stream is processed as a character string without an implicit field or line separation.* The structure is determined via the specification, using regular expressions alone. The line break must be specified explicitly, but, in contrast to other tools, line breaks do not cause the generated program any problems.

Figure 5.4 shows the LEX specification of a program that removes all the HTML tags (including any line breaks that it contains) from a HTML text. The regular expression "`"<"[^>]*>`" recognizes all characters that stand between two angle brackets. (As the first character, "`<`" has a special meaning in LEX (see Section 5.6.2), it must be written as "`"<"`", in order to remove its special meaning.)

Removing HTML
statements

5.5.4 Example: Reading configuration files

The LEX specification from Example 5.3 reads in a configuration file as was described in Section 5.1. Here you can see how the character string

Figure 5.4
*Specification for the
removal of HTML
statements.*

```
$ lex dehtml.l
$ cc -o dehtml lex.yy.c -ll
$ ./dehtml < www.html > www.txt
```

dehtml.l
%%
"<"[^>]*> ;

www.html	www.txt
...at the <A HREF="http://www.uni-passau.de">Uni Passau</A> is...	...at the Uni Passau is...

that matches the regular expression can be used: the program created by
LEX provides a variable yytext, which contains the character string.
(Other such variables are yyleng – the length of the matching character
string – and yylineno – the current line number.) yytext is passed on
to functions that are implemented elsewhere, which process the title and the
definition; if the input does not match, an error function error is called.

Example 5.3
*Specification for
reading configuration
files*

```
%%
^\[[^\]=[]*\]$      process_title(yytext);
^[^\]=[]*=.*$       process_def(yytext);
\n                  ;
.                   error(yytext);
```

*Naming of regular
expressions*

What is striking in Example 5.3 are the complex regular expressions. They
can be simplified by providing common regular expressions with *names*:
in the definition section, recurrent regular expressions can be *predefined* so
that they can be used again later. When doing so, on the left stands the
name under which the regular expression that stands on the right can be
addressed. To refer to the defined regular expression, place its name in
curly braces.

The simplified version can be seen in Example 5.4. Here we use NAME,
to name a sequence of characters, excluding " [", " = " and "] ".

Example 5.4
*Simplified
specification*

```
NAME                [^\]=[]*
%%
^\[{NAME}\]$        process_title(yytext);
^{NAME}=.*$         process_def(yytext);
\n                  ;
.                   error(yytext);
```

5.5.5   Example: Adding up all numbers

Example 5.5 also uses named regular expressions.

```
NUM     [0-9]+
EXP     [Ee][-+]?{NUM}
        #include <stdlib.h>
        float sum = 0.0;
%%
{NUM}("."{NUM})?({EXP})?      sum += atof(yytext);
.        |
\n       ;
%%
main () {
  yylex();
  printf("sum = %f\n", sum);
}
```

Example 5.5
*Adding up read in
numbers*

Here, NUM is defined as a regular expression for integers and EXP as a regular expression for an exponent; they can be reused via "{NUM}" or "{EXP}". In addition, the definition section contains another instruction for the generated program to define the global variable sum in which all numbers are added up by the provided rule. Lines that do not start in the first column are copied 1:1 in to the generated program. Text that shall be copied can also be bracketed by "%{" and "%}", it then may start in the first column.

The remaining two rules for "." and "\n" cause all other symbols to be ignored. In the function section, only the calculated sum is output.

In this example, a *conflict* can arise since a single digit matches both the first rule for numbers and the second rule for single characters. LEX processes the input stream character by character. Further characters are read from the current character onward, as long as there is still a matching rule (*longest match*). If several rules match, the first one is used. Processing then starts again with the first character that does not match. However, it cannot be the case that there are no matching rules, as LEX always generates a rule that outputs characters that have not yet been processed (as we have already seen in Section 5.5.2).

Conflict

Longest match

5.6 Refinements of rule composition

People often want to make the application of a rule dependent on the *context* of the matching character string. The general solution is usually to use a *parser generator*, which can process *context free grammars*, which is dealt with in Chapter 6. For simple problems, LEX provides two ways of taking into account the context on both the right- and left-hand side. In

Context

addition, LEX provides a way of rejecting a rule and by doing so producing *overlapping rules*.

5.6.1　Trailing context

The "$" operation mentioned at the beginning of this chapter is not a genuine operation of a regular expression. For example, a ".$" rule matches all characters at the end of the line and processes the character itself but not the line break. This must be recognized and processed by its own rule using "\n". A regular expression $P\$$ is actually a shortened form of $P/\backslash$n.

Trailing context

In general, *trailing context* is defined as condition for a rule with the help of "/". A regular expression P/Q is then recognized only if PQ matches. However, only the character string that matches P is processed – that which matches Q remains in the input stream.

In Example 5.6, we see a LEX specification comma.l, which splits up numbers into a pre- and post-comma part.

Example 5.6
Use of trailing context in comma.l

```
%%
[0-9]+/"."[0-9]+    printf("Pre-comma %s\n", yytext);
"."                 printf("Comma.\n");
[0-9]+              printf("Post-comma %s\n", yytext);
(.|\n)              ;
```

At first sight, this specification works with no problems:

```
$ lex comma.l
$ cc -o comma lex.yy.c -ll
$ echo 123.456 | ./comma
Pre-comma 123
Comma.
Post-comma 456
$ _
```

Generally, an input such as "123.456.789" does not necessarily lead to the desired results, as "456" is recognized as a *pre-comma part* and not as a post-comma part:

```
$ echo 123.456.789 | comma
Pre-comma 123.456
Comma.
Pre-comma 456
Comma.
Post-comma 789
$ _
```

To correct this, the provision of *left context* is required. Before this is dealt with in the next section, the typical use of the right context will be shown here: In FORTRAN, empty space characters are ignored, "DO 5 I" and "DO5I" *can* both mean the same, but *do not have to*:

DO 5 I = 1.25	means	DO5I = 1.25
DO 5 I = 1,25	means	DO 5 I = 1 , 25

Here, the first case assigns the variable DO5I the value 1.25. The second case describes a loop, whose index I counts from 1 to 25 and carries the jump label 5. In order to identify whether "DO" is a keyword or an identifier, the right context must be taken into account. A possible regular expression would be "DO/[0-9a-zA-Z]*=[0-9a-zA-Z]*," (under the prerequisite that the blank spaces have already been filtered).

5.6.2 Start states

The consideration of *left context* is based on a different concept from that of trailing context. The principle in the case of left context are rules that may only be used in particular *states* – the so-called *start states*. The transition between these states is controlled by BEGIN actions in rules. In Example 5.7, an *LF* state is used (defined by "%S LF") to count (empty) lines.

Left context
Start states

BEGIN

```
%S       LF
%%
\n                      { ++lines; BEGIN LF;}
<LF>[\t ]*/\n  { ++emptylines; BEGIN INITIAL; }
.                       BEGIN INITIAL;
```

Example 5.7
Use of start states

❑ The first rule is not constrained and is executed in every state, as soon as a new line symbol is read. The assigned action increases the number of line breaks and switches to the LF state with "BEGIN LF".

❑ The second rule is only executed if the scanner is in the LF state. This rule only matches lines of blank spaces; its action increases the number of the empty lines and switches back to the start state ("INITIAL").

❑ The third and final rule switches back to the start state in the case of any other character (a line that is not empty).

This example, therefore, counts all lines of a character stream, as well as the lines that only consist of blank spaces. It simulates the behavior of the "^" and the "$" operations, which connects a rule to the whole line. Using these operations, the example is also easier to implement, as you can see in Example 5.8.

Example 5.8
Counting lines and blank spaces

```
%%
^[\t ]*$  ++emptylines;
\n        ++lines;
.           ;
```

5.6.3   Overlapping rules

Rejecting character strings

REJECT

Normally, a character string that matches a rule is only read once. This can be avoided using the REJECT action. If this is used, the character string that matches the current rule is *rejected*, that is, it is taken on as *not yet analyzed*. LEX then uses the rule that matches the *longest prefix* of the character string. This is either

❑ the character string itself, if there is still a subsequent rule that matches this rule exactly or

❑ a rule that matches a prefix of the character string

As an example, we consider the file reject.l from Example 5.9. Here all three-letter words are registered in the second rule and are then rejected.

Example 5.9
Start states in
reject.l

```
%%
.     printf("Accept %s\n", yytext);
...   printf("Reject %s\n", yytext); REJECT;
foo   printf("Match  %s\n", yytext);
\n    ;
```

If the word is "foo", it is accepted by the following rule. Otherwise, the first rule is used on the prefix of the word:

```
$ lex reject.l
$ cc -o reject lex.yy.c -ll
$ echo afoobatz | ./reject
Reject afo
Accept a
Reject foo
Match  foo
Reject bat
Accept b
Reject atz
Accept a
Accept t
Accept z
$ _
```

5.7   Generating scanners

Instead of specifying all actions directly in the rule section, you can use
another property of the code created by LEX. The routine `yylex` can be
defined as a function with a particular return type. `return` instructions of
this type can then be used as actions in the rule section.

yylex

In Example 5.10, for instance, the input text is to be output again – excluding the entries `quit` and `help`, which call the help system or exit the
program respectively.

```
%%
quit      return 0;
help      return 1;
%%
main() {
  while (yylex())
    printf ("No help available.\n");
}
```

Example 5.10
LEX specification
with return

The scanner specification in the Example 5.11 produces a simple scanner
that detects words and numbers in the input stream and returns a corresponding token value. For individual characters, which are neither letters
or numbers nor blank spaces, the scanner returns the ASCII value of the
character.

```
%{
#define NUMBER 256
#define WORD 257
%}
%%
[0-9]+        return NUMBER;
[a-zA-Z]+     return WORD;
[ \t\n]       ;
.             return yytext[0];
```

Example 5.11
Simple scanner
specification

This kind of use of LEX is mainly found when it is used as a *scanner
generator*. The `yylex` routine is then used to split the input stream into
tokens – individual lexical units – and with each call read and return the
next token.

Scanner generator

Token

This kind of generated *scanner* is of course only one part of a large
program that must take on the processing of the tokens that have been
provided by the scanner. The next chapter looks at how such parts of a
program can be generated by means of other tools. It also shows how the
syntactical analysis is performed using the YACC tool.

Concepts

❑ A *nondeterministic finite automaton* (NFA) describes the *syntax* of an input in the form of *state transitions*, which are induced by the characters that have been read in.

❑ A *regular expression* describes an NFA in the form of sequences of characters and *operators*.

❑ A regular expression can be converted at runtime in an NFA, which then recognizes the appearance of the regular expressions in a character string.

❑ LEX connects regular expressions with *actions*, which are then always executed if the corresponding expression has been matched.

❑ A *scanner* created by LEX is used in order to split up input streams into *tokens*, which are then used, for example, as input for the syntactical analysis.

Review exercises

1. Amend the automaton from Figure 5.1 so that it meets the following requirements:

   (a) In the title, in front of a " [" and after a "]" as many blank spaces as desired should be allowed.

   (b) In "*name* = *value*", as many blank spaces as desired should be allowed before and after *name* as well as before *value*.

   (c) In addition, comments should be possible, which start with a "#" and go on to the end of the line.

2. As a supplement to the operators "*" and "+", many libraries for regular expressions offer the additional operation "$\{n, m\}$" (min. n-times, max. m-times occurrences). How can a regular expression containing these operations be converted into an expression that does not contain these operations?

3. For the following constructs, give regular expressions in the variants MODULA-2, JAVA, and C, respectively:

   (a) identifiers

   (b) real numbers

   (c) strings

   (d) operators (arithmetical, logical, comparative, and assigning)

4. Implement the algorithm that executes nondeterministic finite automata.

5. Develop a method to automatically construct a corresponding NFA from a regular expression. (Try on your own at first, before consulting Aho et al. (1988).)

6. Write a LEX specification that replaces all sequences of white spaces (blank spaces, tabulators, and line breaks) with a single blank space.

7. Write a LEX specification that creates a program with the functionality of the "wc" UNIX tool. ("wc" counts the number of characters, words, and lines of the input stream).

8. Write a filter that removes the comments of the following languages:

   (a) C – "/*...*/"

   (b) JAVA – "/*...*/" and "//..."

   (c) MODULA-2 – "(*...*)", may be nested

   (d) PASCAL – "(*...*)" and "{...}", may be nested

   Where are the differences? Which particular problems are there?

9. Why is the REJECT operation so expensive?

Further reading

The first investigation into regular expressions comes from Kleene (1956). They are looked at in more detail in Jeffrey (2002), Hopcroft et al. (2000), and Aho et al. (1986). In addition to this, the application of regular expressions in the construction of scanners is described in the latter, in particular, for LEX specifications. Another good description of LEX can be found in Levine et al. (1992).

The name of GREP originates from the ED command "g/*RE*/p", which in a file that is being processed outputs all lines that match the regular expression *RE*. The tools of the GREP family are compared against each other in Aho (1980). A variant of the GREP family is AGREP, an approximating GREP from Wu and Manber (1992). It allows the search for character strings that do not match exactly, to allow for typing errors in files, for example. The technique that is used is similar to DIFF (see Chapter 2), since AGREP determines the number of changes to the character string that are necessary so that the regular expression that is being used matches.

6 Syntactical analysis with YACC

6.1 Introduction

LEX, which was introduced in Chapter 5, is an excellent tool for processing sequences of individual characters and words. As soon as these sequences take on a complex structure, however, LEX is no longer sufficient. In principle, a data format becomes too complex for LEX, as soon as any kind of *recursion* or *bracketing* is included. The following are some of the tasks that are involved in the processing of such data:

Reading data structures: The data structures of many programs typically consist of atomic objects as well as combined objects that consist of further objects – for example, a vector graphic or a nested document. When reading these kinds of *tree structures* from a file, the structure of the data has to be restored.

Reading tree structures

Recognizing symbolic expressions: One of the tasks of numerous applications is to process *symbolic expressions*, such as arithmetic terms. The correct reading and evaluation of a symbolic expression, in which brackets and rules of priority have to be taken into account, is a demanding task.

Reading symbolic expressions

Processing configuration files: Many applications offer their end users the opportunity to adapt and program them via special *configuration files*. These kind of configuration files are often similar to simple programming languages; the correct reading and processing of these is accordingly complex.

Reading configuration files

Of course, it is possible to write programs that can master these tasks. It is, however, a lot easier to have these programs written automatically. For this purpose, the software tool YACC was developed by Stephen C. Johnson in the seventies. Like LEX, YACC (engl. *yet another compiler compiler*: another compiler compiler) is also a *program generator*: YACC takes a *grammar*, a general description of the structure of a file. From this, YACC creates a *parser*, a program for processing these types of files. YACC, originally designed for processing program text, today belongs to the standard

YACC

Grammar
Parser

toolbox of professional programmers. Most applications, which read non-trivial data structures (including YACC itself), use a YACC-generated parser to do this.

6.2 Describing input using grammars

Context-free grammar

The structure of the input to be processed by YACC, is described using a *context-free grammar*. This kind of grammar is made up of four parts:

Tokens

1. A set of *tokens*, also called terminals

Nonterminal

2. A set of *nonterminals*

Rule

3. A set of productions or *rules*, in which the left side consists of a nonterminal and the right side consists of a sequence of symbols (tokens or nonterminals)

Start symbol

4. A nonterminal labeled as a *start symbol*.

As an example of a grammar, we will first look at simple arithmetical expressions consisting of positive integers, addition, and subtraction – for example, 2+2, 72 or 3+5-8. We begin with the numbers whose structure is described by the following grammar:

Example 6.1
Numbers

$$number \longrightarrow digit$$
$$number \longrightarrow number\ digit$$
$$digit \longrightarrow 0\ |\ 1\ |\ 2\ |\ 3\ |\ 4\ |\ 5\ |\ 6\ |\ 7\ |\ 8\ |\ 9$$

This grammar reads as follows: a *number* can be a *digit* (first rule), but also a *digit*, that follows a *number*. A *digit* is one of the characters 0 ... 9; as in regular expressions, we use the vertical dash (|) to highlight alternatives.

Now to the terms themselves. A term is either a number or a term to which a number is added or subtracted. The complete grammar now looks as follows:

Example 6.2
Terms

$$term \longrightarrow number\ |\ term + number\ |\ term - number$$
$$number \longrightarrow digit\ |\ number\ digit$$
$$digit \longrightarrow 0\ |\ 1\ |\ 2\ |\ 3\ |\ 4\ |\ 5\ |\ 6\ |\ 7\ |\ 8\ |\ 9$$

In this grammar, *term*, *number*, and *digit* are the nonterminals, with *term* as the start symbol; the tokens of the grammar are +, -, as well as 0 ... 9.

YACC now takes this kind of grammar and from this creates a *parser*, which processes input according to the grammar rules. In the process, the

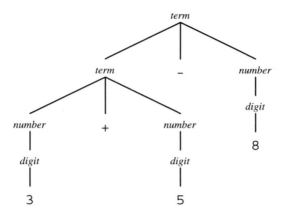

Figure 6.1
A parser tree.

structure of the input can be represented as a *tree*. If YACC, for example, is given the input `3+5-8`, the input will be processed according to the structure in Figure 6.1.

The possible input described by this grammar can also be written as a regular expression (as "`[0-9]+([-+][0-9]+)*`"). If, however, we extend our grammar with further operations and bracketing, it can no longer be written as a regular expression. Example 6.3 shows a simple grammar which, as well as addition and subtraction, recognizes bracketed expressions as well as multiplication (`*`) and division (`/`):

expression	$\longrightarrow$	*operand* | *expression operator operand*
operand	$\longrightarrow$	*number* | (*expression*)
operator	$\longrightarrow$	+ | - | * | /

Example 6.3
Arithmetical
expressions

The start symbol is *expression*; the above rules apply for *number* and *digit*.

Unfortunately, in practice, this kind of grammar is unusable. It writes the syntax of expressions such as `1+2*3+4` correctly. The *structural* information, however, leaves a lot to be desired: all operators are treated the same, regardless of priority. This is clear in Figure 6.2: the expression `1+2*3+4` is bracketed as $(1 + 2) * 3 + 4$ and not as $1 + (2 * 3) + 4$, as one would expect from the "Please excuse my dear aunt sally" rule.

In practice, we would prefer a grammar that gives priority to the multiplication and division operators over the other operators. This can be set up by assigning the grammar separate rules for sums and terms:

expression	$\longrightarrow$	*sum*
sum	$\longrightarrow$	*sum* + *term* | *sum* - *term* | *term*

Example 6.4
Arithmetical
expressions with
priority

Figure 6.2
A parser tree without
priority.

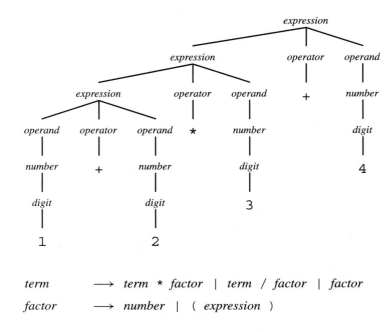

| *term* | $\longrightarrow$ | *term * factor* \| *term / factor* \| *factor* |
| *factor* | $\longrightarrow$ | *number* \| *(expression)* |

We can now use this corrected grammar in YACC in order to write a program that reads and evaluates arithmetical expressions. This is the topic of the next section.

6.3   YACC specification

YACC is given a *YACC specification* as input, which contains the grammar of the input to be processed. From this, YACC generates a C program, from which the C compiler creates an executable program. This program then processes the input according to the grammar and executes defined pieces of the program. The individual steps are shown in Figure 6.3.

Figure 6.3
Creating an
executable program
with YACC.

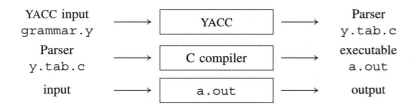

We want to explain the YACC specifications using an example. The program (called `a.out`) takes arithmetical expressions from the input and evaluates them:

```
$ ./a.out
2 + 2
4
27.001 * 8
216.008
1 + 2 * (3.4 + 5)
17.8
$ _
```

This calculation program was generated from the YACC specification in Example 6.5. We will use this specification to explain the general structure. A YACC specification consists of four sections:

Structure of a YACC specification

```
%{
C declarations
%}
YACC declarations
%%
rules
%%
Auxiliary functions
```

The meaning of the four parts will be explained in the following sections.

6.3.1 C declarations

In this section, *C functions are declared, which are required later*. In Example 6.5, for example, the functions of the C library for the input and output in `<stdio.h>` are declared. The YACC-specific macro `YYSTYPE` is explained in Section 6.3.3.

Declaration of necessary C functions

6.3.2 YACC declarations

In this area, the *properties of the grammar* are declared. In our example,

Declaration of grammar properties

```
%token NUMBER
%start input
```

declare the symbol `NUMBER` as a token and the nonterminal `input` as the start symbol. In addition to the tokens declared with "`%token`", character constants (enclosed by "`"`") are also valid as tokens.

Example 6.5
A YACC
specification
grammar.y *for the*
evaluation of
arithmetical
expressions. (Only
the declaration
section and the rules
section are shown;
the additionally
required auxiliary
functions are shown
in Section 6.3.4.)

```
%{
#include <stdio.h>
#define YYSTYPE double
%}

%token NUMBER
%start input

%%
input      :    /* empty input */
           |    input lines
           ;

lines      :    '\n'               /* line end */
           |    expression '\n'    { printf("%g\n", $1); }
           ;

expression :    sum                { $$ = $1; }
           ;

sum        :    sum '+' term       { $$ = $1 + $3; }
           |    sum '-' term       { $$ = $1 - $3; }
           |    term               { $$ = $1; }
           ;

term       :    term '*' factor    { $$ = $1 * $3; }
           |    term '/' factor    { $$ = $1 / $3; }
           |    factor             { $$ = $1; }
           ;

factor     :    NUMBER             { $$ = $1; }
           |    '(' expression ')' { $$ = $2; }

%%
```

The separation between C and YACC declarations is random; in fact, C
and YACC declarations are mixed up arbitrarily. Because of this, a YACC
specification is divided into three sections, in the same way as a LEX
specification.

6.3.3 Rules

Description of the
input structure

The structure of the input processed by YACC is described here. A grammar
rule in the form of

    nonterminal $\longrightarrow$ *symbol-sequence-1* | ... | *symbol-sequence-n* is written in YACC in the form of

> *nonterminal* : *symbol-sequence-1* | . . . | *symbol-sequence-n* ;

Hereby, the symbols ": ", "|", and "; " are typically arranged in one column so that the first rule is formatted as follows:

```
input    :   /* empty input */
         |   input line
         ;
```

Text enclosed by "/*...*/" is a *comment*; the rule, therefore, implies that an input is a (possibly empty) sequence of lines.

In YACC, each rule can be assigned *semantic actions*. These actions – small parts of a C program – will then be executed if the nonterminal has been successfully identified on the left-hand side of the rule. Additionally, each symbol can also be assigned a *value*. In an action, $$ can then be used to refer to the value of the nonterminal on the left-hand side and $*n* to refer to the value of the *n*th token or nonterminal on the right-hand side. In the rule,

Semantic actions

$$
$n

```
line   :  '\n'
       |  expression '\n' { printf("%g\n", $1); }
       ;
```

the value $1, therefore the value of the nonterminal `expression`, is output in the action enclosed by {...} using `printf`.

The typical action of a YACC rule is, however, to determine $$, depending on the separate $*n*. So, in the following rule,

Assignment to $$

```
term   : term '*' factor    { $$ = $1 * $3; }
       | term '/' factor    { $$ = $1 / $3; }
       | factor             { $$ = $1; }
       ;
```

the value pf the nonterminal `term` is determined using the nonterminals `term` and `factor` already read. Incidentally, we would have been able to leave out the last action { $$ = $1; }; it is always automatically created by YACC if no action is given.

The type of the value passed through by YACC via $$ is established using the YYSTYPE macro, which we have defined as `double` (therefore suitable for floating point numbers) in the C-declaration section.

6.3.4 Auxiliary functions

In order to complete our program, we have to provide another three functions, which supplement the Example 6.5. They are appended to the end of the YACC specification `grammar.y` and are separated from the rules by "`%%`".

Providing YACC with tokens

yylex – Reading tokens: We must, at some point, provide YACC with tokens. This is the task of a `yylex` function, which we must provide ourselves. Our implementation overlooks successive blank spaces. If a number then follows, `yylex` returns the NUMBER token. On this occasion, `yylex` then reads in the number using `scanf` and stores its value as a value of the NUMBER token in the YACC variable `yylval`. All other symbols are returned immediately by `yylex`; the return value 0 indicates the end of the input.

Example 6.6
The Auxiliary function `yylex` *reads in tokens*

```
int yylex()
{
    int c;

    /* overlook blank spaces */
    while ((c = getchar()) == ' ' || c == '\t')
        ;

    /* reading numbers */
    if (c == '.' || isdigit(c))
    {
        ungetc(c, stdin);
        scanf("%lf", &yylval);
        return NUMBER;
    }

    /* At the end of the input:return 0 */
    if (c == EOF)
        return 0;

    /* return individual symbols */
    return c;
}
```

Errors in the input

yyerror – output error message: If an error was found in the input, YACC calls this function. Our version simply outputs the error message:

Example 6.7
The Auxiliary function `yyerror` *deals with error messages*

```
int yyerror(char *msg)
{
    fprintf(stderr, "%s\n", msg);
}
```

main – Main program: The parser generated by YACC is called via the function `yyparse`; the return value is 1 for errors, otherwise 0. Our main program `main` simply calls `yyparse` and returns its value to the calling environment:

Calling the YACC parser

```
int main()
{
    return yyparse();
}
```

Example 6.8
Call of the `yyparse` *parser function generated by YACC*

Here, all three functions are kept simple deliberately. In practice, the function `yylex` is often a lot more complicated, for example, because the identifier and comments have to be processed. Anyone wanting to save much work can create `yylex` from a scanner generator such as LEX. In practice, basic lexical units in the rule are processed by the scanner, while the parser is responsible for the larger structure of the input. More about this in Section 6.4.

YACC and LEX

Our `yyerror` is also short and sweet; a more user-friendly implementation could, for example, output the exact position of the error. And since our computer example may typically be a component of a larger application, there is still much to complete for `main`.

6.3.5   Calling YACC

Our YACC specification is now complete. From this, the following steps create a functioning program. We call YACC with our specification in `grammar.y`:

```
$ yacc grammar.y
$ _
```

This creates a parser as a C program in the file `y.tab.c`. We can now compile this C program whereby we link in the YACC auxiliary functions with the option `-ly`.

```
$ cc y.tab.c -ly
$ _
```

Done! Now we can input and evaluate expressions:

```
$ ./a.out
2 + 2
4
$ _
```

6.4   Binding LEX to YACC

In Section 6.3, we wrote a scanner that provides the parser generated by
YACC with tokens. Even for this small task, this has already become quite
expensive. We have already seen that the lexical analysis is carried out
much more easily by a scanner generated by LEX in Chapter 5. Normally,
YACC is used in conjunction with LEX, because LEX provides the exact `yylex` routine that YACC uses. Therefore, in the file `grammar.y`,
we remove the `yylex` function from Example 6.6 and use one of the
scanners generated by LEX, which is specified in Example 6.9 as the file
`scanner.l`.

Example 6.9
Scanner
specification
`scanner.l` *for LEX*

```
%{
#define YYSTYPE double
#include "y.tab.h"
#include <stdlib.h>
extern YYSTYPE yylval;
%}
NUM      [0-9]+
EXP      [Ee][-+]?NUM
%%
{NUM}("."NUM)?({EXP})?    { yylval = atof(yytext);
                                  return NUMBER; }
[ \t]                     ;
.                         |
\n                        return yytext[0];
```

Generating token
definitions

In the next step, the parser is generated again. In the process, via the
option "`-d`" we instruct YACC to create an additional file `y.tab.h` with
the token definitions:

```
$ yacc -d grammar.y
$ _
```

In the LEX specification, the token definition for NUMBER is used by integrating `y.tab.h`. In addition, the parser variable `yylval` is declared
(with type YYSTYPE, `double`) so that it can be used in the scanner and
can pass on the value of the token NUMBER. (Most variants of YACC define
`yylval` in the header file `y.tab.h` already and the declaration can be
omitted.)

The next two steps are the generation of the scanner by LEX and the
compilation of the generated source texts into a program (the LEX specification is in the file `scanner.l`):

```
$ lex scanner.l
```

```
$ cc y.tab.c lex.yy.c -ll -ly
$ _
```

The program a.out that has now been created behaves in the same way
as the original yylex routine that was written manually:

```
$ ./a.out
7 - 3
4
$ _
```

6.5 How a YACC parser works

The parser generated by YACC is known as an *LR parser*. The LR means
that the YACC parser processes its input from left (L) to right and that
generally the nonterminal furthest right (R) is replaced first.

LR parser

The parser generated by YACC works by using a *stack*, in which tokens
and nonterminals are stacked up together with their values. This storing is
traditionally called *shifting*. During reading, the YACC parser shifts tokens
onto the stack until the uppermost tokens on the stack correspond to the
right-hand side of a rule. This rule is then *applied*: the respective tokens are
removed from the stack and replaced by the nonterminal on the left-hand
side of the rule. This replacement is called *reducing*.

Stack
Shifting

Reducing

As an example, we consider our YACC specification from Example 6.5.
Let us assume that the entire input is 1+2*3\n. Table 6.1 shows how the
generated parser processes this input.

1. At the start, the stack is empty and none of the input has been read.

Start state

2. The first action is *shifting*: 1 is read from the input and the NUMBER
   token is put on the stack with the value of the token (displayed as
   $NUMBER_1$).

3. The next action is the *reduction* using the rule factor : NUMBER,
   as the NUMBER token is on top of the stack and matches the right-hand
   side of this rule. The value of the symbol is then copied in accordance
   with the semantic action { $$ = $1; } and the new symbol factor
   is put on the stack along with this value (displayed as $factor_1$).

4. The token now at the top factor matches the right-hand side of the
   rule term : factor and is reduced accordingly. Again, only the
   value is copied as the semantic action here.

5. Now it is reduced again using the rule sum : term.

Table 6.1

Mode of operation of the parser created by YACC. YACC shifts tokens from the input onto the stack until it can reduce the stack by means of a rule

	Stack	Input	Action
1		$1+2*3\backslash n$	
2	$NUMBER_1$	$+2*3\backslash n$	S
3	$factor_1$	$+2*3\backslash n$	$R_{factor\ :\ NUMBER}$
4	$term_1$	$+2*3\backslash n$	$R_{term\ :\ factor}$
5	sum_1	$+2*3\backslash n$	$R_{sum\ :\ term}$
6	sum_1+	$2*3\backslash n$	S
7	$sum_1 + NUMBER_2$	$*3\backslash n$	S
8	$sum_1 + factor_2$	$*3\backslash n$	$R_{factor\ :\ NUMBER}$
9	$sum_1 + term_2$	$*3\backslash n$	$R_{term\ :\ factor}$
10	$sum_1 + term_2*$	$3\backslash n$	S
11	$sum_1 + term_2 * NUMBER_3$	$\backslash n$	S
12	$sum_1 + term_2 * factor_3$	$\backslash n$	$R_{factor\ :\ NUMBER}$
13	$sum_1 + term_6$	$\backslash n$	$R_{term\ :\ term\ '*'\ factor}$
14	sum_7	$\backslash n$	$R_{sum\ :\ sum\ '+'\ term}$
15	$expression_7$	$\backslash n$	$R_{expression\ :\ sum}$
16	$expression_7 \backslash n$		S

6. A further reduction can actually be made here using the rule `expression : sum`; even if we do this, the rest of the input cannot be read, as a line break ("\n") is expected but a plus symbol ("+") appears instead. The next token of the input (the *lookahead*) is used instead to decide whether to shift or reduce using a rule. Therefore, this next "+" token is shifted to the stack.

Lookahead

7. Now there is another shifting, there is no other option.

8. Now there is a reduction, first with `factor : NUMBER` ...

9. ... and then with `term : factor`.

10. At this point, the lookahead is used again to decide that there is not a reduction but a shifting.

11. Now there is another shifting ...

12. ... and the NUMBER token is reduced.

13. Now there is a reduction using the rule `term : term '*' factor` and in the process, by means of the semantic action `{ $$ = $1 * $3 }` a new value is calculated from the two values ($2 * 3 = 6$), which is appended to the new symbol.

14. Reduce again using the rule `sum : sum '+' term` and execute the semantic action `{ $$ = $1 + $3 }`.

15. Reduce using the rule `expression : sum`.

16. Shift again.

17. At last, another reduction using the rule `line : expression`   *End of the input*
    `'\n'` is done. At the same time, the action that outputs the calculated
    value is executed.

The exact mode of operation of the parser generated by YACC can be de-   *Description of the*
scribed by YACC on demand. If, during the call from YACC you enter the   *mode of operation*
option `-v` as well as a parser, YACC creates a file `y.output`, which docu-   *by YACC*
ments the mode of operation. In this case, among other things, `y.output`
contains the entry

```
state 17

    sum    ->   sum '+' term .        (rule 6)
    term   ->   term . '*' factor     (rule 9)
    term   ->   term . '/' factor     (rule 10)

    '*'         shift, and go to state 14
    '/'         shift, and go to state 15

    $default    reduce using rule 6 (sum)
```

Every YACC parser is always in a particular state that is indicated by a
number. The state 17 that is shown here is connected to rules 6, 9, and 10 of
the grammar; the dot " . " shows the respective position during the reading.
In all three cases, a `term` has therefore just been read. If this is followed
by a "`*`" or a "`/`", the symbol is shifted to the stack, and the parser
changes into a new state ("`go to state`"). Otherwise, ("`$default`")
rule 6 is applied in order to determine the sum and reduce the stack. (The
exact format of the `y.output` file is different from implementation to
implementation; we have used the format of the YACC variant from GNU
called BISON.)

6.6   Conflicts and how to resolve them

There are grammars that cannot be converted into a parser by YACC. These   *Ambiguous*
include all grammars that cannot *be clearly deduced*. The reason for am-   *grammars*
biguity is a *conflict* between several possible sequences of parser actions.

6.6.1   Shift/reduce conflicts

A "classic" example is the *dangling else conflict*, which is illustrated in the   *Dangling* else
following grammar:

```
...
statement     : ...
              | if_statement
              ;

if_statement : IF expression THEN statement
              | IF expression THEN statement
                              ELSE statement
              ;
```

Shift/reduce *conflict*

The grammar describes a typical programming language construct, and the (IF) condition, in which the alternative (ELSE) can be omitted. This grammar contains a so-called *shift/reduce* conflict, which YACC displays during the processing:

```
$ yacc -v ifelse.y
conflicts:  1 shift/reduce
$ _
```

We can gather more details about the cause of the error in the file y.output created by YACC:

```
State 7 contains 1 shift/reduce conflict.
...
state 7

    if_statement  ->  IF expression THEN state-
ment .
                                            (rule 3)
    if_statement  ->  IF expression THEN state-
ment .
                                ELSE statement
                                            (rule 4)

    ELSE          shift, and go to state 8

    ELSE          [reduce using rule 3 (if_statement)]
    $default      reduce using rule 3 (if_statement)
```

We can see that the conflict occurs if the parser has processed a statement in the if_statement and an ELSE follows. The parser can now *reduce* the expression, whereby the ELSE is assigned to the first IF. This has the result that a statement

if A then if B then C else D

is bracketed as

$$if\ A\ then\ (if\ B\ then\ C)\ else\ D.$$

The alternative is to shift ELSE onto the stack and then to process the inner statement. By doing so, the ELSE is assigned to the last open IF and the statement is bracketed as

$$if\ A\ then\ (if\ B\ then\ C\ else\ D)$$

This is also the standard in all programming languages that support conditions and alternatives.

If there are *shift/reduce* conflicts, the default for YACC is to give preference to the shifting, which produces the desired results here. The *reduce* alternative that has not been executed is put in y.output in square brackets, which makes it clear that it has not been executed.

Resolving shift/reduce conflicts

To prevent the error message from appearing, the grammar can also be made explicitly clear:

```
%token IF THEN ELSE something
%%
statement      : full_if
               | open_if
               ;

full_if        : something
               | IF expression THEN full_if
                                ELSE full_if
               ;

open_if        : IF expression THEN statement
               | IF expression THEN full_if
                                ELSE open_if
               ;
```

Here it is already guaranteed by the grammar that an ELSE branch is always assigned to the last open IF; there are no longer any conflicts.

6.6.2   Reduce/reduce conflicts

The so-called *reduce/reduce* conflicts occur if the parser has two options of reducing in one state. Reduce/reduce conflicts always indicate a bad error in the grammar. Here is a particularly simple example:

Reduce/reduce conflict

```
%token LISA THOMAS LESLEY
%%
```

```
person    : woman | man;
woman     : LISA | LESLEY ;
man       : THOMAS | LESLEY ;
```

This YACC specification creates the error message:

```
$ yacc -v person.y
conflicts:  1 reduce/reduce
$ _
```

In y.output, we can see where this conflict is:

```
State 3 contains 1 reduce/reduce conflict.
...
state 3


    woman  ->  LESLEY .   (rule 4)
    man    ->  LESLEY .   (rule 6)


    $              reduce using rule 4 (woman)
    $              [reduce using rule 6 (man)]
    $default       reduce using rule 4 (woman)
```

(The "$" symbol stands for the end of the input here.) What happens if the YACC parser has read LESLEY? It can reduce LESLEY to woman (rule 4), but also to man (rule 6). This choice between two reduction options is the reason behind the name "reduce/reduce conflict".

Resolving reduce/reduce conflicts

As can be seen in y.output, the default for YACC is to apply the first matching rule of the grammar (here rule 4). However, this default only rarely leads to suitable solutions. It is better to make the grammar *unambiguous* – for example:

```
%token LISA THOMAS LESLEY
%%
person    : woman | man | uncertain;
woman     : LISA;
man       : THOMAS;
uncertain : LESLEY;
```

6.7   Explicit precedence declarations

The rules required to make a grammar free from conflicts often lead to considerably longer YACC specifications. As an alternative, YACC provides a number of special *precedence declarations*, with which the associativity and precedence of individual symbols can be specified explicitly. Using the declaration

Precedence declarations

```
%left '+' '-'
%left '*' '/'
```

for example, it is agreed that "+", "-", "*", and "/" are associated with the left (left), and that in addition to this, "*" and "/" have a higher precedence than "+" and "-" (because they were declared later). In addition to %left, there is also %right for association with the right, as well as %nonassoc, which declares the respective symbol as being nonassociative.

Precedence declarations can considerably simplify the YACC specifications, like in Example 6.5:

```
...
%left '+' '-'
%left '*' '/'
...
%%
...
expression :
    NUMBER                       { $$ = $1; }
    | expression '+' expression  { $$ = $1 + $3; }
    | expression '-' expression  { $$ = $1 - $3; }
    | expression '*' expression  { $$ = $1 * $3; }
    | expression '/' expression  { $$ = $1 / $3; }
    | '(' expression ')'         { $$ = $2; }
    ;
```

Formally, the grammar remains the same; however, the YACC specification has become considerably shorter due to the precedence declarations.

It is a matter of preference as to whether you use precedence declarations or whether you explicitly formulate the grammar. The use of precedence declarations in arithmetical operations is certainly easy to comprehend; in other tasks, such as the correct arrangement of unbound else, the introduction of an "associativity" or a "precedence" instead of an extended grammar may be unsuitable.

6.8 GLR parser

GLR dissolving of conflicts, discussed in the preceding sections, is not only cumbersome but also partly impossible. If we regard ANSI C, it is undecidable in some places whether "x*y" is a multiplication of two variables that represents x and y or whether it is a declaration of a variable y with type x*. This conflict is dissolvable only by semantic actions in the scanner, which determines for each designator whether it is a variable or a type designator and returns a special token accordingly.

This conflict does not result from the used context-free grammars but by the used algorithms. The GNU version of YACC, BISON, offers therefore an additional approach to repair conflicts – the so-called GLR parsing (*generalized LR parser*).

Parser cloning

If a conflict occurs during GLR parsing, the parser is *cloned* and both parsers process an alternative individually. This can be repeated, so that there can be many parallel parsers at different times.

The parsers continue *synchronized*, that is, if one parser shifts a token, all are shifting the same symbol. The parser can, however, reduce unsynchronized. Each parser can continue until it can neither shift nor reduce (because the rules do not match) or its state is equivalent to the state of another parser. In the first case, the parser simply *dies* and the remaining parsers continue to work normally. In the other case, the two equivalent parsers are merged into one.

As long as there exist several parallel parsers, no semantic actions are executed; instead, the actions are *memorized*. At the time when there is one single parser again, because all others died, the memorized actions are executed belatedly. If two parsers are merged, it cannot be decided which memorized actions are supposed to be executed. If the user in this case did not use the possibility of specifying the behavior, a parse error will be raised.

In order to clarify this, we take up the example from Section 6.6.2 again, change it a little, and insert "'%glr-parser'" at the beginning:

Example 6.10
A GLR parser
specification

```
%glr-parser
%token LISA THOMAS LESLEY MR MRS MILLER SMITH
%%
person: woman name MRS | man name MR ;
name: MILLER | SMITH;
woman: LISA | LESLEY;
man: THOMAS | LESLEY;
```

This specification still generates a conflict message, but this is an indication only with GLR parsers:

```
$ bison person.y
person.y: conflicts:  2 reduce/reduce
$ _
```

This conflict originates, since at token "'LESLEY'" it cannot be decided whether to reduce to "woman" or "man". YACC cannot process this grammar therefore. Since however BISON generates a GLR parser here, this grammar functions perfectly:

```
$ echo lisa miller mrs | a.out
$ echo lisa miller mr | a.out
syntax error
$ echo lesley miller mrs | a.out
$ echo lesley miller mr | a.out
$ _
```

Concepts

❏ The structure of input is described in two levels:

- For the fine structure, *regular expressions* are normally used for the construction of lexical basic elements.

- For the coarse structure, regular expressions are not sufficient; *grammars* are used here.

❏ A grammar consists of a set of *rules* that define the structure of each individual syntactical element.

❏ YACC takes a grammar and from this creates a *parser* that processes the input in accordance with the rules of the grammar.

❏ In YACC, each rule of the grammar can be assigned an *action*, which is called as soon as the corresponding rule is reduced. Typically, the *value* of the syntactical element is determined using the value of its components.

❏ The parser produced by YACC can *shift* read tokens to a stack. The uppermost elements of the stack are *reduced* as soon as they correspond to the right-hand side of a rule.

❏ Ambiguous grammars can lead to *conflicts*:

- In the case of a *shift/reduce* conflict, the parser has the choice of using a token that has been read to shift or reduce.

- A *reduce/reduce* conflict indicates a bad error in the grammar.

❏ GLR parsers do not dissolve conflicts but process alternatives at the same time.

- The analysis is successful if only a faultless alternative remains at the end.

- If several alternatives remain, the user must specify a precedence.

Review exercises

1. The following rule could be given for the recognition of additions and subtractions:

$$term \longrightarrow number \mid number + term \mid number - term$$

This rule is problematic. Why?

Postfix notation

2. Write a YACC program that outputs arithmetical expressions in *postfix notation*. In postfix notation, the operations do not stand between, but *after* their operands; from $a \oplus b$ is $a\ b \oplus$. So, from 1+2*3+4, your program should produce the output 1 2 3 * + 4 +.

3. Imagine that the following YACC specification is given:

```
%token UUUH YEAH BABY BALLA
%%
refrain   : uuuh1 YEAH BABY BALLA BALLA
          | uuuh2 YEAH YEAH YEAH
          ;
uuuh1     : UUUH  { f1(); } ;
uuuh2     : UUUH  { f2(); } ;
```

the grammar is unambiguous but is not accepted by YACC.

(a) Determine the YACC error message as well as its cause.

(b) Indicate an equivalent specification that is accepted by YACC.

(c) Why cannot YACC process the above grammar, even though it is unambiguous?

(d) Is it possible to process the above grammar with a GLR parser?

4. Supplement Example 6.5 with following functions:

(a) Exponential functions. The expression 1+2^3 should produce 9.

(b) One-digit prefixes. "-3" and "+4" should be valid as numbers.

(c) Trigonometrical functions and π. All identifiers should only be one letter long. For example, S stands for sin and P for π, thus S(P/2) should produce the value 1.

(d) User-defined variables. According to the definition "a = 45", the expression "a + 3" produces the value 48.

(e) User-defined functions. In connection to the function definition "f(x) = (2 * x + x - 3)", "f(2)" should produce the value 3. To do this, you must construct the arithmetical expression as a tree during the reading phase, which you store under the function name in order to evaluate it later.

(f) Functions and variables with identifiers of arbitrary lengths. Use the yyname variable in order to access the names read in by LEX in YACC.

First extend the grammar, then if necessary yylex or the LEX specification, and last of all, the actions. If the grammar becomes too complex, use precedence declarations.

Further reading

YACC is a component of every extensive programming environment. The freely available GNU variants from YACC called BISON come with a detailed introduction by Donnelly and Stallman (1995). (The name BISON is a play on words: a bison is a hoofed animal like a yak "YACC".)

An extensive introduction into the use of LEX and YACC is also given by Levine et al. (1992), which as well as numerous practical examples (for example, a parser/scanner combination for SQL) and gives a description of the differences between the different LEX and YACC implementations. Valuable advice on how to avoid conflicts and recognize their causes round the work off.

We have left out how YACC generates a parser from a grammar; the description of this would go beyond the framework of this book. The mode of operation of LEX and YACC is, however, a component of every textbook on the topic of compiler building. A classic work is the "dragon book" by Aho et al. (1986), which also describes how LEX and YACC work. Amongst other things, the basic theory of the formal language is described in Hopcroft et al. (2000).

YACC belongs to the group of the *LR parser generators* (more precisely: YACC is a LALR parser generator). Parser generators are more up-to-date parser generators, which do not work with shifting and reducing but are based on recursive descent. Grammars are usually more cumbersome than LR grammars, but on the plus side, the semantic actions in parser generators are a lot more flexible. The ANTLR generator presented in Chapter 7 is such a parser generator.

Other parser generators

GLR parser is often called Tomita style parser in literature.

7   Lexical and syntactic analysis using ANTLR

LEX and YACC are the classical tools of input processing and accordingly of older date. Unfortunately, they also have a series of disadvantages; for instance, a program can only contain one instance of a scanner or parser. In addition, the generated scanners and parsers do not correspond any longer to the requirements of modern object-oriented computer languages. In the following, we look at a more modern tool of this kind, which has meanwhile established itself as a standard for JAVA programs: ANTLR unites the lexical with the syntactic analysis. Besides, not only scanners and parsers can be generated in JAVA, because ANTLR offers support for C++ and C# in addition.

ANTLR

7.1   Lexical analysis

Instead of a new introduction, we pull up the examples from Chapter 5 and explain the lexical analysis with ANTLR with the same examples, which also eases the comparison of ANTLR to LEX. We begin with the Example 5.1 – a filter that removes expletive words from the input stream.

```
class L extends Lexer;
options { filter=ECHO; }
{
  public static void main (String[] args)
  throws Exception {
    L lexer = new L(System.in);
    Token t;
    do {
      t = lexer.nextToken();
    } while (t.getType() != Token.EOF_TYPE);
  }
}

EMPHASIS: "very" | "quite" | "really" ;
protected ECHO: c:. { System.out.print(c); };
```

Example 7.1
Filter specification
`emphasis.g`

7.1.1   Structure of ANTLR specifications

Structure of a specification

In Example 7.1, we can recognize the structure of an ANTLR specification of a scanner:

> *Preamble*
> class *Name* extends Lexer;
> *Options*
> *Definitions*
> *Rules*

The meaning of these parts is explained in the following.

Preamble: In the preamble, basic options can be specified. It is optional and is missing in Example 7.1.

Name: A specification can define several lexers; hence, every lexer has its own name. Besides, this name serves as a class name and is also used in the generated files.

Options: This (optional) part contains options specifically for the defined Lexer. In the earlier example, it is specified that text matching the rule ECHO should be ignored.

Definitions: If this part exists, it is copied completely into the generated Lexer class. Additional methods and attributes of the Lexer class can thereby be defined. In the example, the main method is defined, which creates a new lexer and requests one token after the other from it. Since ANTLR does not predefine such a method (as for example LEX via "-ll"), it must be defined.

Rules: At the end, the actual lexical rules are defined. Indeed, these resemble the rules from LEX, but there are fundamental differences, which are discussed in the following.

Several specifications may follow one another in a file. These must differ in the name.

The example contains two rules: The upper EMPHASIS rule specifies the three fillers that can be recognized. The lower ECHO rule means that in the semantic action all characters are printed. The "c:" placed in front generates a reference, with which the recognized character can be accessed in the action. This rule must be marked as protected, since it is used *Filter*   as filter. Protected rules have other implications, which are discussed later.

The upper rule does not contain a semantic action; the fillers are regarded as tokens, which are called up and ignored in the main method.

The lower rule leads to no tokens, since matching text is ignored by the `filter` option.

Here we see that the generated filter works:

```
$ java antlr.Tool emphasis.g
$ javac L.java LTokenTypes.java
$ echo "really a very simple example" |
    java L
 a  simple example
$ _
```

The execution of ANTLR generates two files: `LTokenTypes.java` contains the list of defined tokens and `L.java` contains the real lexer. Both files must be compiled, and the generated class `L` contains the usable lexer.

We can specify the example in Figure 5.4 for removal of HTML tags in ANTLR accordingly:

```
class L extends Lexer;
options {
  filter=ECHO;
  charVocabulary='\u0000'..'\uFFFF';
}
{
  ...
}


DEHTML: '<' (~'>')* '>';
protected ECHO: c:. { System.out.print(c); };
```

Example 7.2
Filter specification
`dehtml.g`

Here are some small differences in comparison to a LEX specification: If the generated lexer is not used as a scanner, most often, the alphabet to be accepted must be given. This is done with the `charVocabulary` option, which here declares the whole (Unicode) character range as the input alphabet. Another difference to LEX can be recognized in the `DEHTML` rule:

Input alphabet

There is no character class operation in ANTLR like in regular expressions, and repetition ("`*`") is to be parenthesized.

Let us next focus on the Example 5.3 for reading of configuration files. In contrast to LEX, all rules in ANTLR are named. Example 7.3 shows the according ANTLR specification. There the `NAME` rule specifies a sequence of characters except " [", "=", and "] ". Since there is no character class operation, these characters become grouped (" (...) ") as alternatives (" | "). The negation ("~") is more powerful in ANTLR, because it can be applied to groupings.

The NAME rule is marked as protected – it can be used only in following rules and defines no token. Such rules are visible only in the generated scanner.

Example 7.3
Specification for
reading of
configuration files

```
class L extends Lexer;
options {
  charVocabulary='\u0000'..'\uFFFF';
}
{
  ...
}
protected NAME:  (~( ']' | '=' | '[' ))*;

TITLE: '[' NAME ']' '\n'!
        { Config.processTitle(getText()); };

ENTRY: NAME '=' (~'\n')* '\n'!
        { Config.processEntry(getText()); };
```

The character string matching a rule can be determined in the semantic action via a call of the method getText(). In this example, the matching string is simply handed over to an external class Config for processing. ANTLR does not have LEX's special symbols "^" for the line beginning and "$" for the line end, because left and right contexts are treated differently. The alternative operation "!" indeed removes the preceding matching character or group from the input stream but it does not add it to the text passed to getText(). In the example, the line break is read, but ignored otherwise ("'\n'!").

We also revisit Example 5.5 for adding up read numbers. Example 7.4 shows the equivalent ANTLR version. It consists of a specification of how numbers are represented (specified by NUMBER) and the main routine similar to the one from the beginning of this chapter. We added a variable sum to the lexer class, whose value is printed at the end (in the main routine). In this variable, the values of the numbers are added up (as specified in the semantic action for NUMBER).

7.1.2 Details of rule construction

We have adapted the majority of the LEX examples for ANTLR here, but some examples are missing. The reason is that the details of the rule construction are completely different:

❏ Conflicts are not resolved and can lead to problems. (In LEX, *first longest match* applied.)

❑ There is no possibility to put read characters back into the input stream again (REJECT in LEX).

❑ Trailing context cannot be specified.

❑ There are no explicit start states.

```
class L extends Lexer;
options {
  charVocabulary='\u0000'..'\uFFFF';
}
{
  private static float sum = 0;

  public static void main (String[] args)
  throws Exception {
    L lexer = new L(System.in);
    Token t;
    do {
      t = lexer.nextToken();
    } while (t.getType() != Token.EOF_TYPE);

    System.out.println(sum);
  }
}
protected NUM:  ( '0'..'9' )+;
protected EXP:  ( 'E' | 'e' ) ( '-' | '+' )? NUM;

NUMBER: NUM ( '.' NUM )? ( EXP )?
        { sum += Float.parseFloat(getText()); };
```

Example 7.4
Summation of read numbers

Only the first two points are problematic, because for the last two points more powerful alternatives exist. Start states can be replaced by *semantic predicates*, which we will not present here. Semantic predicates are very powerful and can be used for any contextual situation, for example, to restrict that a rule only matches in the first column or that the current token evaluates to the integer value 3.

Semantic predicates

Instead of the trailing context, in ANTLR, *preceding* context can be specified in the form of syntactic predicates. With the help of the DO problem in FORTRAN, we show that syntactic predicates are equivalent powerful:

Syntactic predicates

```
class L extends Lexer;
...
DO_OR_VAR
```

Example 7.5
Specification of syntactic predicates

```
        :   (DO_HEADER)=> "DO"  { ... }
        |   VARIABLE             { ... }
        ;
protected DO_HEADER options { ignore=WS; }:
    "DO" INT VARIABLE '=' EXPR ','
    ;
protected INT: ('0'..'9')+;
protected VARIABLE: 'A'..'Z' ( 'A'..'Z' | '0'..'9' )*;
protected EXPR: INT ( '.' (INT)? )?;
protected WS: ' ';
```

Here the problem taken up is that in FORTRAN the character sequence
"DO5I=" can be the beginning of a variable assignment to "DO5I" or the
beginning of a loop ("DO 5 I = ...").

This problem is solved by a syntactic predicate. A syntactic predicate
"(P) =>" states that the following rule is used only if the rule P matches
the current input stream. In Example 7.5, the DO_HEADER rule is used
as syntactic predicate. During the analysis of this rule, blanks are ignored
("options { ignore=WS; }"), and the input stream is looked at in
greater detail than the following rules to read the "DO". If the syntactic
predicate does not fit, the following alternative rule is used – in this case,
the application of the VARIABLE rule is tried.

7.2 Syntactic analysis

After we learned how lexers are specified in ANTLR, we now dedicate
ourselves to the syntactic analysis with ANTLR. Therefore, we take up
Example 6.5 for evaluation of arithmetic expressions again and present it
as an ANTLR specification:

Example 7.6
Specification for
evaluation of
arithmetic
expressions

```
class L extends Lexer;
...
EXPRESSION
{ int val; }
    : val=SUM { System.out.println(val); };

protected SUM returns [int val]
{ int tmp; }
    : val=TERM
        ( '+' tmp=TERM { val += tmp; }
        | '-' tmp=TERM { val -= tmp; } )*;

protected TERM returns [int val]
{ int tmp; }
```

```
    : val=FACTOR
        ( '*' tmp=FACTOR { val *= tmp; }
        | '/' tmp=FACTOR { val /= tmp; } )*;

protected FACTOR returns [int val]
    : val=NUMBER
    | '(' val=SUM ')';

protected NUMBER returns [int val]
    : ('0'..'9')+
    { val=Integer.parseInt($getText); };
```

In reality, no parser (such as in YACC) is defined here, but a lexer (like in LEX). Have we not stated at the beginning of Chapter 6 that parenthesizing like in this example is too complex for LEX? This applies furthermore, because LEX is based on regular expressions, while in ANTLR, lexers are specified by context-free grammars that are also used in YACC. Not without reason, the ANTLR specifications resemble rather YACC than LEX specifications.

Why is the lexical analysis still separated from the syntactic one? Problems can already been recognized in Example 7.6. If we actually use this specification, we recognize that *no blanks* may be used in the input. Many such problems exist. Hence, a separation of the lexical analysis, which converts the input stream into a token stream, of the syntactic analysis, which processes the token stream, is sensible.

Separation of the lexical and syntactic analysis

This separation has proved itself and is independent of the kind of analysis. Therefore, we present a parser specification in Example 7.7. There is not much left from the original lexer in this example. It just defines a set of expected tokens and specifies additionally that blanks should be ignored between tokens. Now the parser is similarly constructed like the original lexer, and the rules are almost identical. The biggest difference is that the rule names in the parser must start with small letters – names starting with capital letters are token names of the lexer.

7.3   How recursive descent works

ANTLR is an LL-parser generator. LL-parsers normally work according to the principle of *recursive descent*. With the recursive descent approach, each rule is replaced by an appropriate piece of source code. This fragment decides on the basis of the next characters in the input stream which alternative of the current rule is to be used, and calls the appropriate code.

LL-parser
Recursive descent

We clarified this in the preceding example. We will manually perform the steps that ANTLR normally does for us automatically. In the `main` method, the start rule `input` is called, which we must provide. Thus, we define a suitable method, however, which we do not present yet. Instead, we look at the following rule:

```
expression
{ int val; }
    : val=sum { System.out.println(val); };
```

We transform this rule for `expression` into a suitable method. If we ignore the semantic actions, only `expression:    sum;` remains for the rule. Thus, the suitable method is:

```
public static void expression() {
    sum();
}
```

Example 7.7
Specification for evaluation of arithmetic expressions with lexer and parser

```
class L extends Lexer;
options {
  filter=WS;
}

NUMBER:   ('0'..'9')+;
PLUS:     '+';
MINUS:    '-';
MULT:     '*';
DIV:      '/';
NL:       '\n';
protected WS: ' ';

class P extends Parser;
{
    public static void main (String[] args)
    throws Exception {
        L lexer = new L(System.in);
        P parser = new P(lexer);
        parser.input();
    }
}

input:  (expression | "\n")*;

expression
{ int val; }
    : val=sum { System.out.println(val); };

sum returns [int val]
{ int tmp; val=0; }
```

```
    : val=term
        ( "+" tmp=term { val += tmp; }
        | "-" tmp=term { val -= tmp; } )*;

term returns [int val]
{ int tmp; val=0; }
    : val=factor
        ( "*" tmp=factor { val *= tmp; }
        | "/" tmp=factor { val /= tmp; } )*;

factor returns [int val]
{ val=0; }
    : z:NUMBER { val=Integer.parseInt(z.getText()); }
    | "(" val=sum ")";
```

Because the right side of the rule only contains sum, only that rule fits here; the according method is therefore called. The rule for sum without semantic actions reads:

```
sum: term ( "+" term | "-" term )*;
```

If we suppose that nextToken() delivers the next character or token of the input stream and matchToken() removes the next character from the input stream, we can give the suitable method:

```java
public static void sum() {
    term();
    while (nextToken() == '+' || nextToken() == '-') {
        if (nextToken() == '+') {
            matchToken('+');
            term();
        } else {
            matchToken('-');
            term();
        }
    }
}
```

Here we see how alternatives are represented by if statements and repetitions by while loops. The conversion for term happens analogously. At last, we present the transformation for factor:

```java
public static void factor() {
    if (nextToken() == NUMBER) {
        matchToken();
    } else {
        matchToken('(');
```

```
            sum();
            matchToken(')');
        }
    }
```

Now we can return to the `input` rule. Here we bump into a problem, because we cannot immediately decide for which tokens in the input stream the `expression` alternative has to be chosen. Therefore, we follow successively `expression`, `sum`, `term`, and `factor` and find out that with `factor` either NUMBER or `'('` must be the first token. Because `term` starts with `factor`, these tokens must appear first with `term`, too. This applies also to `sum` and `expression`. We have now identified the set of tokens appearing next in `expression` and can build the method for `input`:

```
public static void input() {
    while (nextToken() == NUMBER
            || nextToken() == '('
            || nextToken() == '\n') {
        if (nextToken() == NUMBER
            || nextToken() == '(') {
            expression();
        } else {
            matchToken('\n');
        }
    }
}
```

Until now we have ignored the semantic actions – however, the given code must just be copied to the suitable places, what we present only for the `sum` rule:

```
sum returns [int val]
{ int tmp; val=0; }
    : val=term
        ( "+" tmp=term { val += tmp; }
        | "-" tmp=term { val -= tmp; } )*;
```

is converted to:

```
public static int sum() {
    int val;
    int tmp; val = 0;
    val = term();
    while (nextToken() == '+' || nextToken() == '-') {
        if (nextToken() == '+') {
            matchToken('+');
```

```
            tmp = term();
            val += tmp;
        } else {
            matchToken('-');
            tmp = term();
            val -= tmp;
        }
    }
    return val;
}
```

At last, the grammar is converted entirely in program text and the input stream can be analyzed by a call of method "input()".

ANTLR proceeds very similar during code production and generates a rather readable source text. In addition, ANTLR offers a large number of other aids, which we cannot present here.

Concepts

❑ ANTLR is both a scanner and parser generator.

❑ The generated lexers as well as the parsers work according to the principle of recursive descent.

❑ Because the lexers are not specified by regular expressions, but by context-free grammars, the lexers generated by ANTLR are more powerful than those of LEX.

Review exercises

1. Explain the advantages and disadvantages of the approach to integrate scanner and parser generator into one tool.

2. Solve task 3 on page 82 (LEX) for ANTLR.

3. Solve task 8 on page 83 (LEX) for ANTLR. Why is the ANTLR solution much easier?

4. The following is a rule for sums and differences:

   term $\longrightarrow$ *term* | *term* + *number* | *term* - *number*

   This rule is problematic. Why?

5. Solve task 2 on page 104 (YACC) for ANTLR.

6. Solve task 4 on page 104 (YACC) for ANTLR. The name can be determined via `getText()` here.

Further reading

The website of ANTLR contains a great deal of information for ANTLR: newcomer's information, documentation, grammars (e.g., for SQL, C++ oder ADA) ... and, of course, ANTLR itself:

```
http://www.antlr.org/
```

Exercises II

In this exercise, you will build programs for text analysis using LEX, YACC, and ANTLR.

1. Adopt two files from this book.

   ❏ The file `grammar.y` shall contain the parser specification from Example 6.5 on page 90 as well as the help functions from Section 6.3.4 on page 91.

   ❏ The file `scanner.l` shall contain the scanner specification from Example 6.9 on page 94.

2. Build a program called `lcalc` from these files.

3. Put this version of your source files under version control with CVS or RCS. Repeat this after each of following tasks.

4. Extend your program by the functions *sin*, *cos*, *tan*, and the constant *pi*. Test this version – so, for example, `sin(pi) = 0` must apply.

5. Extend your program by the *negation* and the *factorial*. Example: `3! * -2 = -12`.

6. Extend your program by *user defined variables*. Accordingly, after the definition "a = 45", the expression "a + 3" produces the value 48. If the variable was not yet defined, an error should be produced. It is sufficient if only the 26 variables a to z can be used.

7. Write a second YACC specification `postfix.y`, which evaluates expressions in postfix notation. From this specification, build a program `pcalc`.

8. Replace the assignment of user-defined variables with the *let* construct: "(let a = 20 in 2 * a) + 2" produces 42.

   (a) Note that outside the *let* construct, the variables defined by `let` are no longer valid.

(b) Overlaying should be allowed:
"`let x = 1 in (let x = 2 in x) + x`" produces 3.

9. Extend your program so that variable names with more than one character are allowed. What happens in the case of the following input?

```
let pi = 3 in let let = 45 in let in = let in pi
```

10. Repeat the preceding tasks with ANTLR in JAVA.

❑ First, you have to convert the specifications from task 1 into one (single) ANTLR specification `grammar.g`.

❑ The main program should still be `lcalc`.

❑ Because of the revision management with CVS or RCS, the ANTLR version should be placed into its own directory.

❑ The postfix specification for ANTLR should be `postfix.g`, the main program `pcalc` again. Consider how you can reuse the scanner specification from `grammar.g`.

Part III

Building Programs

8 Building programs with MAKE

8.1 Building programs out of components

It is rare that the program can be executed and delivered immediately after a change. As a rule, some additional intermediate steps are recommended after a change in order to *build* the program – for example, the conversion of source files to object files or the linking of object files to executable programs. A software product often consists of several programs that all have to be updated after a change. In addition to programs, other components of a software product can also be affected by changes: if, for example, part of the documentation is taken from program texts, a new version of the documentation may have to be produced to reflect changes in the program text.

Reconstruction after change

During the initial construction of a program – or more generally, of a software product – we have a number of *source components*. These are components that have been created manually, for example, program source text or documentation. Components that can be created by the computer without human interaction are called *derived components*, since they are *derived* from other components. Basically, a component *A* is derived from a component *B*, if *A* refers to *B* in some way.

Source components

Derived components

As an example, we will look at a PostScript file with printer instructions; typically, this is derived from another file that has been created by a human operator. An executable program is in turn derived from object files, which in turn are derived from source texts.

As an ongoing example, let us take a program `spellcheck` that consists of two components `grammar` and `dictionary`; both components start off in a C source file `.c` and are then converted into an object file `.o` using the C compiler `cc`; both object files are then linked into the finished program. The C source files `grammar.c` and `dictionary.c` source components are here – all the others (the object files and the executable program) are derived.

Object file

In Figure 8.1, the individual components, together with their derivative relationships, are represented as a *dependency graph*; an arrow *A* ← *B* means that "*A* is derived from *B*". We can infer this derivative relationship directly from the individual construction steps.

Dependency graphs

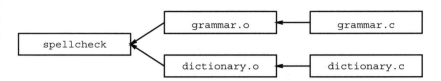

8.2   Incremental construction

The aim of automatic construction is now to create those derived components that are a part of the final product, from the source components. The easiest way of automating the construction is to combine the individual construction steps into a *script*, which can be processed by the computer step by step. In our `spellcheck` example, this would be a sequence of commands that the C compiler `cc` calls accordingly:

*Script for program
construction*

```
cc -c -o grammar.o grammar.c
cc -c -o dictionary.o dictionary.c
cc -o spellcheck grammar.o dictionary.o
```

The disadvantage of such a script is that all construction steps are always executed. When the program is rebuilt after a change, these steps are often superfluous. For example, if we have already created a complete `spellcheck` program and make a change to `grammar.c`, then `dictionary.o` is not recreated since it is not derived from `grammar.c`; executing the steps for the reconstruction of `grammar.o` and `spellcheck` will be sufficient.

As a matter of fact, the derivation relationship also indicates how changes affect the system. A change in component A can only impact the components that are derived from A; these components are therefore also called *dependent* on A. All other components remain independent from the change and do not need to be reconstructed. This knowledge leads to the following theorem:

Dependence

*Reconstruction by
means of
dependencies*

Let A be a derived component, dependent on n other components $A_1, A_2, \ldots, A_n$. The component A has to be rebuilt if

1. A does not exist, or

2. at least one A_i from $A_1, A_2, \ldots, A_n$ has changed, or

3. at least one A_i from $A_1, A_2, \ldots, A_n$ must be rebuilt.

While case 1 and case 2 are trivial, case 3 comes from the assumption that a reconstruction causes a change, which again implies case 2.

In our example, for instance, grammar.o has to be rebuilt if grammar.c has changed; spellcheck also has to be recreated, because grammar.o has to be rebuilt. Such a procedure, which exploits existing results to achieve an aim, is called *incremental*. The above theorem is therefore the basis of *incremental program construction*.

Incremental program construction

8.3 How MAKE works

As a rule, building systems incrementally by hand already fails for small systems – it is simply too difficult to manage the dependencies and construction steps. For this reason, Stuart Feldman from Bell Laboratories developed the software tool MAKE, in 1975, which, today, is one of the most influential and widely used software tools.

MAKE

MAKE realizes incremental program construction using a *system model*. A system model is a description of the software product that lists the individual components together with their dependencies and the steps required for their construction. The system model in MAKE comes in a special file called *Makefile* (engl. *file*: file).

System model

Makefile

A makefile consists of *rules*. A rule indicates on which components one or more components are dependent, as well as the commands that are necessary for building the component(s). It takes the form:

Rules

$$target_1 \ target_2 \ \ldots \ target_n : \ source_1 \ source_2 \ \ldots \ source_m$$
$$command_1$$
$$command_2$$
$$command_3$$
$$\ldots$$

Here $target_1$ to $target_n$ stand for the components to which the rules refer, the so-called *target*. $source_1$ to $source_m$ are the components on which the targets depend. Below the components are the commands that create the respective targets, indented by a tab.

Target

(The fact that commands have to be indented by tabs (and not, for example, blank spaces!) is the biggest stumbling block for beginners wanting to create a Makefile. Stuart Feldman himself apparently encountered the same problems a few days after finalizing the original version of MAKE; MAKE had already been too widely distributed by then for him to be able to correct this design error.)

In our spellcheck example, the Makefile looks as follows:

Example 8.1
Makefile for spellcheck

```
spellcheck: grammar.o dictionary.o
        cc -o spellcheck grammar.o dictionary.o
```

```
grammar.o: grammar.c
        cc -c -o grammar.o grammar.c

dictionary.o: dictionary.c
        cc -c -o dictionary.o dictionary.c
```

MAKE takes a Makefile as input, together with a target A_0 of this Makefile. From the Makefile, MAKE calculates the dependency graph and begins its work with the components A_0. The basic algorithm is a depth-first search into dependency graphs, in which construction steps are executed after every return, if necessary.

❏ Suppose A is the current target component. From the dependency graph, determine the components $A_1, A_2, \ldots, A_n$ on which A depends. If A does not occur as the target in the Makefile, let $n = 0$.

❏ Call the algorithm recursively for each A from $A_1, A_2, \ldots, A_n$.

❏ If one of the components $A_1, A_2, \ldots, A_n$ have changed, or if A does not exist, A has to be rebuilt. For this purpose, the commands associated with A as a target are executed.

Let us explain the procedure with an example. Let us assume that the program spellcheck has already been created once, but now we have changed dictionary.c. What happens during the invocation of MAKE with the target spellcheck?

1. First spellcheck is the current target, dependent on grammar.o and dictionary.o.

2. Now the target grammar.o has to be rebuilt if need be; it is dependent on grammar.c.

3. grammar.c is not a target in the Makefile but it does exist.

4. Since grammar.c has not been changed, grammar.o does not have to be rebuilt either.

5. Now the target dictionary.o is checked; it is dependent on the source file dictionary.c.

6. dictionary.c is also not a target in the Makefile but it does exist.

7. Back at the target, dictionary.o, MAKE determines that the file dictionary.c has been changed: dictionary.o has to be rebuilt. Accordingly, MAKE calls the command cc -c -o dictionary.o dictionary.c.

8. We are back at the target spellcheck again; since dictionary.o has now been changed, spellcheck also has to be recreated; MAKE calls the command cc -o spellcheck grammar.o dictionary.o.

9. With this, the target spellcheck is created; MAKE is finished.

In practice, the whole thing looks like this: MAKE is called with a target of the Makefile. During the run of MAKE, MAKE displays the commands that have been executed.

```
$ make spellcheck
cc -c -o dictionary.o dictionary.c
cc -o spellcheck grammar.o dictionary.o
$ _
```

Until now, we have left one question unasked: how does MAKE actually establish that a file has been changed? The idea is quite simple. In a file system, every file records the time the last change was made . If a component *C* (as a file) shows an earlier date than a component that depends on it, *C* is considered to have been "changed"; the dependent components are recreated. In the above example, we defined dictionary.c to have been changed – according to MAKE, this means that dictionary.c has an earlier date than dictionary.o and has therefore been changed after the last construction of the program.

Time of the change as a basis for reconstruction

If we call MAKE a second time, without changing any of the source components in some way, MAKE does nothing at all. This is due to the fact that after a successful compilation, each source component is older than the components that were derived from it and, therefore, MAKE has nothing more to do:

```
$ make spellcheck
make: nothing to be done for 'spellcheck'.
$ _
```

8.4 Makefiles in practice

For practical use, MAKE provides a number of properties that increase flexibility and reduce the amount of writing that is required.

8.4.1 Variables

If a program is to be compiled in different environments, the construction steps for these environments are also different. For example, if the C

Variables compiler is called cc on one computer and on another gcc, the options for the control of the compilation can also differ from each other. In order to be able to carry out these kinds of changes easily, MAKE *variables*, with which frequently recurring components of Makefiles can be combined and parameterized.

Variables are defined in a Makefile using

> *variable* = *value*

Each further occurrence of $(*variable*) or ${*variable*} is then replaced automatically by *value*.

If, for example, the name of the C compiler is to be parameterized using a variable CC, the spellcheck Makefile looks as follows:

Example 8.2
Makefile with variables

```
CC = cc

spellcheck: grammar.o dictionary.o
        $(CC) -o spellcheck grammar.o dictionary.o

grammar.o: grammar.c
        $(CC) -c -o grammar.o grammar.c

dictionary.o: dictionary.c
        $(CC) -c -o dictionary.o dictionary.c
```

The meaning of the Makefile is still unchanged; each occurrence of $(CC) is replaced by cc. At the invocation of MAKE, however, a new value for the CC variable can be specified. The call

> $ **make CC=gcc spellcheck**

executes all construction steps for spellcheck, whereby, however, gcc is executed instead of cc.

Variables need not only refer to commands; each part of a Makefile can be parameterized by means of variables. For example, long lists of object files are frequently combined in a variable. So, for example, usage of an OBJECTS variable can make sure that there is precisely one list of object files in one location:

Example 8.3
Makefile with lists of object files

```
OBJECTS = grammar.o dictionary.o

spellcheck: $(OBJECTS)
        $(CC) -o spellcheck $(OBJECTS)
     ⋮
```

In this example, OBJECTS need only be changed in one place in order to bring the dependencies and the construction command up-to-date.

8.4.2 Implicit rules

Another simplification of Makefiles becomes apparent if one considers the fact that components are frequently built in the same way. In our example, the construction steps for `dictionary.o` and `grammar.o` are the same; only `dictionary` and `grammar` are exchanged. In order to combine such equal-type rules, MAKE offers *implicit rules*.

An implicit rule is applied on a number of components that are given via a definite name pattern. Name patterns mark files through their *suffix*: so, for example, `.o` is a pattern that contains all files that end with `.o` (object files) and `.c` is a pattern for all files that end with `.c` (C source text files).

Implicit rules

An implicit rule has the form

> $.suffix_1.suffix_2:$
> > *command*

In this case, $suffix_1$ is the suffix of the source and $suffix_2$ is the suffix of the target. An implicit rule for compiling C source text files in object files would therefore take the form

> `.c.o:`
> > *command*

Since an implicit rule is used for a whole number of components, in the *command*, special *implicit variables* have to be used, which stand for the respective components. The implicit variable `$@` therefore stands for the current target and the implicit variable `$<` for the first source. As a result, an implicit rule for the compilation of C files in object files can be given:

Implicit variables

> `.c.o:`
> > `$(CC) -c $(CFLAGS) $(CPPFLAGS) -o $@ $<`

This rule is always applied if MAKE is searching for a target that ends in ".o" and a file exists with the same basic name but ends in ".c", but no *explicit rule* has been entered for this target in the Makefile. The variables `CFLAGS` and `CPPFLAGS` are also used here to control the C compiler and the C preprocessor.

In fact, this rule is already predefined in MAKE, together with suitable values for the variables used. As a result, the entire Makefile for the `spellcheck` project can be shortened to:

```
OBJECTS = grammar.o dictionary.o

spellcheck: $(OBJECTS)
        $(CC) -o spellcheck $(OBJECTS)
```

Example 8.4
Makefile with implicit rules

The rules for `dictionary` and `grammar` no longer have to be explicitly specified; they are automatically derived from the predefined implicit `.c.o` rule. In the case of the variables, we can also rely on the predefined values from MAKE.

The file suffixes used in a Makefile have to be defined in a special rule. All sources of the *installed target* `.SUFFIXES` are used as the file ending for implicit rules – therefore,

```
.SUFFIXES: .c .o
```

This is particularly important if you wish to define your own implicit rules.

8.4.3 Pattern rules

Pattern rule

As a more powerful alternative to file-ending rules, some MAKE variants, in particular GNU MAKE, offer the option of working with *patterns*. In a *pattern rule*, the percentage sign "`%`" in the target stands for an arbitrary character string. With patterns, the implicit rule for compiling C files into object files can be expressed as

```
%.o: %.c
        $(CC) -c $(CFLAGS) $(CPPFLAGS) -o $@ $<
```

Pattern rules have the advantage that additional dependencies can be accommodated – for example, a dependency of all C files from a header file `defs.h`:

```
%.o: %.c defs.h
        $(CC) -c $(CFLAGS) $(CPPFLAGS) -o $@ $<
```

MAKE and RCS

In pattern rules, "`%`" actually stands for arbitrary character strings; the usage is not only limited to prefixes or suffixes. If the target consists of just one percentage sign "`%`", this rule applies *to all targets*. The following rule, for example, executes an RCS check out (Chapter 3), if the RCS file is newer than the target file itself:

```
% :: RCS/%,v
        $(CO) $(COFLAGS) $<
```

The MAKE variable CO is defined here as `co`; COFLAGS stands for `co` options. The double colon (`::`) is used to instruct MAKE not to reconstruct missing sources. Thus, MAKE does not need to check for every file whether there is a way to create its RCS file.

8.4.4 MAKE for installation

In practice, MAKE is also used for the automation of tasks in the *associated field* of program construction. It is therefore normal to define a *pseudotar-* *get* called `install`, which installs the finished program on a computer, and therefore makes it available to everyone. A pseudotarget does not create a file but simply executes a number of commands.

Pseudotarget

```
# Installation program
INSTALL_PROGRAM = install

# General prefix for customer-sided
# installed programs and data
prefix         = /usr/local

# Prefix for machine-specific
# programs and data
exec_prefix    = $(prefix)

# Prefix for machine-specific programs
bindir         = $(exec_prefix)/bin

install: spellcheck
        $(INSTALL_PROGRAM) spellcheck $(bindir)/spellcheck
```

Example 8.5
Installation rules
in Makefile

Note the use of variables to parameterize name and location of the installed program. If the variables are not changed, the `spellcheck` program is installed in the directory `/usr/local/bin` – whereby the `install` dependency of `spellcheck` guarantees that`spellcheck` is up-to-date.

```
$ make install
install spellcheck /usr/local/bin/spellcheck
$ _
```

Besides `install`, a number of other pseudotargets are commonly used. Table 8.1 lists the most important ones.

8.4.5 Recursive MAKE

In large projects, it is not unusual to split up a system into *subsystems*, which are built as individual units and then combined. When building a system, it is normal to also construct a subsystem. This is done via a *recursive call* of MAKE. As an example, we look at a subsystem called `readline`, which can be found in a subdirectory of the same name and within which its construction is taken care of by MAKE. In the *Makefile* of

Table 8.1
Standard target
in MAKE.

Command	Effect
make all	Constructs the whole program.
make install	Installs the program on a computer.
make uninstall	Deletes the program from the computer.
make clean	Deletes the program and all derived files.
make distclean	Like "clean"; but also reverses platform-specific adaptations of the source text.
make dist	Creates a source text package (distribution).
make check	Carries out suitable tests.
make depend	Recalculates dependencies.
make love	outputs "not war?".

the main system, we find the following targets:

```
READLINE_TARGETS = readline/libreadline.a \
                   readline/readline.h
```

```
readline $(READLINE_TARGETS):
        cd readline && $(MAKE)
```

In the variable READLINE_TARGETS, targets from the readline subsystem are defined – in this case, for example, a library (libreadline.a) and a header file (readline.h).

MAKE *variable*   The MAKE variable MAKE here stands for the original MAKE call – that is, the MAKE program with a complete path and, if need be, MAKE options. If, for example, MAKE is called as

$ gmake CC=gcc readline

$(MAKE) expands to gmake CC=gcc. MAKE executes the command

```
cd readline && gmake CC=gcc
```

and by doing so makes sure that the MAKE parameter is also taken into account in the subsystem.

Unfortunately, recursive MAKE arranged in this way is inefficient: for each target that depends on readline.h, MAKE is called once. The efficiency can be increased by omitting the dependencies, which is done at the expense of the flexibility. In our example, one can, for example, remove readline.h from the list of the targets:

```
READLINE_TARGETS = readline/libreadline.a
```

```
readline $(READLINE_TARGETS):
        cd readline && $(MAKE)
```

With this kind of rule, the recursive MAKE call would only take place if libreadline.a is required during the final linking of the program. However, if readline.h is a derived file, MAKE cannot and will not reconstruct it in the main system.

In practice, people do their best to construct subsystems one after the other according to their dependencies. Typically, the uppermost directory of a product contains rules for the construction of the whole system:

Building subsystems

```
MODULES = termcap readline main


all install uninstall clean distclean::
        for dir in $(MODULES); do \
            (cd $$dir && $(MAKE) $@); \
        done
```

The entire system is constructed using the call make all: The for command of the UNIX command interpreter calls MAKE in the subdirectory with the given target once for every subsystem from the MAKE variables MODULES; this applies to all standard targets. The subsystems in MODULES are arranged in such a way that later subsystems are dependent on earlier subsystems.

Does this scheme also work for complex dependencies? The scheme requires the subsystems to be sorted by means of their dependencies (topological). More complex (cyclic) dependencies lead to more complex command sequences. If several runs are necessary, *Makefile* is not very different from a normal nonincremental script. The approaches introduced here should be sufficient for normal projects though.

8.5 Determining dependencies

In practice, a derived component not only changes if its respective source components change. In fact, incremental construction must also take into account changes *in other components that are being used* as well as *in the construction process itself*:

Hidden dependencies

Dependency of components used: Every component that is accessed during the construction process can have an effect on the derived components. If, for example, a C file uses the header file spellcheck.h, every change in spellcheck.h can affect the derived object file.

Dependency of construction tools: If the compiler is changed, all object files have to be recompiled. This is similar if there are changes in the *invocation* of the tools (for instance, invoking the compiler with or without activated optimization) as well as for changes in the *context* (for example, environmental variables).

Figure 8.2
Another dependency graph. Additional "hidden" dependencies are listed here.

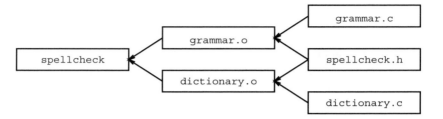

To start with, we will look at the first area, the dependency of used components. Practically, every program uses definitions and declarations of other program components. A C program, for instance, requires special declarations for the input and output, which are combined in the header file <stdio.h>. This means that the executable program is dependent not only on the C source text files but also on <stdio.h>.

A system file like <stdio.h> changes so rarely that the dependency can be ignored. Things are much more complicated with header files that are part of the project. If, for example, in our spellcheck example, both grammar.c and dictionary.c use definitions from a general header file spellcheck.h, then the dependency graph has to be *extended*, as shown in Figure 8.2.

In a Makefile, these new dependencies are expressed by further rules:

```
grammar.o: grammar.c spellcheck.h
dictionary.o: dictionary.c spellcheck.h
```

Tracking such dependencies manually can be very tedious, as the use can be very arbitrarily nested: referred components can again refer to other components. If, for example, a new reference to pidgin.h were to be introduced in spellcheck.h, all dependencies of the components that use spellcheck.h would have to be extended to include pidgin.h. For this reason, dependencies should be automatically determined whenever possible.

Automatically determining dependencies

UNIX C compilers provide an *automatic method for determining dependencies*. The option "-M" causes a MAKE rule to output a list that indicates all the dependencies of the components that were processed – a list of the files that were opened by the C preprocessor while it was being run:

```
$ cc -M grammar.c
grammar.o: grammar.c
grammar.o: ./spellcheck.h
$ _
```

This property of cc can be used in a Makefile to bring the dependencies up-to-date automatically using make depend. For example, the following rule could be found in a Makefile:

```
depend::
        (for file in $(SOURCES); do \
            $(CC) -M $$file; \
        done) > Makedeps
```

```
include Makedeps
```

Example 8.6
*Automatic
determination of
dependencies*

The `for` command (in brackets) of the UNIX command interpreter calls `cc -M` once for every file from the MAKE variable `SOURCES`; the corresponding dependencies are output in the file `Makedeps`. The MAKE instruction `include Makedeps` is replaced by the content of `Makedeps` when reading the Makefile; thus, the determined dependencies become part of the Makefile. The dependencies must always be recalculated as soon as some component introduces a new dependency.

A problem that is not taken into account sufficiently by MAKE are the dependencies of the *tools* being used and their context. A change from `cc` to `gcc`, as well as general changes in the Makefile, are not detected by MAKE. Therefore, after changes in the Makefile, one must check whether derived files have to be deleted in order to force a reconstruction.

Dependency of tools

8.6 Additions and extensions

MAKE has produced and inspired countless successors, offering improved functionality – in particular, for determining dependency and for archiving derived components.

8.6.1 Language-specific knowledge

The determination of dependencies, as outlined in Section 8.5, became integrated into successors of MAKE right from the beginning. The software tool ODIN, for example, uses language-specific knowledge to automatically produce dependency graphs; C and C++ files, for example, are searched for `#include` instructions. Other programming environments rely on knowledge about the programming language used in order to determine the effects of changes: thus, for instance, changes to comments do not lead to reconstruction.

ODIN

8.6.2 Automatically determining dependencies

A very elegant way of dealing with dependencies is carried out using the already mentioned CLEARCASE system. During the construction of the program, the virtual file system logs the files that have been opened by the construction tools. In doing so, dependencies that otherwise remain hidden

CLEARCASE

from developers are brought to their attention – for example, configuration files that are opened internally by the compiler used or help programs that are called during the construction of other tools. The big advantage of this is that all the files that are used are always seen and dealt with automatically.

8.6.3 Changes in the construction

A problem with MAKE is that changes to the *Makefile* itself only lead to a reconstruction if the dependency to the *Makefile* is explicitly specified

Changes in construction commands

in the *Makefile*. In order to include changes in the construction, for every derived component, many successors and expansions of MAKE, therefore, memorize the command that was used for their construction. A change in the command (as a result of a change in the Makefile) then leads to a reconstruction.

Changes in the construction context

The CLEARCASE tool (mentioned above) not only logs file accesses but also the invocations of the respective construction tools as well as their *environment variables.* Any change in the construction tools or their environment automatically leads to a reconstruction. There is a reason why the environment of the construction tools is also taken into account: in many operating systems, for example, the environmental variable PATH determines where executable programs are searched for; a change is therefore highly likely to have an impact on the finished product.

Unfortunately, CLEARCASE cannot log which programs access which environmental variables, so that, in the case of doubt, an *arbitrary* change in the environment leads to a new construction. CLEARCASE, therefore, makes a distinction between *critical* environmental variables (which cause a change in derived components) and *uncritical* environmental variables (whose change has no influence).

8.6.4 Archives for derived components

Binary pools

Binary pools are archives, in which derived components are filed together with their construction context. If the components are to be restored to the same configuration at a later date, they can be copied directly from the binary pool; there is no need to reconstruct them. This is particularly useful if there are several developers who all hold their own copy of the program in their work area. When the first developer constructs the program initially, all the construction steps are executed. Each subsequent developer can, however, fall back on the derived components in the binary pool – the construction time is reduced to zero. (Management of the binary pool adds a small overhead.)

Normally, the management of a binary pool requires *revision control* to be used, as the source configuration of every derived component must be known – this means that for every derived component, the MAKE-like tool must memorize the revisions of the files concerned. In advanced SCM systems, derived files are therefore versioned automatically; during the reconstruction of a particular configuration, derived files are also reconstructed – either from a binary pool or using a MAKE-like mechanism.

MAKE and revision control

8.7 ANT: A framework for program construction

Another weak point of MAKE is the direct linkage of *commands* and *targets:* To create a target, it is mandatory to execute specific commands. Granted, one can create flexible commands by means of variables and implicit rules; but life would be much easier if the construction tool itself knew how to perform a specific task – and if such tasks could be added and extended at will.

Exactly, this is the aim of ANT (from *another neat tool*). Rather than specifying commands, an ANT user specifies *tasks* that realize a specific target. Each task knows which tools and commands to use to realize the target. ANT comes with more than 100 predefined tasks that include the following:

Compilation: Javac (Compile a JAVA program), JspC (Execute JSP compiler)

Tasks in ANT

Archives: Jar (create Jar archive), Zip (create Zip archive), Rpm (create RPM archive)

Documentation: Javadoc (Create a JAVADOC documentation; see Section 10.2)

File management: Checksum (create check sum), Copy (copy files), Delete (delete files), Move (rename files), Mkdir (create directory), Tempfile (create temporary file)

Tests: JUnit (Run tests; see Chapter 13)

Just as in MAKE, a system model defines the components of the system – in ANT, it is called a *Buildfile*. A Buildfile consists of the following parts:

Buildfile

❑ A Buildfile has exactly one *project*. Every project has a *name* and a *default target* – a target that is used unless some other target is specified.

❑ Every project has one or more *targets*. ANT targets are similar to MAKE targets, but much more coarse-grained. Rather than files to be constructed, an ANT target refers to some general *activity*.

Every target has a name and optional *dependencies*. The dependencies list targets that must be realized before the actual target. An archive as a target, for instance, will typically be dependent on earlier compilation.

❏ Every target is realized by a number of *tasks* – activities that must be conducted to realize the target.

The Buildfile itself is written in *XML format*. This allows simple creation and processing by other tools.

Example 8.7 shows a Buildfile named build.xml for a simple project named SimpleProject. The compile target uses two Tasks to create a directory (mkdir) and to invoke the JAVA compiler (javac). Additional XML attributes define *task parameters* – for instance, the name of the directory (dir) to be created in the mkdir task.

Example 8.7
An ANT Buildfile

```
<project name="SimpleProject" default="dist">
  <target name="compile">
    <mkdir dir="classes"/>
    <javac srcdir="." destdir="classes"/>
  </target>
  <target name="dist" depends="compile">
    <mkdir dir="lib"/>
    <jar jarfile="lib/simple.jar" basedir="classes"/>
  </target>
  <target name="clean">
    <delete dir="classes"/>
    <delete dir="lib"/>
  </target>
</project>
```

Example 8.8
Building with ANT

```
$ ant
Buildfile: build.xml

compile:
    [mkdir] Created dir: /src/moore/classes
    [javac] Compiling 3 source files
            to /src/moore/classes
dist:
    [mkdir] Created dir: /src/moore/lib
      [jar] Building jar: /src/moore/lib/simple.jar

BUILD SUCCESSFUL

Total time: 3 seconds
$ _
```

If we invoke ANT using the Buildfile from Example 8.7, we obtain the activities shown in Example 8.8:

1. The default target of `build.xml` is `dist`.

2. The target `dist` depends on `compile`, so `compile` must be realized first.

3. The `compile` target is realized by the two tasks `mkdir` and `javac`, which must be executed first.

4. Now the tasks of `dist` can follow – `mkdir` and `jar`.

5. All targets are realized – the build was successful.

Just like MAKE, ANT works incrementally – with every new build, only those targets are realized whose dependencies have changed. In contrast to MAKE, though, incrementality is not built into the tool but *must be realized by the individual task implementation*. The `javac` task, for instance, determines the dependencies between JAVA programs automatically and builds just those classes that must be reconstructed. ANT is, thus, just a *framework* to organize the individual tasks; the actual intelligence regarding construction (and in particular incremental reconstruction) is in the tasks.

ANT can be easily extended by additional tasks. ANT comes with a JAVA class `Task` that can be subclassed to realize new tasks. Since existing complex tasks also come as `Task` subclasses, they can be further subclassed to create new extensions or adaptations. Finally, ANT can also be configured at runtime. For instance, the original JAVA compiler can be easily replaced by another variant.

These properties have made ANT the most popular construction tool for JAVA programs. Unfortunately, there are only few ANT tasks for other programming languages. If ANT is not available, MAKE can step in.

Concepts

❏   The aim of automatic program construction is to create all derived components from a number of source components, which are an integral part of the finished software product.

❏   If a component has changed, all the components derived from it must be rebuilt.

❏   MAKE is a tool for building programs, during the course of which existing derived files are reused as much as possible.

❏ MAKE uses the date when components were changed in order to detect changes.

❏ The basis of MAKE is a Makefile, a system description that lists the components of the system as well as their dependencies and construction steps.

❏ Makefiles can be simplified and parameterized using variables and implicit rules.

❏ Later improvements and extensions refer to the automatic determination of dependencies as well as the automatic management of versions of derived components.

❏ Frameworks for program construction such as ANT allow specific extensions by the user as well as by third parties.

Review exercises

1. Program construction is not always successful. What alternatives does MAKE have if one of the commands in a *Makefile* cannot be ended correctly? What must MAKE take into account if the target file has already been partially created but the creating command is ended with an error code?

2. If the object files `grammar.o` and `dictionary.o` in our MAKE example are deleted, but `spellcheck` is kept, during the next run, MAKE recreates `spellcheck` and all object files again – even if the source files are unchanged. Suggest a modification of the MAKE algorithm that does not recreate the given target if there are unchanged source files and missing intermediate files. Are there cases where this optimization is unreasonable?

3. In order to avoid the purely time-oriented change mechanism of MAKE, many developers of MAKE files use the following trick: during the reconstruction of a component A, a component called A' is created and compared with the existing A. If A' and A are different, A' is copied to A. Otherwise, A remains unchanged, including the date that it was changed, and the files that depend on A do not have to be recreated because of A.

   (a) With this kind of process, can the steps that will be necessary be determined before the actual construction of the program?

   (b) A MAKE that follows the rule for reconstruction from Section 8.2 exactly would nevertheless recreate the components that depend on *A*. Why? What must MAKE take into account so that this trick works?

4. Our colleague Smith complains about having to regularly enter `make depend` in order to bring the dependencies up-to-date. "It would be a lot better if the dependencies were not managed centrally, but individually for each component – a `Makedeps` file for every individual component, so to speak." Can this be done using MAKE? How would these kinds of dependency files be created? When would they have to be rebuilt?

5. Design a tool similar to MAKE, which does not detect the changes by means of the date when it was changed but by means of the actual content of the components. To do this, for every derived component *A*, you must remember the content of all components $A_1, \ldots, A_n$, on which *A* depends. Should *A* be reconstructed, you can compare the current and the previous content of the component A_i; *A* only actually has to be reconstructed if there are differences in the content. How can you use the techniques from Chapters 2 to 4 to save space?

6. Write an ANT task that creates a "Hello, world!" JAVA program. How can you replace `javac`, the standard JAVA compiler, by an alternative (say, `jikes`)?

7. Sketch an ANT task named `cc` that compiles C programs automatically. What are the requirements for such a task? In particular, consider easy configurability as well the automatic detection of dependencies.

Further reading

The first extensive description of MAKE is found in Feldman (1979). Since this original version, MAKE has been extended many times, and is available in numerous variants and extensions. Almost the entire toolbox of all of the existing MAKE extensions are realized*** GNU MAKE, which is freely available from Stallman and McGrath (1995).

The dependency management of CLEARCASE is described in Leblang (1994). ODIN was introduced by Clemm (1988). The difficulty of using MAKE recursively and efficiently is described by Miller (1997).

Not every change in a program must lead to recompilation – for example, changes in comments. This so-called *smart recompilation* is investigated in articles by Tichy (1986), Schwanke and Kaiser (1988), as well as Shao and Appel (1993).

Smart recompilation

Integration with
version control　　　　The future of software construction lies in the tight integration with version control. Outstanding examples of this include the codeveloped SHAPE from Mahler (1994) as well as the CAPITL programming environment, described in Rich and Solomon (1991) as well as Adams and Solomon (1995). Recent theoretical approaches can be found in Gunter (1996) as well as Zeller (1998).

ANT and its documentation can be found on the Web at

$$\texttt{http://ant.apache.org/}$$

Other tools for program construction

MAKE and ANT are typically integrated into programming environments – for instance, the ECLIPSE programming environment described in Chapter 20. However, several *commercial* variants and extensions are also available, which normally include the basic functionality described here.

Tools for building programs that go beyond MAKE are frequently components of systems for configuration management. You can find a selection of these on Page 59.

9 Configuring software automatically with AUTOCONF

9.1 Introduction

Variants are a common source of problems in software development. Variants are product versions that have to be created and maintained alongside an existing version. Variants are created for many reasons:

Variations in the hardware environment: A program should support new hardware – such as a new graphics card or a new input device.

Variations in the software environment: A program should work on a number of operating systems or with various graphic user interfaces.

Variations in the program construction: Depending on the environment, different tools and commands may be needed for building the program.

In general, dependency on variation in the program should be kept to a minimum, as testing expenses increase with every variant. The common, nonvarying part must be as large as possible and the varying part as small as possible. This can be achieved using *abstraction* of varying properties, especially by creating and using generally available and standardized *interfaces*. In particular, object-oriented *design patterns* provide appropriate abstraction that supports variation in class hierarchies.

Variant management becomes complicated if, for technical reasons, the variation cannot be handled at runtime but must take place at *compilation time*. It is not usually possible to get a WINDOWS program to run on a UNIX computer or vice versa. Variation results in (at least) two executable programs, including a number of other variations impeded by the operating system.

But even if it is possible to rely on a common interface, technical reasons may lead to creating variants that are tailored for a specific environment – such as program variants, which are optimized to the performance characteristics of the corresponding processor. Rather than create all-purpose executables, where only a part of the code is tailored for the specific environment, it may be preferable to include only such code that will actually be executed.

Variations, therefore, not only lead to various executable programs but also cause many differences in source code, which must be resolved at compilation time. These differences in the source text and during the building of the program need to be detected and dealt with.

9.2 Explicit variant management

A simpler way to manage variants is to copy the varying software components and allocate them their own identifiers. Thus, the operating system—specific parts of the program could be set out in modules (files, directories...) such as `macos`, `windows2000`, `windowsxp`, or `unix`. All modules provide the same services; the final program only integrates the suitable module.

Variation facets

However, this simple approach fails in practice owing to one major problem: *variations have many facets.*. The variation of the environment extends not only to the basic properties but also to the details. Because of this, the operating system can only provide certain services in certain versions. Optional drivers and libraries can provide varying services. And finally, specific versions of the environment may contain errors, which must be worked around.

If each of these facets is encapsulated in an individual module, several difficult-to-handle modules are soon generated. However, if modules are created that differ from each other in detail only, we get common sections in modules that require multiple maintenance and organization.

9.3 Creating variants from templates

Template for creating variables

One way to avoid this problem is not to manage variants explicitly but to generate them from a more abstract *template* according to demand. A template can be understood as a form – it contains sections that are filled according to the variant as well as sections that are used together for several, or even for all, of the variants. The explicit variant is therefore created implicitly from the template at compilation time – it is said that the template is *instantiated*.

The following three tools have become established for instantiating templates:

❏ SED is useful for simple substitution tasks.

❏ M4 is a macro processor for any given files.

❏ CPP is a macro processor specifically for program files.

9.3.1 SED

The *stream editor* SED applies a sequence of commands on a character stream. SED is mainly used for replacing character strings. The SED command s, *old*, *new*, g, for instance, replaces all occurrences in the text *old* with the text *new*.

Replacing character strings with SED

Here is an example: in a *Makefile* template (see Chapter 8) called Makefile.in, the C compiler is parameterized:

```
CC = @CC@
```

Using the following SED call, the concrete Makefile is instantiated from the Makefile.in template by replacing the symbolic entry @CC@ with the concrete program gcc:

```
$ sed 's,@CC@,gcc,g' < Makefile.in > Makefile
$ _
```

Using SED, for instance, the concrete values for make variables such as CC could be set or determined externally in order to instantiate the *Makefile* template.

9.3.2 M4

The macro processor M4 also manipulates a text, whereby *macros* inserted into the text are replaced by other texts. A number of useful macros have already been predefined:

Macro replacement with M4

Replacing text: The M4 macro define (*macro*, *text*) causes all further occurrences of *macro* to be replaced by *text*. *text* can contain additional macros.

Inserting text: include (*filename*) is replaced by the contents of the file *filename*.

Conditional conversion: ifdef (*macro*, *text₁*, *text₂*) is replaced by $text_1$, if *macro* is the name of a defined macro, and by $text_2$, if *macro* is not defined.

The replacement of *macro* can be suppressed using a single exclamation mark ('*macro*').

Here is an example: the manual.in text file template describes the basic variants as well as the professional revisions of a product. This can be expressed using M4 as follows:

```
define('VERSION',
   ifdef('PROF', 'professional', 'basic') version)
Thanks for choosing the VERSION!
```

Example 9.1
Text file template manual.in *with M4 macros*

```
ifdef('PROF',
'This VERSION provides the following features:',
'This VERSION does not contain the following features.
  However, you can acquire them at an additional charge:')
...
```

If M4 is now called with defined macro PROF, we obtain the `professional` variant; otherwise, we get the `basic` variant:

```
$ m4 -DPROF < manual.in
Thanks for choosing the professional version!
This professional version provides the following features:
...
$ m4 < manual.in
Thanks for choosing the basic version!
This basic version does not contain the following features.
However, you can acquire them at an additional charge:
...
$ _
```

Instead of two separate files, one must manage only one file; common parts remain in one position.

Owing to its efficient macro language, M4 is popular for variant management, especially if one must parameterize and instantiate other files than programs.

9.3.3 CPP

The C preprocessor (CPP) is a macro processor specially designed for C and C++. Like M4, it provides ways of replacing text, inserting files, and conditional compilation. The relevant CPP statements have the same name as the macros in M4.

Replacing text: The command #define *macro* *text* means that all additional occurrences of *macro* are replaced by *text*. The definition is canceled by #undef *macro*.

Inserting text: The #include *filename* command is replaced by the contents of the file *filename*.

Conditional compilation: The #ifdef *macro* *text*$_1$ #else *text*$_2$ #endif string is replaced by *text*$_1$, if *macro* is the name of a defined macro, and by *text*$_2$, if *macro* is not defined. #ifndef *macro* *text*$_2$ #else *text*$_1$ #endif is equivalent to this.

Macro replacement using CPP   In contrast to M4, CPP does not always replace macros. Macro replacement is suppressed in C comments, character strings, and CPP statements. For this reason, unlike M4, CPP does not require any speech marks in order to suppress replacement.

Here is a typical application of CPP: The `config.h` file defines macros, which tell us whether certain system files are present. For example, if the `time.h` file is available, then `config.h` defines the HAVE_TIME_H macro. In practice, this then looks as follows:

```
#include "config.h"

#ifdef HAVE_TIME_H
#include <time.h>
#endif
#ifdef HAVE_SYS_TIME_H
#include <sys/time.h>
#endif
```

Example 9.2
Conditional
compilation
with CPP

Besides such variant-specific applications, the use of CPP (and macro processors in general) should be limited as far as possible. Wherever possible, one should rely on the features of the actual programming language.

As an example of the dangers of CPP, we look at *parametric macros*, used in C to simulate "efficient functions". The macro `square(x)`, for instance, should calculate x^2:

Parametric macros

```
#define square(x) x * x
```

`square(2)` actually produces the value `2 * 2` – that is, 4. The above definition may cause problems, because `square(a + b)` is consequently replaced by `a + b * a + b`. Even the "corrected" version

```
#define square(x) ((x) * (x))
```

still has the drawback that in `square(f())` the `f` function is called twice – possibly with unpleasant side effects. As a result, in the successor C++, the macro capabilities of CPP were made superfluous by C++-specific language resources – with constants, `inline` functions, and code templates. But still, CPP is (and must be) used for handling variation at compile-time.

9.4 Determining properties

By using SED, M4, and CPP, we can instantiate templates for concrete variants. However, we must also know how to call these tools, and how we can use the respective macros.

A method that is often chosen is to assign each variable an *individual name*. In fact, CPP provides some *predefined macros*, which indicate the machine type and the operating system. These macros can also be used for configuration. The disadvantage of this, however, is that *each variant has to be listed separately*, which leads to programs that are hard to maintain.

As a deterrent, we will look at an extract from the XLOAD program, which displays the current CPU load as a component of the X Window system. Example 9.3 displays the source text, teeming with system-specific statements: depending on the system, a different name for the kernel variable, in which the current load is located, is chosen for each C preprocessor. This carries on for dozens of lines, as the access method to the kernel memory and the name of the kernel must still be determined – all this is enclosed by system-specific #if... #endif statements.

*Example 9.3
Extract from the
XLOAD program*

```
#ifndef KERNEL_LOAD_VARIABLE
#    ifdef alliant
#        define KERNEL_LOAD_VARIABLE "_Loadavg"
#    endif /* alliant */
#    ifdef CRAY
#        if defined(CRAY2) && OSMAJORVERSION === 4
#            define KERNEL_LOAD_VARIABLE "avenrun"
#        else
#            define KERNEL_LOAD_VARIABLE "sysinfo"
#            define SYSINFO
#        endif /* defined(CRAY2) ... */
#    endif /* CRAY */
#    ifdef hpux
#        ifdef __hp9000s800
#            define KERNEL_LOAD_VARIABLE "avenrun"
#        endif /* hp9000s800 */
#    endif /* hpux */
#    ifdef umips
#        ifdef SYSTYPE_SYSV
#            define KERNEL_LOAD_VARIABLE "avenrun"
#        else
#            define KERNEL_LOAD_VARIABLE "_avenrun"
#        endif /* SYSTYPE_SYSV */
#    endif /* umips */
#    ifdef sgi
#        define KERNEL_LOAD_VARIABLE "avenrun"
#    endif /* sgi */
#    ifdef AIXV3
#        define KERNEL_LOAD_VARIABLE "sysinfo"
#    endif /* AIXV3 */
#    ifdef MOTOROLA
```

```
#       if defined(SYSV) && defined(m68k)
#           define KERNEL_LOAD_VARIABLE "sysinfo"
#       endif
#       if defined(SYSV) && defined(m88k)
#           define KERNEL_LOAD_VARIABLE "_sysinfo"
#       endif
#       ifdef SVR4
#           define KERNEL_LOAD_VARIABLE "avenrun"
#       endif
#   endif /* MOTOROLA */
#endif /* KERNEL_LOAD_VARIABLE */
```

In practice, however, instead of this *explicit list of configurations*, it has proved worthwhile to assign an attribute to each varying property of a product – that is, to *each facet of the variant*. This includes:

Configuration from varying attributes

❏ *intrinsic* properties of the variant such as the availability of debugging output, the selection of a particular algorithm, or compilation with activated optimization, as well as

❏ *extrinsic* properties of the environment such as a specific client or a specific operating system.

To describe a specific configuration (of the variant or its environment), one uses a collection of attributes that are defined with a specific value.

In practice, this looks as follows. The `config.h` file contains a number of macros, each of which indicate a specific property of the system:

```
    . . .
    /* Define if 'getpgrp' takes no argument.  */
    #undef GETPGRP_VOID

    /* Define to 'int' if <sys/types.h> doesn't.  */
    #undef gid_t

    /* Define if you have alloca.  */
    #define HAVE_ALLOCA 1
    . . .
```

Now each of these macros can be defined (as the above HAVE_ALLOCA) or undefined (as in the other two); in later code, one of the versions of the code is selected depending on the facet by using `#ifdef ... #endif`. In the XLOAD case from Example 9.3, one macro may stand for the name of the kernel variable, one for the access method, and one for the name of the kernel.

In practice, a configuration can be defined by several of these attributes. An application such as the C compiler GNU CC is controlled by no less than

200 attributes, each representing a varying property. But where exactly do we get all these attributes from? Essentially, there are three methods for doing so.

Attributes from a global database

❏ System attributes are placed in a *global database*. This approach is taken by IMAKE, the configuration program of the X Window System: Each X installation contains a database from which a Makefile can be generated automatically. The *registry* in WINDOWS can also be thought of as such a kind of database. The XLOAD example from Example 9.3 also contains explicitly coded system knowledge.

The *advantage* of this method is that you can access the attributes of the system very rapidly. The *disadvantage* is that the information that is found in the database need not necessarily be correct.

Obtaining attributes

❏ When creating the system, *the user is asked for possible attributes*, whereby suitable defaults can be suggested. This occurs with META-CONFIG, for instance, the configuration program of the language PERL.

The *advantage* of this method is that the user is given full control over the configuration of the system. The *disadvantage* is that the configuration cannot be automated – and users may become overwhelmed by questions.

Automatic determination

❏ A special *configuration script* determines the properties of the system entirely automatically. This is what happens using AUTOCONF.

The *advantage* of this method is that the script can determine the current state of the system. The *disadvantage* is that this configuration requires time, and that the user has only limited influence over the outcome.

In practice, the third approach has proved to be the most successful – automatic configuration with AUTOCONF.

9.5   Using configuration scripts

AUTOCONF

We will now look at AUTOCONF from the user's point of view. A source package managed by AUTOCONF contains a script called `configure`, which executes a sequence of tests to establish the properties of the system:

Example 9.4
Calling the
`configure` *script*

```
$ ./configure
checking whether build environment is sane... yes
checking for a BSD compatible install... install -c
checking host system type... i686-pc-linux-gnu
```

```
checking for gcc... gcc
checking whether the C compiler (gcc) works... yes
checking whether the C compiler (gcc) is a
    cross-compiler... no
checking whether we are using GNU C... yes
checking whether gcc accepts -g... yes
checking for working alloca... yes
checking for <sys/wait.h>... yes
  ⋮
```

In this example, `configure` checks

❏ whether the system clock is correct (`build environment is sane`)

❏ for a suitable installation program (`install`)

❏ what the C compiler is called (`gcc`)

❏ whether the C compiler accepts the `-g` option

❏ whether the `alloca()` function is available

and several others tests. `configure` finally creates two files:

❏ The file `config.h` is created from the `config.h.in` template; it   `config.h` contains the attribute definitions required for program compilation.

In our case, the `config.h` file contains:

```
/* Define if you have alloca.  */
#define HAVE_ALLOCA 1

/* Define if you have <sys/wait.h>. */
#define HAVE_SYS_WAIT_H 1
```

with which, after including `"config.h"`, we can accurately select the sections of the source text that match the environment – using `#ifdef HAVE_ALLOCA ...   #endif` and similar instructions.

❏ The file `Makefile` is created from the template `Makefile.in`; it   `Makefile` contains the construction rules for the MAKE program (capital 8).

In our case, `Makefile` is almost identical to `Makefile.in`; only the character strings `@CC@`, `@CFLAGS@`, and `@INSTALL_PROGRAM@` are replaced by the values `gcc` determined by `configure -g` and the installation program `install -c`.

How configure
works

How does configure work? For a start, configure is a large script in the script language of the operating system that is used. This script calls tests, each marked by the output checking for....

How tests work

Each test is carried out in a different way. Some tests search the path for specific programs. But most consist of one test program, which is compiled and, if necessary, executed. However, if we are to check whether the remove function is available, configure creates and compiles a program, which calls remove. Only if the program can be compiled without any errors is remove actually available.

To check whether remove does what it is supposed to – namely deleting files – configure could also create a test file and execute a program that uses remove on the test file. This type of test would be used if we knew that remove did not work properly in certain environments.

Instantiating tem-
plates

During the test, configure accumulates a string of attributes, each with a certain value. All these attributes are eventually applied to the templates.

❏ In Makefile.in, all occurrences of @*name*@ are replaced by the value of the *name* attribute.

❏ In config.h.in, all lines of the form #undef *name* are replaced by #define *name*, and the value of the attribute – as long as the attribute also actually has a value.

This replacement is carried out quite effortlessly, by configure calling SED using suitable replacement commands.

9.6   Creating configuration scripts

Specific tests

The configure script and the config.h.in file are both created from a template called configure.in. configure.in contains a number of tests for different purposes – in our example, for example:

AM_SANITY_CHECK ensures that the date of a newly created file is more recent than that of a source file.

AC_PROG_INSTALL gives the INSTALL attribute the name of a suitable installation program.

AC_PROG_CC determines a functioning C compiler in the CC attribute and sets CFLAGS to -g if the C compiler accepts this option.

AC_FUNC_ALLOCA checks whether a functioning alloca() function is present; if so, HAVE_ALLOCA is defined.

All these names are M4 macros, which expand into the actual tests.

The `configure.in` file thus looks like this: after a compulsory initialization header

AC_INIT (*name of any given program file*)
AC_CONFIG_HEADER(config.h)

come the individual tests, which should execute `configure`:

AM_SANITY_CHECK
AC_PROG_INSTALL
AC_PROG_CC
AC_FUNC_ALLOCA

and finally a footer with which the individual files are created:

AC_OUTPUT(Makefile)

The actual `configure` file is then created from `configure.in` using the `autoconf` program:

```
$ autoconf
$ _
```

The `autoconf` program calls M4 to `configure.in` and a collection of macros. Each M4 macro used in `configure.in` is replaced by its definition – a complete test, which is written in the `configure` script.

Even the `config.h.in` file, which serves as the template for `config.h`, is created automatically:

```
$ autoheader
$ _
```

The `autoheader` program automatically creates `config.h.in` from `configure.in` and a collection of attributes complete with documentation. Like `autoconf`, `autoheader` calls M4, but with changed macro definitions; instead of the tests, only the possible attribute definitions are collected. Then, for each attribute, a description complete with #undef line is written in `config.h.in`.

This is the summarized procedure:

1. `autoconf` creates `configure` from `configure.in` with M4.

2. `autoheader` creates `config.h.in` from `configure.in` with M4.

3. `configure` creates `config.h` from `config.h.in` as well as `Makefile` from `Makefile.in` with SED.

Figure 9.1
*Creating and using
configuration scripts.
(Executable
programs are labeled
with "*". File
fragments with which
the procedure can
be parameterized
further are put in
parenthesis.)*

Preparation of a `configure.in` file:

$Sources \rightarrow$ `autoscan`$^* \rightarrow$ `(configure.scan)` $\rightarrow$ `configure.in`

Preparation of a package for a release:

```
configure.in   ⎫ ⎫
(aclocal.m4)   ⎪ ⎪ → autoconf* → configure
(acsite.m4)    ⎬ ⎬
(acconfig.h)   ⎪ ⎪ → autoheader* → config.h.in
(config.h.top) ⎪ ⎪
(config.h.bot) ⎭ ⎭
```

Configuration of a package in the target environment:

```
config.h.in  ⎫                    ⎧ config.h
Makefile.in  ⎬ → configure* →     ⎨ Makefile
             ⎭                    ⎪ (config.status*)
                                  ⎩ (config.log)
```

4. MAKE creates the executable program using `Makefile`. The program text is piped through CPP; CPP selects suitable code parts using the definitions in `config.h`.

Steps 1 and 2 must only be executed once for each `configure.in`; the Steps 3 and 4 must be repeated for each environment.

All these steps can be adapted individually by further file fragments. Figure 9.1 gives an overview.

9.7 Further automation possibilities

Using AUTOCONF as a base, a set of additional tools have arisen that further automate the configuration process.

❑ The `autoscan` program creates a pattern for `configure.in` by searching through the source texts in the current directory for program sources – in our example, for instance, the use of `alloca()`. This is a good starting point for making existing projects configurable.

❑ The `aclocal` tool allows adding further tests to AUTOCONF. The `aclocal` program maintains a database of tests, which can be added as required. This way, AUTOCONF users can easily publish their own tests as well as integrate tests from other users.

❏ AUTOMAKE is a package that generates *Makefiles* automatically from simple templates. The *Makefiles* created by AUTOMAKE have a full set of configurable rules for building and installing the program.

9.8   Variant management with RCS or CVS?

In Chapters 3 and 4, we became familiar with the RCS and CVS tools with which the *variants* and *configurations* resulting from a software project are managed and controlled. Why do we not use these tools? In particular, we have seen that RCS and CVS also support variants using branching, which forms an *alternate path* in the variant tree.

The answer to this question is that alternate paths are useful, but, in practice, have a key disadvantage: *the number of variants to be used increases with each alternate path.* This becomes annoying if the common part between the variants is large and, therefore, duplicated. If versions 1.2.1.1 and 1.4 in Figure 9.2 share the same code, a change must be made to the common code in both versions – and with each new alternative path, there is another variant to use.

Using variants in alternate paths

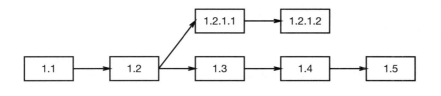

Figure 9.2
Multiple changes with branches. If versions 1.2.1.1 *and* 1.4 *share code, changes must be made to both variants.*

Creating variants in alternative paths is only worthwhile if their lifetime is restricted from the outset, for instance, because the changes arising here are to be *integrated* into the main path at some point, or the version managed in the alternative path is to be replaced with a new version. Variants whose lifetimes are restricted in this way are therefore called *temporary variants*.

For *permanent variants* with unrestricted lifetimes, RCS and CVS offer no support, as they merely name and archive variants – we would have to rely on explicit variant management, as described in Section 9.2. In practice, templates are therefore preferred, which should of course, be subject to version control.

Permanent variants

Concepts

❏ Variation should be dealt with at runtime as far as is possible and necessary.

❏ Each aspect of the variant should be controlled by its own attribute.

❏ SED, M4, and CPP are tools with which templates can be instantiated into concrete variants using attributes.

❏ A configuration script carries out tests and instantiates code files and *Makefiles* using the attributes of the environment determined in this way.

❏ AUTOCONF generates a configuration script from a list of predetermined tests.

❏ The variant management of CVS and RCS are only suitable for temporary variants, whose lifetimes are limited from the outset.

Review exercises

1. CPP and some M4 versions have a number of predefined, system-specific macros. GNU CPP thus defines, amongst other things:

```
#define __GNUC__ 2
#define __GNUC_MINOR__ 7
#define sparc 1
#define sun 1
#define unix 1
```

(a) What effect does it have if you apply CPP to normal text files? For example, on this text:

```
Suddenly, a light, brighter
than the sun, came
from my sparc unix system.
```

(b) Does it make sense to compile conditionally with these kind of names, for example, as #ifdef sun...#endif? Discuss the advantages and disadvantages of the character-oriented approach.

2. Give suitable MAKE rules for rebuilding *Makefiles* from configure.in.

3. Should the scripts created by AUTOCONF be managed by RCS or CVS? Discuss the advantages and disadvantages.

4. Design an AUTOCONF script for the configuration of XLOAD. The complete XLOAD source code can be found at:

```
ftp://ftp.x.org/pub/unsupported/programs/xload/
```

Further reading

AUTOCONF was developed by MacKenzie et al. (1994). CPP, M4, and SED have long been an integral part of the UNIX operating system.

Object-oriented design patterns with which variants can be encapsulated at runtime are described in Gamma et al. (1994).

The Mahler (1994) article is one of the few that deal with the general problem of variation. The SHAPE system Mahler and Lampen (1988) is an experimental integration of MAKE and variant management.

Zeller (1998) looks at general problems of the integration of variables in system models.

10 Documenting programs with JAVADOC

10.1 Program documentation

The creation of a program also requires the preparation of the *program documentation*. This is perhaps one of the most unpopular tasks faced by the programmer. He has worked long and hard at programming, knows his software by heart, and has very little appetite for such a "dull" task. However, documentation is important not just for later use but also for the programmer, for whom preparation of the documentation can lead to better understanding and to better design of the software. The process of documenting a system for others forces the programmer to take another point of view, focusing less on the internal details and more on the functionality provided to the user or programmer.

The primary goal of program documentation is to support programmers who use the documented software for the first time. Nowadays, a programmer usually spends more than half of his or her available time simply trying to *understand* software. One rule of thumb says that a line of code is read a hundred times more often than it is written or changed!

10.1.1 Kinds of documentation

There are different kinds of documentation with different purposes, and written for different readers. For the programmer, the following documents have been the most useful:

Design documents

Ideally, this kind of document is constructed before any code is written. It contains overviews and abstractions of the program in the form of narrative text, diagrams to convey its overall structure and anticipated construction, with references to the documented purposes and requirements that the design is intended to implement. This documentation is vitally important for any programmer who works on the project after its initial development, and especially for those who perform sustaining engineering on the program; so it should be kept absolutely current, being updated any time the software design changes.

Tutorial

Normally, one thinks of a tutorial only as an introduction document for end users of the system. However, a programmer is also an end user – of the internal libraries and interfaces of the system. A tutorial, which introduces the usage of these libraries and interfaces, explaining them via the use of easy-to-understand examples, is helpful for new programmers.

Reference manual

Again, this is not the manual for the end user, but rather a reference documentation of the interfaces, subsystems, and so on. The reference manual should describe all interfaces, document the precise semantics, and explain the purpose of the use of each. The reference manual should also indicate any restrictions or specific features of the use of the interface, subsystem, and so on.

10.1.2   Requirements for the Documentation

Experience shows that the program code itself is the best documentation. Every attempt to maintain the documentation and the program code independently of each other inevitably leads to the documentation being obsolete, incomplete, or inaccurate. In addition, independent documentation requires the programmer to change constantly between code and documentation, and thereby increases the risk that the programmer will lose the focus while switching between the two. To keep documentation and code in a single file requires both support by the programming language to integrate the two and the availability of tools to generate independent documentation.

Comments   The simplest support of the programming language are *comments*. These can facilitate the reading of programs considerably. However, a compiler cannot check whether the comment is sensible, current, or fits with the program at all.

Comment properly   To use comments properly in a program is an art, for they are mostly used too much or too little. The developer of C++, Bjarne Stroustrup, suggested the following in 1997:

❑   A comment for every source file

❑   A comment for every class

❑   A comment for every nontrivial function,

- which expresses the function's purpose

- which, if necessary, describes the approach (= the algorithm)

❏ A comment for every (global) variable and constant

❏ Comments for not-evident or not-portable points

❏ "Very little else".

This list can be summarized basically in two rules of thumb:

1. Keep comments brief and precise.

2. If I can express something in the program code, I need no comment.

10.1.3 How not to comment

Often, one sees comments that attach more importance to the external form than to the contents. Example 10.1 is such a specimen:

```
/*****************************************************
* Start of function S Q R T  (= "square root")      *
* SQRT takes an argument:                            *
* - double X: the number to be squared (X >= 0)      *
* SQRT returns:                                      *
* - the square root of X                             *
* (c) 2003 H. Becker, Burbach - all rights reserved *
*****************************************************/
```

Example 10.1
An example of poor programming

A change to the above comment not only requires extensive adaptations to the frame but also fails to document the most important information – that the square root is calculated. It would be far better to have a comment in the following form, which presents all the important information:

Bloated comments

```
// Return the square root of X
double sqrt(double x) {
    . . .
```

Instruction blocks often have superfluous comments – comments should only explain what is not clear from the source text.

Superfluous comments

```
n += 1;    // Increment n by one
a *= n;    // Multiply a with n
return a;  // Return the value of a
```

Here the comments only mirror exactly what the instructions themselves state – hence, the comments are superfluous. Indeed, it remains unclear what *purpose* the instructions have. Only comments that explain the purpose of the instruction are useful.

```
int d;              // Current number of daffodils
d = num_d();        // Compute number of daffodils
assert (d == 2);  // We expect two daffodils
```

Indeed, in this example, the comments are important to make the purpose of the instructions clear. However, one should have expressed this in the *program code*, by using sensible variable names:

Sensible identifiers

```
int current_daffodils = number_of_daffodils();
int expected_daffodils = 2;
assert (current_daffodils == expected_daffodils);
```

The correct, sensible naming of identifiers during programming is probably one of the most important activities. However, unfortunately, no tools can help create sensible names; this is entirely up to the programmer.

10.2 Documenting with JAVADOC

During the development of JAVA, it was emphasized from the beginning that the interface documentation in the source code is supported by suitable tools and guidelines. Therefore, the JAVADOC tool, which extracts documentation from special comments and converts it into hypertext (HTML), was developed very early in the creation of JAVA. This approach to generating documentation from source text offers two clear advantages:

JAVADOC
Documentation
extraction

❏ The documentation becomes a part of the system and can be maintained and constructed with automated tools.

❏ A strong cohesion is established between documented parts of a program and their documentation, making it more likely that a programmer will keep the documentation current.

Cohesion between
documentation and
source text

JAVADOC looks only at special comments, which are initiated by "/∗∗". These comments refer to the next declaration of a class, method, or other element. Such comments must be written in a particular form, which is explained in the following example.

Example 10.2
A JAVADOC
comment for a sqrt
method

```
/**
 * Returns the square root.
 * The argument is not allowed to be negative.
 * @param x a nonnegative number.
 * @return the square root of parameter <code>x</code>
 */
public double sqrt(double x) {
```

The first sentence of such a comment is a short description, which is used with overviews. The whole text describes the method in detail.

Also, special tags are used to describe certain attributes of the documented   *Tags*
method. These tags are initiated by "@". In the above example, the parameter "x" of the method is documented by the tag "@param", the method's
return value is documented by "@return".

JAVADOC will generate an overview for every class in the source text
with comments in this form. The overview for each class contains a list of
methods, and is followed by a detailed description. Both Figures 10.1 and
10.2 show examples of the generated HTML documentation for a class.

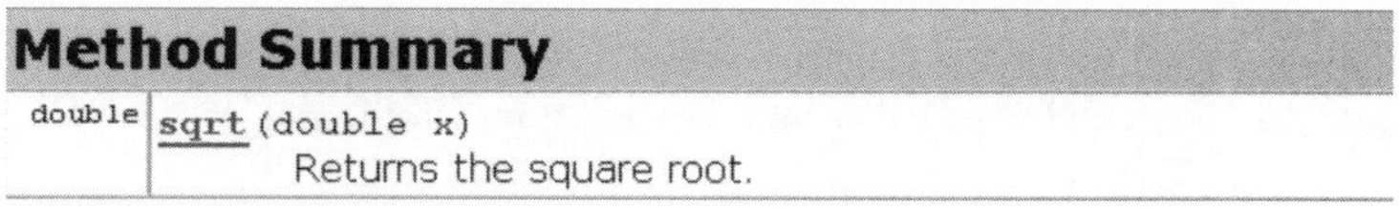

Method Summary

double | sqrt(double x)
        Returns the square root.

Figure 10.1
*Short description of
the* sqrt *method in
the method
overview.*

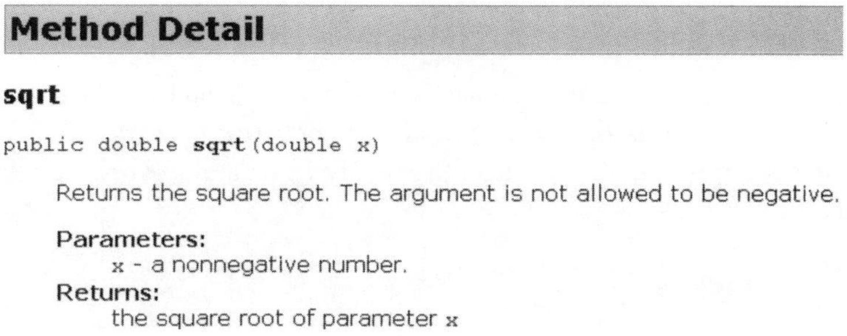

Method Detail

sqrt

public double **sqrt**(double x)

Returns the square root. The argument is not allowed to be negative.

Parameters:
    x - a nonnegative number.
Returns:
    the square root of parameter x

Figure 10.2
*Detailed description
of the* sqrt *method.*

10.2.1   Structuring

Within these comments, a large number of HTML commands may be used
in order to structure the documentation. For example, inserting paragraphs
in the documentation is accomplished by including a "<p>" tag in the
comment. You can also modify the font attributes within the documentation
using other familiar HTML markup tags:

❑ *Italic* – <i>text</i>

❑ **Bold** – text

❑ Typewriter type – <code>text</code>

Enumerations may be generated by "<ul>" and "<li>". In addition,
example source code can be embedded in the documentation by surrounding
it with "<pre>...</pre>" tags.

10.2.2 The most important tags

JAVADOC offers a large set of useful tags. Among the most common – and most useful – are:

@author specifies the author of a class.

@version contains the version of a class. Usually this tag is followed by a revision like that described in Chapters 3 and 4.

@deprecated marks methods, which will be removed in future versions.

@since indicates the time, when the documented element has been introduced.

@see, @link creates cross-references to other elements.

@param documents the parameters of a method.

@return documents a method's return value.

@exception documents the possible exceptions, which can occur during the execution of a method (`@throw` is a synonym).

These tags can be used to document not only classes and methods but also packages, interfaces, or fields. Not all tags are functional in all contexts, but it is easy to identify the tags that apply to or are appropriate for any given piece of documentation.

10.2.3 Doclets

Documentation generated by JAVADOC is normally in HTML format. This is sensible, since HTML makes quick navigation of the documentation possible. However, neither the output format nor the form of the output is user-selectable. Therefore, a method has been introduced to extend JAVADOC, called *Doclets*. The main task of doclets is to provide other output formats or new tags. Hence, doclets exist for output in LaTeX, PDF, DocBook, or MIF (Framemaker). Another doclet (iDoclet) provides tags for invariants as well as pre- and postconditions ("`@pre`", "`@post`", etc.).

Doclet

DocCheck
DocLint

Because this interface is rather adaptable, special doclets have been created that check the structure of the comments and reveal places where the comment does not conform to the required format. *DocCheck* and *DocLint* are such doclets.

10.2.4 Additional tags

Despite the flexibility of doclets, it is very complicated and laborious to introduce and handle new tags. Hence, there are two further mechanisms for the treatment of new tags, which are demonstrated in the following.

Let us suppose that you want to create a new tag, "@reviewed", to specify when and by whom a section of code was reviewed. Let us see how this tag is used in the following example.

```
/**
 * Returns the square root.
 * The argument is not allowed to be negative.
 * @param x a nonnegative number.
 * @return the square root of parameter <code>x</code>
 * @reviewed Arthur Dent, 30.2.2003
 */
public double sqrt(double x) {
```

Example 10.3
A method documentation with @reviewed *tag*

The first possibility simply consists of specifying new tags on the command line:

```
$ javadoc -tag reviewed:m:"Reviewed by:"
...
```

This call defines a new tag, which can be used in methods only (":m:"). The text following the tag "@reviewed" is output in the documentation below the "Reviewed by:" segment.

Unfortunately, it is not possible with this easy mechanism to influence the format of the text following the tag. If we want to print the text in green, for instance, we must fall back on the *Taglet* mechanism. Taglets resemble Doclets, but are considerably simpler. A taglet is a special class, which must provide a small set of methods.

Taglet

Example 10.4 shows the use of a taglet, again providing a "@reviewed" tag, but this time the text following the tag is printed in bold and green. The "register" method has the task to register the tag with JAVADOC. The other method performs the desired output. In reality, this class has to provide some other methods, which are not important for this example.

Using this taglet is simply done by an indication on the command line; integration happens automatically:

```
$ javac ReviewedTaglet.java
...
$ javadoc -taglet ReviewedTaglet *.java
...
```

Figure 10.3 shows the result.

Example 10.4
A taglet providing a @reviewed *tag*

```
public class ReviewedTaglet implements Taglet {

    private static final String NAME = "reviewed";
```

```
private static final String HEADER = "Reviewed by:";

public static void register(Map tagletMap) {
    ReviewedTaglet tag = new ReviewedTaglet();
    Taglet t = (Taglet) tagletMap.get(tag.getName());
    if (t != null) {
        tagletMap.remove(tag.getName());
    }
    tagletMap.put(tag.getName(), tag);
}

public String toString(Tag tag) {
    return "<DT><B>" + HEADER + "</B><DD>"
           + "<strong><font color=green>"
           + tag.text()
           + "</font></strong></DD>\n";
}
}
```

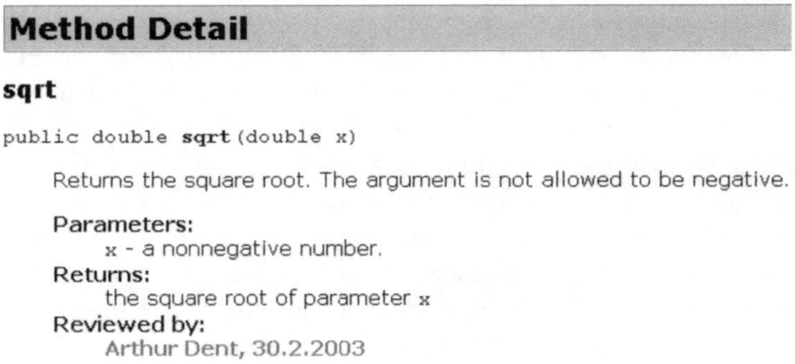

Figure 10.3
Output generated by
JAVADOC with
Reviewed taglet.

Method Detail

sqrt

`public double sqrt(double x)`

> Returns the square root. The argument is not allowed to be negative.

> **Parameters:**
>   x - a nonnegative number.
> **Returns:**
>   the square root of parameter x
> **Reviewed by:**
>   Arthur Dent, 30.2.2003

10.3   Documenting with DOXYGEN

Unfortunately, JAVADOC documents only JAVA source files; support for other programming languages is not planned. However, the usefulness of JAVADOC has inspired the creation or adaption of a number of similar tools: Before JAVADOC, there was a large number of tools, which extracted documentation from source text, but many of the newer tools have adopted both JAVADOC's philosophy and commenting syntax. The result is that these tools can now be divided into two groups: those that support the JAVADOC way of creating documentation, and all others.

DOXYGEN   A popular tool in the first group is DOXYGEN, which has its own format for documentation comments and also supports the JAVADOC style. A significant advantage of DOXYGEN is its broad support of programming languages: Though originally created to work with C and C++, DOXYGEN also supports IDL and (of course) JAVA. In addition to its JAVADOC-like capabilities, DOXYGEN can also generate inheritance and collaboration diagrams.

A typical DOXYGEN documentation comment thereby looks as follows:

```
/*! \fn int read(int fd, char *buf, size_t count)
    \brief Read bytes from a file descriptor.
    \param fd The descriptor to read from.
    \param buf The buffer to read into.
    \param count The number of bytes to read.
    \retval The number of bytes read.
*/
```

Example 10.5
Function documentation for DOXYGEN

This example demonstrates DOXYGEN's "free form" style of function documentation. In contrast to the JAVADOC style, which insists that the documentation for a program element (in this case a function) immediately precede that element in the source file, DOXYGEN's free-form documentation style allows the comment block for an element to be located anywhere in the source file or even elsewhere in the source tree.

In this example, the "\fn" tag tells DOXYGEN that the signature of the function being documented is not to be extracted from the source code, but rather from the "\fn" tag comment itself. The remaining tags inside this comment resemble the suitable JAVADOC comments (e.g., "\brief" indicates the short description of the function). In DOXYGEN, the symbols "\" and "@" can be used interchangeably; there is no difference between "\param" and "@param".

The generated documentation specified by this comment looks as follows:

int read(int fd, char *buf, size_t count)

Read bytes from a file descriptor.

Parameters:

fd The descriptor to read from.
buf The buffer to read into.
count The number of bytes to read.

Returns: The number of bytes read.

Example 10.6
Documentation generated by DOXYGEN

DOXYGEN also offers mechanisms to structure the generated documentation in chapters or sections. Dedicated tags are used to define these sections, as seen in the following example. This capability is typically used to create general documentation that is not tied to specific source elements, such as an introduction, tutorial, or other related documentation. The definition of these sections is typically stored in a separate file for ease of maintenance.

Example 10.7
Structuring of documentation with dedicated tags

```
/*!
  \mainpage Title
  ...
  \section sec1 First Chapter
  ...
  \section sec2 Second Chapter
  ...
*/
```

Besides a clearly extended set of tags, one additional advantage of DOXYGEN in comparison to JAVADOC is that several different output formats can be chosen. In addition to HTML format for presentation in browsers, output in LaTeX for reference manuals or in RTF or MAN format is supported.

However, these advantages are offset by a set of disadvantages: unfortunately, DOXYGEN offers no extension interface to define new tags or to support other output formats.

10.4   Literate Programming

JAVADOC and DOXYGEN are tools to extract documentation from source text. It is possible to do it the other way, though – to *extract the program from documentation*. This is the idea of *Literate Programming*. Here, it is assumed that the documentation is the central element of programming, and the program is only an artifact of a good documentation of the solution. Therefore, one first concentrates on and writes the documentation of the system and only after that is complete does one embed the code fragments such that they can be extracted and be combined together to create a program.

WEB
WEAVE
TANGLE

The first system of Literate Programming was Donald E. Knuth's WEB, which produces both a printable version of the documentation (via TeX) and compilable Pascal source code to create the executable program. It uses two tools, WEAVE and TANGLE, for this purpose.

Example 10.8 contains a fragment of the documentation for the `wc` tool in a WEB file. (Here, the CWEB variant is used for the programming language C.) From this file, the C source code is extracted by a calling TANGLE, which is compiled afterward. The documentation is processed by calling WEAVE (and subsequently TeX) to create printable documentation as shown in Figure 10.4.

Example 10.8
`wc.w` – *A fragment of a WEB file*

```
...
@ Most \.{CWEB} programs share a common structure.
It's probably a good idea to state the
```

```
overall structure explicitly at the outset,
...
@c
@<Header files to include@>@/
@<Global variables@>@/
@<Functions@>@/
@<The main program@>

@ We must include the standard I/O definitions, since we
@ want to send formatted output to |stdout| and |stderr|.

@<Header files...@>=
#include <stdio.h>

@ The |status| variable ....
```

> **2.** Most CWEB programs share a common structure. It
> explicitly at the outset, even though the various parts
> code if we wanted to add them piecemeal.
>   Here, then, is an overview of the file wc.c that is de
>
> ⟨ Header files to include 3 ⟩
> ⟨ Global variables 4 ⟩
> ⟨ Functions 20 ⟩
> ⟨ The main program 5 ⟩
>
> **3.** We must include the standard I/O definitions, sir
> *stderr*.
>
> ⟨ Header files to include 3 ⟩ ≡
> #**include** <stdio.h>
> This code is used in section 2.
>
> **4.** The *status* variable will tell the operating system

Figure 10.4
Printable CWEB
documentation.

Donald E. Knuth has implemented its TEX system completely in WEB and has thus proved that the system works: Literate Programming "documents" the implementation piece by piece, and so supports the understanding of the overall system. However, if one only wants to *use* a component, the documentation of the *interfaces* is far more important – and for this, Literate Programming offers no support.

Concepts

❏ Important rules for commenting:

– *Bad comments are worse than no comments!*

– *Keep comments brief and precise.*

> – *If I can express something in program code, I need no comment.*

❏ If the documentation becomes part of the source text,

  – it can be maintained and edited with tools,

  – it is easier to keep the documentation current.

❏ JAVADOC extracts documentation from source text and uses special comments for this.

❏ *Doclets* and *taglets* are defined interfaces for JAVADOC extensions. DOXYGEN, on the other hand, does not support such mechanisms.

❏ JAVADOC supports JAVA, DOXYGEN and also other programming languages like C, C++, C#, and IDL.

❏ *Literate Programming* extracts source code from the documentation.

Review exercises

1. The extraction of the documentation from comments is normally done via an interaction of scanner and parser (see Chapter 5, 6, and 7). Consider how this interaction works.

2. Try and explain why Literate Programming is virtually not found for object-oriented programming languages.

3. Document your programs from the previous chapters in the JAVADOC style. Generate the documentation for your JAVA programs once with JAVADOC and once with DOXYGEN. Which version do you like better? Why?

4. With DOXYGEN, formulae can be used in TEX notation. Develop a taglet for a "`@formula`" tag, which fulfills the following requirements:

   (a) Process the text following the tag with TEX.

   (b) Convert the TEX output into a bitmap graphic.

   (c) Include the bitmap graphic in the output via "`<IMG>`".

Further reading

Besides a reference manual for JAVADOC from Sun Microsystems, Inc. (2002), there is also a collection of conventions on how documentation in comments should be designed: the "Java Code Conventions" – Sun

Microsystems, Inc. (2000). The original design decisions and background are presented in Friendly (1995).

In Sewell (1989), Literate Programming with the WEB system is described in detail. The appendix contains the listings of the two WEB tools WEAVE and TANGLE (which are developed with Literate Programming themselves).

DOXYGEN can be found on the web site

```
http://www.doxygen.org/
```

where documentation and other introducing material are provided.

Everything about JAVADOC is found on Sun's JAVA pages:

```
http://java.sun.com/j2se/javadoc/
```

Additional tools for documentation

JAVADOC is integrated in most development environments for JAVA. For other programming languages exists a series of similar tools: DOXYGEN was split off of an early version of DOC++, which offers a similar functionality. KDOC is another system for C++ and IDL and originates from the KDE project.

Exercises III

In this exercise, you can automate the building of the program `lcalc` from Exercises II using MAKE and AUTOCONF. In addition, you shall document your programs using JAVADOC and DOXYGEN; an ANTLR variant is to be built by ANT.

1. Create a *Makefile* for `lcalc` that

   ❏ creates the files `grammar.c` and `grammar.h` from `grammar.y`; to do so, have the *Makefile* invoke YACC and rename the resulting files `y.tab.c` and `y.tab.h`;

   ❏ creates the file `scanner.c` from `scanner.l`; to do so, your *Makefile* has to invoke LEX and rename the resultant file `lex.yy.c`;

   ❏ creates the file `grammar.o` from `grammar.c`;

   ❏ creates the file `scanner.o` from `scanner.c`;

   ❏ creates the program `lcalc` from `scanner.o` and `grammar.o`.

   The call `make` without any further arguments should create `lcalc`. Use *explicit* rules and *explicit* tools.

2. Set up the *Makefile* so that `make clean` removes all files created by MAKE.

3. Make the tools of your *Makefiles* configurable so that users can provide tools during the call of MAKE – for instance

   ```
   $ make CC=gcc LEX=flex
   ```

4. Use implicit rules that

   ❏ convert YACC and LEX files into C files

   ❏ convert C files into object files.

5. Make the `lcalc` packet configurable so that the C compiler and the YACC and LEX tools are automatically determined by a configuration script. Take note of the following:

❏ You can take on the file `Makefile.in` from `Makefile`, in which you can use appropriate dummies for the tools (`@CC@`, `@LEX@`, `@YACC@`).

❏ In `configure.in`, you need the AUTOCONF macros `AC_INIT`, `AC_PROG_CC`, `AC_PROG_LEX`, and `AC_PROG_YACC`.

❏ A file `config.h` is not required. The same goes for the macros `AC_CONFIG_HEADER` and `AM_SANITY_CHECK`.

❏ For details, see the section "Particular Program Checks" in the AUTOCONF documentation.

6. Insert rules into your *Makefile* so that

    $ **make Makefile**

    the *Makefile* is automatically recreated from `configure.in`.

7. Document all files with DOXYGEN. Note that you have to use the "free form" style of function documentation for all files except C source files.

8. Include the DOXYGEN invocation in your *Makefile*, such that the documentation is created automatically.

9. DOXYGEN is not supported by AUTOCONF. Design appropriate macros.

10. Create an ANT specification `build.xml` for the ANTLR exercise. ANTLR is supported directly by ANT.

11. Document your JAVA files using JAVADOC. Extend your ANT specification such that the documentation is generated automatically.

Part IV

Prototyping

11 Creating prototypes using Tcl/Tk

11.1 Prototypes and script languages

Many of the tools that are dealt with in this book coordinate the work of several developers. This division of work is a relatively new phenomenon. Until the early sixties, programs were mostly developed by users and were only used by themselves. There was no distinction between customers, developers, and users, and, if errors were found, they could often be identified on the spot and could be eliminated by the user-developer.

By the middle of the 1960s, the situation had become completely different: the considerable increase in computer power and sinking prices allowed much larger programs to be used on many more computers. This brought two large *risks*, and the end of the sixties led to the so-called *software crisis* and the birth of the expression *software engineering*:

Misunderstandings in the development: Modern software systems are so complex that it is impossible for individual developers to grasp all the details. Software systems are therefore developed in groups; each developer creates one part of the system. The division of a task into several individual solvable subproblems is called *software design* and one of the major areas of software engineering.

Misunderstandings in the requirements: The division into users and developers often makes it difficult to record the requirements accurately. Developers are, as a rule, not experts in the field in which the program will be used, and the reverse face of this coin is that users seldom have knowledge of the internal construction and development of their programs.

Both risks are still core issues in software engineering today. In this chapter, we wish to concentrate on the second risk: how can we guarantee that users get the program they want?

An important approach is the creation of *prototypes*. The idea is to present the customer and selected users with running parts of the system early on, which means that customers can provide more accurate feedback and future users can be integrated into the design process. These prototypes

Prototypes

are revised until the requirements are finalized, whereupon the development of the actual system can be started.

Kinds of prototypes   Depending on the subset of the software system that is produced by a prototype, one can distinguish between various kinds of prototypes:

- ❏ A *vertical prototype* only realizes a few functions of the system to be built; however, each function comes with complete or almost complete functionality. Using a vertical prototype, one can check whether critical functions satisfy the requirements.

  The name "vertical prototype" is based on the assumption that a software system is organized in layers, with layers organized from bottom (the machine's functions) to top (the user interface). A vertical prototype crosscuts all layers of the software system.

- ❏ A *horizontal prototype* only realizes a subset of the layers; the layers, however, are mostly programmed completely. What this kind of prototype lacks is the actual functionality, which is produced in the lower layers.

  Typically, a horizontal prototype realizes the *user interface*. Since the lower layers are still incomplete, many user interface elements are mock-ups without actual functionality. With a horizontal prototype, one can check whether the program can cope with the user's typical work procedures.

Features of script   The essential feature of prototypes is that they can be created quickly and
languages   can be changed easily. Therefore, for programming prototypes, so-called *script languages* are often used, which have the following features:

No static type checks: In contrast to normal programming languages, script languages do not have *type declarations* and, thus, no type checking at compilation time. Variables and functions may accept and return arbitrary types; type correctness is only checked at runtime.

Simple reuse: Script languages have functions that essentially facilitate the conversion of data from one format into another – for instance, regular expressions can easily be extracted from character strings. This simplifies the integration of other programs that use text as an input and output format.

Interpreting instead of translation: In general, script languages are *interpreted* or translated into executable code at runtime. This means that recompilation after changes are made is no longer necessary, which speeds up the development; scripts from external sources can also be read, assembled, and processed at runtime.

Higher degree of abstraction: Script languages are not meant to implement basic system functions. Low-level system features such as pointers or direct memory manipulation are therefore searched for in vain. Instead, script languages have *versatile data types* such as lists, character strings, and associative fields with which functions can be produced quickly. Coupled with efficient and easy-to-use libraries, an application in a script language requires, on average, only 10% of the code written in a conventional programming language.

Data types

These properties have their price:

Disadvantages of script languages

❏ The lack of static type checking causes a high *risk of runtime errors*.

❏ *Complex data structures* are difficult to realize in a safe way.

❏ Interpreted code is usually *slower* than native machine code.

There is no reason, though, to use exclusively conventional programming languages or script languages: the success lies in combining the strengths of both the approaches. This is the aim of the script language *Tcl*, which is introduced in this chapter.

11.2   Tcl: Commands and scripts

Tcl is an abbreviation for *Tool command language*, a *script language* developed by John K. Ousterhout in 1988. A Tcl program consists of a number of *Tcl commands*, which produce the individual functions of the program. The simplest form of a Tcl program is a *Tcl interpreter*. A Tcl interpreter uses the *Tcl parser*, to read and process command calls and call the appropriate commands. As an example, consider the Tcl interpreter `tclsh` ("Tcl Shell"), which is a component of Tcl and reads commands from the keyboard:

Tcl

```
$ tclsh
% _
```

The percentage sign "%" is the `tclsh`'s prompt, at which we can now enter Tcl commands. The `puts` command outputs a character string:

`puts`

```
% puts hello
hello
% _
```

The first word of a line is the command name (here `puts`), all other words, separated by empty spaces, are arguments of this command (here `hello`).

set   The Tcl set command assigns a value to a variable:

```
% set pi 3.1415
3.1415
% _
```

Tcl only has character strings as values; pi now formally stands for the *character string* 3.1415, not, for example, for the numerical value 3.1415. However, pi is normally interpreted numerically, as we will see later.

Every Tcl command has a result that is also output by tclsh – the result of the set commands, for example, is the assigned value, while the result of puts is the empty character string.

In order to access the value of the variables, we place a dollar sign "$" in front of the name:

```
% puts $pi
3.1415
% _
```

Variable substitution   In fact, the Tcl parser replaces every character string of the form $*name* with the value of the *name* variable. This replacement is called *variable substitution*. The above example is therefore equivalent to:

```
% puts 3.1415
3.1415
% _
```

Arithmetic in Tcl   Tcl does not have a built-in arithmetic – this is the task of a special command. expr takes an expression in the usual notation from other programming languages, evaluates it, and outputs the result:

```
% expr $pi * 2
6.283
% _
```

Command substitution   The result of expr is usually further processed within the program. For this, we use *command substitution:* Each character string of the form [*command*] is replaced by the result of the *command* command. For example, in order to assign the variable 2pi the result of the evaluated expression, we write:

```
% set 2pi [expr $pi * 2]
6.283
% puts $2pi
6.283
% _
```

As we can see, blank spaces as well as "$" and "[...]" have a special *Backslash*
meaning in Tcl. The special meaning of these signs can be canceled by
putting a backslash in front of the characters "textt\". For example, in
order to output a text with blank spaces, we can write:

```
% puts The\ result\ is\ $2pi
The result is 6.283
% _
```

If we do not insert the backslashes, an error message is produced, as puts
is called with incorrect arguments:

```
% puts The result is $2pi
wrong # args: should be
    "puts ?-nonewline? ?channelId? string"
% _
```

In practice, however, it is tiresome to put a backslash in front of every   *Double quotation*
blank space. Tcl therefore has the special form *"text"*, in which all empty *marks*
spaces within *text* are dealt with as ordinary characters, and, therefore, are
not used to separate arguments. All other substitutions remain unchanged.

```
% puts "The result is $2pi"
The result is 6.283
% _
```

Within double quotation marks, all substitutions are still available and can
be turned off, if necessary, using backslashes. Quotation marks within
quotation marks can also be entered as ordinary characters:

```
% set price 20
20
% puts "The book \"Tcl/Tk\" costs \$$."
The book "Tcl/Tk" costs $20.
% _
```

If *all* characters are to be seen as normal characters, and therefore all kinds   *Curly braces*
of substitutions remain turned off, the text can be put between curly braces
"{...}".

```
% puts {The car costs $300.}
The car costs $300.
% _
```

Curly braces are used mainly to define *command sequences* that are to be   *Command*
evaluated at a later date – for example, to define *functions*. The proc   *sequences*
command defines a new command; it is given a command name, a list of
parameters, and a function body that is given as a sequence of commands:

```
% proc plus {a b} {expr $a + $b}
% plus 2 5
7
% _
```

Regular expressions in Tcl

Here is a complex example. The command `grep` is used to output all lines from a file containing a specific text pattern. Let us look at the American English text from Example 2.2 in the file `ae`. We could use `grep` to look for the regular expression $i[zs]$:

```
% grep {i[zs]} ae
The change impact was minimized
by localizing the most
% _
```

How does one implement `grep`? The two arguments are `pattern` for the regular expression and `file` for the file. First of all, we open the file using `open` and assign the variable `fd`, a file descriptor. Then, we read a line from the file `line` using `gets`; as long as this works well (`while`), we check (`if`) whether the regular expression matches the line (`regexp`). If so, we output the line (`puts`). At the end of the loop, the file is closed again (`close`).

Example 11.1 GREP command in Tcl

```
% proc grep {pattern file} {
   set fd [open $file r]
   while {[gets $fd line] >= 0} {
     if [regexp $pattern $line] {
       puts $line
     }
   }
   close $fd
}
% _
```

Compared with a conventional programming language, the example is extremely short: We do not need declarations (particularly, type declarations) and can use powerful functions (for example `regexp` here). Also, we do not have to worry about allocating and freeing memory or care about buffer overflows. All of this is already taken care of by Tcl.

It is interesting that `while` and `if` are actually Tcl commands. They are both passed an expression and a sequence of commands as arguments. When required, the arguments (i.e., the `while` and `if` bodies) are evaluated by the interpreter. This is done using the Tcl command `eval`:

```
% set cmd {puts hello}
puts hello
% eval $cmd
hello
% _
```

Using `eval`, command sequences can also be composed at runtime and can be executed when needed; it is also possible to define new control structures similar to `if` and `while`. The special Tcl command `uplevel` makes it possible for control structures to access the variables of calling commands.

11.3 Extending Tcl itself

Using the means introduced until now, one can by now write a program of any size exclusively in Tcl. This is, however, not what was intended by the inventor. Instead, Tcl should only establish the *connection* between parts of the program that already exist, which were developed in a conventional manner – Tcl acts as the glue between these parts.

Tcl as a glue function

The connection between the conventional parts of the program and Tcl is made by *self-defined Tcl commands*. Here is an example for a Tcl command `eq`, which is used to test the equality of its two arguments. It is implemented in C:

Self-defined Tcl commands

```c
#include <tcl.h>

int EqCmd (ClientData clientData,
    Tcl_Interp *interp,
    int argc, char *argv[])
{
    if (argc != 3)
    {
        interp->result = "wrong # args";
        return TCL_ERROR;
    }

    if (strcmp(argv[1], argv[2]) == 0)
        interp->result = "1";
    else
        interp->result = "0";

    return TCL_OK;
}
```

The arguments are submitted eq in the array argv. It contains the name of the command (in argv[0]) as well as all arguments (in argv[1], argv[2], ...). argc is the number of array elements in argv — eq is therefore called using two arguments, and argc has the value 3.

If eq does not have two arguments, an error message is returned; otherwise, the text of the two arguments is compared (using strcmp) and depending on the result of the comparison, the return value is 1 (equal) or 0 (unequal).

In order to use the function thus defined, it must be integrated into the interpreter again. The classic way of doing this is to extend the tclsh by implementing a variant of the function Tcl_AppInit:

```
#include <tcl.h>

int Tcl_AppInit(Tcl_Interp *interp)
{
    if (Tcl_Init(interp) == TCL_ERROR)
        return TCL_ERROR;

    Tcl_CreateCommand(interp, "eq", EqCmd,
        (ClientData) ZERO,
        (Tcl_CmdDeleteProc *) ZERO);

    return TCL_OK;
}
```

The key function here is Tcl_CreateCommand, which associates the self-defined C function EqCmd with the Tcl command eq. Let us assume that EqCmd and Tcl_AppInit are defined in myAppInit.c. If myAppInit is now linked to the Tcl library under the name mytclsh, the main function main predefined in the Tcl library is used, which calls Tcl_AppInit and then feeds the commands that have been read into the Tcl interpreter.

Thus, the self-defined eq command in mytclsh can then be accessed:

```
$ cc -o mytclsh myAppInit.c -ltcl -lm
$ ./mytclsh
% eq 2 2
1
% eq foo bar
0
% _
```

Tcl extensions   The possibility of extending Tcl by its own commands is the main reason for its success. Currently, there are extensions for access to databases, network programming, simulation of user input, and much more. Special extensions for testing regression with EXPECT and DEJAGNU are introduced in Chapter 12.

11.4 Tk: Buttons and commands

The most remarkable and widely distributed Tcl extension is *Tk,* a library for the simple creation of graphical user interfaces. In Tk, user interfaces are put together out of basic elements, which are called *widgets* (evoking "window gadget"). Widgets accomplish a variety of basic functions; some Tk widgets are shown in Figure 11.1.

Tk

Widgets

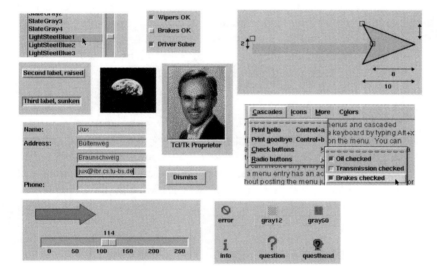

Figure 11.1
Some Tk widgets.

Widgets are divided into *classes* according to their appearance and behavior, for example, buttons, scrollbars, or text windows. To create a single widget, the widget class is given as a command, followed by the name of the widget and, if necessary, other options; the `pack` command adds the newly created widget to the main window.

Widget classes

Here is an example that uses the Tcl interpreter `wish` (from "windowing shell") that has been extended by Tk:

```
$ wish
% button .b -text "Hello, world!"
.b
% pack .b
% _
```

You only need these two commands to create the window shown in Figure 11.2.

Figure 11.2
A "Hello, world!"
application. (The
decorative title bars
come from the
window manager.)

As a Tk developer, you do not need a time-consuming initialization, or long-winded work with widget properties, or a long compilation – you can immediately and even interactively see the result of your work.

What exactly happens here? The `button` command creates a new button called `.b`. Using further arguments, certain properties of the newly created widget can be specified – in our example, the text to be displayed. *Widget options*   Since these additional arguments can also be omitted, they are called *options*. Options frequently have their own argument; in our `button` example, the option is `-text` with the argument `"Hello, world"`. The `button` class has about 20 properties that can be set using the options.

Widget commands   Each widget has some of its own commands with which its properties can be queried and changed retrospectively. These commands are joined at the end of the widget names. The `configure` command allows properties to be entered again in the form of options; these are the same options that were entered during the creation of the widget. We can, for example, use `configure` to enter a *command* that has to be executed when the button is clicked:

```
% .b configure -command {puts "Hello!"}
.b
% _
```

From now on, with every click, the character string `Hello!` is output.

Changing properties   `configure` can also be used to change properties that have already been entered. The following command can be used to change the text that is displayed.

```
% .b configure -text "Goodbye, world!"
.b
% _
```

Linking variables to widget properties   In order to change properties at runtime, another method is normally used in Tcl: Properties are not changed by commands directly, but are instead linked to *variables*. Here is a brief example with several widgets.

```
$ wish
% checkbutton .bold -text Bold -variable bold
.bold
% checkbutton .italic -text Italic -variable italic
.italic
% checkbutton .underline -text Underline \
  -variable underline
.underline
% pack .bold .italic .underline -side top -anchor w
% _
```

This input creates the window in Figure 11.3.

Figure 11.3
A small menu for the creation of text properties.

The three options of the checkbutton widget class can either be on or off. Their status is *linked* to a variable using the -variable option: each change in the status of the widget causes a change of the value of the variable, and vice versa. The bold variable then has the value 1 if the .bold option is on and value 0 otherwise.

Let us assume that Figure 11.3 shows the current status of the window. This results in the following values for the variables:

```
% puts "$bold $italic $underline"
1 0 0
% _
```

The link between variables and widgets works in both directions: by changing the variables, the status of the menu can also be changed. The following Tcl commands, for instance, turn on all three options.

```
% set bold 1
% set italic 1
% set underline 1
% _
```

As already explained, the widgets can be linked not only to variables but also to *Tcl functions*. The basic idea is always to execute a function if a

widget is *activated*. To "activate" means that a certain *event* occurs with
reference to this widget – typically user actions such as the pressing of
a key while the mouse pointer points to this widget. During the process,
Tcl/Tk allows an arbitrary combination of events and functions.

Example 11.2 shows the file power.tcl, which produces a complete
application with several widgets.

```
proc pow {base p} {
  set result 1
  while {$p > 0} {
    set result [expr $result * $base]
    set p [expr $p - 1]
  }
  return $result
}

entry .base -width 6 -textvariable base
label .label1 -text "to the power"
entry .power -width 6 -textvariable power
label .label2 -text "is"
label .result -textvariable result
pack .base .label1 .power .label2 .result -side left \
  -padx 1m -pady 2m
bind .base  <Return> {set result [pow $base $power]}
bind .power <Return> {set result [pow $base $power]}
```

Example 11.2
*Calculating powers
in the file*
power.tcl

We can source the commands from the file power.tcl by calling wish
using the option -f:

$ **wish -f power.tcl**

We get the image in Figure 11.4. After entering a number in one of the
two text windows and pressing the Return key, the power is automatically
calculated on the right-hand side.

Figure 11.4
*A graphical user
interface for the
calculation of
powers.*

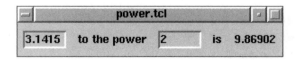

This application consists of five widgets: two text windows (.base and
.power) as well as three labels (.label1, .label2, and .result).

In one text window (widget class `entry`), users can input and edit character strings. The `-textvariable` option links the text window to the variables `base` and `power`.

The two labels `.label1` and `.label2` display constant character strings that are set using the `-text` option; the label `.result` indicates the current value of the `result` variable, which is linked to the label using `-textvariable` in the same way as with text windows.

The `pack` command is used in the same way on all five widgets; using the `-side` option, it is arranged so that the specified widgets are arranged from left to right. The other options determine the thickness of the outer border.

Using the `bind` command, the `pow` command is linked to the text window. Its arguments are a widget, an event description, and a command sequence. In our case, the event description is `<Return>`: if the `Return` key is pressed in the widget specified, the command sequence is executed, which in this case recalculates the value of the `result` variable.

Once again, the example is surprisingly concise but very clear. In fact, scripts are written so quickly that programs for the *interactive* arrangement of user interfaces (so-called *GUI builder*) for script languages have not yet managed to gain much of a foothold. At any rate, there are some. SpecTcl (from spectacle), shown in Figure 11.5 creates interfaces for Tcl and JAVA. Widgets are dragged from a menu onto the desktop; the

GUI builder

SpecTcl

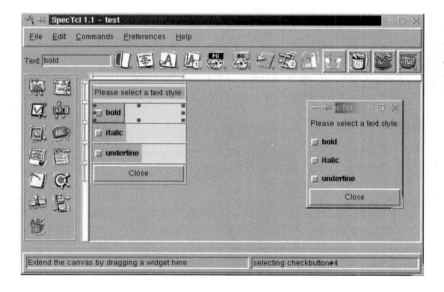

Figure 11.5
Designing a graphical user interface using SpecTcl.

prototype program can be executed any time for testing. SpecTcl is written entirely in Tcl/Tk.

Whether typed or clicked, details of the application can be changed quickly and easily, until both the customers and users are happy. As soon as the user interface is stable, prototype-based (and slow!) implementations in the script language (such as pow) can be replaced by efficient implementations, which have been produced in "traditional" programming languages.

11.5   Tcl/Tk as a prototype language

Incremental program development using Tcl

The Tk examples show, even more clearly that the Tcl examples, how quickly prototypes can be created using Tcl/Tk. However, we may not ignore the fact that applications that are only programmed in Tcl can cause big problems as far as maintenance is concerned. To develop programs incrementally using Tcl/Tk, the following steps are therefore recommended:

1. Develop a *horizontal prototype* for the coordination of the user interface with customers and users.

2. In parallel with the above, define the *interface* between user interfaces and self-defined Tcl commands.

3. Realize the Tcl commands using Tcl alone, typically with a significantly reduced functionality or none at all.

4. While the prototype is being refined further, *(re)implement* the Tcl commands in a conventional programming language. The normal design, implementation, and test phases apply.

5. Provided that no unusual demands are made on the *user interface*, this can remain written in Tcl/Tk.

The end product then consists of two parts:

1. A number of conventional Tcl commands, which cover the functionality of the application, and are independent from a particular representation.

2. A user interface in Tcl/Tk, which invokes the Tcl commands of the application and presents results to the user.

Division between user interface and functionality

Tcl favors a clear distinction between user interfaces and actual functionality; the application can be reused independently from a particular user interface in any context. As a "glue language", Tcl binds the application together with the user interface as well as, if need be, other applications.

Because the individual Tcl commands are programmed completely conventionally in the end product, one still has the overall safety and efficiency of standardized, compiled programming languages. Finally, users can extend and adapt their interface as they like, without having to get familiar with the details of the application or compile the application themselves – they only need to know the specific Tcl commands of the application.

11.6   Other script languages

The biggest weakness of Tcl is that, besides character strings and associative arrays, it does not support any built-in data type – even numbers can only be processed as character strings. Therefore, other script languages for prototyping have been established in addition to Tcl.

11.6.1   Perl

PERL, from Larry Wall (also the author of PATCH, as discussed Chapter 2), is an efficient prototype language with outstanding abilities in word processing and system programming; PERL is particularly used on WWW servers.

PERL is famous, if not infamous, for its syntax and its versatility: the author of PERL claims that having more than one way to write a program is a big advantage ("there's more than one way to skin a cat"). Example 11.3 shows four different ways of copying data from one source m$fp into another $conn.

PERL syntax

```
while (1) {
    $buf = $fp->read($blocksize);
    if (not $buf) { last }
    $conn->send($buf);
}

LOOP:
while (1) {
    $buf = $fp->read($blocksize);
    if (!$buf) {
        last LOOP;
    }
    $conn->send($buf);
}

while (1) {
    last unless $buf = $fp->read($blocksize);
    $conn->send($buf);
```

Example 11.3
Four ways of writing the same function in PERL. (This example was published in 1995 by Tom Christiansen in the newsgroup `comp.lang.perl`.*)*

```
        }

        while (1) {
            last unless $buf = read $fp $blocksize;
            send $conn $buf;
        }
```

Data structures
in PERL
In contrast to Tcl, PERL has a number of typical data structures at its disposal, such as lists, associative arrays and records, which can also be used to implement object-oriented programming with inheritance. The combination of these basic elements to make up complex data structures is, however, quite difficult and is, thus, the topic of frequently answered questions. The countless built-in language gimmicks are also difficult to combine; each one of them seems to have been created to solve a specific problem.

As a demonstration, we will implement a *matrix multiplication* in PERL, shown in Example 11.4.

```
sub mmult {
    my ($m1,$m2) = @_;
    my ($m1rows,$m1cols) = (scalar @$m1, scalar @{$m1->[0]});
    my ($m2rows,$m2cols) = (scalar @$m2, scalar @{$m2->[0]});

    unless ($m1cols == $m2rows) {  # raise exception, actually
        die "IndexError: matrices don't match: $m1cols != $m2rows";
    }

    my $result = [];
    my ($i, $j, $k);

    for $i (0 .. ($m1rows - 1 )) {
        for $j (0 .. ($m2cols - 1 )) {
            for $k ( 0 .. ($m1cols - 1)) {
                $result->[$i]->[$j] +=
                    ($m1->[$i]->[$k] * $m2->[$k]->[$j]);
                }
            }
        }

    return $result;
}
```

Example 11.4
matrix multiplication
in PERL

The PERL constructs have the following meaning:

❏ The construct my defines a local variable. (Note: by default, therefore without my, variables are global; local is used to modify global variables temporarily in order to produce dynamic scoping.)

❏ @_ is the list of function arguments.

❏ l->[n] is used to get the nth element of the list l.

❏ unless is an if with a negated condition.

❏ for starts a loop.

❏ a += b means the same as a = a + b.

We leave the judgment of the syntax to the reader – at least, the program works. PERL comes with a Tk module and, thus, allows for the fast creation of user interfaces.

11.6.2   Python

PYTHON from Guido van Rossum is also a script language; as efficient as PERL, it boasts a clear syntax, inspired by MODULA-2. In PYTHON, each functionality is covered by precisely one language construct; there are fewer language constructs than in PERL but those available are more orthogonal (combinable) than those in PERL.

The "There is only one way" character from PYTHON is expressed not only in the language constructs but also in the syntax: here, *indents* are used for structuring – instead of curly braces (like in C, Tcl, or PERL) or BEGIN...END blocks (like in Modula or Ada). This feature, often initially perceived as unorthodox. provides for clean, unified formatting.

PYTHON syntax

Example 11.5 shows the program for matrix multiplication that we already know from PERL – this time in PYTHON. The only construct that needs to be explained is the form [e] * l, which creates an array of the length l, in which each element has the value e.

```
def mmult(m1, m2):
    m2rows, m2cols = len(m2), len(m2[0])
    m1rows, m1cols = len(m1), len(m1[0])
    if m1cols != m2rows:
        raise IndexError, "Matrices do not match"

    result = [None] * m1rows
    for i in range(m1rows):
        result[i] = [0] * m2cols
```

Example 11.5
Matrix multiplication in PYTHON

```
            for j in range(m2cols):
                for k in range(m1cols):
                    result[i][j] = \
                        result[i][j] + m1[i][k] * m2[k][j]

        return result
```

PYTHON data types   Like PERL, PYTHON brings efficient data types such as lists, tuples, links, and associative arrays. It also offers full object orientation and modularization, with which the PYTHON programs can easily progress from the prototype stage.

PYTHON also comes with support for Tk and can easily be extended with new commands written in C.

To conclude, can we also write a matrix multiplication in Tcl? Yes, we can, as shown in Example 11.6.

```
proc mmult {m1 m2} {
    set m2rows [llength $m2];
    set m2cols [llength [lindex $m2 0]];
    set m1rows [llength $m1];
    set m1cols [llength [lindex $m1 0]];
    if { $m1cols != $m2rows || $m1rows != $m2cols } {
        error "Matrix dimensions do not match!";
    }
    foreach row1 $m1 {
        set row {};
        for { set i 0 } { $i < $m2cols } { incr i } {
            set j 0;
            set element 0;
            foreach row2 $m2 {
                incr element \
                    [expr [lindex $row1 $j] * [lindex $row2 $i]];
                incr j;
            }
            lappend row $element;
        }
        lappend result $row;
    }
    return $result;
}
```

Example 11.6
matrix multiplication
in Tcl

In this example, the following Tcl commands are used:

llength *l* returns the length of a list *l*.

lindex *l n* returns the *n*th element of a list *l* (beginning with 0).

foreach *e l b* executes *b* for every value *e* from *l*.

for *i j p b* is a loop in C style: First, the initialization *i* is carried out. As long as the condition *p* is met, the loop body *b* and the increment statement *j* are repeated.

incr *n* increases *n* by 1.

incr *n m* increases *n* by *m*.

lappend *l e* appends *e* and the list *l*.

The example clearly shows the limits of command orientation in Tcl: for each assignment and each access to an element, a separate Tcl command has to be called, which does not make the program easier to read. The PYTHON variants are a lot more readable!

Concepts

❑ A *prototype* realizes a subset of a software system, precising the customer's ideas. Users can produce feedback on the design at an early stage.

❑ *Script languages* such as Tcl are well suited to creating prototypes quickly. The development is accelerated by the lack of declarations, as well as increased reuse and abstraction. Script languages are, however, unsuitable for highly efficient or complex applications.

❑ Tcl comes with a *methodology* for the creation of prototypes: missing functions are first produced rudimentally in Tcl and then programmed in a conventional programming language.

❑ The *user interface* can also be produced using Tcl/Tk in the end product. Since every function is assigned its own Tcl command, there is a good possibility of reuse.

❑ PERL and PYTHON provide more complex data structures than Tcl, which only supports character strings. While the strength of PERL lies in its simple scripts for word processing and system programming, PYTHON is suitable for developing larger programs, owing to modularization and object orientation.

Review exercises

1. Your boss has got hold of a case study in which a PERL program has been developed ten times quicker than a program written in a non-scripting language. He now demands that you immediately program entirely in PERL. Tell him about the five dangers of this method.

2. If the signature of a function is changed in a conventional programming language, this will be notified as soon as the remainder of the program is recompiled. What happens in the case of script languages? How can developers of libraries for script languages maintain the compatibility with earlier versions?

3. Imagine that you face the following requirements. Think about how to split the system into individual components. Which components would you implement in Tcl, and which would you implement in a conventional programming language? Using incremental program development, which components would you develop first, and which would you develop last?

   (a) An interactive program for creating, managing, and sending electronic mail.

   (b) A program for controlling a cash dispenser that must communicate with a central computer.

   (c) A graphical user interface for CVS (Chapter 4).

   (d) A program for the displaying the status of several weather stations.

Further reading

The benchmark to Tcl/Tk is the book by Ousterhout (1994), on which this chapter is based. Tcl/Tk enjoys a large community of users and widespread commercial support. John Ousterhout established the *Scriptics* company, which currently develops Tcl/Tk; the WWW page

`http://www.scriptics.com/`

contains links to numerous other Tcl/Tk resources; SpecTcl, which is also shown in Figure 11.5 is available here.

The standard book about PERL is the book from Larry Wall (1996); anyone wanting to understand the numerous PERL tricks should supplement this with the book from Christiansen and Torkington (1998). The official PERL web site

`http://www.perl.com/`

contains links to a vast amount of other resources.

The official PYTHON web site

```
http://www.python.org/
```

is the first source of good documentation on PYTHON. You can also find the on-line tutorial from van Rossum (1999) here. People who may prefer printed books should take a look at Himstedt and Mätzel (1999).

Other prototyping tools

In addition to Tcl/Tk, PERL, and PYTHON, a number of other prototyping script languages are in use:

- ❏ LISP, one of the oldest programming languages, is used everywhere where *symbols* are processed; lastly, LISP is also established as a script language by the EMACS editor and the graphic system GIMP.

- ❏ The modern LISP revision SCHEME is the basis for the GUILE project – a universal script language as the basis for programmable tools.

- ❏ PROLOG is popular as a script language for deductive reasoning, in particular, for mechanical problem solving.

- ❏ The functional language HASKELL offers high abstraction capabilities with unequaled elegance.

The following languages provide efficient programming environments with GUI builders:

- ❏ VISUAL BASIC from *Microsoft* is script language number 1 in the WINDOWS world. VISUAL BASIC comes with a programming environment that is easy to learn, and with which simple interfaces can be built quickly. Its weaknesses lie in the lack of portability and system-related functions.

- ❏ SMALLTALK is more a whole *system* than a language – all details of the graphical interface can be set up and manipulated in an object-oriented way.

Furthermore, GUI builders are typically components of *programming environments*. Page 360 gives an overview.

Exercises IV

In this exercise, you can create a simple pocket calculator using Tcl/Tk.

1. Create an application `calc.tcl`, which reads an arithmetical expression and evaluates it. By pressing the `Return` key in the input field, the expression is evaluated:

Tips:

❑ Base the structure of the program on the `power` program in the script.

❑ Use the Tcl/Tk command `expr` for the evaluation of arithmetical expressions.

2. Define a `lexpr` command that calls your `lcalc` program from the exercises of Part II. Integrate `lexpr` into `calc.tcl`.

Notes:

❑ The Tcl command

   `exec` *program* `<<` *expression*

calls *program* and passes *expression* to it as input.

❑ In your case, *expression* must end with a new line character (\n), so that `lcalc` accepts it as valid input.

❑ After the output of the result, `lcalc` has to exit (by means of the call of `exit(0)`), so that `exec` is also brought to an end.

3. (For readers with experience in C) Build a variant from `tclsh`, which has a built-in `lexpr` command.

For this, you have to

(a) alter the `lcalc` program so that it reads its input from a character. Depending on the LEX variant, you either have to

❑ redefine the macros `input` and `unput`: `input()` returns a character; `unput(x)` saves a character `x` in a buffer, which is then read during the next `input()`.

❑ redefine the macro `YY_INPUT(buf, result, max_size)` so that it writes the size `max_size` until the `result` character in a text `buf`.

(Some suggestions for creating this program are given below)

(b) define the Tcl command `LexprCmd` in a similar way as `EqCmd` in the script.

(c) bind together your own variant of `tclsh` by compiling `LexprCmd` and your own `Tcl_AppInit` and linking them with `-ltcl`.

Here is a LEX extension that reads from `input_ptr` instead of from the standard input:

```
%{
/* INPUT_PTR points to the input text */
static char *input_ptr = ...;

/* Buffer for pushed back characters */
static char pushback[BUFSIZ];
static char *pushback_ptr = pushback;

/* push back C character */
static int do_unput(char c)
{
    if (c != '\0')
        *pushback_ptr++ = c;
    return c;
}

/* read character from INPUT_PTR */
static int do_input()
{
    if (pushback_ptr != pushback)
        return *--pushback_ptr;

    if (*input_ptr != '\0')
```

```
            return *input_ptr++;
        else
            return 0;
    }

    /* LEX wants its input like this: */
    #ifdef input
    #undef input
    #define input do_input
    #endif

    #ifdef unput
    #undef unput
    #define unput do_unput
    #endif

    /* FLEX wants its input like this: */
    #ifdef FLEX_SCANNER
    #undef YY_INPUT
    #define YY_INPUT(buf, result, max_size) \
    {\
        int c = do_input(); \
        result = (c == '\0') ? \
            YY_ZERO : (buf[0] = c, 1); \
    }
    #endif
    %}
```

Note: On some systems, the linker may not find the main function in the Tcl library – this leads to an error message indicating that the main function is missing.

In this case, an explicit reference to main helps the process along. Therefore, in myAppInit.c from Section 11.3, the following lines can be added:

```
#include <tcl.h>

extern int main();
int *tclDummyMainPtr = (int *) main;
```

This explicit reference makes sure that main is loaded from the Tcl library.

Part V

Testing and Debugging

12 Software tests with DEJAGNU

12.1 My program ran yesterday – will it run today?

After its first delivery, a software product has to be continually *changed* – either to correct bugs or simply to adapt it to a changed environment. In this *maintenance phase*, it is important to assess the *effects of changes* properly: In contrast to earlier development stages, the program is already in use, and a small change can endanger the whole operation of the program. Therefore, one must always ensure that after a change, *at least the earlier functionality* is preserved.

Maintenance

Effects of changes

Using modern software design methods, the effects of changes can be limited and controlled effectively. Concepts such as modularization, object-oriented programming, and even encapsulation using functions and procedures are all suitable for hiding changes behind a well-defined interface.

In practice, another technique is used: the *regression test*. The aim of the regression test is to show differences in the functionality of the program after a change. The basic idea is to have a *number of test cases*, which cover the *existing functionality* of the program. Each test case consists of a number of input data and an (expected) set of output data – for example, the output produced by the version of the program being used at the time.

Regression test

Coverage of the existing functionality

After a change, the input data saved earlier is fed into the program. Each difference between the *observed* output and the *expected* output (as recorded earlier) points out a change of the functionality of the program. These differences must then be examined manually as to whether they are intended or not.

Difference in the behavior of programs

In this chapter, we focus on tests that execute the program as a whole and compare its output – so-called *system tests*. As an example, we will look at a simple regression test for the UNIX interpreter bc. The program bc reads an arithmetical expression from the standard input, evaluates it, and writes the result on the standard output. We use two files that hold the input (bc.in) and the expected output (bc.out) (Figure 12.1).

System test
Regression test for bc

Let us now assume that we have changed the program bc to bc.new and that we want to check whether the previous functionality is preserved.

Figure 12.1

Input bc.in *and*
expected output
bc.out *for the* bc
program.

bc.in	bc.out
2 + 2	4
7 * 9	63
3 - 7	-4
9 / 3	3

We use the input bc.in on bc.new and mark its output in bc.new.out. Finally, we compare the actual output bc.new.out with the expected output bc.out.

```
$ bc.new < bc.in > bc.new.out
$ diff bc.out bc.new.out
$ _
```

Since the DIFF output is empty, bc.out and bc.new.out are identical – the functionality written in bc.in and bc.out is unchanged in the new program bc.new. However, bc.in and bc.out with their four test cases are unrealistically small and cover the functionality of bc only inadequately. In fact, *absolute safety* cannot be achieved using tests; as Dijkstra says:

> A test can only point out the presence of errors, but not their absence.

Test coverage In practice, one, nonetheless, attempts to discover as many errors as possible. Therefore, one forms the test cases such that the functionality of the program being tested is covered as much possible, in order to increase the *probability of the discovery of errors*. Each new version of the GNU C compiler, for example, is fed with a test amount of 40,000 C programs before its release, which make good use of all the properties and peculiarities of the C language. In our example, the test cases also would have to cover the entire bc vocabulary to preserve the basic functionality of bc.

12.2 Programmed dialogs with EXPECT

The "stubborn" comparisons of expected and actual outputs by means of DIFF brings a number of problems in practice:

Syntactic and semantic differences **Irrelevant differences:** The comparison of the output using DIFF only checks *syntactic* differences, while the *semantics* of the output may be unchanged. For example, we change bc so that before every output of the character string "Output = " the semantic remains unchanged; DIFF would, however, see a difference in every individual test case.

Complicated user interface: Many programs, interactive programs, in particular, cannot process a list of inputs easily – they can only be invoked or used in a *dialog*. It is not enough here to send input and compare output. Before inputting, one has to wait for a *prompt*; perhaps additional *questions* ("Are you sure?") have to be answered.

Interactive programs

Both these problems can be simplified considerably by using a tool for *programmed dialog*. The basic idea is to automate a dialog using a sequence of *send/expect* actions:

Programmed dialog

❑ A *send* action (engl. *to send*: to send) sends an input to an interactive program using a *virtual terminal* – usually a keyboard entry.

Virtual terminal

❑ An *expect* action (engl. *to expect*: to expect) links specific actions (in particular, *send* actions) to certain outputs of the interactive program.

The whole dialog, thus, can be expressed as a sequence of *expect* and assigned *send* actions.

A widely distributed tool for programmed dialog tracking is the EX-PECT program from Don Libes. EXPECT extends Tcl (Chapter 11) with special `send` and `expect` commands for the automation of dialogs. All acceptability of Tcl such as variables, check-flow control, and so on, are available. The executable program `expect` is a Tcl interpreter extended with EXPECT commands, which can process the EXPECT scripts (Tcl scripts with EXPECT commands).

EXPECT

EXPECT and Tcl

As an example, we will look at a simple EXPECT script for automated dialog tracking using the UNIX file transfer program (FTP). FTP is a shell with which individual files can be transferred between computers. At the start of FTP, the user must first indicate the computer from which he wants to download files; then, she has to input the name and password.

Automation of the FTP program

Publicly accessible FTP servers provide *anonymous FTP*: As a username, `anonymous` is sufficient, and the e-mail address is usually entered as the password. This process is often tedious, but can be automated via an EXPECT script, like `ftp.exp`, which is shown in Example 12.1.

```
# Start FTP
spawn ftp

# Wait for FTP prompt
expect "ftp> "

# Send open command
send "open ftp.gnu.org\r"
```

Example 12.1
The EXPECT script `ftp.exp` *automates the anonymous log-on to an FTP server*

```
while 1 {
  # send name and password if required.
  expect {
    "Name *:"   { send "anonymous\r" }
    "Password:" { send "user@somewhere.com\r" }
    "*ftp> "    break
    timeout     exit
  }
}

# Send binary and hash commands
send "binary\r"
expect "*ftp> "
send "hash\r"
expect "*ftp> "

# Switch to user interaction
interact
```

The script ftp.exp uses the following EXPECT commands:

Program start   **spawn** normally stands at the beginning of an EXPECT script; it starts the program to be automated (such as ftp).

Expecting output   **expect** waits for a certain output of the program:

❑ In the simple form, expect *character string* waits for EXPECT until the program has output a *character string* (here the prompt ftp>).

❑ In the more complex form, expect *pattern₁ action₁ pattern₂ action₂* ... waits for EXPECT until the program output meets a pattern *patternᵢ*, and then executes the assigned command in *actionᵢ*. In this form, a *pattern* can contain "?" as a placeholder for a single character and "*" as a placeholder for any number of characters.

Sending character   **send** sends the given Tcl character string to the program (here for example:
strings   open ftp.gnu.org, followed by a return sign).

Submitting control to   **interact** submits the control to the user; all input from the user is passed
users   on to the program.

We will now look at the process of ftp.exp in detail. First, the FTP program is started using spawn; then the FTP prompt appears, and EXPECT then sends an open command to FTP:

```
$ expect ftp.exp
spawn ftp
ftp> open ftp.gnu.org
Connected to ftp.gnu.org.
220 ProFTPD Server [gnudist.gnu.org]
```

Now, the request for the input of a name and password appears, which complies with the EXPECT script:

```
Name (ftp.gnu.org:zeller): anonymous
331 Anonymous login ok,
send your complete e-mail address as a password.
Password:
230-Welcome, archive user!
230 Guest login ok, access restrictions apply.
```

Lastly, our script sets a few more FTP parameters before it submits control to us and we can browse the FTP archives (for example, pub/gnu) interactively:

```
ftp> binary
200 Type set to I.
ftp> hash
Hash mark printing on (1024 bytes/hash mark).
ftp> cd pub/gnu_
```

12.3 EXPECT in regression tests

The ability of EXPECT to automate routine dialogs is used for automated regression tests. As an example, we will look at the UNIX interpreter bc. again. Example 12.2 shows a possible script for the test case 2+2.

```
# Start BC
spawn bc

# Leave a little time for initial messages
sleep 1

# The pass and fail procedures
```

Regression tests using EXPECT

Example 12.2
The EXPECT script
2+2.exp *tests whether* bc *the arithmetical expression* 2+2 *is correctly evaluated*

```
# output the test outcome:
# PASS = "Test is successful"
# FAIL = "Test has failed"
proc pass {a} { puts "PASS $a" }
proc fail {a} { puts "FAIL $a" }

# Send expression to bc
send "2+2\n"

# Ignore echo
expect "2+2\r\n"

# Check correct output
expect {
   "4\r\n"      { pass "2+2" }
   "*\r\n"      { fail "2+2" }
   timeout      { fail "(timeout) 2+2" }
}
```

The `sleep` command interrupts the execution of the script for one second, in order to give `bc` an opportunity for printing initial messages. The `pass` and `fail` commands print the outcome of the test. We use a separate `expect` command to handle the echo of the input.

Opening messages   What is the `sleep` command required for? Without the `sleep` command, initial messages may be interpreted as *error messages* later. Normally, one would wait for an explicit prompt, as in the FTP example. With `bc`, this is not the case, however, since `bc` does not use a prompt. As an alternative, we could use an `expect` command to expect and check the initial message of `bc`.

Since we have more test cases, we can write a procedure `bc_test` for individual test cases that have arithmetical expressions and expected outputs as arguments. This could then look as shown in the script `bc.exp` in Example 12.3.

Example 12.3
The EXPECT script
`bc.exp` *tests several*
arithmetic
expressions

```
# Start BC
spawn bc

# Leave a little time for initial messages
sleep 1

# The pass and fail procedures
# output the test outcome:
# PASS = "Test is successful"
```

```
# FAIL = "Test has failed"
proc pass {a} { puts "PASS $a" }
proc fail {a} { puts "FAIL $a" }

# bc_test expr result sends expr to BC
# and checks whether BC's output is result
proc bc_test {expr result} {
  send "$expr\n"
  expect "$expr\r\n"

  # The option '-gl' makes sure that a
  # pattern beginning with '-' is not interpreted as a
  # expect option.
  expect {
     -gl "$result\r\n" { pass "$expr" }
     "*\r\n"           { fail "$expr" }
     timeout { fail "(timeout) $expr" }
  }
}

# Individual test cases
bc_test "2+2"   "4"
bc_test "7*9"   "63"
bc_test "3-7"   "-4"
bc_test "9/3"   "4"
```

Using this EXPECT script, we can now test the bc program:

```
$ expect bc.exp
spawn bc
2+2
4
PASS 2+2
7*9
63
PASS 7*9
3-7
-4
PASS 3-7
9/3
3
FAIL 9/3
$ _
```

Surprise – the test run shows a failure! What has happened? Actually, the error is not in the bc program, but in the script: For the expression 9/3, the result 4 is expected, although bc correctly calculates 3. This example shows that differences in the expected and the actual result are not necessarily indications of an error in the program.

12.4   DEJAGNU – a framework for regression tests

Using the pass, fail, and bc_test procedures from bc.exp, we have defined a *framework* in which any number of other test cases can be embedded. We now want to introduce a ready-made framework, which is built on EXPECT and has a wide functionality for the execution and assessment of regression tests: DEJAGNU.

DEJAGNU extends the EXPECT functionality with Tcl commands, which execute and evaluate test cases. In addition, DEJAGNU provides a program called runtest, which runs a given set of test cases automatically. (The name DEJAGNU is a play on word, inspired by the expression *Déja vu* (frz. *already seen once*; and *Déja-vu experience*) and means the behavior of the program that existed earlier – the basis of the regression test.)

DEJAGNU was produced after the POSIX standard 1003.3, which defines one of the five possible outcomes for test cases:

Success   **PASS:** The test was completed successfully; the program behaves as expected.

Failure   **FAIL:** The test has failed; the behavior of the program is not what was expected.

Indefinite   **UNRESOLVED:** The result of the test is indefinite – neither success nor failure. The final assessment needs to be carried out by a human operator who will decide between PASS or FAIL.

Untested   **UNTESTED:** The test was not carried out. This is a dummy for a (still) nonexistent test.

Unsupported   **UNSUPPORTED:** The test cannot be carried out because the environment does not provide sufficient services.

Each one of these five cases is assigned a Tcl command, which contains the name of the test output and the name of the test case as an argument. The commands defined in bc.exp, pass, and fail are therefore predefined by DEJAGNU. In addition to the output of a message, they also update statistics on the test cases that have been executed.

In DEJAGNU, the tests are divided into a number of EXPECT
scripts, which are distributed over various directories. In `config/` *Initialization script*
`default.exp`, there is an *initialization script*, which starts the program
that is to be tested and defines important commands. The following
commands have to be defined for DEJAGNU:

name_load loads a test into the program *name*.

name_start starts the program to be tested.

name_exit exits the program to be tested.

name_version prints the version of the program.

In addition to these four functions, the initialization script can contain
other self-defined Tcl commands. At the end of the initialization script,
the program to be tested is started up. (The `config/` directory can
also contain other initialization scripts for specific architecture as well
as `default.exp`. So, for example, on UNIX machines, instead of
`config/default.exp`, the script `config/unix.exp` is executed.)

In Example 12.4, we have edited the script `bc.exp` for DEJAGNU and
created a `config/default.exp` file for bc. The command `bc_start`
starts `bc` and the command `bc_exit` exits it; `bc_test` is the already
known auxiliary function for easy testing. `pass` and `fail` are available
in DEJAGNU.

```
# Load test
proc bc_load { arg } {
    #
}

# Start program
proc bc_start {} {
    global spawn_id
    spawn "bc"
    sleep 1
}

# Exit program
proc bc_exit {} {
    send "quit\n"
}
```

Example 12.4
A file
`config/default.exp`,
with which the
DEJAGNU is set up
for the testing of bc

```
# Return program version
proc bc_version {} {
    return "unknown"
}

# Own functions
proc bc_test {expr result} {
  send "$expr\n"
  expect "$expr\r\n"

  expect {
     -gl "$result\r\n" { pass "$expr" }
     "*\r\n"           { fail "$expr" }
     timeout { fail "(timeout) $expr" }
  }
}

# Finally: Start program
bc_start
```

The actual test cases are defined in EXPECT scripts, which are stored in subdirectories in the form of *name.suffix*. In our example, DEJAGNU would process all scripts in subdirectories with the name bc.*suffix*. We create a separate file called bc.test/expr.exp, which combines the four test cases already known, shown in Example 12.5.

Example 12.5
The test file
bc.test/expr.exp,
which contains the
actual test cases

```
# Some test cases
bc_test "2+2"    "4"
bc_test "7*9"    "63"
bc_test "3-7"    "-4"
bc_test "9/3"    "4"
```

This is all we need. The command runtest --tool *name* executes all tests that are assigned to the program *name*, in our case, therefore, runtest --tool bc. The additional option --all makes sure that, in addition to the failed tests, the successful tests are also output.

```
$ runtest --all --tool bc
Test Run By zeller on Mon Jul  7 17:57:59 1997
Native configuration is sparc-sun-sunos4.1.4
```

```
                    === bc tests ===

Running ./bc.test/expr.exp ...
PASS: 2+2
PASS: 7*9
PASS: 3-7
FAIL: 9/3


                    === bc Summary ===

# of expected passes        3
# of unexpected failures    1
$ _
```

Like the original EXPECT script bc.exp, DEJAGNU displays the test outcome and also gives *statistics* on the test outcome. The results from DE-
JAGNU are logged in history files and can be forwarded to other developers.
Therefore, in numerous companies, it is standard practice to automatically
check out the latest version of the developed program, to compile it, and
to carry out regression tests. The uniform format of DEJAGNU outputs
and the easy automation help identify problems in the code as early as
possible.

Statistics

Nightly tests

12.5 Testing programs with graphical user interaction

The examples we have dealt with so far are suitable for batch-oriented
programs, as well as for programs that communicate with the user over
a terminal interface. But what happens for programs that come with a
graphical user interface? These types of programs can also be automatically tested – as long as they have an interface available by which they can
be controlled and run from a remote program.

The Tk toolkit introduced in Section 11.4 does provide such an interface via its interactive wish interpreter. While the interactive program
is running, the status can be requested via wish and be manipulated.
As a simple example, we will look at a test for the "Hello World" program from Figure 11.2. The file hello.tcl contains the command in
Example 12.6.

```
button .b -text "Hello, world!"
pack .b
```

Example 12.6
A Tcl script
hello.tcl

After invoking wish with hello.tcl, we can query the status of the program and all buttons using suitable Tcl commands – such as the title of the button .b:

```
$ wish
% source hello.tcl
% .b cget -text
Hello, world!
% _
```

Furthermore, we can *remote control* the program. The action invoke has the same effect as a mouse-click on the button – namely, the output of "Hello, world!".

```
% .b invoke
Hello, world!
% _
```

These two properties – the displayed text and the result of invoke – can thus be tested. We create an initialization script config/default.exp for hello.tcl, shown in Example 12.7.

Example 12.7
A file default.exp
for testing
hello.tcl

```
# Load test case
proc hello_load { arg } {
    #
}

# Start program
proc hello_start {} {
    global spawn_id
    spawn "wish"
    expect "% "
    send "source hello.tcl\n"
}

# Exit program
proc hello_exit {} {
    send "exit\n"
}

# Output program version
proc hello_version {} {
    return [info tclversion]
}
```

```
# Functions
proc hello_test {cmd result} {
  send "$cmd\n"
  expect {
    "*$result\r\n% " { pass "$cmd" }
    "*% "            { fail "$cmd" }
    timeout          { fail "(timeout) $cmd" }
  }
}


# Finally: start program
hello_start
```

The commands required by DEJAGNU are all available; the self-defined command `hello_test` checks whether a Tcl command shows the expected result. Since `wish`, in contrast to `bc`, has a separate prompt (namely "% "), `hello_start` can use the safe `expect` command instead of a `sleep` call; the `expect` call in `hello_test` can also be formed more easily.

Now to the test cases. We check that the button displays the correct text. We create a test case file (for example, with the name `hello.test/label.exp`), in which we insert:

```
hello_test ".b cget -text" "Hello, world!"
```

In addition, we can ensure that activating the button results in the output "'Hello, world!'":

```
hello_test ".b invoke" "Hello, world!"
```

Invoking `runtest` shows that the program actually has the required properties.

```
$ runtest --all --tool hello
Test Run By zeller on Mon Jul  7 20:31:27 1997
Native configuration is sparc-sun-sunos4.1.4

                === hello tests ===

Running ./hello.test/label.exp ...
PASS: .b cget -text
PASS: .b invoke
```

```
                              === hello Summary ===

         # of expected passes          2
         $ _
```

Internal status

A number of issues till remain, though. On one hand, there are a number of *technical problems:* the `hello` window still has to be positioned on the screen; it also needs a screen on which `hello` can run. On the other hand, we must be aware that we query the *internal status* (a variable value) rather than the external status of the program (the text shown on the screen). Test cases are therefore very fragile with respect to internal changes, which may have no effect on the externally visible behavior. If, for example, `.b` is renamed to `.button`, the appearance of the program remains unchanged; however, test cases that refer to `.b` must also be changed accordingly.

Remote control of user interfaces

Testing the actual graphical output of an interactive program remains a challenge. Most current user interfaces are *remote controlled* – in addition to the Tcl/Tk introduced here, the WINDOWS and MacOS operating systems have outstanding script abilities. Alternatively, one can *record* the *interactions* of the user – such as key strokes and mouse movements – and later *play them back* (so-called *Capture/Replay*). However, it is difficult to automate the *status* of a program merely by recognizing its graphical interface and reacting to this after the event; it is also very susceptible to change.

Capture/Replay

Considering all these challenges, it appears more useful either to directly access the program status (and to accept a strong coupling of program and test cases) or to implement a special interface just for automation. Making the core functionality available for automation (including queries of the program status!) via a well-defined interface can be very useful here – for example, as a Tcl command, as outlined in Section 11.5.

Concepts

❑ *Regression tests* are used to uncover unintended changes in the functionality of the program after a change to the code.

❑ When designing regression tests, a program for automating dialog tracking such as EXPECT helps

– mastering variations in program output (and thus distinguishing *semantic* changes from *syntactic* changes), as well as

– dealing with complex dialogs and user interfaces.

❑ DEJAGNU is an example of a general *testing framework* in which individual test cases can be included in an easy and standard way.

❑ Regression testing of programs with graphical user interfaces works best if *interfaces for automation* are available.

Review exercises

1. If, in an `expect` command, a pattern is preceded by `-re` instead `-gl`, the pattern will be interpreted as a *regular expression*. Extend the script `bc.exp` with regular expressions so that

   (a) after the result, there can be any number of blank spaces,

   (b) in front of the result, there can be any number of blank spaces,

   (c) in front of the result, there can be any number of characters, which must not be mistaken for the result.

2. Use the `expr` function of Tcl to compare the actual and expected results in `bc.exp` *numerically*. What are the advantages of this method? What are the disadvantages?

3. Because of the final representation of numbers in the computer, real and rational numbers cannot be tested for equality with a meaningful result. Design a procedure `bc_real_test`, which obtains a percental deviation as an additional argument, which, when exceeded, is judged as an error.

4. A change in a program frequently means a change in the regression test. How can you use a version control to link these changes to each other?

Further reading

The article from Onoma et al. (1998) shows the industrial use of the regression test: *regression testing is today one of the most important and common test strategies in the industry.*

Zeller (1999) describes a technique with which one can systematically and automatically determine the changes that have caused the error after a failed regression test. This so-called *delta debugging* should be used after every failed regression test.

EXPECT was developed by Libes (1990); Libes (1992) describes its use in regression tests. Libes (1994) is an extensive book about EXPECT.

DEJAGNU as a common test frame was developed by Savoye (1996) in a company called CYGNUS for executing regression tests for the GNU tools GCC and GDB. DEJAGNU is used in a number of companies today.

Other testing tools

In addition to DEJAGNU, there are also a number of other *commercial* tools for testing. We have arranged a selection of these in the following list.

❑ TESTSUITE from *Mercury Interactive* is an efficient test environment for numerous platforms, in particular, WINDOWS and UNIX. The products WINRUNNER and XRUNNER offer *Capture/Replay* for WINDOWS or UNIX. Owing to character recognition, the tools can extract the displayed text from dialog boxes, which simplifies automation. A test management program TEST DIRECTOR is also included.

❑ SILKTEST from *Segue Software* also offers *Capture/Replay* in conjunction with *4Text*, an object-oriented script language. In a *test frame*, every graphical object is assigned an identifier, which can be used by test cases and, thus, abstracts from internal object properties. SILKTEST is available for WINDOWS and UNIX and can test cross-platform.

❑ TEAMTEST from *Rational* (formerly *SQA Suite*) is a test frame for WINDOWS. The tool RATIONAL ROBOT automates component tests using the cross-platform script language *SQABasic*, a variant of VISUAL BASIC. Scripts can automatically be created by *Capture/Replay*.

❑ VISUAL TEST from *Rational* (taken over by *Microsoft*) is a simple *Capture/Replay* tool for WINDOWS with a good integration of WINDOWS development tools.

13 Component tests with JUNIT

13.1 From system tests to component tests

Chapter 12 has discussed DEJAGNU – a tool to automate program testing. Such automated tests are definitely useful to detect failures early. But once a failure has been found, it can be difficult to *narrow down* the cause of the failure – which component is responsible for the failure? For this reason, it is useful not only to test the system as a whole but also to test its *components* – and even better, to compose the system from tested components.

Component tests

Just like system tests, component tests should run *automatically,* such that undesired effects of changes can quickly be detected. Since a component typically does not execute on its own, we need a *testing framework for components* that

❑ provides the required environment for the component,

❑ executes the individual services of the component,

❑ compares the observed program state with the expected program state,

❑ reports any deviations from the expectations,

❑ and does all of this automatically.

In general, a testing framework for components does not differ from a framework for systems, as realized in DEJAGNU. The difference is in the language: System tests are typically written in a scripting language (such as Tcl in DEJAGNU). In contrast, component tests are specified in a programming language that is supported by the component interface – typically, the language in which the component is written.

13.2 Validating program states

The main tool of component tests is the *comparison* of the observed state with the expected state. For this purpose, one uses a special programming technique, the so-called *assertion.*

Assertion   An assertion expresses some expected property of the program state. Upon execution, the assertion checks whether the property holds; if not, the assertion generates a failure. In C, C++, and JAVA (JDK 1.4 and later), assertions are realized using the *assert* function. Its general form is

$$\texttt{assert}(b)$$

When the `assert` function is executed, it evaluates the boolean expression b. If b is true, nothing happens – the assertion passes. If b is false (the assertion fails), a *runtime error* occurs – the execution is aborted. In C and C++, this typically takes place using the `abort()` function; in JAVA, an `AssertionError` exception is raised.

Here is an example of how to use assertions in test cases. Let us assume you manage a Java class for rational numbers, called `Rational`. This class has a constructor that takes a numerator and a denominator: the code `Rational(1, 3)` creates the rational number $\frac{1}{3}$.

Suppose you want to test the comparison of rational numbers. Some properties you would like to see are

Identity. Is $\frac{1}{3} = \frac{1}{3}$?

Different representations. Is $\frac{2}{6} = \frac{1}{3}$?

Integers. Is $\frac{3}{3} = 1$?

Nonequality. Is $\frac{1}{3} \neq \frac{2}{3}$?

To realize these tests, we could easily extend the `Rational` class by a dedicated testing method. It is better, though, to separate application code and testing code – especially because tests and applications can thus be maintained separately. Therefore, we create a class `RationalAssert` that uses assertions to test the above examples.

```
class RationalAssert {
  public static void main(String args[]) {
    assert new Rational(1, 3).equals(new Rational(1, 3));
    assert new Rational(2, 6).equals(new Rational(1, 3));
    assert new Rational(3, 3).equals(new Rational(1, 1));
    assert !new Rational(2, 3).equals(new Rational(1, 3));
  }
}
```

When translating this class, we must specify the JAVA-Version (currently 1.4); earlier JAVA versions do not support `assert`.

```
$ javac -source 1.4 RationalAssert.java
$ _
```

In JAVA, assertions are *disabled* by default. To have the JAVA interpreter execute them, one must specify a special option -enableassertions (or short -ea).

```
$ java -ea RationalAssert
Exception in thread "main" java.lang.AssertionError
    at RationalAssert.main(RationalAssert.java:3)
$ _
```

Oops! Obviously, our Rational class still has room for improvement – the first assertion in Line 3 has failed. (In C/C++ programs, assert also outputs the location of the failing assertion). The next task is to narrow down the failure cause – this is also a task where assertions come in handy (see Chapter 15 for more on debugging).

13.3 Executing component tests

Testing with standard assertions, as discussed in Section 13.2, is not well suited for larger test tasks:

- ❏ If a test fails, the subsequent test cases are no longer executed.

- ❏ One should be able to run test cases individually, independent of other test cases.

- ❏ One should be able to group tests into *test suites*.

- ❏ One should be able to grasp immediately whether tests have failed, and if so, which ones.

All these are requirements for *any* test framework. Therefore, what we need is a test framework that uses assertions to organize tests. The standard of such test frameworks for JAVA is JUNIT (from JAVA unit test), developed by Kent Beck and Erich Gamma. Several variants exist for various programming languages, such as CPPUNIT for C++ programs. JUNIT's strengths lie in its simplicity and versatility: Developers can quickly write, execute, and evaluate tests.

Figure 13.1 shows the JUNIT graphical user interface. Clicking on the *Run* button starts the tests; the progress bar below shows how many tests have been executed so far. A green bar stands for "no failures so far"; if the bar turns red, the window below gives more information about the failures that have occurred.

13.4 JUNIT test cases

How does one specify tests in JUNIT? In JUNIT, tests are organized into *test cases*. Each test case is realized by its own class derived from the

Figure 13.1
JUNIT with Swing
GUI.

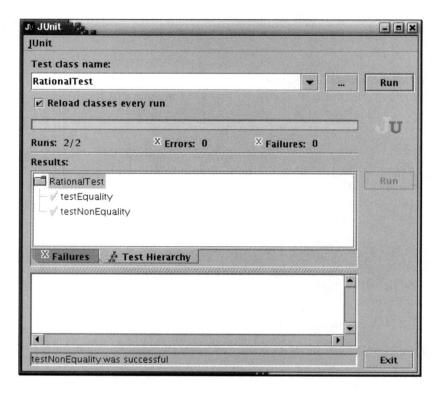

Figure 13.1
JUNIT with Swing GUI.

JUNIT `TestCase` class. The constructor takes the name of the test case as an argument; typically, it simply invokes the constructor of the parent class.

```java
import junit.framework.*;

public class RationalTest extends TestCase {
  // Create new test
  public RationalTest(String name) {
    super(name);
  }

  (more methods (see below))
}
```

Each test of the test case is realized by its own *method* whose name starts with `test...`. Thus, a method `testEquality` could summarize the equality assertions for the `Rational` class. The `assertTrue()` method, inherited from `TestCase`, has the same meaning as the `assert()` function discussed above; however, instead of aborting execution, `assertTrue()` just reports the failed assertion to JUNIT.

```
// Test for equality
public void testEquality() {
  assertTrue(new Rational(1, 3).equals(
    new Rational(1, 3)));
  assertTrue(new Rational(2, 6).equals(
    new Rational(1, 3)));
  assertTrue(new Rational(3, 3).equals(
    new Rational(1, 1)));
}
```

Besides `assertTrue()`, JUNIT provides a number of predefined assertion methods, listed in Table 13.1. Using the `assertEquals()` method, for instance, simplifies comparison:

```
// Test for equality
public void testEquality() {
  assertEquals(new Rational(1, 3), new Rational(1, 3));
  assertEquals(new Rational(2, 6), new Rational(1, 3));
  assertEquals(new Rational(3, 3), new Rational(1, 1));
}
```

Method	Effect
`fail(msg)`	Failure named `msg`
`assertTrue(msg, b)`	Failure if `b` is false
`assertFalse(msg, b)`	Failure if `b` is true
`assertEquals(msg, `v_1`, `v_2`)`	Failure if $v_1 \neq v_2$
`assertEquals(msg, `v_1`, `v_2`, `ϵ`)`	Failure if $\lvert v_1 - v_2 \rvert > \epsilon$
`assertNull(msg, obj)`	Failure if `obj` is not null
`assertNonNull(msg, obj)`	Failure if `obj` is null
`assertSame(msg, `o_1`, `o_2`)`	Failure if o_1 and o_2 do not refer to the same object
`assertNotSame(msg, `o_1`, `o_2`)`	Failure if o_1 and o_2 refer to the same object

Table 13.1
Assertions in JUNIT.

The message `msg` can also be omitted.

A test case (class) can hold an arbitrary number of tests (methods). The JUNIT GUI (Figure 13.1) allows the enabling or disabling of tests and test cases individually.

```
// Test for nonequality
public void testNonEquality() {
```

```
    assertFalse(new Rational(2, 3).equals(
      new Rational(1, 3)));
}
```

Having set up all tests, we must take care that the test case can actually be executed. The `main` method of the `TestRunner` class takes care of this – in our case, using a graphical user interface (`swingui`):

```
// Invoke GUI
public static void main(String args[]) {
  String[] testCaseName =
    { RationalTest.class.getName() };
  junit.swingui.TestRunner.main(testCaseName);
}
```

This completes our test case. To compile and execute `RationalTest`, we need the package `junit.jar`, whose path must be included in the JAVA class path (`-classpath`). Eventually, we obtain the GUI in Figure 13.1.

```
$ javac -classpath .:wherever/junit.jar \
        RationalTest.java
$ java -classpath .:wherever/junit.jar \
        RationalTest
$ _
```

The alternate `TestRunner` text user interface (`textui`) is much less comfortable, but useful for batch execution – for instance, in a nightly batch job. If, in `main`, we replace the invocation

```
junit.swingui.TestRunner.main(testCaseName);
```

by

```
junit.textui.TestRunner.main(testCaseName);
```

we get

```
$ javac -classpath .:wherever/junit.jar \
        RationalTest.java
$ java -classpath .:wherever/junit.jar \
        RationalTest
..
Time: 0.009

OK (2 tests)
$ _
```

The two dots being printed stand for successful tests; failing test would have been output as F or E.

13.5   Setting up fixture

Tests frequently need some *fixture* to execute. Typical examples include:

❑ configuration files that must be read and processed,

❑ external resources that must be requested and set up,

❑ services of other components that must be initialized.

If multiple tests need such a fixture, how do they get it? Of course, every test could set up its own fixture. However, maintaining all these fixtures can quickly cause more work than maintaining the actual tests. Therefore, JUNIT provides special methods for setting up the fixture for the tests:

Setting up: The method `setUp()` is called *before* each test of the class; its purpose is to set up common fixture.

Tearing down: The method `tearDown()` is called *after* each test. It is used for *releasing* fixture – for instance, to deallocate or to close additional resources.

In our `Rational` case, a fixture can be useful to set up frequently used values – for instance, an attribute `a_third` that holds the value $\frac{1}{3}$:

```
public class RationalTest extends TestCase {

    private Rational a_third;

    // Set up fixture
    // Called before each testXXX() method
    protected void setUp() {
      a_third = new Rational(1, 3);
    }

    // Tear down fixture
    protected void tearDown() {
      a_third = null;
    }
        ⋮

}
```

The attribute `a_third` can then be used as fixture in all other test cases:

```
// Test for equality
public void testEquality() {
  assertEquals(new Rational(1, 3), a_third);
```

```
assertEquals(new Rational(2, 6), a_third);
assertEquals(new Rational(3, 3), new Rational(1, 1));
}
```

Using the same pattern, the setUp() method can set up arbitrary fixture, which can then be accessed by all tests of a test case. Note, though, that the tests must remain *independent of each other* – executing a test must neither influence nor require other test executions.

13.6 Organizing test cases

JUNIT tests need not necessarily be executed via a JUNIT interface. JUNIT provides methods that allow executing the individual tests directly. For this purpose, one must pass the name of the test method as an argument to the class constructor; the run() method executes the test:

```
TestResult result =
    (new RationalTest("testEquality")).run();
```

Test suite If multiple test cases are to be executed, these multiple test cases can be grouped into a *test suite*. A test suite is a *container* for multiple test cases. The following piece of code creates a test suite, composed from the individual tests of the RationalTest class:

```
TestSuite suite = new TestSuite();
suite.addTest(new RationalTest("testEquality"));
suite.addTest(new RationalTest("testNonEquality"));
TestResult result = suite.run();
```

In CPPUNIT and other JUNIT variants, a test suite must actually be created this way: Each single test must be specified explicitly. JUNIT, however, also provides a shortcut. If the Testsuite constructor gets a class name as argument, then all methods of the class whose name begins with test... are added to the test suite. Thus, the above piece of code can be shortened as follows:

```
TestSuite suite = new TestSuite(RationalTest.class);
TestResult result = suite.run();
```

This behavior can be useful to define the suite of tests to be executed by TestRunner. This is done using the suite() method:

```
public class RationalTest extends TestCase {
  :
  // Define test suite
  public static Test suite() {
    TestSuite suite = new TestSuite(RationalTest.class);
```

```
        return suite;
    }
    :
:}
```

However, the code above is exactly the default behavior, which is why we could also omit the `suite()` method. If we want to invoke tests from other classes, though, we can explicitly add them in our own `suite()` method. Thus, we can create a class `AllTests` that integrates the test suite from `RationalTest` and the tests from some other class named `MoreRationalTests`:

```
public class AllTests extends TestCase {
    :

    public static Test suite() {
        TestSuite suite = new TestSuite();
        suite.addTest(RationalTest.suite());
        suite.addTest(MoreRationalTest.suite());
        return suite;
    }
    :
    :
}
```

If we execute `TestRunner` on the `AllTests` class, then the test suite of `RationalTest` and the test suite of `MoreRationalTest` will be executed.

Figure 13.2 shows the UML diagram of the classes provided by JUNIT. A `Test` is either a `Testcase` or a `Testsuite`, which again contains `Tests` – a classical *composite* design pattern.

Composite

13.7 A test-driven development process

Automated tests enable new methods of software development. In particular, one can validate the system's functionality after each single change – that is, one can run a regression test as discussed in Chapter 12. Such regression tests should be designed such that a maximum of code is actually being executed (or *covered*) during the test: At least each statement (or better, every control transition between two statements) should be executed by at least one test. Section 16.4 discusses this in more detail.

Component tests, though, do not only facilitate regression testing of existing code; the test cases can also be used for *testing code that has not been written yet*. In other words, the test cases serve as *specification* of the component to be tested.

Figure 13.2
The JUNIT classes.

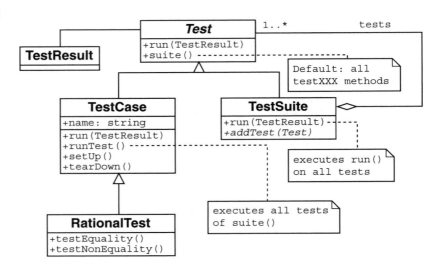

As an example, consider the `Rational` class, as described by the tests above. Just by reading the test cases, a programmer could implement the `Rational` class such that it satisfies all tests – in our case, the constructor and the `equals()` method. If we included further test cases that cover, say, basic arithmetic, these test cases would become part of the specification, and would have to be satisfied by the implementation.

Specifying program behavior by test cases can naturally only cover *examples*, instead of specifying the general behavior for all kinds of input. Test cases, though, have significant advantages over specifications in natural language: They can be validated by a machine – simply by executing the tests. Since the validation takes place automatically, it can be repeated after each change. And finally, the test cases can serve as *documentation* on typical uses of the component.

Test-first approach   A software process in which test cases are written before the actual code, is called *test-first approach*. Following Link (2002), these are the typical characteristics of an ideal test-first approach:

❏ Before writing one line of production code, a test motivating that code is created.

❏ One writes just as much production code as required by the test. In other words, once the test runs, the code is ready.

❏ Development takes place in small steps, in which testing and coding alternate. Such "micro iterations" do not take longer than 10 minutes.

❏ Upon integration of the components into the complete system, all component tests must pass.

The advantages of a test-first approach are clear:

The code can be tested automatically. This increases confidence into one's own work.

Debugging is significantly easier. Every new code is tested after 10 minutes at most. If failures occur later on, it is the rule to first write a test case that reproduces the failure.

The code is as simple as possible. The code is no more complex than needed to satisfy the tests. (Of course, complex test cases result in complex code.)

Test cases as specification are fun. The multiple value of automated test cases – first as specification, then as validation device, and then as documentation – motivates developers to make use of them.

The *test-first approach* is part of *extreme programming* – an approach to programming that promotes extreme flexibility. While some parts of extreme programming are heavily discussed (such as ruthless restructuring in order to obtain the simplest possible system), the value of the test-first approach is hardly ever questioned. One should keep in mind, though, that creating automated test cases is work; if one knows that the software will no longer change, manual tests may come cheaper.

Extreme programming

In the best of all worlds, we would also have precise specifications that describe the *complete* behavior of a system. But just as in real life, it is the mix of general *rules* (as in a precise specification) and concrete *examples* (as in test cases) that result in the best understanding.

Concepts

❏ The programming language of component tests typically is the language in which the component is written.

❏ To write tests, the most important language tools are *assertions* that express an expected program state.

❏ In component tests, *methods* represent tests and *classes* represent test cases; *test suites* group multiple tests.

❏ Component tests can serve as specifications that are written before the actual component (*test first*).

Review exercises

1. Collect arguments for and against the following (heavily discussed) questions:

    (a) Should one test nonpublic methods? Why? Why not?

    (b) Should one test one-line functions (which can easily be scanned for errors)? Why? Why not?

    (c) Should tests access nonpublic attributes and methods to query the internal state of a component? Why? Why not?

2. Use the JUNIT `assertEquals()` method to compare observed and expected results in `Rational` *numerically*. What are the advantages and disadvantages of this approach?

3. A change in a program frequently induces a change in the component tests. How can you use version control to couple these changes?

4. Consider *exceptions* that may be thrown by tested code. Should these be caught within the test case?

5. Are there applications for which *test first* is not useful? Why?

Further reading

As a reference for beginners, we recommend Link (2002). This book not only has several details on the *test-first* approach but also contains useful hints on how to deal with persistent and distributed data as well as on testing parallel and interactive programs.

The latest and greatest information about JUNIT can be found at

$$\texttt{http://www.junit.org/}$$

This page also contains further examples that introduce JUNIT.

More testing tools

Automatic component tests are now available for almost every programming language. Here are some examples:

❏ SUNIT is a component test framework for SMALLTALK programs. SUNIT is JUNIT's grandfather: all JUNIT concepts originated in SUNIT and still are reflected today. SUNIT is available at:

$$\texttt{http://sunit.sourceforge.net/}$$

❏ CPPUNIT is a framework for component testing C++ programs. The general approach is as in JUNIT – tests become methods, test cases become classes. The `test...` methods must be compiled manually into a test suite; the package provides helpful macros for this purpose. CPPUNIT is available with an introduction and documentation at:

```
http://cppunit.sourceforge.net/
```

❏ Component tests are available for several languages besides JAVA, C++, and SMALLTALK – from A as in ADA to X as in XSLT. An overview can be found at:

```
http://www.xprogramming.com/software.htm
```

14 Tracking problems with BUGZILLA

14.1 Tracking and managing problems

In Chapters 12 and 13, we have presented testing tools like DEJAGNU and JUNIT, which allow for the quick and systematic detection of program failures. Unfortunately, not every software problem is detected during testing. Instead, the problems are experienced (or, more precisely, suffered) by the users. In general, users cannot or must not fix problems themselves, but must be satisfied by having the problem fixed. To do so,

1. the user must *inform* the vendor about the problem,

2. the vendor must *reproduce* the problem,

3. the vendor must *isolate* the problem circumstances,

4. the vendor must *fix* the defect at the user's site.

This life cycle must be organized in some way. In particular, the vendor must be able to answer questions like:

Which problems are currently open? An open problem indicates that there probably is some defect in the software that must be fixed.

Which are the most severe problems? Typically, the most severe problems are the first to get fixed.

Did similar problems occur in the past? If there were similar problems, there may be a solution at hand that only needs to be delivered.

Furthermore, the *user* may want to know the state of her problem – and be quickly informed about any progress made.

Systems that handle all this are called *problem tracking systems*. In this chapter, we discuss the life cycle of a problem – from the initial report over to management up to the (hopefully successful) resolution.

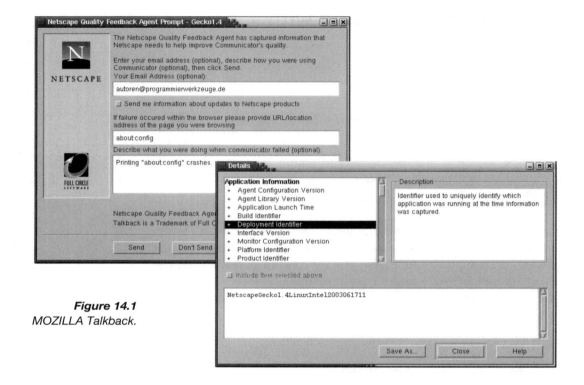

Figure 14.1
MOZILLA Talkback.

14.2 Reporting problems

Before we discuss *managing problems,* we first examine how a problem gets reported from user to vendor.

Problem report   In order to fix the problem, the developer must first be able to *reproduce it* – because otherwise, she would have no way to inquire further details about the problem, and, worse, there would be no way to tell that the problem is fixed. The information required for this task is called a *problem report* (PR), also known as *change request* (CR) or simply *bug report*.

14.2.1 What's relevant?

Open source projects (and commercial projects interested in customer feedback) typically invite users to report any problems. The basic principle is "State all the relevant facts", with "relevant" meaning "relevant for reproducing the problem". But determining the relevant facts can impose problems. How should the user know what is relevant or not?

Real-life problem reports frequently include *too much,* such as gigantic core dumps, entire hard disk contents, even entire drives. But they may also include *not enough:* "Your program crashed. Just wanted to let you

---

Product release: Typically, this is the version number or some other unique identifier – for instance, the configuration name of a CVS version. Using this information, the developer can re-create a local copy of the program in the version as installed in the user's environment.

Environment: Typically, this is version information about the operating system. As problems may occur because of interactions between third-party components, information about such components may be useful as well. Using this information, the vendor can re-create the user's environment.

Problem history: This is a description of what has to be done to reproduce the problem, as a minimal set of steps necessary. Typically, this also includes any accessed resources, such as input or configuration files.

Expected behavior: This describes what should have happened according to the user. This information is important to decide whether the behavior is actually an error.

Observed behavior: These are the *symptoms* of the problem – that is, what has happened in contrast to the expected behavior. Using this information, the developer can verify whether the problem was faithfully reproduced.

Table 14.1
Typical items in problem reports.

---

know." – a real-life problem report which the authors of this book received in 1999 (probably about the GNU DDD debugger).

To get the right amount of information, it is usually a good idea to have a list of *specific items* that should be included in every single problem report (Table 14.1). Some products include specific functionality or stand-alone tools to produce standardized problem reports. Figure 14.1 shows the *Talkback* dialog, which appears when the MOZILLA web browser experiences a fatal failure. Clicking on *Send* forwards all relevant information (shown in the *Details* dialog) to the MOZILLA developers.

14.2.2 What has happened?

If the error occurs after a long series of events, it is often difficult for the user to retrace all the steps from the program invocation to the failure.

This problem can be addressed by having the program *record* important events in a *log file*. These events can later be examined and reproduced by the vendor. The user should be enabled to *authorize* both the logging as well as the forwarding of logs to the vendor.

Whether the user herself fills in a problem report, or whether this is done by a special maintenance team – eventually, all problem reports must be processed by the vendor. This is the time for problem tracking systems like BUGZILLA.

14.3   BUGZILLA – a problem tracking system

Most developer teams keep track of the current problems in their system using a single *"problem list" document* that lists all the open or unresolved problems to date. Such a document is easy to set up and easy to maintain. However, there are a number of associated problems:

Only one person can work on the document at a time. Exception: The document is in a *version control system* that allows parallel editing and later merging, such as CVS (Chapter 4).

History of earlier (and fixed) problems is lost. As a consequence, one cannot recall which problems are (still) present in earlier versions and which ones have been fixed. Exception: The document is in a version control system and evolves together with the product.

Does not scale. One cannot track hundreds or thousands of different issues in a simple text document.

Problem database   The alternative to keeping a document is to use a *problem database* that stores all problem reports. Problem databases scale up to a large number of developers, users, and problems.

Figure 14.2 shows an example of such a problem tracking system – *BUGZILLA,* the problem tracking system for the MOZILLA web browser. BUGZILLA uses a web browser as user interface, which means that it can be accessed from anywhere (and anyone, as MOZILLA is an open source project). BUGZILLA is also an open source project itself, such that you can even install it for your own project.

14.4   Classifying problems

Let us assume that we want to report a problem in BUGZILLA (either because we are expert users and know how to enter a problem on a web site, or because we are in charge of processing a user problem report). To report a problem, we must not only supply the required information (Section 14.2) but also *classify* the problem. The attributes BUGZILLA uses to classify problems are typical for problem tracking systems:

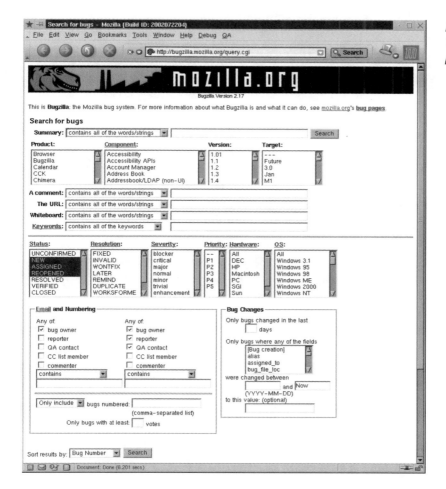

Figure 14.2
The BUGZILLA problem database.

Severity

Each problem is assigned a *severity*, which described the impact of the problem on the development or release process. BUGZILLA knows the following severity levels, from the most impact to the least:

Blocker Blocks development and/or testing work. This highest level of severity is also known as *Showstopper*.

Critical Crashes, loss of data, severe memory leak.

Major Major loss of function.

Normal This is the "standard" problem.

Minor Minor loss of function, or other problem where an easy workaround is present.

Trivial Cosmetic problem like misspelled words or misaligned text.

Enhancement Request for enhancement. This means that the problem is not a failure at all, but rather a desired feature.

Ideally, a product is not shipped unless all "severe" problems have been fixed – that is, major, critical, or blocker problems have been resolved. If a product is to be released at a fixed date, functions that still cause problems can be disabled.

Priority

Each problem is assigned a specific *priority* – the higher the priority, the sooner the problem is going to be addressed. The priority is typically defined by the management – in fact, it is the *main means* for management to express what should be done first, and what later. The importance of the priority attribute when it comes to control the process of development and problem-solving cannot be overemphasized.

Identifier

Each problem gets a unique *identifier* (a *PR number*; in BUGZILLA, the *bug number*) such that developers can refer to it within the debugging process – in e-mails, change logs, status reports, and attachments.

Comments

Every user and developer can attach *comments* to a problem report – for instance, to add information about the circumstances of the problem, to speculate about possible problem causes, to add first findings, or to discuss how the problem should be fixed.

Notification

Developers and users can attach their e-mail address to a problem report; they will get notified automatically every time the problem report changes.

14.5   Processing problems

Let us now assume that someone has entered a new problem report into the problem database. This problem report must now be *processed*. During this

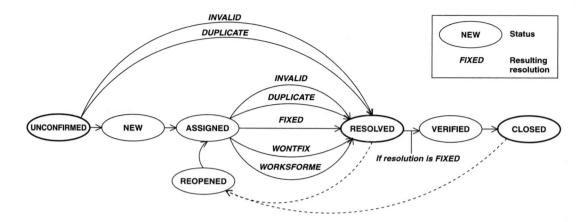

process, the problem report runs through a *life cycle* (Figure 14.3) – from UNCONFIRMED to CLOSED. The position in the life cycle is determined by the *state* of the problem report:

Figure 14.3
The life cycle of a problem in BUGZILLA.

UNCONFIRMED This is the state of any new problem report, as entered into the database.

NEW The problem report is *valid:*

- ❏ It contains the relevant facts. (Otherwise, its *resolution* becomes *INVALID* – see below.)

- ❏ It is not an obvious *duplicate* of a known problem. (Otherwise, its resolution becomes *DUPLICATE* – see below.)

A NEW problem need not necessarily be reproducible. This is being taken care of in the remainder of the life cycle.

ASSIGNED The problem is not yet resolved, but already assigned to a developer (in BUGZILLA, the *bug owner*).

RESOLVED The problem is resolved; the *resolution* tells what has become (for now) of the problem report:

FIXED The problem is fixed.

INVALID The problem is not a problem, or does not contain the relevant facts.

DUPLICATE The problem is a duplicate of an existing problem.

WONTFIX The problem described is a problem that will never be fixed. This may also be the case for problems that turn out as features rather than failures.

(Here is a *WONTFIX* example: The MOZILLA browser does not display ALT texts for images as tooltips, which many consider a problem – but the MOZILLA developers say this behavior is mandated by web standards and, thus, won't fix the "problem". See bug #25537 on bugzilla.mozilla.org)

WORKSFORME All attempts at reproducing this problem were futile. If more information appears later, the problem may be reopened.

If the resolution is *FIXED*, the fix must be verified (state VERIFIED) and finally delivered (state CLOSED).

VERIFIED The problem is fixed; the fix has been verified as successful. The problem remains VERIFIED until the fix has been delivered to the user (for instance, by shipping a new release).

CLOSED A new release of the product was shipped; in this release, the problem no longer occurs.

REOPENED If a problem occurs again, it is assigned a state of REOPENED rather than NEW; it must be assigned again.

A Scenario

How does a problem report run through all these states? Here is a typical scenario:

1. Olaf is a happy user of the Perfect Publishing Program – until it suddenly crashes.

2. Olaf reports the failure to Sunny at customer support.

3. Sunny enters the failure details as a new problem report into the problem database. She reports on how Olaf can reproduce the failure, inquires the relevant facts about Olaf's configuration, and sets the severity to "normal". She also reports Olaf's contact address.

4. The problem gets a PR number (say, PR 2074). Its initial state is UNCONFIRMED – nobody has tried yet to reproduce it.

5. Programmer Violet finds that PR 2074 was not known before and sets its state to NEW.

6. Mr Poe, the manager, asks Violet to solve PR 2074; the state is now ASSIGNED.

7. Violet is unable to reproduce the PR 2074 in her environment. She documents her attempts in additional comments to the problem report, sets the resolution to WORKSFORME and the state to RESOLVED. However, could it be that Olaf has the product configured to use the metric system? She asks Sunny whether she could get further data.

8. Sunny requests further information from Olaf and sets the state of PR 2074 to REOPENED.

9. Violet is still responsible for PR 2074 (state ASSIGNED); with the new data, she can finally reproduce and fix the problem. The state becomes RESOLVED; the resolution is FIXED.

10. Tester Klaus reviews Violet's fix; he gives his OK to integrate the fix in the current production release. The state of PR 2074 becomes VERIFIED.

11. Finally, the fixed release is delivered to Olaf. The state is CLOSED.

12. If further users contact customer support about the problem, Sunny can look up the problem in the problem tracking system and point them to the new release.

14.6 Managing problem tracking

As shown in the scenario, a good problem tracking system is the base for all daily work on problems and failures. If nobody files in problem reports, it is useless; if nobody marks problems as resolved, it will quickly be filled with outdated information. Therefore, the following issues should be resolved:

Who files problem reports? This could be support personnel only; in general, though, it is probably useful if any developer can add new entries. Advanced users and beta testers may also be enabled to file problem reports.

Who classifies problem reports? The *severity* of a problem can be extracted from the initial report; sometimes, the severity is only determined after the problem could be reproduced.

Who sets priorities? To determine the priority of a problem, management must assess the *impact* of a problem – that is, not only its severity but also

- ❑ its likelihood,
- ❑ the number of users affected, and
- ❑ the potential damage.

Hence, the priority need not be correlated with the severity of a problem: A "blocker" problem in an alpha release may have lower priority than a "major" problem in a widely distributed product.

Many organizations use a *software change control board* (SCCB) to set priorities – a group of people who track problem reports and take care of their handling. Such a group is typically composed of developers, testers, and configuration managers.

Who takes care of the problem? All problem tracking systems allow *assigning* problems to individual developers. This is also the task of an SCCB or a like group.

Who closes issues? This can be the SCCB or a like group, the individual tester, or some quality assurance instance that verifies fixes (as in the scenario above).

What is the life cycle of a problem? The BUGZILLA model, as shown in Figure 14.3, is typical for problem databases, but by no means the only possible one. Depending on your individual needs, one can design alternate states and transitions; problem tracking systems may be configured to incorporate such processes.

Software development as problem solving

A good problem tracking system can *summarize* the problem database in the form of statistics (How many problems are still open, how many problems are being assigned to whom, etc.). A problem tracking system may even be the *primary tool* to organize the debugging process, or even the development process. Problem #1 is "the product is missing"; this problem can then be decomposed into several subproblems, all of which describe properties of the product to be built. If a component is implemented, which solves a subproblem, the subproblem is marked as FIXED. Just as in the "test first" development process discussed in Section 13.7, we find that the product is ready for shipping when all problems are resolved – indicated by problem #1 being FIXED, too.

14.7   Relating problems and tests

Problem reports and test outcomes

Many developers use problem tracking systems not only for problems as reported by end users but also for problems encountered in-house; that is, as soon as a developer stumbles across a problem, she reports it just as if an end user had told her about the problem.

In principle, this is a good thing, since no problem stays unreported. However, the main way by which developers find problems is by *testing* the program, as discussed in Chapters 12 and 13. And this induces a conflict between test outcomes and problem reports: Should a failing test be tracked in the problem database? And if so, how are we going to *synchronize* the problem database with the test outcomes?

Unless you have a problem tracking system that neatly integrates with your test suite, we recommend keeping test outcomes separate from problem reports. There are a number of reasons for doing so:

❏ Test outcomes occur frequently – possibly (and hopefully) far more frequently than user's problem reports. Storing these test outcomes in the problem database would quickly flood the database – and divert from the actual problems in the field.

❏ If you use automated tests (Chapters 12 and 13), you can check test outcomes for any version, any time at the press of a button – so there is no need for storing that information.

❏ Supposing a test fails: If you can find the defect and fix it right away, there is no need to enter a record in the problem tracking system.

All this boils down to one point: *Test cases make problem reports obsolete.* If a problem occurs during development, do not enter it into the problem tracking system. Instead, write a *test case* that exposes the problem. This way, the test case will show that the problem is still present, and you can always check for the problem by running the test.

You *can* always use the problem tracking system, though, for storing *ideas* and *feature requests* – that is, for anything that does not immediately translate into code or a test case. As soon as you start implementing the feature request, start writing a test case that exposes the lack of the feature and close the entry in the problem tracking system. Once the feature is implemented, the succeeding test case can be used to determine whether it meets expectations.

Concepts

❏ A problem report must contain all information that is *relevant to reproduce the problem.*

❏ A *problem tracking system* uses a *database* to organize and classify problem reports. Typical classification items include:

    – the *problem identifier*

    – the *severity* of the problem – from *blocker* to *enhancement*

    – the *state* of the problem – from *unconfirmed* to *closed*

    – the *resolution* – from *invalid* to *fixed.*

❏ Problem tracking systems can organize not only the problem resolution but the *entire development process*: The lack of a component yet to be written is defined as a problem – and tracked until it is fixed.

❏ Whenever a new problem arises, one should create a *test case* that *reproduces* the problem.

❏ To relate problems and tests, *make a problem report obsolete* as soon as a test case exists. When a problem occurs, prefer writing test cases to entering problem reports.

Review exercises

1. Visit the MOZILLA problem tracking site at

> `http://bugzilla.mozilla.org/`

and answer the following questions:

   (a) How many problems have been entered as NEW into BUGZILLA in the past three days?

   (b) How many of these are critical (or even blocking)?

   (c) How many of these are invalid? Why?

   (d) How many unresolved or unconfirmed problems are there in the currently released version?

   (e) Which is the worst currently unresolved problem?

   (f) According to problem priority, which problem should you address first as a programmer?

2. What are the major differences between a dedicated problem tracking system like MOZILLA and a general organizing and messaging tool such as Microsoft Outlook?

3. Which other problems (beside software) could be managed using a problem tracking system?

Further reading

Regarding problem tracking systems, there is not too much information available except from those provided by vendors. Mirrer (2000) addresses the issue of obsolete test cases. For him, organizing a problem tracking system is like "organizing your socks": Once in a while, an overflowing sock drawer has to be cleaned up.

Kolawa (2002) comments on the relationship between problem tracking systems and testing. He states that problem tracking systems "should be used exclusively as a place to store feedback when you cannot immediately modify the code"; otherwise, you should create a reproducible test case.

The BUGZILLA problem tracking system can be found at

`http://www.bugzilla.org/`

Its specific incarnation for MOZILLA is available for browsing at

`http://bugzilla.mozilla.org/`

PHPBUGTRACKER is a lightweight problem tracking system, simpler to install and manage than BUGZILLA. If you want to toy with a problem tracking system at your site, PHPBUGTRACKER might be your choice.

`http://phpbt.sf.net/`

Advanced problem tracking systems partially integrate with version control systems. The *Software Configuration Management FAQ* for the `comp.software.config-mgmt` newsgroup contains a large list of problem tracking systems and their integration within software configuration management:

`http://www.daveeaton.com/scm/`

If you are interested in automated project organization beyond simple problem tracking, the two following systems provide discussion forums, public CVS archives, user management, mailing lists, and so on.

❏ The SAVANNAH project provides a home for open source projects; a simple registration suffices. It is also available as open source itself and can be installed at other sites – but only to manage open source projects.

`http://savannah.gnu.org/`

❏ The SOURCEFORGE project is the largest home for open source projects; here, too, a simple registration suffices. SOURCEFORGE is available as a commercial version to be installed at other sites and to manage commercial projects.

`http://www.sf.net/`

Finally, if you want to keep your customers happy, see Phil Verghis' help desk FAQ at

`http://www.philverghis.com/helpdesk.html`

15 Debugging with GDB and DDD

15.1 Systematic debugging

Oops! Something is going wrong. My program prints out random characters, runs in an endless loop, or just crashes. What now?

No one should be ashamed if the program they have just created does not run the first time. Errare humanum est: errors occur with all technical systems and these are more likely to occur the more *complex* the system is. The complexity comes from the number of components and the possible interactions between these components. In this sense, software is one of the most complex things that man has created – and therefore also one of the most error-prone.

Errors and complexity

But how does one identify errors? First of all, you must make sure that an error *manifests* itself, so that it becomes visible as a *failure*. (This is done by reading the code – and of course by testing it, as described in Chapters 12 and 13.)

Observing failures

Once a failure is observed, the aim of *debugging* is to relate this failure to a specific piece of code, whose change fixes the error. In order to do this, we need *an insight into the execution of the program.*

Debugging
Fix

Human beings typically cannot grasp all details of the execution of a technical system. The analysis must therefore be limited to a *carefully selected subset* of the system or its execution. Within these subsets, one sets up *hypotheses* – for example, that an error occurs in this subset. These hypotheses are then *tested*, confirmed or disproved, in order to isolate the causes of the problem.

Setting up hypotheses

Here is an example: When printing a manuscript, random characters appear on the pages following Page 249. A possible hypothesis could be that Page 249 contains some control code that causes the printer to produce an incorrect readout. This hypothesis can now be tested – for example, by printing out Page 249 alone. If the failure occurs again, we can *isolate* the error further by only printing out a part of this page – until we have eventually found the code that causes the failure.

Isolating failure causes

Figure 15.1
*The scientific
method of
debugging.*

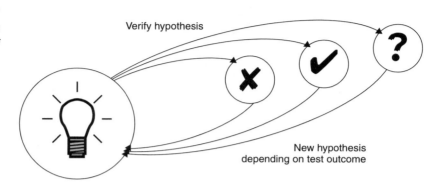

Figure 15.1
*The scientific
method of
debugging.*

Scientific method   This systematic isolation of causes is also called the *scientific method* of debugging. It works as follows:

*Setting up
hypotheses*

1. Set up a hypothesis about the failure cause. (In our example: *Page 249 contains an escape code that causes failures.*)

*Checking
hypotheses*

2. Test this hypothesis using the program execution. (*Only print out Page 249.*) As in systematic tests (Chapter 12), we distinguish different test outputs (Figure 15.1):

Refining hypotheses

The test fails (FAIL, ✗): (*The page is printed incorrectly.*) This confirms our hypothesis, which we can now *refine*. The refined hypothesis will test a *subset* of failure causes. (*New hypothesis: "The control code that causes the failure is in the upper half of Page 249."*)

Antithesis

The test is successful (PASS, ✔): (*The printout is free from errors.*) This disproves the hypothesis, which is why we continue with the *antithesis*. This will test the *complement set* of failure causes. (*New hypothesis: "The control code that causes the failure is not on Page 249."*)

*Alternative
hypothesis*

Inconsistence (UNRESOLVED, ?): The test outcome is indefinite – it shows neither correct nor incorrect behavior. (*Page 249 is not printed at all.*) We try an *alternative hypothesis*, which makes a definite test outcome more likely. (*New hypothesis: "The initialization code from Page 1 has to be added."*)

3. Continue with the new hypothesis with step 2 until the failure cause has been adequately isolated.

This isolation process can be shown graphically as a plane of possible failure causes, which are separated by a line (the hypothesis) and are divided

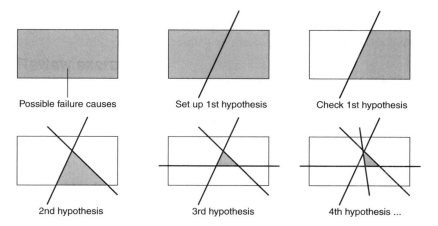

Figure 15.2
Systematic isolation of possible failure causes.

Possible failure causes   Set up 1st hypothesis   Check 1st hypothesis

2nd hypothesis   3rd hypothesis   4th hypothesis ...

into two areas (Figure 15.2). With every definite test output, we choose one of these areas, which is then isolated by the next hypothesis.

The success of the scientific method depends on the *choice of hypotheses*. A hypothesis is more effective, *Choice of the hypothesis*

❏ the fewer failure causes it leaves when proved correct, and

❏ the more failure causes it rules out when refuted.

If proving and refuting the hypothesis are both equally probable, the most effective types of hypotheses are the ones that include *half* of the causes of errors – and so with every step of the scientific method, the remaining number of failure causes is halved.

But what if a failure is caused by a *combination of several causes?* In our printer example, several control codes may well interact to cause the error – an control code on Page 1, followed by a control code on Page 249. Here, the hypothesis (printing of Page 249) as well as the antithesis (printing of all other pages) would be refuted. In this case, one has to specifically *search for combinations*: for example, the printing of Page 249 together with Pages 1–10. This can also be carried out systematically – for example, by excluding possible failure causes individually until only a failure-causing core remains. Similar strategies are useful for indefinite test outputs. *Combination of error causes*

15.2 Setting up and testing hypotheses

Unfortunately, it is not so easy to set up hypotheses that definitely include or exclude failure causes. Debugging is like solving a crime: without concrete proof, the criminal cannot be convicted. And in order to get proof, there must be time-consuming *investigations* – in our case *investigations of the* *Observing program execution program execution.* In contrast to an actual criminal case, though, we can usually *repeat* the program execution at will. In the following, we describe some basic techniques that provide us with further information.

15.2.1 Outputting the program status

Debugging instructions

The most basic debugging technique is to insert specific instructions at selected places in the program, which log part of the program status for the programmer – for example, the contents of variables, function names, or arguments. These *debugging instructions* are usually set up such that they can be turned on or off at compilation time or runtime.

Here is an example: In a C program, we find the instruction

```
#ifdef DEBUG
    fprintf(stderr, "x = %f, y = %f\n", x, y);
#endif
```

The `fprintf` instruction outputs the variables x and y on standard error (`stderr`) so that the programmer can check the values (and, by the way, find out that the instruction was actually reached).

By bracketing this with `#ifdef DEBUG`, the debugging instruction is inserted into the final program (and executed) if and only if the CPP macro (Section 9.3.3) `DEBUG` is defined at compilation time.

It is worthwhile to leave these types of debugging instructions in the final code, such that subsequent maintainers can use them. If the code becomes cluttered with debugging instructions, though, *assertions* are a better choice.

15.2.2 Validating program states

Debugging instructions bring a major disadvantage: The program state as logged must be *validated by the programmer* – that is, the programmer must check whether the state meets her expectations. This comparison of observed state versus expected state can be tedious and error-prone; therefore, one should aim to automate that task.

The classical technique to validate program states automatically is the use of *assertions,* as discussed in Section 13.2. The general process is as follows:

❑ Introduce assertions and invariants at "suspect" places in the program.

❑ Each new assertion validates another subset of the program state.

❑ Narrow down the moment in time when the program state first became faulty. Let us assume some program state is first validated by an assertion; later, though, some assertion on the same program state fails. In this case, some statement must have been executed between these two assertions that invalidated the program state.

How does one use assertions? As an example, consider a C++ function called `divide`, which divides a number `dividend` by `divisor` and returns its result in the parameters `quotient` and `remainder`.

```
void divide(int dividend, int divisor,
            int& quotient, int& remainder)
{
    // Precondition
    assert(divisor != 0);

    // Actual computation ...

    // Postcondition
    assert(quotient * divisor + remainder ==
           dividend);
}
```

In case the precondition is violated – for instance, because `divide` is called with a `divisor` equal to zero – the `assert` function aborts the program while stating the violated assertion:

```
divide.cc:4: failed assertion 'divisor != 0'
IOT instruction (core dumped)
```

Likewise, `divide` aborts if the computation was incorrect – that is, the postcondition was violated. If `divide` returns, though, the result satisfies the postcondition. During debugging, a return of `divide` means that we can rely on `divide` being correct – and thus search elsewhere for the error.

Assertions on complex data structures require special validation functions that verify the *invariants* of the data structure – properties of the data structure that must always hold.

Invariants

As an example, consider a simple tree data structure, in which a node refers to the parent as well as a left and a right child:

```
struct Tree {
    struct Tree *parent;  /* parent node */
    struct Tree *left;    /* left child */
    struct Tree *right;   /* right child */
};
```

What is the invariant here? On the one hand, the children of a node k refer to their parent k. And of course, in turn, the children themselves have to be valid trees.

We check all these using a `tree_ok` function, which only returns 1 (true) if all these conditions are met:

```
/* Invariant */
int tree_ok(struct Tree *tree)
{
    return tree == NULL ||
        (tree->left  == NULL ||
            tree->left->parent  == tree) &&
        (tree->right == NULL ||
            tree->right->parent == tree) &&
        tree_ok(tree->left) &&
        tree_ok(tree->right);
}
```

Validation function   Such *validation functions* can now be used in assertions, for instance, to guarantee consistency before and after a function:

```
void balance(struct Tree *tree)
{
    assert(tree_ok(tree)); /* Precondition */
    :                             /* Function */
    assert(tree_ok(tree)); /* Postcondition */
}
```

The program will be aborted as soon as `balance` is called with an invalid tree (violated precondition), or if `balance` itself makes the tree invalid (violated postcondition).

Overall, assertions kill multiple birds with one stone:

❑ Assertions are *persistent* – in contrast to debugging instructions and interactive debuggers discussed below, assertions can remain in the program code and thus validate state whenever necessary.

❑ Assertions are *explicit* – expectations about the program state do not only take place in the head of the programmer, but are coded explicitly.

❑ Assertions *document* the program – and thus foster program understanding. Deviations between assertions and actual program state are quickly uncovered.

Assertion functions such as `assert` take up a lot of time at runtime – particularly if they look at large data structures, such as in `tree_ok`. Therefore, in C and C++, `assert` is implemented as a macro, such that by defining a special CPP macro (typically `NDEBUG`) all assertions can be switched off. This normally happens in production code, to improve efficiency. In JAVA, assertions are turned off by default; they must be enabled explicitly. Using the JAVA interpreter `java`, this is done using the `-enableassertions` option, which can be abbreviated as `-ea`.

One should keep in mind, though, that efficiency gained by disabling assertions reduces the security of the program. And although a program that aborts due to a failing assertion is not particularly user friendly, a program that computes a bad result without noticing it can have far worse consequences.

Assertions and invariants are an approved means of recognizing faults and isolating their causes. We can only recommend that you provide a validation function for every data structure, and use assertions lavishly all over the code.

15.2.3 Changing program state

A third technique for examining the program state is to *explicitly change* it, and deduce failure causes from the resulting outcome. Such changes can be made in various ways:

Explicitly changing the program state

Changing the program environment: Most bugs only appear in a certain *environment*. This environment includes all data that influences the behavior of the program – first of all, the input data, but also other resources such as the computer configuration or personal user settings. Here, one can try to isolate the failure cause by using a *systematic change* of the environment.

Systematic change of the program environment

Example: A word processing program terminates after loading a large document after a few keystrokes. By changing the input – of the document as well as the keystrokes – the failure cause can be systematically isolated.

Since one alters the *external state* of the program, the mapping to the *internal state* must be made by the programmer. On the other hand, meaningful descriptions of the failure-causing environment are valuable aids for finding errors.

Changing the program code: Specific changes to program code can help find the cause of an error. Such changes do not mean a *repair – this should only take place once the exact circumstances are known.* Systematic *removal of functionality*, though, can help isolate failure causes.

Removing program functionality

Example: We suspect that a tree-balancing function is corrupting the memory. We test the hypothesis by replacing the function by a *dummy* without functionality; if the problem has now disappeared, we have successfully isolated the problem cause.

Differences between old and new program versions

Changing the program version: Changing code is of course only possible if an appropriate alternative is available. A special case occurs if an old version of the program works fine, but the new version fails ("Yesterday my program worked, today it does not – why?"). In such a case, it helps to examine the *differences* between old and new versions.

Failure-inducing changes

Example: After the changes, the export of data no longer works. By examining the changes, (beginning with the functions that are responsible for the export) the *failure-inducing change* can be found.

15.3   Debugging with DDD: An example

Debugger

If one wants an insight into the program execution without extending the code (which is time-consuming), there are special tools that can help, called *debuggers*. A debugger *controls a program's execution.* Using a debugger, it is possible to

❏ *execute* the program in a defined environment,

❏ make the program *stop* on specified conditions,

❏ *observe* the state of the stopped program, and

❏ *change* the state of the stopped program.

GDB

In this chapter, we discuss one of the most powerful debuggers, the GNU debugger (GDB). GDB is an interactive program that is controlled via a *command line*. In order to simplify interaction with GDB, numerous *graphical interfaces* are available, which provide buttons and menus for the GDB commands, and which process the GDB outputs. We look at one of the most comfortable interfaces for GDB, the GNU *Data Display Debugger* or DDD.

DDD

In order to get an overview of how debuggers are used, we look at a simple DDD scenario. Example 15.1 shows the C program `sample.c`, a program for sorting numbers.

Example 15.1
`sample.c` – a (faulty) sorting program

```
1    /* sample.c - a simple sorting program
2
3    #include <stdio.h>
4    #include <stdlib.h>
```

```
5
6   static void shell_sort(int a[], int size)
7   {
8       int i, j;
9       int h = 1;
10      do {
11          h = h * 3 + 1;
12      } while (h <= size);
13      do {
14          h /= 3;
15          for (i = h; i < size; i++)
16          {
17              int v = a[i];
18              for (j=i; j>=h && a[j-h]>v; j-=h)
19                  a[j] = a[j - h];
20              if (i != j)
21                  a[j] = v;
22          }
23      } while (h != 1);
24  }
25
26  int main(int argc, char *argv[])
27  {
28      int *a;
29      int i;
30
31      a = (int *)malloc((argc - 1) * sizeof(int));
32      for (i = 0; i < argc - 1; i++)
33          a[i] = atoi(argv[i + 1]);
34
35      shell_sort(a, argc);
36
37      for (i = 0; i < argc - 1; i++)
38          printf("%d ", a[i]);
39      printf("\n");
40
41      free(a);
42      return 0;
43  }
```

This program has an error: Normally, sample should sort and print its arguments numerically, as in the following example:

```
$ ./sample 8 7 5 4 1 3
1 3 4 5 7 8
$ _
```

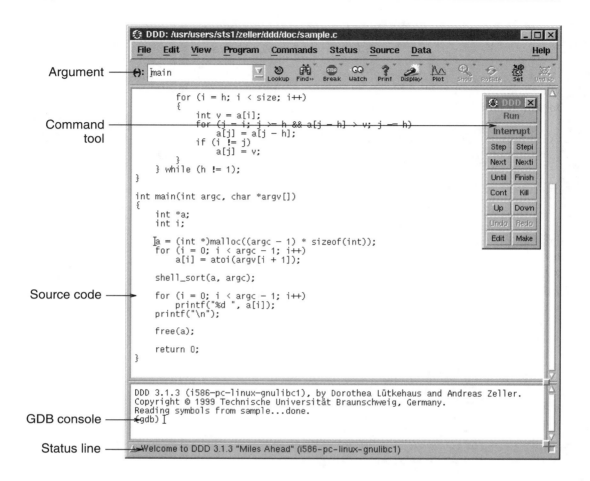

Argument

Command
tool

Source code

GDB console

Status line

Figure 15.3
The DDD interface

However, with certain arguments, this goes wrong:

```
$ ./sample 8000 7000 5000 1000 4000
1000 1913 4000 5000 7000
$ _
```

Although the output is sorted and contains the correct number of arguments, some arguments are missing and are replaced by bogus numbers; here, 8000 is missing and is replaced by 1913. (Actual numbers and behavior on your system may vary.)

15.3.1 Executing programs

Debugging information

Using DDD, we can now find out what happens in sample. First of all, we have to enrich the program with *debugging information*. This is done

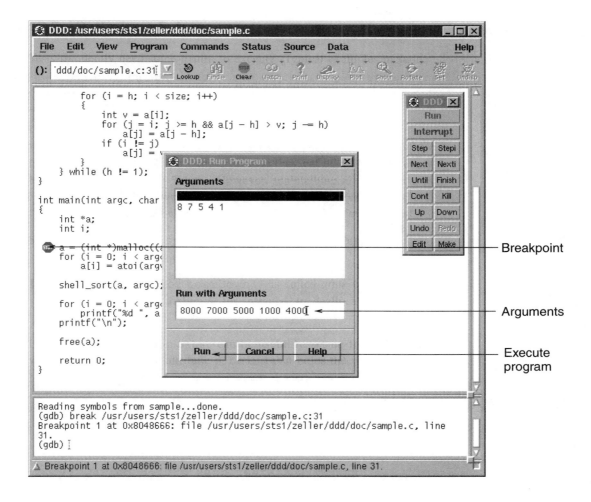

Figure 15.4
Execute program
under DDD

during compilation using the option -g:

```
$ gcc -g -o sample sample.c
$ _
```

Now we can invoke DDD on the executable:

```
$ ddd sample
```

Figure 15.3 shows the DDD interface. The *source code* sample.c is displayed in the central area. The *GDB console* (on the bottom edge) shows the DDD version and the GDB prompt (gdb).

Now we can execute the program under DDD (and GDB). In order to extract the program state, GDB has to stop the program within the execution.

Break point   GDB has several possibilities for specifying *stop conditions*. The easiest condition is to have the program as soon as a specific statement is executed: At this place in the code, one sets a *breakpoint*.

Our first hypothesis is "The transfer of the values from the command line is faulty". We want to test this hypothesis by *setting a breakpoint* at the appropriate place. We click on the empty space next to the initialization

Argument   of a. The *argument* "():" now contains the position sample.c:31. By clicking on *Break*, we set a breakpoint in the position indicated by the argument, that is, in Line 31.

Now we have to start the program. Using *Program → Run*, we begin the execution. We can also enter arguments in the dialog (Figure 15.4) – in our case the failure-causing arguments, namely, 8000 7000 5000 1000 4000. Click on *Run* to start execution with the arguments you just entered.

GDB now starts sample. Execution stops after a few moments as the breakpoint is reached. The current state and the commands sent by DDD to GDB are reported in the GDB console.

```
(gdb) break sample.c:31
Breakpoint 1 at 0x8048666: file sample.c, line 31.
(gdb) run 8000 7000 5000 1000 4000
Starting program: sample 8000 7000 5000 1000 4000

Breakpoint 1, main (argc=6, argv=0xbffff918)
at sample.c:31
(gdb) _
```

The current execution line is indicated by a green arrow (here "⇒"):

$$\Rightarrow \text{ a = (int *)malloc((argc - 1) * sizeof(int));}$$

15.3.2 Analyzing data

As soon as the program stops, we can examine the current variable values. The easiest way of doing this is to point to a variable name using the mouse; the value is displayed in a small window. The variable argc, for example, should have the value 6; the variable a, however, is not yet initialized.

Executing the   In order to execute the current line, click on *Next* in the command tool.
current lines   As Figure 15.5 shows, a is now initialized correctly.
Output in the GDB   In order to print out the individual values of a, GDB has a print
console   command available, which is activated in DDD via the *Print* button. Enter a[0] in the argument field, and click on *Print* in order to display the value

in the GDB console:

```
(gdb) print a[0]
$1 = 0
(gdb) _
```

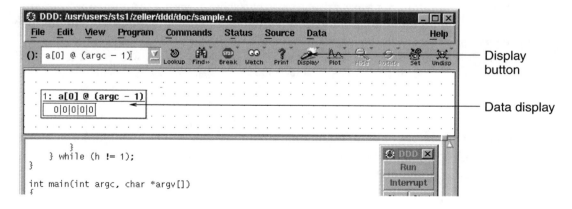

Execution position

Value pop-up

Figure 15.5
Displaying variable values by moving the mouse pointer onto the names

(By doing this on your machine, you can also obtain another value – remember that a is not yet initialized.)

In order to examine *all elements* of a, you have to tell GDB the *size* of the array. (Since the size of a is determined at runtime, GDB cannot derive the size from the debugging information.) To do this, you can use the special @ operator: $a[n]@m$ outputs the elements $a[n]\ldots a[n+m-1]$. In our case, we want to output all elements of a:

The @ operator

```
(gdb) print a[0] @ (argc - 1)
$2 = {0, 0, 0, 0, 0}
(gdb) _
```

(You can either enter this command in the GDB console or click on *Print* with a[0] @ (argc - 1) in the argument field.)

Figure 15.6
Permanent data display in DDD

Permanent display   Explicitly printing variable values can be quite tiresome; it is much easier for the variables to be displayed automatically with every stop. Therefore, GDB and DDD have *permanent displays*, in which variable values are automatically refreshed.

While the argument field contains a[0] @ (argc - 1), click on *Display*. The contents of a now have to be shown in the *data window* (Figure 15.6). Using *Rotate*, the field can be ordered horizontally to save space.

Using *Next*, we get to the initialization of a:

```
⇒   for (i = 0; i < argc - 1; i++)
            a[i] = atoi(argv[i + 1]);
```

By clicking on *Next* again, you can track how the values of a change during initialization. Using *Until*, GDB continues the execution until the loop is exited.

```
⇒   shell_sort(a, argc);
```

We establish that the contents of a are correct. We have to reject our hypothesis; the error is somewhere else. Maybe it is in shell_sort? By clicking on *Next*, we execute shell_sort and end in:

```
⇒   for (i = 0; i < argc - 1; i++)
            printf("%d ", a[i]);
```

Now a has the value 1000, 1913, 4000, 5000, 7000 – our hypothesis is confirmed, shell_sort has mixed up the values of a.

15.3.3   The call stack

Now we have to *refine* the hypotheses: what exactly in shell_sort caused the faulty state? shell_sort has already been executed; we have
Delete breakpoint   to restart the program. In order to do so, we delete the old breakpoint (click on the breakpoint, followed by *Clear*) and set a new one next to the call of shell_sort. Using *Program* → *Run Again*, we execute the program again, and end next to the call:

```
⇒   shell_sort(a, argc);
```

Jump into the   This time, we want to examine closer what shell_sort is doing. Using
function   *Step*, we step into the call to shell_sort. This leaves your program in the first executable line of shell_sort, or

```
⇒   int h = 1;
```

whil GDB tells us exactly where we are:

```
(gdb) step
```

```
shell_sort (a=0x8049878, size=6) at sample.c:9
(gdb) _
```

This output is part of the *call stack* of the programs while the execution of the called function, their arguments, and their local variables are stored.

Call stack

You can use *State → Backtrace* to see where you are in the stack as a whole; selecting a line (or clicking on *Up* and *Down*) will let you move through the stack (Figure 15.7).

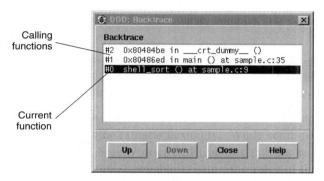

Figure 15.7
The call stack in DDD

The GDB and DDD debuggers only show the local variables that are defined in the current function. For example, the local variable a is only shown if main is selected in the call stack.

Before we look at the insides of shell_sort, let us first test the arguments. Our new hypothesis reads: "The call of shell_sort is faulty". We select shell_sort in the call stack and examine the array argument a:

```
(gdb) print a[0] @ size
$4 = {8000, 7000, 5000, 1000, 4000, 1913}
(gdb) _
```

Surprise! Where does the additional value 1913 come from? Simple answer: The array size as passed in size to shell_sort is *too large by one* – 1913 is a bogus number that happens to reside in memory after a. And this bogus number is being sorted in as well. Our hypothesis is therefore confirmed.

15.3.4   Changing the program state

In order to exclude other failure causes, we *correct* the incorrect size value manually by selecting size in the source code and clicking on *Set*. In the dialog (Figure 15.8), we can now replace the incorrect value 6 with the correct value 5. Using *Finish*, we resume execution of shell_sort:

Setting variables

```
(gdb) set variable size = 5
(gdb) finish
```

Finish function

Set button

Select variable

Edit value

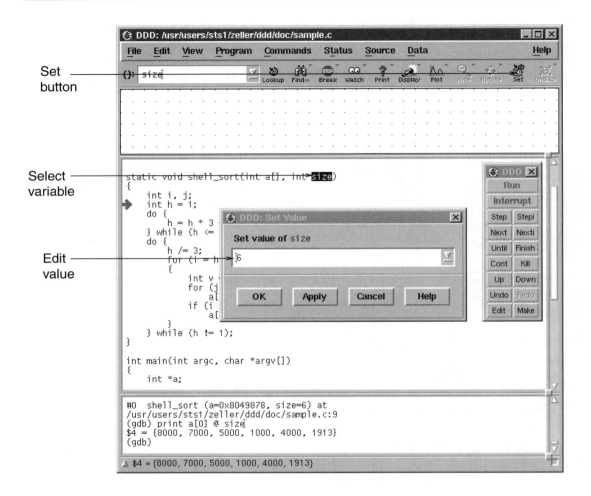

Figure 15.8
Changing the program state in DDD

```
Run till exit from #0
    shell_sort (a=0x8049878, size=5)
    at sample.c:9
0x80486ed in main (argc=6, argv=0xbffff918)
    at sample.c:35
(gdb) _
```

Continuing execution   Success! Now a has the correct value (Figure 15.9). Using *Cont*, we continue execution and see that sample actually outputs the values just observed:

```
(gdb) cont
1000 4000 5000 7000 8000
```

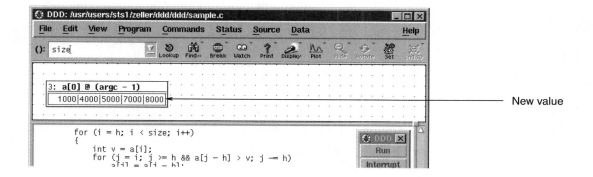

New value

```
Program exited normally.
(gdb) _
```

Figure 15.9
Corrected program
run

Now we can fix the error. Using *Edit* (or a text editor of your choice), load sample.c and change the lines

```
shell_sort(a, argc);
```

Editing program text

to the correct version

```
shell_sort(a, argc - 1);
```

After recompilation,

```
$ gcc -g -o sample sample.c
$ _
```

We can start the program again in DDD (using *Program* → *Run Again*) and see whether we were successful:

```
(gdb) run
'sample' has changed; rereading symbols.
Reading in symbols...done.
Starting program: sample 8000 7000 5000 1000 4000
1000 4000 5000 7000 8000

Program exited normally.
(gdb) _
```

This error has now been fixed. Exit the DDD session using *Program* → *Exit* or Ctrl+Q.

15.4 Other debugger functionalities

In the scenario from Section 15.3, we saw how to use a debugger in order to output the state of the program. A debugger is therefore a good alternative to debugging instructions – especially since we can do without the time-consuming recompilation.

How about the other techniques for testing hypotheses, such as those that were introduced in Section 15.2? It shows that for most techniques, equivalent debugger functions are available.

15.4.1 Validating the program state

Validating the program state in the debugger

In Section 13.2 we, discussed the `assert` function with which the program state can be validated. Debuggers can also call *validation functions*. The normal way of doing this is to use a *conditional breakpoint*: debuggers (also GDB) offer the option of connecting breakpoints with *conditions* – the breakpoint is then only active if the condition is met when the breakpoint is reached. With the GDB command

```
(gdb) break if x < 0 || y < 0
(gdb) _
```

a breakpoint is set in the current line, which stops the program only if the given condition is met.

15.4.2 Watching program state

Permanent watching of the program state

If the consistency violation cannot be associated with a certain point in the program code, debuggers offer the option of *permanent watching*: After every individual computer instruction, an expression is evaluated; in the case of a change, the program is stopped. This property can be used to call validation functions. By doing so, it can be ensured that a data structure remains consistent:

```
(gdb) watch tree_ok()
(gdb) _
```

The catch with constant watching is that the program is now considerably slower since `tree_ok()` must be run after every single instruction. Even if we watch only one single variable (`watch` outputs every value change), the program is slowed down by a factor of 1000. Therefore, this technique can only be used for short sections of the program.

The good news is that some processors (particularly the Intel x86 family) can watch certain memory cells on their own. The debugger can use this feature in order to display the change of simple variables quickly. On such a processor, the command

```
(gdb) watch a[0]
(gdb) _
```

makes sure that every change of a[0] brings the program to a halt – without the program running being slowed down.

15.4.3 Changing program execution

In Section 15.3, we saw how to change variable values while the program is running. Besides this, a debugger offers further possibilities of intervening in the execution of the program. By using the GDB-return command, for instance, each function can be made to return immediately. With jump, one can skip sections of functions – in DDD, this also works by dragging the execution arrow to another position.

Changing program execution

These commands can also be associated with breakpoints, whereby certain areas of the program can be completely excluded from the execution – in a similar way to the removal of code from Section 15.2.3. If we assume, for example, that a certain function corrupts memory, we can set a breakpoint at the beginning of the function and couple the breakpoint with a return command. With every subsequent call, the breakpoint makes sure that the function returns straight away – the actual function is never executed.

15.4.4 Changing the program code

With some debuggers, the program code can be changed *during execution*. Any failure causes found during execution can be fixed when the program is stopped, and the success of the fix can be checked after resuming execution. GDB offers this feature in a few variants only, but can automatically reread a recompiled program without losing any settings.

Changing program code

15.4.5 Postmortem debugging

Finally, one of the most important properties of debuggers: After a program has crashed, the *last state* of the program can be investigated. On UNIX, the program is terminated if there are fatal errors. In order to make a diagnosis, the content of the memory of the program that has crashed is written in a file called core (from "core memory"). This core file can be read in later by a debugger, so that the programmer can examine the faulty program state. Often, displaying the call stack is all it needs – where has the error occurred? – to isolate the error.

Investigating program state after it has crashed

core file

15.5   How GDB and DDD work

Control of the
execution of the
program

Every debugger must be able to control the *execution of the program*, that is, to start and stop the program. Furthermore, the debugger needs access to the *program state*. In this section, we discuss how these basic functions are realized in GDB; furthermore, we will briefly talk about the internals of DDD.

15.5.1   Process control

Generally, it is the duty of the operating system to execute programs as processes. Therefore, the debugger requires some support of the operating system to control execution.

ptrace

The UNIX operating system provides an interface called `ptrace`, which allows executing a child process in a controlled manner. Basically, the child process is executed until it is given a signal – the parent process (the debugger) can therefore keep on running in the meantime.

Here are the most important commands of the `ptrace` function:

PTRACE_TRACEME: Prepare the child process for controlled execution. The child process has to issue this command so that it can be controlled by the debugger. This works as follows:

❏ The debugger process is forked into a parent process and a child process.

❏ The child process calls `ptrace(PTRACE_TRACEME)`.

❏ Using `exec`, the child process replaces itself by the program to be controlled.

The other commands are executed by the parent process (the debugger):

Reading data

PTRACE_PEEKTEXT, PTRACE_PEEKDATA: Reads data from the memory of the child process. The `TEXT` variant accesses the executable program code, and the `DATA` variant accesses the program memory. (Many UNIX variants offer a `/proc` file system as an alternative – a virtual file system from which the memory contents of a process can be read in the same way as from a file. Access via the `/proc` file system is faster and easier.)

Writing data

PTRACE_POKETEXT, PTRACE_POKEDATA: Write data into the memory of the child process.

PTRACE_CONT: Continue executing the child process (by sending a signal, if necessary). *Continuing execution*

PTRACE_SINGLESTEP: Turn on or off single step execution. If this option is active, the process is stopped by a signal after every execution of an instruction. *Single step execution*

But how does the debugger make sure that once the child process is started it also actually stops? On one hand, the debugger can send *signals* to the process that is being investigated. In GDB, for example, this happens if the user enters an interrupt signal via the keyboard (typically Ctrl+C). On the other hand, the program can run into a *breakpoint*. These are realized by the debugger by inserting special *breakpoint instructions* into the machine code of the program – instructions which, when being executed, have the operating system interrupt the process with a special signal. This signal is intercepted by the debugger, which can now investigate the process state. *Signal*

Breakpoint instructions

If the debugger resumes execution, it has to replace the breakpoint instruction with the original instruction. This instruction is then executed in one step. Subsequently, the breakpoint instruction is inserted again and the execution is continued until the next signal. Some processors have special *breakpoint registers* in which breakpoints can be saved; with such registers, there is no need to alter the machine code.

15.5.2 Data access

With `ptrace`, a debugger can access any memory location of the program in question. But how does the debugger establish the connection between the program memory and the variables used in the original source text?

This is where the *debugging information* that was generated during compilation comes into play. If we compile the `sample` program from Example 15.1 to assembler (`sample.s`), in addition to the actual machine code we also find a large number of `.stabs` instructions: *Debugging information*

```
$ gcc -g -S sample.c
$ more sample.s
.stabs "/home/zeller/tmp/",100,0,0,.Ltext0
.stabs "sample.c",100,0,0,.Ltext0 ...
```

These `.stabs` instructions are those from which the debugger gets information about the program. They come in STABS format (from "symbol tables"). A `.stabs` instruction has the following format: *STABS format*

.stabs *"string"*, *type*, *extension*, *description*, *value*

In the first `.stabs` instruction, the *type* has the value `100` – this stands for the path (`/home/zeller/tmp/`) and the name `sample.c` of the source file. All STABS instructions are taken on in the object file (and thus in the executable file) so that GDB can associate machine code with the appropriate source code.

Further down in `sample.s`, we find the debugging information for native C types:

```
.stabs "int:t(0,1)=r(0,1);0020000000000;0017777777777;",128,0,0,0
.stabs "char:t(0,2)=r(0,2);0;127;",128,0,0,0
.stabs "long int:t(0,3)=r(0,1);0020000000000;0017777777777;",
     128,0,0,0
.stabs "__caddr_t:t(7,34)=(7,35)=*(0,2)",128,0,82,0
```

Example 15.2

Debugging information for native C types

This information tells GDB the basic type names (`t`): `int` is given the number `(0,1)`. With the suffix `r`, `int` is declared as a subrange of the type `(0,1)` – that is, itself. (This may not sound very logical, but is a historical convention.) This is followed by the value range of `int`. The same happens for all other native C types – and also for user-defined types such as `__caddr_t`, which are defined as pointers to `(0,2)` (`char`).

After all the types, the machine code for `shell_sort` follows, closing with the debugging information for `main`:

```
.stabs "main:F(0,1)",36,0,27,main
.stabs "argc:p(0,1)",160,0,26,8
.stabs "argv:p(0,21)=*(7,35)",160,0,26,12
```

The type `36` defines a function name – such as `main`. The type `160` defines a parameter – in our case, `argc` and `argv`. `argc` has the type `(0,1)` (`int`) and is at position 8 during the call. The *description* of `argc` is `26` – this is the number of the line in which `argc` is defined. `argv` is a pointer (`=*`) to the type `(7,35)` – `__caddr_t`, a pointer to individual characters.

At end of `main`, we find the information

```
.stabs "a:(0,20)",128,0,28,-4
.stabs "i:(0,1)",128,0,29,-8
```

with which the local variables (type `128`) are defined: `a` is defined in line `28` and is at position `-4`; `i` follows one line later.

This example will suffice for now to get an idea of debugging information. In fact, for every concept of programming language, there is an adequate coding in the STABS format. The fact that the debugger can process all of these and interpret any expression of the programming language shows how much happens behind the scenes of GDB.

15.5.3 Graphical data representation

Now that we have seen how GDB accesses the data of the debugged program, let us look at how this data is presented to the user in an appropriate form. This is the task of DDD.

Visualization in DDD

GDB outputs the data in a textual form. As seen in Example 15.3, this is not always easy to read:

```
*tree = {value = 7, _name = 0x8049e88 "Ada",
  _left = 0x804d7d8, _right = 0x0,
  left_thread = false, right_thread = false,
  date = {day_of_week = Thu, day = 1, month = 1,
    year = 1970,
    _vptr. = 0x8049f78 ⟨Date virtual table⟩},
  static shared = 4711}
```

Example 15.3
Textual value output in GDB

DDD, in contrast, creates a structured display in which details can be unfolded (Figure 15.10).

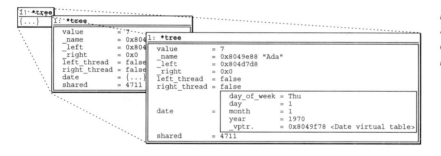

Figure 15.10
Structured value output in DDD with increasing details

How does DDD create such an image? DDD communicates with GDB via the command line and receives data values from GDB in textual form. When parsing the GDB output, DDD assigns a rectangular area to every data value that is output – an area called a *box*. Structures that are nested within each other are represented by boxes nested within one another, which, when not unfolded, are being replaced by dummies.

Representation in boxes

Furthermore, DDD can also visualize *relations* between data. If some data *d'* is displayed as originating from an existing data *d* – for example by the *dereferencing* of a pointer in *d* – DDD displays the relation by means of an arrow from *d* to *d'*. This allows for the representation of complex data structures (Figure 15.11).

Visualizing relationships

Normally, a maximum of one arrow points to every new datum that has been created – the representation is therefore reduced to tree structures. By

Alias detection

activating a special *alias detection*, DDD can also display more complex data structures. The idea is to *merge* all boxes of data that are found at the same addresses in the memory (*Aliases*), thus allowing several references to one piece of data.

Figure 15.11
Structures in DDD

As an example, we take another look at the data from Figure 15.11. The comparison of the pointer values make it clear that the self pointer refers to the nodes themselves; in addition, the last next pointer is assigned to the first element on the list. After the alias detection has been switched on (using *Data → Detect Aliases*), DDD fetches all the memory addresses for the displayed data and merges their boxes. The result can be seen in Figure 15.12 – the image clearly shows to which data the pointers refer, without their addresses having to be compared first.

Figure 15.12
Structures with alias detection

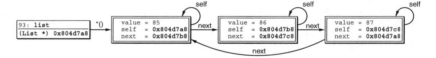

15.6 Validating memory

Some properties of a program must hold *during the entire execution* – for instance, the integrity of the program code or its data. If the fundamental techniques for accessing memory no longer work, it becomes hard to isolate individual failure causes.

In C and C++ programs, misuse of the *heap* memory is a common source of errors. In C and C++, the heap is a source for arbitrary amounts of memory; this is the place where new objects are allocated. If an object is no longer required, the appropriate heap memory must be deallocated (or *freed*) explicitly; the memory thus becomes available for other objects. The programmer must take care, though, that deallocated memory is no longer used; also, deallocated memory must not be deallocated again. Both actions result in *time bombs* – faults that manifest themselves only several instructions later and, thus, are hard to isolate, regardless of the debugging technique being used.

Fortunately, there are a number of useful tools that help validate the state of the heap. It is a good idea to always have these tools ready during development and to apply them at the slightest suspicion – it makes little sense to reason about individual variable values if the structure of the heap is not sound. The catch of these tools is that they increase memory and time requirements and, thus, cannot be used in production code.

15.6.1   Validating the heap with MALLOC_CHECK

Using the GNU C runtime library (default on LINUX systems), one can avoid common errors related to heap usage simply by setting an environment variable called MALLOC_CHECK_. For instance, one can detect multiple deallocation of heap memory:

```
$ MALLOC_CHECK_=2 myprogram myargs
free() called on area that was already free'd()
Aborted (core dumped)
$ _
```

The core file generated at program abort can be read in by a debugger (Section 15.4.5), such that one is directly pointed to the location where free() was called the second time.

15.6.2   Avoiding buffer overflows with Electric Fence

The ELECTRIC FENCE library effectively prohibits buffer overflows. Its basic idea is to allocate arrays in memory such that each array is preceded and followed by a nonexisting memory area – the actual "electric fence". If the program attempts to access this area (i.e., an overflow occurred), the program is aborted.

Using ELECTRIC FENCE, one can quickly narrow down the overflowing array in sample (Example 15.1). We compile sample using the efence library and call the resulting sample-with-efence program with two arguments; as soon as a[2] is accessed, the program is aborted.

```
$ gcc -g -o sample-with-efence sample.c -lefence
$ sample-with-efence 11 14
Electric Fence 2.1
Segmentation fault (core dumped)
$ _
```

Again, the core file can be read in by a debugger – unless one runs sample-with-efence directly from within the debugger.

15.6.3   Detecting memory errors with VALGRIND

VALGRIND (the holy entrance to Valhalla, the home of Odin) provides the functionality of ELECTRIC FENCE, plus a little more. VALGRIND detects the following:

❏ Read access to noninitialized memory

❏ Write or read access to nonallocated memory

❏ Write or read access across array boundaries

❏ Write or read access in specific stack areas

❏ Memory leaks (areas that were allocated, but never deallocated)

If we apply VALGRIND to the `sample` program from Example 15.1, we obtain a message stating that `sample` accesses memory in an illegal manner. This access takes place in `shell_sort` (Line 17), called by `main` and `__libc_start_main`.

```
$ valgrind sample 11 14
Invalid read of size 4
  at 0x804851F: shell_sort (sample.c:17)
  by 0x8048646: main (sample.c:35)
  by 0x40220A50: __libc_start_main (in /lib/libc-2.3.so)
  by 0x80483D0: (within /home/zeller/sample)
```

The remaining message gives some details about the invalid memory area: It is close to the memory area allocated by `main` (Line 31) – the memory area `malloc`'ed for `a[0...1]`.

```
Address 0x40EE902C is 0 bytes after a block alloc'd
  at 0x4015D414: malloc (vg_clientfuncs.c:103)
  by 0x80485D9: main (sample.c:31)
  by 0x40220A50: __libc_start_main (in /lib/libc-2.3.so)
  by 0x80483D0: (within /home/zeller/sample)
$ _
```

How does this work? VALGRIND *interprets* the machine instructions of the program to be debugged, and keeps track of the used memory:

❏ Each memory bit is associated with a controlling *value-bit* or, in short, V-bit. Each V-bit is initially unset; it becomes set as soon as the associated memory bit is being written.

❏ In addition, each byte is associated with an *allocated-bit* or, in short, A-bit, which is set if the corresponding byte is currently allocated. When some memory area is deallocated, the A-bits are cleared.

Whenever the program tries to read some memory whose A-bits or V-bits are not set, VALGRIND flags an error.

Figure 15.13 shows the situation in which the above error message for the `sample` program is generated. `a[0]` and `a[1]` are allocated and initialized – their A- and V-bits are set (shown in dark). In contrast, `a[2]` is neither allocated nor initialized – accessing it causes VALGRIND to issue an error message.

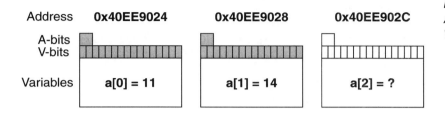

Figure 15.13
*A- and V-bits in
VALGRIND.*

15.7 Avoiding errors

The usage of assertions and dedicated tools to check memory usage is the undisputed best practice to detect failure causes. The usage of interactive debuggers such as GDB and DDD is disputed, though. Basically, *constructive measures* such as good design, a higher degree of abstraction, or a precise specification are clearly more suitable for *avoiding errors from the start* rather than attempting to fix errors with debugger. (In plain terms: "Prevention is better than cure" – and assertions, of course, are part of the prevention). Also, debuggers should not be used to correct a program until it is running (the dreaded "debugging into existence"). On this topic, Harlan Mills says the following:

> An interactive debugger is an outstanding example of what is *not* needed – it encourages trial-and-error hacking rather than systematic design, and also hides marginal people barely qualified for precision programming.

So can we do without debuggers? No! The more the components of a software system are interrelated and the more third-party components are added, the more one has to deal with errors *induced* by third-party software or caused by the *interaction* of all these components. Often, only debuggers can help understand what is actually happening.

For your own software, it is best not to activate the debugger first, but to activate you own brain. McConnell (1993) thinks:

> A debugger is not a substitute for good thinking. But in some cases, thinking is not a substitute for a good debugger either. The most effective combination is good thinking and a good debugger.

Concepts

❏ The aim of debugging is to relate an externally observable state (the *failure*) to a certain moment during execution, whose change (the *fix*) eliminates the failure.

❑ The *scientific method of debugging* consists of the systematic creation and testing of hypotheses.

❑ In order to test a hypothesis and to get an insight into the program execution, one can

– enrich the code with *debugging instructions* or

– use a debugger.

❑ Typical investigation techniques include

– *outputting program state* at suitable points, for example, in a debugger after *stopping* the program;

– *validating program state*, the best techniques being preventive such as *assertions*; and

– *changing program state*, such as disabling program fragments.

❑ Debuggers use specific *interfaces of the operating system* in order to control the process that is being investigated, as well as *debugging informations* that map process data onto elements of the programming language.

❑ Some tools are specialized to detect errors in memory management effectively. Such tools should be applied before all other methods of debugging.

❑ Debuggers are not a substitute for good thinking.

Review exercises

1. In order to find an error, you insert debugging instructions, as shown in Section 15.2.1. After you have found the error, you can

   (a) remove the debugging instructions from the code,

   (b) leave the instructions in the code so that they can be activated at compilation time,

   (c) leave the instructions in the code so that they can be activated at runtime.

   What are the points in favor and against the different options?

2. Preconditions and postconditions can be described not only in the form of assertions but also in the form of *program comments.* Discuss the advantages and disadvantages.

3. Why are assertions removed in the end-product? Consider the efforts for computation and the space needed for assertions, as well as the user friendliness of assertions from the point of view of the end user.

4. Produce a system that automatically determines the changes that are causing errors in a revision tree (Section 15.2.3). Use CVS to access earlier configurations, MAKE to build the programs, and DEJAGNU or JUNIT to test them.

5. Write a program that creates a list of all functions (parameters / local variables / ...) from the STABS information of an object file.

Further reading

An introduction to the topic is given by *The Debugging Scandal* from Lieberman (1997). This version of the *Communications of the ACM* contains numerous secondary articles on the topic.

Rosenberg (1996) describes the general construction of debuggers and their interaction with the (WINDOWS) operating system.

Zeller (1999) describes how the *Delta Debugging* method automatically finds error-causing changes.

GDB was written by Stallman and Pesch (1998) and is maintained by *Red Hat* (formerly CYGNUS).

DDD was developed by Zeller and Lütkehaus (1996). The scenario in Section 15.1 is taken from the DDD handbook from Zeller (2000).

The STABS format is described by Menapace et al. (1998).

In the early days of computer development, it was thought that there were insects (bugs) in the computer which caused errors. According to Hopper (1981), in 1947 a moth was found that got caught in a relay.

Other debugging tools

Interactive debuggers such as GDB and DDD are usually not available as separate tools but are components of the programming environment delivered with a compiler – for example, the WINDOWS debugger is provided together with the WINDOWS development environment. As a rule, the debuggers can only be used in their own environments.

As an exception, GDB can process the debugging information of numerous compilers. Therefore, commercial support is also available for GDB:

❏ *Red Hat* (formerly CYGNUS) provides commercial support for GDB.

❏ *Insight* from *Red Hat* is another graphical interface that is closely connected to GDB. *Insight* is available free of charge; *Red Hat* also provides commercial support.

Other useful commercial debugging tools include:

❏ PURIFY from *Rational* is one of the most efficient tools for discovering errors at runtime – in particular, errors in the management of memory. On LINUX, PURIFY is an alternative to VALGRIND.

❏ INSURE++ from *ParaSoft* also discovers memory management errors at runtime, but combines this with *static analysis* in order to isolate failure causes more accurately. INSURE++ can be used for WINDOWS and UNIX platforms.

❏ BOUNDSCHECKER from *NuMega* discovers memory management errors on WINDOWS platforms; its functionality can be compared to ELECTRIC FENCE and VALGRIND.

The tools introduced in Chapter 18 for *static analysis* can also be used to find errors in programs.

Exercises V

In this exercise, you can test the lcalc program created in the earlier practical exercises as well as the Rational class from Chapter 13.

1. Create an EXPECT script lcalc.exp, which tests your lcalc program with a script similar to bc.exp from Example 12.3 on page 210. Suggest appropriate test cases.

2. Set up DEJAGNU as testing environment for lcalc, as described for bc in Chapter 12. Use lcalc.exp as a starting point.

3. Try to provoke failures in lcalc. In particular, test overflows as well as division by zero. Use a debugger to find and eliminate the cause of the error.

4. Create a RationalTest class as described in Chapter 13.

   ❏ If you want to program in C++, define the test cases in C++ using CPPUNIT.

   ❏ If you want to program in JAVA, define the test cases in JAVA using JUNIT.

5. Create a Rational class that satisfies the test cases. Validate the class using JUNIT or CPPUNIT, respectively.

6. Create a RationalArithTest class that contains basic arithmetic tests (methods add, subtract, multiply, divide).

7. Extend the Rational class such that it also satisfies the test cases from RationalArithTest.

8. Create an AllRationalTests class, which, as a test suite, combines the tests from RationalTest and RationalArithTest. Check whether your Rational class passes AllRationalTests.

Part VI

Program Analysis

16 Profiling using GPROF and GCOV

16.1 Improved performance due to profiling

An important part of program creation is *tuning* – the systematic increase of the performance of a program. In this case, "systematic" means that it is not optimized "randomly". Instead, by using determined specific *profiling*, one determines

Tuning
Profiling

❑ the *locations* at which the performance can be increased and

❑ the *effect* of possible optimizations on the runtime.

In this chapter, we will discuss three tools that carry out this kind of profiling in various degrees of detail:

TIME determines the runtime of *processes*.

GPROF shows how the runtime is split across *functions*.

GCOV counts how often individual *program lines* are executed.

16.2 General runtime measurement using TIME

Let us begin with a look at how the runtime of *processes* is determined. The TIME program executes the command passed as an argument and then outputs the runtime that was required by the process. As an example, we will look at some huffencode program, which is written in C++ and outputs a text in Huffman coding. The COPYING text file is used as a test input.

TIME

```
$ c++ -o huffencode huffencode.C
$ time ./huffencode COPYING > COPYING.huff.C
real    0m0.465s
user    0m0.420s
sys     0m0.010s
$ _
```

The times indicated in the TIME output are:

real: the total time elapsed

user: the CPU time used to execute the command

sys: the CPU time consumed by system overhead (such as kernel functions)

Increase in speed through optimization

TIME is useful to get a rough idea of the runtime of a process and, for example, for checking the effect of different compiler options. If we compile huffencode with optimization enabled (-O), we get the following picture:

```
$ c++ -O -o huffencode huffencode.C
$ time ./huffencode COPYING > COPYING.huff.C
real    0m0.735s
user    0m0.130s
sys     0m0.010s
$ _
```

We see that the CPU time for user functions has dropped to a third – the program, therefore, runs at about three times the speed. At the same time, however, the real runtime has increased. Why? There are several possible reasons for this – for example, other processes could be running, which also require CPU resources. Alternatively, it may take a moment for the newly created program to be loaded into memory.

For this reason, it is generally not very useful to consult the actual runtime for a comparison, unless you can define the status of a computer accurately or form a suitable *statistic mean average value* through an adequate number of tests. Even the system time can vary depending on the system load – for instance, there can be delays if memory has to be swapped to and from the hard drive. Only the user CPU time is wholly reliable and independent of the current load.

Incidentally, TIME itself only measures the actual time elapsed; the CPU time is tracked by the operating system for each individual process.

16.3 Program profiles with GPROF

GPROF
Program profile

While we have a general procedure to measure the runtime of a program using TIME, we also need to know how the runtime of the program is divided between its components. A first approximation is given by the program GPROF, which evaluates the *program profile*.

A program profile is created by an executable program while it is running; it shows which functions have been called and how often, and how much time they required. This is done in three steps:

1. During compilation, the program is *set up* for profiling.

2. When the program is executed, a *program profile* is created.

3. The program profile is analyzed by GPROF.

16.3.1   A program for setting up GPROF

The first step is to *set up* a program for profiling – this means compiling it *Setting up a profile* so that it creates program profiles when executed. This is done by using the compiler option -pg. (The option -pg must be given when the program is being linked as well as when it is compiled.)

```
$ c++ -O -pg -o huffencode huffencode.C
$ _
```

The second step is now to execute the program by feeding it with as *Executing and* much representative data as possible. The program works in the usual *profiling* way – maybe a little slower. At the end, a file gmon.out is automatically created, which contains the program profile:

```
$ ./huffencode COPYING > COPYING.huff.C
$ ls -l gmon.out
-rw-r--r--   1 zeller       21176 Jun 29 11:09 gmon.out
$ _
```

In the third step, the data in gmon.out is analyzed by GPROF. In order *Analysis of the profile* to do this, we call GPROF and submit the program from which the profile in gmon.out comes as an argument. GPROF writes the results of the analysis in the standard output.

```
$ gprof ./huffencode
⋮
GPROF output
⋮
$ _
```

The output from GPROF consists of two parts:

❏ A *flat profile*, which indicates how the runtime is divided into individual functions.

❏ A *structured profile* in which the functions that have been called and are to be called are indicated.

16.3.2   Flat profiles

Example 16.1 shows the *flat program profile*, as it is generated by GPROF. *Flat program profile* The flat program profile indicates which functions need the most runtime, and which are therefore candidates for possible optimizations – the functions that need the most time are shown at the beginning.

% time	cumulative seconds	self seconds	calls	self us/call	total us/call	name
33.33	0.02	0.02	47110	0.42	0.42	string_Scat
16.67	0.03	0.01	10674	0.94	0.94	bits_to_byte
16.67	0.04	0.01	10673	0.94	0.94	string::at
16.67	0.05	0.01	1	10000.00	42298.03	encode
16.67	0.06	0.01	1	10000.00	17668.44	read_input
0.00	0.06	0.00	10983	0.00	0.00	string_Salloc
0.00	0.06	0.00	256	0.00	0.00	compare
0.00	0.06	0.00	154	0.00	0.00	string::op char *
0.00	0.06	0.00	154	0.00	0.44	_cook
0.00	0.06	0.00	153	0.00	0.00	extract_min
0.00	0.06	0.00	153	0.00	0.00	insert
0.00	0.06	0.00	78	0.00	0.00	string_Scopy
0.00	0.06	0.00	1	0.00	0.00	global destructors
0.00	0.06	0.00	1	0.00	0.00	global constructors
0.00	0.06	0.00	1	0.00	0.00	string::from
0.00	0.06	0.00	1	0.00	0.00	huffman
0.00	0.06	0.00	1	0.00	64.53	init_codes
0.00	0.06	0.00	1	0.00	0.00	initial_queue
0.00	0.06	0.00	1	0.00	0.00	length
0.00	0.06	0.00	1	0.00	60000.00	main
0.00	0.06	0.00	1	0.00	0.00	write_encoding
0.00	0.06	0.00	1	0.00	33.54	write_huffman

Example 16.1
A flat program profile. For each function, f, the runtime quota and the number of calls is listed.

Let us look at the profile in Example 16.1 more closely. The most important details are:

self seconds: the user runtime used in this function

% time: the percentage of the total runtime

calls: the number of calls of this function

The leader, the string_Scat function, takes up a third of the runtime itself and with more than 47 000 calls is also the most frequently called function. Optimizations in the following functions, bits_to_byte, string::at, encode, and read_input can also increase the performance of the huffencode program.

Library functions   Altogether, 0.06 s of runtime were measured; before this, TIME recorded 0.13 s of runtime. Where are the remaining 0.07 s? They were needed by *library functions* – in our case, the input and output functions of the C++ standard library. In order to include them in the profile, the program must be linked with library variants that are compiled with -pg and thus specially set up for profiling.

16.3.3   Structured profiles

With a more accurate analysis of the program, we can establish that there is hardly anything that can be improved with the function string_Scat – the function does nothing more than concatenate two character strings. Instead, we ask ourselves: how is it that so many time-consuming character string operations are executed? Here we need the *structured program profile* generated by GPROF, shown in Example 16.2.

Structured program profile

The structured program profile is essentially more detailed than the flat program profile. For each individual function *f*, it indicates

❏ what share *f* and the functions called by *f* have of the entire runtime (%time).

Share of total runtime
Calling functions

❏ which functions *f* are called and how often, as well as *f*'s individual share of their runtime (these functions are listed *above f*)

❏ which functions *f* have been called and how often, and what share of *f*'s runtime they have (these functions are listed *below f*)

Called functions

As an example, we look at the entry for the string_Scat function, listed under the index [4] in Example 16.2. string_Scat does not call any other function (at least none that are set up for profiling); of the 47 110 calls, 18 063 come from the read_input function and 28 737 come from the encode function. Perhaps these are two suitable candidates for optimization? A detailed analysis of the functions may be useful here, discussed in Section 16.4.

```
index % time    self  children    called     name
                0.00    0.06       1/1            _start [2]
[1]    100.0    0.00    0.06       1          main [1]
                0.01    0.03       1/1            encode [3]
                0.01    0.01       1/1            read_input [5]
                0.00    0.00       1/1            write_huffman [10]
                0.00    0.00       1/1            huffman [17]
                0.00    0.00       1/1            write_encoding [20]
-----------------------------------------------------
                                               <spontaneous>
[2]    100.0    0.00    0.06                  _start [2]
                0.00    0.06       1/1            main [1]
-----------------------------------------------------
                0.01    0.03       1/1            main [1]
[3]     70.5    0.01    0.03       1          encode [3]
                0.01    0.00    28737/47110        string_Scat [4]
                0.01    0.00    10674/10674        bits_to_byte [6]
                0.01    0.00    10673/10673        string::at [7]
```

```
              0.00      0.00      1/1            init_codes [9]
              0.00      0.00      77/154         _cook [8]
              0.00      0.00      10752/10983    string_Salloc [11]
              0.00      0.00      256/256        compare [12]
              0.00      0.00      1/1            string::from [16]
              0.00      0.00      1/78           string_Scopy [15]
        ----------------------------------------------------
              0.00      0.00      152/47110      init_codes [9]
              0.00      0.00      158/47110      _cook [8]
              0.01      0.00      18063/47110    read_input [5]
              0.01      0.00      28737/47110    encode [3]
[4]    33.3   0.02      0.00      47110          string_Scat [4]
        ----------------------------------------------------
              0.01      0.01      1/1            main [1]
[5]    29.4   0.01      0.01      1              read_input [5]
              0.01      0.00      18063/47110    string_Scat [4]
        ----------------------------------------------------
```

⋮

16.4   Coverage measurement with GCOV

In order to establish which parts were executed particularly frequently within a function, there is a special program called GCOV, which measures the *line coverage* – it calculates how often each line of the program was run.

Like profiling, coverage measurement occurs in three stages:

1. During compilation, the program is set up for coverage measurement.

2. During the execution of the program, coverage measurement information is generated.

3. The coverage information is analyzed by GCOV.

In order to set up a program for coverage measurement, a special compilation option must be specified. In the case of GCC, these options are -fprofile-arcs and -ftest-coverage.

Using these options, two *auxiliary files* called *file* .bb and *file* .bbg are created for every source file *file.suffix*. These auxiliary files contain the *Control flow graphs* (cf. Chapter 18) and its mapping to the source code – in our case, the files huffencode.bb and huffencode.bbg. Furthermore, the options set up the executable program so that coverage information is created at runtime.

```
$ c++ -g -fprofile-arcs -ftest-coverage
        -o huffencode huffencode.C
$ ls -l huffencode.bb*
-rw-r--r--  1 zeller    2464 Jun 29 11:56 huffencode.bb
-rw-r--r--  1 zeller    5096 Jun 29 11:56 huffencode.bbg
$ _
```

In the second step, the program is executed; the coverage information is written in the file *file*.da:

Executing the program

```
$ ./huffencode COPYING > COPYING.huff.C
$ ls -l huffencode.da
-rw-r--r--  1 zeller    1496 Jun 29 12:03 huffencode.da
$ _
```

In the third step, the coverage information is finally analyzed using the program GCOV. For every source file *file* given as an argument, GCOV creates a file *file*.gcov.

Analysis of the coverage information

```
$ gcov huffencode.C
96.69% of 121 source lines executed
Creating huffencode.C.gcov.
$ _
```

```
          // Fill CODES[C] with a [01]+ string denoting
          // the encoding of C in TREE
          static void init_codes(string codes[UCHAR_MAX + 1],
                                 HuffNode *tree,
                                 string prefix = "")
   153 {
   153     if (tree == 0)
######        return;

   153     if (tree->isleaf)
    77         codes[(unsigned char)tree->l.c] = prefix;
          else
    76     {
    76         init_codes(codes, tree->i.left,  prefix + "0");
    76         init_codes(codes, tree->i.right, prefix + "1");
          }
      }

          // Encode TEXT using the Huffman tree TREE
          static string encode(const string& text, HuffNode *tree)
     1 {
     1     string codes[UCHAR_MAX + 1];
```

```
    1      init_codes(codes, tree);
    1      string bit_encoding;
    1      for (int i = 0; i < text.length(); i++)
18063         bit_encoding += codes[(unsigned char)text[i]];

    1      string byte_encoding;
    1      for (int i = 0; i < bit_encoding.length() - BITS_PER_CHAR;
              i += BITS_PER_CHAR)
           {
              byte_encoding +=
10673            bits_to_byte(bit_encoding.at(i, BITS_PER_CHAR));
10673      }
    1      byte_encoding += bits_to_byte(bit_encoding.from(i));

    1      return byte_encoding;
       }
```

Example 16.3

*A program profile.
Before every line, the
number states how
often it has been
executed*

Example 16.3 shows a section of the file huffencode.C.gcov created by GCOV. For every program line, the GCOV file indicates how often it has been executed; lines that have not been executed are marked with "#####". Now we can also see from where the numerous calls of string_Scat come from: character strings are made up of two loops that contain the entire text coding. The first loop is executed once for every character of the input – precisely 18 063 times; the second for each character of the output – precisely 10 673 times. These two critical positions can now be optimized – for example, by using an alternate data structure optimized for the frequent appendage of character strings.

The number 96.69%, which is output by GPROF, means that the whole code was executed – except for 3.3% of the code. Using suitable arguments, the remaining lines can also be covered.

In contrast to GPROF, the coverage information is not overwritten with every new program run but is appended to the old file. In this way, with every run, the number of executions for the individual lines are added up until the .da file is deleted.

16.5　How GPROF and GCOV work

*Code
instrumentation*

The general idea of GPROF as well as GCOV is to have the compiler produce *instrumented code* – that is, the code is enriched with certain instructions for profiling. The options that are specified during compilation are used for this purpose.

In the case of GPROF, functions are compiled so that every function that is called leaves an entry showing when and from where it was called.

This information is used later by GPROF to output the structured profile. In the case of GCOV, each node in the control flow graph is provided with a counter that is incremented during the run of the program. With both GPROF and GCOV, the information that is gained is output as a file at the end of the program.

The *profiling* of GPROF is not produced via instrumentation. Instead, a special function analyzes the current program counter at specific intervals – for example, 100 times per CPU second – and marks which functions have just been executed. Instead of the accurate counting of function calls, this is a sample that is subject to statistical inaccuracies.

Samples via program counters

16.6 Testing with GPROF and GCOV

The data gained in the profiling can also be used for systematic *tests*. We know, for example, that the length of the input file is 18 063 characters, so the loops have to be executed over text 18 063 times – which the GCOV output in Example 16.3 confirms. The GPROF output in Example 16.2 shows that string_Scat is called 18 063 times by read_input – once for every character.

Testing

By means of a repeated execution of the program that is being examined, one can strive for a *minimum coverage* using GCOV. For instance, by using GCOV, one can ensure that a test executes 95% of all statements at least once – thus making a statement about the quality of the test suite. This kind of *statement coverage* (also called C_0 test) is, however, only a minimal criterion. In practice, it is usually required that each *branch of the control flow graph is run at least once* (so-called *branch coverage*, C_1 test). For this, GCOV has the -b option at its disposal, using which it can also indicate how often the individual branches were executed:

Minimum coverage

Statement coverage

Branch coverage

```
$ gcov -b huffencode.C
 96.69% of 121 source lines executed
 75.00% of 100 branches executed
 69.00% of 100 branches taken at least once
 92.36% of 144 calls executed
Creating huffencode.C.gcov.
$ _
```

If GCOV is given the option -b, the .gcov file contains details about how often the individual branches were executed, as shown in Example 16.4. Here you can see the following:

❏ The branch of the term tree == 0 was executed in 100% of all runs.

❑ The branch from `return` to the end of the function was never executed (since the `return` statement was never executed either).

❑ The branch of the term `tree->isleaf` "branch 0" was executed in 50% of all runs.

❑ The following branch to the end of the function "branch 1" was executed in 100% of all cases.

❑ The last branch to the end of the function "branch 2" was also executed in all runs.

In addition to how often the branches are run, GCOV also indicates how often the functions return in the .gcov file. In a structured program, this should always be the case – unless the function aborts execution.

```
        // Fill CODES[C] with a [01]+ string denoting
        // the encoding of C in TREE
        static void init_codes(string codes[UCHAR_MAX + 1],
                        HuffNode *tree,
                        string prefix = "")
153 {
153     if (tree == 0)
branch 0 taken = 100%
#####         return;
branch 0 never executed

153     if (tree->isleaf)
branch 0 taken = 50%
 77     {
 77           codes[(unsigned char)tree->l.c] = prefix;
branch 1 taken = 100%
        }
        else
 76     {
 76           init_codes(codes, tree->i.left,  prefix + "0");
 76           init_codes(codes, tree->i.right, prefix + "1");
branch 2 taken = 100%
        }
    }
```

Example 16.4
A program profile
with branch
coverage

Concepts

❑ The aim of *tuning* is the systematic increase in the performance of a program, with which the critical positions are identified and optimized.

❏ TIME determines the *general runtime* of a process and, thus, the global effect of optimizations.

❏ The flat profile of GPROF shows how *the runtime is divided into individual functions*.

❏ The structured profile of GPROF shows how the runtime of a function is divided *into subfunctions it has called*.

❏ Using GCOV, it is possible to establish *how often individual lines and branches were executed*.

❏ While the GPROF profiling is based on *sampling*, the number of calls and executions reported by GPROF and GCOV are *accurate*.

Review exercises

1. In C, there are three ways of increasing an integer i by 1 : i = i + 1, i += 1, and i++. Check to see whether the variants differ from each other in their runtime. Should you draw logical conclusions for your programming?

2. Why should you identify the critical points of a program first? Does it not make more sense to implement each function as optimally as possible from the start?

3. You have compiled a program with activated optimization and a coverage test. GCOV shows, to your surprise, that in the following piece of code *both* branches are apparently always executed 100 times:

```
100 if (a == b)
100     c = true;
100 else
100     c = false;
```

How does something like this happen? Consider that optimization may combine several source code instructions into one machine instruction!

4. Write a program that analyzes the .bb and .bbg files created by GCOV and visualizes the program flow graph. You can find notes on the data format in Stallman (1998b).

5. Extend your program created in Exercise 4 such that the coverage information is evaluated, too. As an example, you could highlight edges that have not yet been covered.

Further reading

GPROF was originally developed by Graham et al. (1982); a detailed description can be found in Graham et al. (1983). Traditional GPROF only produces structured profiles, while flat profiles are analyzed by PROF; the implementation from Fenlason and Stallman (1997) that is introduced here unites both functionalities in one program.

Since version 2.8.0, GCOV has been a component of the GNU Compiler Collection GCC. GCOV and GCC as well as the data formats used by GCOV are described in Stallman (1998b).

Kernighan and Plauger (1974), Chapter 7, and Bentley (1982) are classics on the topic of efficient programming. Test methods are described by Liggesmeyer (1990).

The `huffencode` program used here is a component of the debugger DDD from Zeller and Lütkehaus (1996) (cf. Chapter 15); the analyses described were actually carried out to increase performance.

Other analysis tools

Tools that are similar to GPROF and GCOV are often delivered together with the respective compilers, but are also available separately. The following commercial tools provide profiling and coverage measurement.

- ❏ JCOVERAGE from *Jcoverage Ltd* is an open source tool for measuring the coverage of JAVA programs, similar to GCOV. An extended version is available commercially.

- ❏ CLOVER from *Cortex eBusiness Ltd* also checks the coverage of JAVA programs; it provides a multitude of statistical functions and reports.

- ❏ QUANTIFY from *Rational* is a professional implementation of GPROF. With QUANTIFY, the data is not only available in textual form but can also be graphically edited and filtered.

- ❏ PURECOVERAGE from *Rational* also provides for a comfortable processing of the test coverage data, as is also produced by GCOV. Statistical functions, filters, and coverage reports make life a lot easier; in the program, coverage can be activated or disabled when desired via a programmer interface.

- ❏ INSURE++ from *ParaSoft* also provides coverage tests. More on Page 278.

17 Checking style with CHECKSTYLE

17.1 Programming guidelines

Programming in a team means that the individual parts of a system will be worked on by different authors over time. If each author uses a different programming style, a system is created in which no uniform programming style exists. New authors will find it difficult to orient themselves in such a system, because the basic principle of *consistency* is violated.

Principle of consistency

Therefore, it is prudent for teams to create a set of *programming guidelines* to which the team members adhere. If these guidelines are reasonable and consistent, then it will be much easier for the programmers to read and maintain unfamiliar programs.

Programming guidelines

If a set of programming guidelines is introduced late (in the project), it is likely that the programmers will be upset and oppose it, because they do not view style as a problem and are biased toward their own particular style.

To ensure that such a problem cannot develop, Sun Microsystems has established programming guidelines for the JAVA programming language – the "Java Code Conventions". This set of guidelines provides direction for questions such as:

Java Code Conventions

❑ How should files, classes, variables, and so on, be named?

❑ Where should comments be placed and where not?

❑ How should source text be indented and word-wrapped?

❑ Where is white space required and where is it prohibited?

The adherence to such guidelines is difficult as violations easily creep in. A good policy is to examine the existing source texts against existing guidelines. Often enough, such checks require expensive *reviews* or *audits*, where groups of programmers and/or consultants meet to conjointly examine source texts. A substantial part of the guidelines can be checked automatically – for example, it is possible to check the source texts with a scanner for required or prohibited white space.

17.2   CHECKSTYLE usage

CHECKSTYLE   CHECKSTYLE is a tool to check JAVA source code for compliance to programming guidelines. It is highly configurable; the default configuration conforms to the "Java Code Conventions". To explain the tools usage, we will analyze the file `Notepad.java` from the examples of SUN's "Java Development Kit" in the following exercise.

```
$ java -jar checkstyle-all-3.0.jar \
  -c sun_checks.xml Notepad.java
Starting audit...
Notepad.java:37:20: Line contains a tab character.
Notepad.java:61:5: Missing a Javadoc comment.
Notepad.java:73:5: Missing a Javadoc comment.
Notepad.java:74:1: Line contains a tab character.
Notepad.java:76:1: Line contains a tab character.
 . . .
```

We have used the configuration file `sun_checks.xml` here, to check the source code against the "Java Code Conventions". Almost 500 warnings are issued! Two rule offenses lead to this large number:

❏ The configuration prohibits tabs in sources, despite that it is allowed in the "Java Code Conventions".

❏ A bulk of the methods, variables, and so on, are not documented with JAVADOC comments.

For our next test run, we will switch off these two checks. To accomplish this, we will create our own configuration file using the configuration `sun_checks.xml`. Then, we remove the corresponding modules from our configuration file. The following lines are commented out or deleted:

```
<module name="JavadocMethod"/>
<module name="JavadocType"/>
<module name="JavadocVariable"/>
<module name="TabCharacter"/>
```

With the new configuration, the test run still creates 43 warnings. If we examine these warnings more closely, we discover that the programmer has violated a set of guidelines. For example, the white spaces are not placed consistently. Sometimes there is a whitespace between "`if`" and "`(`" and at other times there is none. In this situation, the "JAVA Code Conventions" require that "`if`" and "`(`" are separated by whitespace (the same holds for "while" and "for"). After the insertion of white spaces at these places, five fewer warnings accrue. In this way, we can improve the program step-by-step. This process can continue so that eventually the source code no longer violates any of the guidelines designated in the configuration file.

Code smells

Many CHECKSTYLE rules not only inspect the programming style but also search for *Code Smells*. A code smell is an indicator of a problem in the source code. Two typical examples are:

Code smells

❑ If a class overloads equals, then it must overload hashCode too.

❑ Local variables or parameters should not cover fields.

Code smells may be problems that can be recognized simply, like the problems uncovered by CHECKSTYLE, or they may be profound problems, where a complex program analysis is needed for detection. We will get to know a few of such complex problems in Chapter 18.

17.3 Creating a new check

CHECKSTYLE transforms the source code, with the aid of ANTLR (see Chapter 7), into an abstract syntax tree. This syntax tree gets traversed (depth-first), and every node is checked against the configured guidelines. To illustrate this, we will create a new check. This check will be integrated via the designated CHECKSTYLE interface. The guideline that shall be implemented is: *"No class or interface shall define more than 30 methods."*

Syntax tree

First, we have to receive an impression on the parts of the syntax tree for class and interface definitions. CHECKSTYLE provides a tool for this purpose, which can be used to visualize and navigate the syntax tree of a JAVA program.

Figure 17.1 shows such a syntax tree. Most of the subtrees are folded beneath the nodes. Only the nodes for call definition ("CLASS_DEF") and the list of variable and method definitions ("OBJBLOCK") are unfolded. Now, we can see how the guideline check can be implemented: the OBJBLOCK node below a CLASS_DEF node should not contain more than 30 METHOD_DEF nodes.

The source code of the actual implementation is shown in Example 17.1. To integrate this check, it suffices to add one line to the configuration file:

```
<module name="MethodLimitCheck">
```

Figure 17.1
A syntax tree
visualized by
CHECKSTYLE.

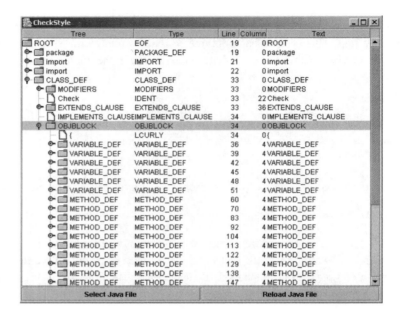

```
import com.puppycrawl.tools.checkstyle.api.*;

public class MethodLimitCheck extends Check {

    private int max = 30;

    public int[] getDefaultTokens() {
        return new int[]{TokenTypes.CLASS_DEF, TokenTypes.INTERFACE_DEF};
    }

    public void visitToken(DetailAST ast) {
        DetailAST objBlock = ast.findFirstToken(TokenTypes.OBJBLOCK);

        int methodDefs = objBlock.getChildCount(TokenTypes.METHOD_DEF);

        if (methodDefs > max) {
            log(ast.getLineNo(),
                "too many methods, only " + max + " are allowed");
        }
    }
}
```

Example 17.1   If we repeat the testing of Notepad.java, our new check will be applied
Implementation of a   too. The guideline is not violated and no warning is issued. Normally,
check

custom checks are created and deployed to their own `jar` archives file. In this case, the CLASSPATH has to be extended.

Concepts

❏ A *consistent* programming style ease the orientation in unfamiliar code.

❏ SUN has provided a set of guidelines for JAVA, the *JAVA Code Conventions*.

❏ CHECKSTYLE checks a set of accepted guidelines.

❏ *Code smells* are typical programming problems.

❏ CHECKSTYLE can be extended by own checks.

Review exercises

1. Test all of your (so far realized) JAVA programs with CHECKSTYLE using the default configuration file. How many and which violations of the guidelines do you observe?

2. Consider which rules of the "JAVA Code Conventions" are also relevant for C or C++. Which are not? Why?

3. Implement a check that ascertains that all methods have a "@reviewed" tag (see Chapter 10).

4. Compare the features of CHECKSTYLE to the DocCheck and DocLint doclets in respect to JAVADOC comments.

Additional tools for guideline checking

A set of (mostly commercial) tools for style and guideline checking exist.

❏ From the open source community for JAVA, the following tools originate:

JLINT   `http://artho.com/jlint/`
PMD   `http://pmd.sourceforge.net/`
JCSC   `http://jcsc.sourceforge.net/`

Corresponding tools for C or C++ do not exist.

❏ The GCC compiler for C++ contains a set of style checks, which can be enabled through appropriate "`-W...`" command line options. In particular, some of the guidelines of Meyers (1997) have been implemented.

❏ CODEWIZARD, C++TEST, JTEST, and so on, from *ParaSoft* uncover violations of predefined guidelines.

❏ The QA products of *Programming Research* check C, C++ or JAVA source texts against guidelines.

❏ Together, now owned by *Borland*, provides an auditing tool.

18 Static program analysis with LINT

18.1 Introduction

In the previous chapters, we introduced programming tools that are used to avoid or fix problems when building large systems. In this chapter, we will look at *programming language* tools, which support the creation and maintenance of source code. We will look at problems such as:

Programming language tools

Typing mistakes such as incorrectly declared functions

Data flow problems such as uninitialized variables

Pointer problems such as memory leaks

All of these tools work *statically* – they examine the program code without executing it (*dynamically*).

Static analysis

18.2 Type checking using LINT

As an introduction, we will discuss a problem that occurred in June 1997, when a Masters student from TU Braunschweig wanted to show his work to one of the authors. The (simplified) program shown in Example 18.1 should calculate the number of iterations used to reduce the probability under a value of 0.00005% starting from a probability of 100%. This is done by multiplying probabilities caused by chance. The standard function `drand48` was used for this, which returns a pseudo random number between 0 and 1 (of type float).

```
1    #include <stdlib.h>
2    #include <stdio.h>
3    void main ()
4    {
5        float f = 1.0;
6        int n = 0;
7        while (f > 0.0000005) {
8            n = n + 1;
```

Example 18.1
Example program
`rand.c`

```
 9              f = f * drand48();
10          }
11          printf ("%d iterations.\n", n);
12      }
```

The following example is based on a "problem" present in SunOS 4 due to incomplete header files. The successor of SunOS 4, Solaris, does no longer have that problem.

The Masters student had developed the respective program on his own computer running LINUX and wanted to demonstrate it on the SunOS computer of the department. There were no problems compiling the program on the LINUX or the SunOS system, and on the LINUX system also it ran smoothly:

```
linux$ cc -o rand rand.c
linux$ ./rand
12 iterations.
linux$ _
```

However, the system did not terminate on the SunOS system:

```
sunos$ cc -o rand rand.c
sunos$ ./rand
...
```

LINT

Where is the problem here? Identifying the problem by looking at the source code requires subtle understanding and persistence. Static analysis tools can automate this process. *LINT* is such a tool. It examines the C source code for possible errors, style, and portability problems (LINT removes "fluff" from programs). LINT produces a list of warnings for the example program:

```
sunos$ lint rand.c
...(Warnings)...
sunos$ _
```

The warnings are listed and discussed here one by one:

```
rand.c(12): warning: main() returns random value
                 to invocation environment
```

Function without return value

The function `main` is not defined in the normal way. It is defined as a function that does not return a value, but the standard requires that `main` returns an `int` value.

```
drand48 value used inconsistently
        llib-lc(198)   ::   rand.c(9)
```

Inconsistent usage

The usage of `drand48` is inconsistent with the definition in the library (as we shall see later).

```
drand48 value declared inconsistently
        llib-lc(198)  ::  rand.c(9)
```

> Through the usage, *drand48* is declared implicitly; this declaration is not compatible with the definition in the library (an explanation will follow).

Inconsistent declaration

```
printf returns value which is always ignored
```

> The return value from `printf` – an indication as to whether the function was successful – is ignored.

Ignored return value

While the warnings regarding `main` and `printf` are fairly minor, the warnings of `drand48` point to a serious problem.

On the LINUX system, the `drand` function is declared in the standard header file as `double drand48(void);`. On the SunOS system, however, the declaration is missing; it is not found in any standard header. In C, functions can be used without declarations; `int` is then assumed to be the type and it allows arbitrary parameters to be passed. Thus, on the SunOS system, the function is implicitly declared as `int drand48();`, which does not match the declaration in LINT's library.

In our case, however, this acceptance has fatal effects: when compiling, the incorrect implicit declaration is produced and used as `int drand48();`. The floating point number delivered by `drand48` is consequently interpreted as an integral number in the generated program. Hence, the generated value is always larger then 1, the value `f` increases instead of decreases, and the program does not end as the abort condition can never be fulfilled.

The first incarnation of LINT was developed shortly after the first C compiler. The idea behind this was to keep the computation effort low by separating compilation and checking. Many traditional LINT checks are now integrated into compilers. In the GNU C compiler, GCC, there are several warnings activated by means of the `-Wall` option. In the case of Example 18.1, GCC on the SunOS system produced warnings that are sufficient for identifying the error:

LINT and compiler

```
$ gcc -o rand rand.c -Wall
rand.c: In function 'main':
rand.c:9: warning:
        implicit declaration of function 'drand48'
rand.c:11: warning:
        implicit declaration of function 'printf'
$ _
```

The warnings show that there are no declarations for `drand48` or `printf`, thus trapping the problem.

18.3   Data flow analysis

The *Fibonacci function* *fib*(n) calculates the *n*th member of the Fibonacci sequence 1, 1, 2, 3, 5, 8, ..., in which every element is presented as the sum of its two antecessors. It is recursively defined as

$$fib(n) = \begin{cases} 1, & \text{for } n = 0 \lor n = 1 \\ fib(n-1) + fib(n-2), & \text{otherwise .} \end{cases}$$

In Example 18.2, we find an iterative implementation that computes *fib*(n).

Example 18.2
fibo.c – *computing*
Fibonacci numbers

```
1   #include <stdio.h>
2   int fib (int n)
3   {
4       int f, f0 = 1, f1 = 1;
5       while (n > 1) {
6           n = n - 1;
7           f = f0 + f1;
8           f0 = f1;
9           f1 = f;
10      }
11      return f;
12  }
13
14  int main ()
15  {
16      int n = 10;
17      while (n-- > 1)
18          (void) printf("fib(%d)=%d\n", n, fib(n));
19      return 0;
20  }
```

Unfortunately, the implementation in Example 18.2 is not quite correct:

```
$ cc -o fibo fibo.c
$ ./fibo
fib(9)=55
fib(8)=34
fib(7)=21
fib(6)=13
fib(5)=8
fib(4)=5
fib(3)=3
fib(2)=2
fib(1)=134513905
$ _
```

The last value for *fib*(1) is incorrect, as *fib*(1) = 1 must hold. If we used the tools previously mentioned in this chapter, they would not help us:

```
$ lint fibo.c
$ _
$ gcc -o fibo fibo.c -Wall
$ _
```

An analysis of the program behavior shows that if $n = 1$, the variable f is not initialized, which leads to an undetermined result. To recognize such problems, a *data flow analysis* is useful. Data flow analyses collect information that is as accurate as possible about the use of results and variables of a program. The *data flow information* produced is needed mainly in program optimization – to notice which variables are best kept in registers and when the values of the variables are actually needed. The same information, however, can also be used to detect uninitialized variables and other programming mistakes.

Data flow analysis

18.3.1 Control flow graph

The first step in data flow analysis is to create a *control flow graph*. A control flow graph shows in which *order* the statements can be executed:

Control flow graph

❑ The instructions of a program are mapped to nodes (or vertices).

❑ A series of statements that must be executed in sequence can be combined into a *basic block* node.

Basic blocks

❑ Edges (or arcs) connecting the nodes represent the possible *control flow* between the instructions – a possible execution sequence of statements.

❑ An entry and exit node represent the beginning and the end of the program or function.

In Figure 18.1, the control flow graph for the Fibonacci function from Example 18.2 is shown.

18.3.2 Data flow analysis

With the help of the control flow graph, the actual data flow analysis is carried out, which describes the behavior of variables or values in the program. The data flow information is normally displayed in *data flow sets*. These are sets of variables or other objects. The basic sets are:

Data flow sets

❑ *gen*(*S*) is the *generated* set – the set of variables that are newly defined in a node *S*.

Figure 18.1
Control flow graph.

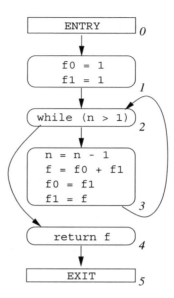

- ❏ *kill*(*S*) is the *destroyed* set – the set of variables that are made un-defined in a node, and whose status is therefore unknown after the node. These include, for example, control variables of FOR loops in Pascal, which have an undefined status after the end of the loop.

- ❏ *in*(*S*) is the *incoming* set, which is the set of variables that are defined before entering the node.

- ❏ *out*(*S*) is the *outgoing* set, which is the set of variables that are defined at the end of the node.

The relationships between these sets are described by *data flow equations*:

- ❏ The *outgoing* set *out*(*S*) contains the variables defined in this node (*gen*(*S*)) or defined before entering the node (*in*(*S*)) that are not destroyed in the node (*kill*(*S*)):

$$out(S) = gen(S) \cup (in(S) - kill(S))$$

- ❏ The *incoming* data flow *in*(*S*) depends on the outgoing set of the preceding node. If you look at the data flow that *must* be present in any case (here the set of variables that must be initialized independently of the execution of the program), this is the *intersection* of the outgoing data flows of all preceding nodes:

$$in(S) = \bigcap_{S_i \in \mathbf{pred}(S)} out(S_i)$$

(Alternatively, you could also view the *possible* data flow – in our case, the set of variables that *may* be initialized. An example for such a *may problem* is found in Chapter 19. See also the exercises at the end of this chapter.)

To solve a data flow problem, the *gen* and *kill* sets are fixed for all nodes; additionally, the sets *in* and *out* are calculated in accordance with the preceding equations.

18.3.3 An example

As an example, we will calculate the initialized variables for the Fibonacci function in every case. By doing so, we can identify the complement – the *possibly noninitialized* variables.

Calculation of noninitialized variables

We will start with the determination of $gen(S)$ and $kill(S)$ for every node S, as shown in Figure 18.1. The set $gen(S)$ contains all variables that are assigned to in node S. The set $kill(S)$ is empty, as no variables are undefined in our program.

		Initialization		1. run		2. run	
S	$gen(S)$	$in(S)$	$out(S)$	$in(S)$	$out(S)$	$in(S)$	$out(S)$
S_0	{n}	Ø	{n}	Ø	{n}		
S_1	{f0, f1}	Ø	{f0, f1}	{n}	{n, f0, f1}		
S_2	Ø	Ø	Ø	{n, f0, f1}	{n, f0, f1}	{n, f0, f1}	{n, f0, f1}
S_3	{n, f, f0, f1}	Ø	{n, f, f0, f1}	{n, f0, f1}	{n, f, f0, f1}	{n, f0, f1}	{n, f, f0, f1}
S_4	Ø	Ø	Ø	{n, f0, f1}	{n, f0, f1}	{n, f0, f1}	{n, f0, f1}
S_5	Ø	Ø	Ø	{n, f0, f1}	{n, f0, f1}	{n, f0, f1}	{n, f0, f1}

Table 18.1
Calculation of the data flow sets.

The sets $in(S)$ and $out(S)$ cannot be immediately computed because of the cycle in the control flow graph – they are recursively dependent on each other.

We solve this problem using *fix point iteration*: starting from the suitable initial values, we alternately determine $in(S)$ and $out(S)$ in several runs until the values no longer change.

Fix point iteration

1. For initialization, we make a conservative assumption: The incoming data flow of every node is empty and no variables are defined in the entry. The initial outgoing flow can be calculated from an analysis of the code.

2. In the first iteration, we determine the new values from $in(S)$ and $out(S)$ for every node S using the data flow equations. In order to do this, we go from top to bottom, so that the values of $out(S_0)$

that have already been calculated can be used for the calculation of $in(S_1)$.

Only in the case of $in(S_2)$ do we need to rely on the possible incorrect initialization value of $out(S_3)$.

3. In the second iteration, the calculated value of $out(S_3)$ from the first can be used for $in(S_2)$. Since the values no longer change, we now have the final results.

And what do the final values tell us? The set $out(S_4)$ does not contain the variable f, although f is given as a return value. It is therefore possible that the returned value is undefined – a clear case for a warning.

Use of warning options   In practice, it looks like this: when the optimization is activated by the option -O in GCC, a data flow analysis similar to the one described is carried out – and now the errors are recognized by GCC:

```
$ gcc -o fibo fibo.c -Wall -O
fibo.c: In function 'fib':
fibo.c:4: warning: 'f' might be used
              uninitialized in this function
$ _
```

In this and the previous examples, you can see that *all warning possibilities of the compiler should always be used*. Every warning must be followed and the code improved, until the last warning has vanished. There is the danger that new warnings are overlooked if warnings are left – or the warnings are switched off completely.

18.4 Specifications

The previous sections have demonstrated how a tool can recognize some aspects of the behavior of a program. This behavior should be exactly what the programmer was thinking while creating the program. However, in programming languages, these wishes can only be formulated in a limited way, and this can lead to implementation errors. These kinds of errors can only be recognized by their *symptoms*, and they often do not give any indication of the *cause* of the problem.

In our example, there are two possible reasons for the problem. On the one hand, the programmer could simply have forgotten to initialize f, because if f is initialized with the value 1, the Fibonacci function returns the correct values for 0 and 1. On the other hand, it may also be that the function is only used for values larger than 1, since the values for 0 and 1 are defined explicitly.

Assertion   However, the programmer should have dealt with this kind of exception in the program – by using *assertions*, which are covered in Section 13.2.

Example 18.3 shows a version of the Example 18.2, with an assertion inserted at line 6. The assertion documents that the Fibonacci function is defined only for values > 1.

```
1    #include <stdio.h>
2    #include <assert.h>
3    int fib (n)
4    {
5        int f, f0 = 1, f1 = 1;
6        assert(n > 1);
7        while (n > 1) {
8            n = n - 1;
9            f = f0 + f1;
10           f0 = f1;
11           f1 = f;
12       }
13       return f;
14   }
```

Example 18.3
fibo-assert.c –
Fibonacci function
with assertion

If this program is executed by calling *fib*(1), the assertion will fail and the program will terminate with a runtime error:

```
$ cc -o fibo-assert fibo-assert.c
$ ./fibo-assert
fib(9)=55
fib(8)=34
fib(7)=21
fib(6)=13
fib(5)=8
fib(4)=5
fib(3)=3
fib(2)=2
fibo-assert.c:6: failed assertion 'n > 1'
zsh: 2040 IOT instruction
      (core dumped)  fibo-assert
$ _
```

One can view an assertion as a specification of the requirements of a program. Unfortunately, this has three serious disadvantages:

1. Assertions are checked *dynamically*, that is, faulty behavior can only be recognized by executing test cases.

2. Assertions are limited to properties that can be expressed as a C expression.

3. Assertions are in the code, not in the interface documentation (the header file).

Specification   *Specifications* have none of these disadvantages. They can be checked *statically* against the program text, and offer a much more flexible notation of conditions. Unfortunately, strictly formal specifications are not used by many programmers since they are often unwieldy. A tool that is not quite

SPLINT   so formal but programmer-friendly is SPLINT, which permits specifications in the form of *annotations* (special comments) directly in the source text. In addition, SPLINT offers a rich vocabulary of specifications, which is targeted to the needs of the software developers.

18.4.1 Buffer overflow

Today, buffer overflows are probably the largest security problem; almost every attack seems to exploit a buffer overflow. The reason lies with the commonly used programming language, C. In the first place, C does not automatically check that every access to an array element lies within the array's borders. Yet, C also offers unsafe library functions like "gets". The "gets" function is problematic, because it copies unchecked user input into an array, without guaranteeing that the input actually fits into the array. This function is so unsafe that current compilers criticize calls of "gets" automatically:

```
$ gcc input.c -o input
In function 'input':
the 'gets' function is dangerous and should not be used.
$ _
```

Buffer overflows can also occur when array elements are accessed directly:

Example 18.4
nine.c – *Program*
with undetected
buffer overflow

```
1    #include <stdio.h>
2    #define SIZE 256
3    static char line[SIZE];
4    static int val;
5    int main()
6    {
7      val = 999999;
8      line[SIZE] = '\0';
9      printf("%i\n", val);
10     return val;
11   }
```

If we test this program, the following happens:

```
$ gcc -Wall nine.c -o nine
$ ./nine
```

```
999936
$ _
```

Instead of the expected output of 999999, another number is printed, 999936. We can identify the reason by using SPLINT, if we enable the checks for buffer overflows ("+bounds"):

```
$ splint +bounds nine.c
Splint 3.0.1.6 --- 14 Oct 2002

nine.c: (in function main)
nine.c:8:3: Possible out-of-bounds store:
    line[256]
    Unable to resolve constraint:
    requires 255 >= 256
     needed to satisfy precondition:
    requires maxSet(line @ nine.c:8:3) >= 256
  A memory write may write to an address beyond
  the allocated buffer.
  (Use -boundswrite to inhibit warning)

Finished checking --- 1 code warning
$ _
```

SPLINT tells us here that in line 8 ("line[SIZE]='\0';") a buffer overflow can take place, since it is not guaranteed that the access index "SIZE" is smaller or equal to the array upper limit of 255. Here, the access is outside the storage area of the variable "line", and instead is the location of the variable "val". The correct code would have been "line[SIZE-1]='\0';". Such wrong accesses, which go one location beyond the allocated size, are very frequent and are called *"off by one"* errors.

18.4.2 Abstract data types

The C programming language offers little support for implementing abstract data types. All types are known in the complete program, and there is no possibility of hiding information. Additionally, there is little distinction between interface and implementation – header files are in no way comparable with, for example, *definition modules* from MODULA-2 .

SPLINT offers a remedy here, as user-defined types can be declared *abstract*. This takes place by means of an annotation in the header file directly within the definition of the type. In the file implementing the type (which has the same name as the header file), this has no effect, but the use of the type is limited in other files to the defined interface. The type representation is protected by an *abstraction barrier*, which may not be penetrated. The actual implementation remains visible to the programmer, but may not be used. On the other hand, the program remains real C source, which can be delivered and compiled without SPLINT – nobody is forced to use SPLINT. Example 18.5 shows the implementation of a list data type that has been equipped with SPLINT annotations:

Example 18.5
list.h – *List interface with SPLINT annotations*

```
1    typedef /*@abstract@*/ struct _list
2    {
3       /*@only@*/ char* this;
4       /*@only@*/ struct _list* next;
5    } *list;
6
7    void list_addh (list l, /*@only@*/ char* e);
```

The data type list is declared as abstract using the annotation /*@abstract@*/. The actual implementation as a pointer to a structure with the fields this and next may not be used by a user of this type. Only the declaration, the assignment operator "=", and functions made available via the interface are allowed on abstract types. (The meaning of the annotation /*@only@*/ is explained in the next section.)

Example 18.6
list-use.c – *List usage*

```
1    #include "list.h"
2
3    void print_front (list l)
4    {
5       printf("%s\n", l->this);
6    }
```

Example 18.6 shows the usage of the type list. In line 5, the actual implementation of the type is used. SPLINT recognizes this as violation of the abstraction barrier:

```
$ splint list-use.c
Splint 3.0.1.6 --- 14 Oct 2002

list-use.c: (in function print_front)
list-use.c:5:19: Arrow access of non-pointer (list):
  l->this Types are incompatible.
  (Use -type to inhibit warning)

Finished checking --- 1 code warning
$ _
```

18.4.3   Memory management

Problems with using incorrect pointers

The vast majority of programming errors in C are due to the *faulty use of pointers* – unused memory is not released, the pointer accesses the wrong object, a pointer is dereferenced that still refers to memory already released, and so on. Problems such as these are very hard to detect, since the cause can be far from the appearance of a symptom.

To detect these problems, SPLINT combines the data flow analysis with a special *access model*. There must always be a pointer to an allocated object and its owner has the *obligation* to release the memory of the object after it has been used. This obligation can only be satisfied by actually releasing the memory or passing the obligation to another pointer that is prepared for this. The programmer must document memory-management decisions using annotations. For example, the /*@only@*/ annotation declares a reference that has an obligation to release memory.

Access models in SPLINT

Obligation of releasing

In Example 18.5, the fields of the list nodes this and next are annotated with /*@only@*/, so they take on the obligation of releasing memory. In addition, the function for appending an element to the list list_addh takes on the obligation for the element passed as its second parameter. A caller, therefore, transfers the release obligation for the appended element and may no longer use it. Example 18.7 shows an implementation of the function list_addh.

```
1   #include "list.h"
2
3   extern /*@out@*/ /*@only@*/ void* smalloc(size_t);
4
5   void list_addh (list l, /*@only@*/ char* e)
6   {
7     if (l != NULL) {
8       while (l->next != NULL) {
9         l = l->next;
10      }
11      l->next = (list) smalloc(sizeof(*l->next));
12      l->next->this = e;
13    }
14  }
```

Example 18.7
list.c – *Implementation*
of list_addh

The function smalloc is a "safe" version of malloc, which produces a runtime error if the requested memory cannot be provided. Therefore, it always returns a pointer to an allocated object and also assigns the release obligation to the caller. The second annotation /*@out@*/ documents that the allocated object is not yet initialized.

The function list_addh searches for the end of the list first and then requests a new list node that is appended to the list. However, this function is faulty, as SPLINT reports in Example 18.8:

❑ The first error is based on a faulty treatment of an empty list: the function will only work correctly if the list already contains an

Memory management

element. This leads to the obligation for the parameter e only being satisfied for the lists that are not empty, by assigning this to the this field to transfer the obligation. If the list is empty, then the obligation is left unfulfilled.

Missing initialization ❏ The second error is that the pointer to the next element is not initialized in the newly created object. It would have been correct to assign this field with NULL.

```
$ splint list.c
Splint 3.0.1.6 --- 14 Oct 2002

list.c: (in function list_addh)
list.c:13:3: Variable e is kept in true branch, but not kept in
  continuation. The state of a variable is different depending on
  which branch is taken. This means no annotation can sensibly be
  applied to the storage. (Use -branchstate to inhibit warning)
  list.c:12:5: Storage e becomes kept
list.c:14:2: Storage *(l->next) reachable from parameter contains
  1 undefined field: next
  Storage derivable from a parameter, return value or global is not
  defined. Use /*@out@*/ to denote passed or returned storage which
  need not be defined. (Use -compdef to inhibit warning)

Finished checking --- 2 code warnings
$ _
```

Example 18.8
SPLINT analysis of
`list.c`

18.5 Annotations in practice

With the help of annotations, static analysis tools like SPLINT can easily and efficiently uncover numerous errors – programmers just have to take the trouble to express their intentions using annotations. The Microsoft company made substantial progress in code security with such techniques and static analysis tools – once the programmers realized the benefits, they were not to dissuade from annotating.

Concepts

❏ *Static program analysis* can identify common errors at compile time.

❏ The *type checking* by LINT reports inconsistent declarations and uses of functions.

❏ As a side effect of the program optimization, *data flow analysis* can reveal the use of uninitialized variables.

❏ *Assertions* guard against incorrect program status. They can be used to check the compliance of pre- and postconditions during runtime.

❏ The specifications of SPLINT extend conventional programming languages with abstraction barriers and assumptions about memory management, whose compliance can be checked statically.

Review exercises

1. Find out which warning options your compiler has. Switch them all on and check what you can do to improve the code. Are there warnings that you regard as nonsensical?

2. Data flow analysis can also show that a variable is not defined in *any case*. To do this, look at the *possible* data flow – the set of the variables that *may* be initialized – and determine the complement. The possible data flow is formed like the *union* of the outgoing data flows:

Possible data flows

$$in(S) = \bigcup_{S_i \in \mathbf{pred}(S)} out(S_i)$$

The calculation is carried out in a similar way to the method that is described. Determine $out(S)$ for all nodes from Figure 18.1, and determine whether there are variables, which have never been initialized.

Investigate other possible initializations of $in(S)$ and their effects.

Further reading

The history and development of the programming language C are presented in Ritchie (1993). There is also a Section about LINT. LINT itself was invented by the YACC developer Johnson (1977).

A comprehensive introduction to the data flow analysis is given in Aho et al. (1986). The application of error detection was recognized by Fosdick and Osterweil (1976), whose system DAVE (Osterweil and Fosdick (1976)) analyzed FORTRAN programs.

Several other tools have used and analyzed later specifications, such as *Omega* from Wilson and Osterweil (1985), *Cesar* from Olender and Osterweil (1992), or *Inscape* from Perry (1989).

Evans and Larochelle (2002b) provides a brief overview of SPLINT. Evans and Larochelle (2002a) describes how SPLINT was used to uncover faults in the FTP server "wu-ftpd". The predecessor of SPLINT was LCLint. The ability of LCLint to discover errors in the use of pointers is introduced in Evans (1996). In addition, it also shows how these capabilities were taken advantage of in order to eliminate faults in the memory management of LCLint itself. These faults could be eliminated within a matter of days. It took more than a week of unsuccessful searches with conventional means.

For modern languages, tools such as LINT are not as important, as they offer sufficient means for abstraction. (Exception: C++; through its compatibility with C it has exactly the same problems as C.) Therefore, CCEL of Duby et al. (1992) also works in a similar way to SPLINT. In EIFFEL, assertions in the form of preconditions, postconditions, and invariant are part of the language definition. Meyer (1992) offers the underlying theory of the *design by contract*.

ESC/Java, described in Detlefs et al. (1998), is a static analysis tool for JAVA.

19 Program slicing using UNRAVEL

19.1 Slices and data flow

A program has a faulty output. What do you do? A frequently used strategy is to determine *how the faulty value has occurred.* This is a tedious task even with a debugger, as shown in Chapter 15. Luckily, there are tools that help solve these kinds of *data flow problems*. These problems include:

Data flow problems

❏ The recognition of *dependences* between input and output

❏ The identification of instructions that *influence* the others

❏ The isolation of the effects of *code changes*.

Example 19.1 shows a simple program that calculates the sum (sum) and the product (mul) of all numbers in an interval [a, b] and outputs both values.

```
1    int main() {
2       int a, b, sum, mul;
3       sum = 0;
4       mul = 1;
5       a = read();
6       b = read();
7       while (a <= b) {
8          sum = sum + a;
9          mul = mul * a;
10         a = a + 1;
11      }
12      write(sum);
13      write(mul);
14   }
```

Example 19.1
Calculation of sums
and product

The aim is, starting from the output, to find all instructions that influence the value that is output.

These kinds of tasks can be dealt with efficiently using a special technique called *program slicing*. Program slicing attempts to remove irrelevant instructions of a program, or to mark relevant instructions. It is therefore a piece, a *slice*, cut out from the program.

Program slicing

Slice

Slicing criteria
Calculation of slices

The calculation is set via the *slicing criterion* (v, n). It specifies the slice for a variable v using an instruction n. A slice is calculated, in which as many instructions of the program are *deleted* as possible, without changing the calculation of the value for the variable v in the instruction

Executable slice

n. An *executable slice* is a slice that produces an executable program.

In order to find the instructions that influence the product, we can therefore calculate a slice for the criterion (mul, 13). For this, the instructions of lines 3, 8, and 12 are deleted. Perhaps the declaration of the variable sum can be removed from line 2. The resulting slice is shown in Example 19.2 (a). In a slice for (sum, 12), the instructions 4, 9, and 13 are removed and for (a, 7) the instructions 3, 4, 6, 8, 9, 12, and 13 are removed.

Example 19.2
Forward and
backward slices

```
1   int main() {              1   int main() {
2       int a, b, sum, mul;   2       int a, b, sum, mul;
3                             3
4       mul = 1;              4
5       a = read();           5
6       b = read();           6       b = read();
7       while (a <= b) {      7       while (a <= b) {
8                             8           sum = sum + a;
9         mul = mul * a;      9           mul = mul * a;
10        a = a + 1;          10          a = a + 1;
11      }                     11      }
12                            12      write(sum);
13      write(mul);           13      write(mul);
14  }                         14  }
```

(a) Backward slice for (mul, 13)   (b) Forward slice for (b, 6)

If the instructions that may influence the value of a variable at a position in a program are being computed, this is called *backward slicing*, since one looks *backward* at the effects of earlier instructions.

The reverse of this is *forward slicing,* if one has determined all statements that are affected by a change to the variables v in the instruction n and thus looks *forward* at the effects in the program.

Example 19.2 shows a forward slice in Part (b) for (b, 6). The slice contains the complete While-loop, since the value of the variable b decides how often the loop will be run.

19.2 Program slicing using UNRAVEL

UNRAVEL

An example of a program slicing tool is UNRAVEL from the National Institute of Standards and Technology of the United States. It will help understand C programs. It can analyze ANSI-C programs and calculate backward slices for them. The calculated slices are visualized by displaying contained instructions in the source text inversely. The user then has the option of navigating in the source text of the program and examining the affected instructions more closely.

Figure 19.1 shows the visualization of the slice (mul, 13) of our Example 19.1. The contained instructions are displayed *inversely*. In contrary to Example refbsp:unravel/slice.c, the slice computed by UNRAVEL is not mandatory executable, so that among others the variable declarations of line 2 are omitted.

Visualizing slice

If more than one source belongs to the program, they are visualized as appended to each other in this window. Since the window can normally only display one section, there is a navigation bar on the right-hand side.

The bar on the left of this is an abstract representation of the slice in the whole program. The bar stands for the whole program, in which the parts contained in the current slice are inverted in this bar. This bar can also be used for *navigation*: A mouse click in this bar jumps to the corresponding place in the program and the corresponding area is shown in the source text window.

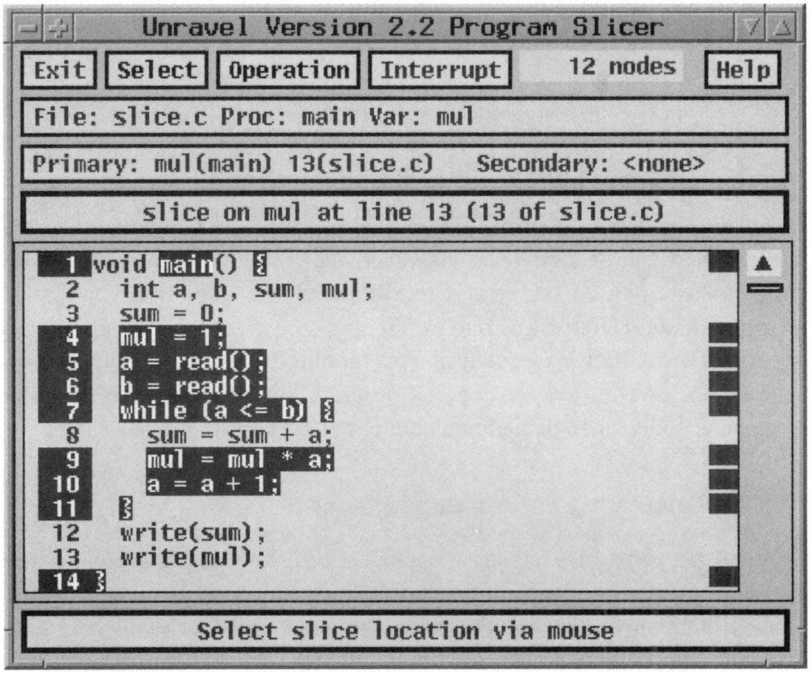

Figure 19.1
Slice interface
of UNRAVEL

19.3 Program dependence graphs

Program slices are calculated using *data flow analysis*, which was introduced in Section 18.3. The two most common techniques are:

❑ Data flow analysis *alone*

Program Dependence Graph (PDG)

❑ Calculation via *PDGs* (*Program Dependence Graphs*)

PDGs are constructed in a similar way to control flow graphs; however, their edges do not indicate the control flow, but *control* and *data depen-*

Control dependence

dences between the instructions that are represented by the nodes. Between two instructions, there is a *control dependence* if one of the instructions

Data dependence

influences whether or how often the other instruction is executed. Between two instructions, there is a *data dependence* if a variable has been assigned a value in an instruction and this value is used in the other instruction (by the evaluation of this variable).

Calculation of the PDG

A PDG is calculated in four steps:

1. Determination of the control flow graphs

2. Insertion of the edges for control dependences

3. Calculation of the data dependences and insertion of the edges

4. Deletion of the control flow edges.

These four steps are examined more closely below.

19.3.1 Determination of the control flow graphs

Determining the control flow graph

The determination of control flow graphs is done in a similar way to the process shown in Section 18.3. However, the instructions cannot be combined to basic blocks, such that a maximum of one side effect can appear per node (assignment of a variable).

Figure 19.2 shows the control flow graphs for Example 19.1. Each node is labeled with a corresponding program line number. (Line 2 is not assigned a node, since declarations are excluded here.)

19.3.2 Calculating control dependences

Calculating control dependences is fairly easy. You determine the nodes whose predicates make decisions about the execution of following instructions – for example, those nodes that correspond to the `if` and `while` instructions. From these nodes, you can put the edges to all controlled instructions. In particular, the `ENTRY` node controls all other instructions – only if it gets executed, the other instructions can execute too.

In the example, the nodes 3–7 and 12–13 are control-dependent on the `ENTRY` node 1, and the nodes 8–10 are control-dependent on the `while` statement in node 7.

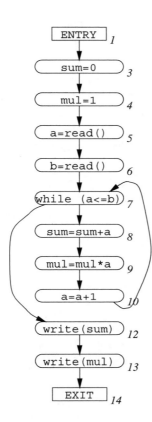

Figure 19.2
*Control flow graph
without basic blocks.*

In fact, the calculation is not as easy as this, as certain unstructured jumps (e.g., `goto`) make the calculation more difficult. For appropriate methods, refer to the literature at the end of the chapter.

19.3.3 Calculation of data dependences

For the data dependences, we fall back on the *data flow sets* from Section 18.3. The calculation of data dependences describes a *possible* data flow, shown in the following equations:

Possible data flow

$$out(S) = gen(S) \cup (in(S) - kill(S))$$

$$in(S) = \bigcup_{S_i \in \mathbf{pred}(S)} out(S_i)$$

In a similar way to the method shown in Section 18.3.3, where we use data flow analyses for the determination of noninitialized variables, we must now establish the *gen* and *kill* sets:

❑ The *generated data flow gen(S)* for a node S consists of the pairs *Generated data flow*
(v, S) for all variables v that are assigned in node S.

Destroyed data flow   ❏ The *destroyed data flow kill*(S) of a node S consists of the pair (v, S′) for all nodes S′ of the graph and for all variables v that are assigned in the node S.

Thus, at a node assigning a new value to a variable v, the previous origin is overwritten. A new origin for a data dependence edge is created; all origins of this variable, which reach this node, are destroyed.

Table 19.1 shows the sets that arise. The short form v_i stands for the pair (v, S_i) – the variable v that is assigned in node S_i.

Table 19.1
gen and kill set

S	gen(S)	kill(S)	S	gen(S)	kill(S)
S_1	$\emptyset$	$\emptyset$	S_8	$\{\text{sum}_8\}$	$\{\text{sum}_3\}$
S_3	$\{\text{sum}_3\}$	$\{\text{sum}_8\}$	S_9	$\{\text{mul}_9\}$	$\{\text{mul}_4\}$
S_4	$\{\text{mul}_4\}$	$\{\text{mul}_9\}$	S_{10}	$\{a_{10}\}$	$\{a_5\}$
S_5	$\{a_5\}$	$\{a_{10}\}$	S_{12}	$\emptyset$	$\emptyset$
S_6	$\{b_6\}$	$\emptyset$	S_{13}	$\emptyset$	$\emptyset$
S_7	$\emptyset$	$\emptyset$	S_{14}	$\emptyset$	$\emptyset$

From the *gen* and *kill* sets, we can now, by means of the data flow equations, calculate the *in* and *out* sets. After initialization using $\emptyset$, we carry out a fix point iteration in a similar way to the method in Section 18.3.3. Table 19.2 shows the first run and Table 19.3 shows the second and last run.

Table 19.2
in and out sets,
first run

S	in(S)	out(S)
S_1	$\emptyset$	$\emptyset$
S_3	$\emptyset$	$\{\text{sum}_3\}$
S_4	$\{\text{sum}_3\}$	$\{\text{sum}_3, \text{mul}_4\}$
S_5	$\{\text{sum}_3, \text{mul}_4\}$	$\{a_5, \text{sum}_3, \text{mul}_4\}$
S_6	$\{a_5, \text{sum}_3, \text{mul}_4\}$	$\{a_5, b_6, \text{sum}_3, \text{mul}_4\}$
S_7	$\{a_5, b_6, \text{sum}_3, \text{mul}_4\}$	$\{a_5, b_6, \text{sum}_3, \text{mul}_4\}$
S_8	$\{a_5, b_6, \text{sum}_3, \text{mul}_4\}$	$\{a_5, b_6, \text{sum}_8, \text{mul}_4\}$
S_9	$\{a_5, b_6, \text{sum}_8, \text{mul}_4\}$	$\{a_5, b_6, \text{sum}_8, \text{mul}_9\}$
S_{10}	$\{a_5, b_6, \text{sum}_8, \text{mul}_9\}$	$\{a_{10}, b_6, \text{sum}_8, \text{mul}_9\}$
S_{12}	$\{a_5, b_6, \text{sum}_3, \text{mul}_4\}$	$\{a_5, b_6, \text{sum}_3, \text{mul}_4\}$
S_{13}	$\{a_5, b_6, \text{sum}_3, \text{mul}_4\}$	$\{a_5, b_6, \text{sum}_3, \text{mul}_4\}$
S_{14}	$\{a_5, b_6, \text{sum}_3, \text{mul}_4\}$	$\{a_5, b_6, \text{sum}_3, \text{mul}_4\}$

19.3.4   Calculation of the PDG

By using the calculated *in* sets, we can now determine the data dependence edges. We start with the control flow graphs. Here we determine for every variable v used in a node S the node S′, for which $(v, S') \in in(S)$ is valid. Then, for every node S′, we insert a data dependence edge $S' \rightarrow S$.

S	$in(S)$	$out(S)$
S_1	$\emptyset$	$\emptyset$
S_3	$\emptyset$	$\{sum_3\}$
S_4	$\{sum_3\}$	$\{sum_3, mul_4\}$
S_5	$\{sum_3, mul_4\}$	$\{a_5, sum_3, mul_4\}$
S_6	$\{a_5, sum_3, mul_4\}$	$\{a_5, b_6, sum_3, mul_4\}$
S_7	$\{a_5, a_{10}, b_6, sum_3, sum_8, mul_4, mul_9\}$	$\{a_5, a_{10}, b_6, sum_3, sum_8, mul_4, mul_9\}$
S_8	$\{a_5, a_{10}, b_6, sum_3, sum_8, mul_4, mul_9\}$	$\{a_5, a_{10}, b_6, sum_8, mul_4, mul_9\}$
S_9	$\{a_5, a_{10}, b_6, sum_8, mul_4, mul_9\}$	$\{a_5, a_{10}, b_6, sum_8, mul_9\}$
S_{10}	$\{a_5, a_{10}, b_6, sum_8, mul_9\}$	$\{a_{10}, b_6, sum_8, mul_9\}$
S_{12}	$\{a_5, a_{10}, b_6, sum_3, sum_8, mul_4, mul_9\}$	$\{a_5, a_{10}, b_6, sum_3, sum_8, mul_4, mul_9\}$
S_{13}	$\{a_5, a_{10}, b_6, sum_3, sum_8, mul_4, mul_9\}$	$\{a_5, a_{10}, b_6, sum_3, sum_8, mul_4, mul_9\}$
S_{14}	$\{a_5, a_{10}, b_6, sum_3, sum_8, mul_4, mul_9\}$	$\{a_5, a_{10}, b_6, sum_3, sum_8, mul_4, mul_9\}$

Table 19.3
in and out sets, second run

If we now remove the control flow edges from the graph, the PDG in Figure 19.3 arises.

Figure 19.3
Program dependence graph.

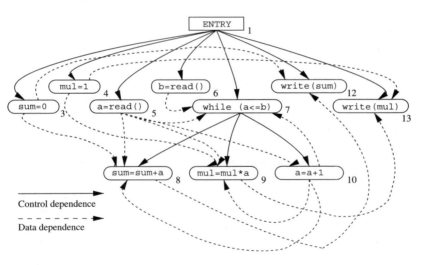

Control dependence

- - - - - - - →
Data dependence

19.3.5   Slicing by means of PDG

If the PDG exists, the slicing itself is only a reachability problem. First of all, a slice criterion in a graph only consists of one node n, which also stands for the variable assigned in this node.

❏ A *forward slice* then consists of the subgraph that contains all the nodes that can be reached from n.

Forward slice

Figure 19.4
Slice for (mul, 13)
in PDG.

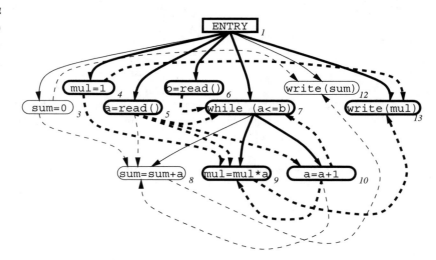

Backward slice

❑ A *backward slice* consists of the subgraph that contains all nodes that can reach *n*.

In Figure 19.4, the backward slice for node 13 is highlighted in the PDG. This stands for the slice from the criterion (mul, 13).

Program slicing using program dependence graphs offers many more applications than program comprehension. Other important areas are the integration of changes (see Section 2.4), debugging, and software testing. Slicing is also available for object-oriented, functional, or logical programming languages.

19.4   Set operations using slices

Slices as sets of
instructions

Slices are not only used on their own. They can also be seen as *sets of instructions* on which various *set operations* can be performed. In Part (a) of the Figure 19.5, a program is shown as a set of instructions, with two labeled points X and Y, which are to display the two calculations and the equivalent slice criteria. The corresponding slices α for criterion Y and β for criterion X are displayed in parts (b) and (c). Set operations can be used on both of these slices, whose result is shown in Part (d). Thereby, the following holds (θ is not displayed):

$$
\begin{aligned}
\delta &= \alpha \cap \beta \\
\gamma &= \beta - \delta &= \beta - \alpha \\
\epsilon &= \alpha - \delta &= \alpha - \beta \\
\theta &= \alpha \cup \beta &= \delta \cup \gamma \cup \epsilon
\end{aligned}
$$

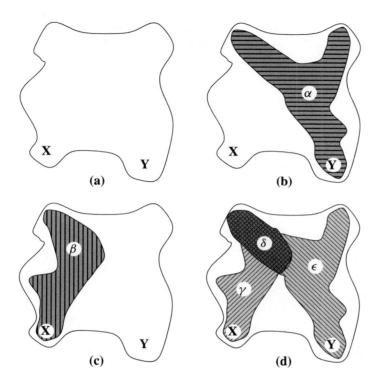

Figure 19.5
Different slices.

❑ The *union* θ of two slices α and β is interpreted as the set of instructions, which is influenced by the criterion for α *or* for β. Since this operation is used frequently, slicing criteria are often specified as sets of pairs of variables and instructions.

Combination

❑ The *intersection* δ of two slices α and β stands for the commonly used instructions and is also called a *backbone slice*.

Intersection
Backbone slice

❑ The slice ϵ, which is the result of the *subtraction* of two slices α and β, consists of the instructions that influence one criterion, but not the other. This kind of slice is also called a *dice*.

Subtraction

Dice

❑ The intersection between a forward and a backward slice is called a *chop*. A chop can identify the instructions exactly, through which a certain input may influence an output.

Chop

In Part (a) of Example 19.3, the *backbone slice* is displayed for the criteria (sum, 12) and (mul, 13). It contains the instructions relevant for calculating sum as well as mul. Part (b) shows the corresponding *dice,* which contains the instructions that are only relevant for the calculation of mul.

In UNRAVEL, backbone slices and dices can be determined and visualized using the commands in the *operation* menu. The base for this is selecting a *primary* and a *secondary* slice that can then be connected.

Example 19.3
Backbone slice (a)
and dice (b) for the
criteria (sum, 12) *and*
(mul, 13)

```
1    int main() {               1    int main() {
2       int a, b, sum, mul;     2       int a, b, sum, mul;
3                               3
4                               4       mul = 1;
5       a = read();             5
6       b = read();             6
7       while (a <= b) {        7
8                               8
9                               9          mul = mul * a;
10         a = a + 1;           10
11      }                       11
12                              12
13                              13         write(mul);
14   }                          14   }
```

(a) backbone slice   (b) Dice

Concepts

❏ A *slice* is the section of a program that is relevant for the value of a variable at a point:

  – A *backward slice* consists of the instructions that may influence the value of a variable at a particular place in the program.

  – A *forward slice* consists of the instructions affected by a change of a variable at a particular place.

❏ Slices are determined by a *program dependence graph* (PDG), which shows the control and data dependences in a program.

❏ The data dependences for the PDG are determined using the *possible* data flow, in which the data flow set consists of a pair of variables and assignment positions.

❏ Using *set operations* on slices, instruction sets can be isolated more accurately.

Review exercises

1. For Example 19.1, calculate the backward slice for (mul, 9). Why is line 10 included, which is executed after line 9?

2. Which procedure for retrieving the reachable node is better: a depth-first or a breadth-first search?

3. Think about how you can calculate slices without program dependence graphs. Note: you can fall back on the sets of variables used in an instruction, and the assigned variables. In addition to this, you can set up rules to create a number of new criteria from one criterion.

4. Why is there a difference between normal and executable slices?

5. Why is slicing for *purely* functional programming languages considerably easier than for imperative?

6. Use UNRAVEL on your own programs.

Further reading

Reengineering is a wide field, for which Arnold (1993) gives an overview. New work on the topic of program comprehension can be found in Cimitile and Müller (1996).

Program slicing was invented by Mark Weiser, who in 1982 examined how programmers find errors. In Ottenstein and Ottenstein (1984), dependence graphs for slicing were used for the first time. An overview of program slicing is given in Tip (1995) as well as in Binkley and Gallagher (1996), and Berzins (1995) combines important articles.

UNRAVEL is presented in Lyle et al. (1995) in detail.

Other tools for program slicing

In addition to UNRAVEL, there are also a number of additional research prototypes. An overview is given by Hoffner et al. (1996).

Besides these, there exists only one industrial-strength tool: CODE-SURFER from *Grammatech* allows the navigation of the program dependences, similar to navigation with a WWW browser. CODESURFER supports the programming language C; other languages will be supported in the future.

CODESURFER is probably the most usable program slicing tool. Besides slicing, it offers additional functionality for program comprehension, for example, structured visualization of the program's variables or the visualization of the call graph (Figure 19.6). The visualization of the slices does not differ much from UNRAVEL: Figure 19.7 shows the same program piece as in Figure 19.1.

Figure 19.6
Call graph in
CODESURFER

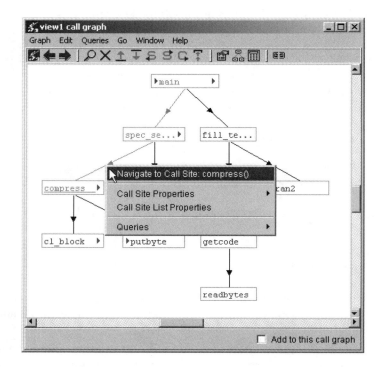

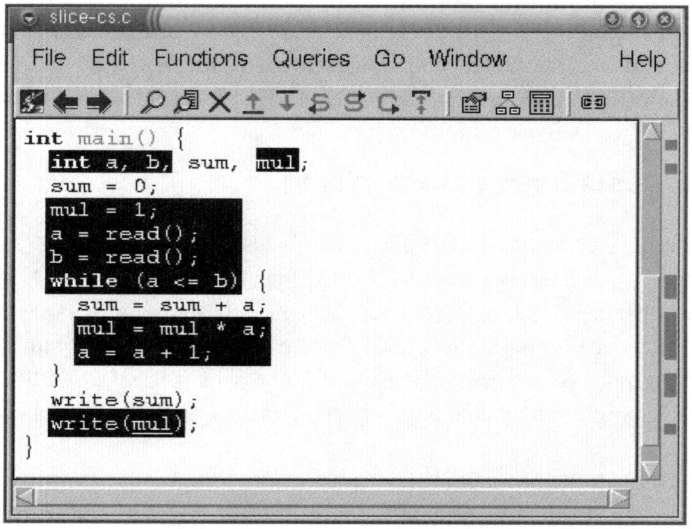

Figure 19.7
Slice interface
of CODESURFER

Another freely available slicing tool is **SPRITE/ICARIA** from Atkinson and Griswold (2001). This tool also analyses C programs.

Exercises VI

In this exercise, you shall try out GCOV and UNRAVEL and get to know different uses of slices.

1. Have a look at the program `lcalc` from Exercise . Extend `lcalc.exp`, so that

   (a) every *statement* is executed at least once,

   (b) every *edge* is executed at least once.

   You can omit statements that have been generated by LEX and YACC; only examine program text written by yourself. Use GCOV to check the coverage.

2. Consider your class `Rational` from Exercise . Extend your test cases, so that

   (a) every *method* is executed at least once,

   (b) every *statement* is executed at least once,

   (c) every *edge* is executed at least once.

   Use GCOV (for C++) and JCOVERAGE (for JAVA) to check the coverage.

3. The program `primecount` from Example 19.4 counts all prime numbers up until a given number n:

```
$ gcc -o primecount primecount.c primelib.c -lm
$ ./primecount 20
Number of prime numbers: 8
Number of others:        12
Sum of prime numbers:    70
$ _
```

4. Install the program code of `primecount`, which you can find at

   http://www.programmierwerkzeuge.de/

   in a separate directory.

5. Setup `primecount` for coverage analysis and evaluate the protocols generated by GCOV.

6. Call UNRAVEL. In the UNRAVEL main window that appears, choose the analyzer and have the C source examined. Look at the history of the analysis (in the main window under *Review History → Last Analysis*).

7. Create a slice for variable *b* in line 8 (function `makeoutput`). Using *select*, set the first slice as *primary* and the second as *secondary*.

8. Form a *dice* from the two slices just created, and look at it. Which errors are now easier to spot?

9. How can you find out which points influence the output of *a* as well as of *b*?

10. Create a union of the two output variables *a* and *b*. Can you delete all unmarked lines in order to remove the calculation of *c*?

11. Try to form a *forward slice* using UNRAVEL.

12. Compute the slice from `arr2` in line 43 (`main`). The variable `arr1` will contain prime numbers in the fields `arr1[0]` to `arr1[a - 1]`. Find the error in the slice.

13. Correct the program and form a new slice in as few steps as possible.

Example 19.4
Example program
`primecount.c`

```
1    #include "primelib.h"
2    #include <math.h>
3
4    void makeoutput(int a, int b, int c)
5    {
6        printf("Number of prime numbers: %d\n", a);
7        printf("Number of others:        %d\n", b);
8        printf("Sum of prime numbers:    %d\n", c);
9    }
10
11   int main (int argc, char *argv[])
12   {
13       int i, j, a, b, c, n;
14       int arr1[1024];
15       int arr2[1024];
16
17       for(i = 0; i < 1024; i++) {
18           arr1[i] = 0;
19           arr2[i] = 0;
20       }
```

```
21
22          n = atoi(argv[1]);
23          a = 0;
24          b = 1;
25          for(i = 2; i <= n; i++) {
26              if (isPrim(i)) {
27                  arr1[a] = i;
28                  a++;
29              }
30              else {
31                  b++;
32              }
33          }
34
35          c = b;
36          send(arr2, arr1, a);
37          for (j = 0; j < a - 1; j++) {
38              c = c + arr2[j];
39          }
40
41          makeoutput(a, b, c);
42
43          return 0;
44      }
```

```
1       extern void send(int* to, int* from, int count);
2       extern int gcd(int a, int b);
3       extern int isPrime(int a);
4       extern int fact(int a);
```

Example 19.5
Auxiliary file
primelib.h

```
1       #include "primelib.h"
2       #include <stdlib.h>
3       #include <stdio.h>
4       #include <math.h>
5
6       void send(int *to, int *from, int count)
7       {
8           /* Duffs Device */
9           int n = (count + 7) / 8;
10          switch (count % 8) {
11          case 0:  do { *to++ = *from++;
12          case 7:         *to++ = *from++;
```

Example 19.6
Auxiliary file
primelib.c

```
13          case 6:        *to++ = *from++;
14          case 5:        *to++ = *from++;
15          case 4:        *to++ = *from++;
16          case 3:        *to++ = *from++;
17          case 2:        *to++ = *from++;
18          case 1:        *to++ = *from++;
19          } while (--n > 0);
20          }
21      }
22
23      int gcd(int a, int b)
24      {
25          int result;
26
27          if (a < b)
28              result = gcd(b, a);
29          else if (a % b == 0)
30              result = b;
31          else
32              result = gcd(b, a % b);
33
34          return result;
35      }
36
37      int isPrime(int a)
38      {
39          int i;
40          i = floor(sqrt(a));
41          return gcd(fact(i), a) == 1;
42      }
43
44      int fact(int a)
45      {
46          int result = 1;
47          int i = 1;
48
49          if (a >= 13 || a <= 0) {
50              fprintf(stderr, "factorial overflow!\n");
51              result = 0;
52          }
53          else {
54              for (i = 1; i < a; i++)
55                  result = result * i;
56          }
57          return result * a;
58      }
```

Part VII

Integrated Environments

20 Integrated development with ECLIPSE 3.0

In the previous chapters, we presented a number of tools that are helpful when working on software projects. However, these tools differ from each other in the operation and in the presentation of outcomes. *Integrated environments* try to combine these tools using a uniform graphical interface and make them intuitively operational. The following requirements apply for integrated environments:

Integrated environments

Intuitive operation. It should be possible to use it without a handbook or any training.

Automation. Routine tasks should be carried out as automatically as possible or by using short commands (a keystroke).

Interoperability. It should be possible to use the outcomes and data of a tool in other tools, without any difficulties.

Abstraction. The environment should support as many programming languages, operating systems, and kinds of tools as possible.

Functionality. It should support as many phases of the software development as possible.

Most commercial compilers come in an *integrated development environment (IDE)*. However, they rarely provide more than support in the *edit-compile-debug cycle*. Furthermore, IDEs are mostly connected to a specific programming language, a specific compiler and debugger, and a specific operating system; they do not provide any way to integrate external tools – therefore, they are referred to as a *closed* environment. On the other hand, an *open* environment provides a way to integrate other tools, as well as interfaces for accessing data and functions of the environment. An environment of this kind is ECLIPSE, which we will introduce in this chapter.

Integrated development environment, IDE

Open and closed environments

ECLIPSE has been developed by Object Technology International (OTI) and was donated as open source by IBM. During the e-hype, the name

ECLIPSE was chosen to express that ECLIPSE outshines existing IDEs. However, in order to invite SUN to join ECLIPSE and avoid a renaming, the official source for the name is the Pink Floyd album "Dark Side Of The Moon" which contains a song called "Eclipse".

Plug-ins — ECLIPSE refers to itself as "an IDE for anything, and for nothing in particular". The design of ECLIPSE reflects this principle: The core of ECLIPSE is small and compact, and the actual functionality is realized in *plug-ins*. By the use of the plug-in concept, ECLIPSE is extensible and allows a seamless integration of third-party tools into the ECLIPSE user interface.

Although ECLIPSE is implemented in JAVA, it does not run on all operating systems that are supported by JAVA. The reason is the *Standard Widget Toolkit* (SWT), which is only available for WINDOWS, MacOS, LINUX, and some UNIX variants. SWT is faster than the JAVA widgets and closer to the *look and feel* of the operating system. ECLIPSE itself only supports the development for the JAVA programming language. However, additional third-party plug-ins extend ECLIPSE for further programming languages, such as C, C++, PYTHON, PERL, and PHP.

ECLIPSE can be used in all phases of software development, especially in phases that deal with source code. These are the later phases of software development, like implementation and maintenance. ECLIPSE provides tool support for most activities that were introduced in previous chapters: version management (CVS), program building (ANT), software testing (JUNIT), and debugging. Furthermore, ECLIPSE provides various ways of visualizing source code properties and supports the refactoring of existing source code.

20.1 Projects in ECLIPSE

Software products consist of thousands of source files and dozens of libraries; therefore, they need to be divided into manageable parts. Most *Projects* — IDEs offer *projects* for this kind of structuring. Each project has a *project directory*, which contains the files belonging to the project. Besides source code, make files, and documentation, this directory also contains a *project description*. The project description consists of specific information on the project, such as the version management used, or dependencies to other projects.

Workspace — In ECLIPSE, each user has a *workspace* that contains one or more projects. For instance, Figure 20.1 shows the workspace for ASPECTJ. The *Projects in ECLIPSE* — ASPECTJ tool consists of several modules, which are realized as projects in ECLIPSE. For each project, there are directories for the source files (`src`) and the binary files (`bin`). Furthermore, each project has a file

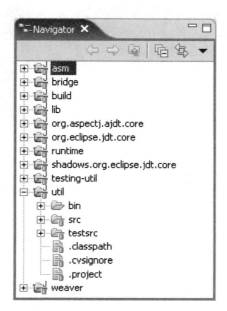

Figure 20.1
A sample workspace.

called .project with project settings, and in some cases, a file called .classpath that contains the JAVA classpath. An additional project called lib collects all libraries used by ASPECTJ, and is included by the other projects.

The term *resources* summarizes projects, directories, and files in ECLIPSE. Resources can be tagged with *markers*. Internally, ECLIPSE uses such markers to highlight errors, warnings, or bookmarks in the source code.

Resources

20.2 The user interface

The graphical user interface of ECLIPSE is called the *workbench*. Besides the mandatory menu bars, tool bars, and status bars, the ECLIPSE workbench consists of *editors*, *views*, and *perspectives*.

Workbench

20.2.1 Editors

With an *editor*, a developer opens and changes files. An editor follows the *open-modify-save-cycle*. This means, only opened files can be modified and changes do not take effect until they are saved. Editors usually extend the ECLIPSE menu bars and tool bars with additional entries.

Editors

In Figure 20.2, three editors are open: one for HelloWorld.java, ASTView.java, and UpdateViewAction.java, respectively. How-

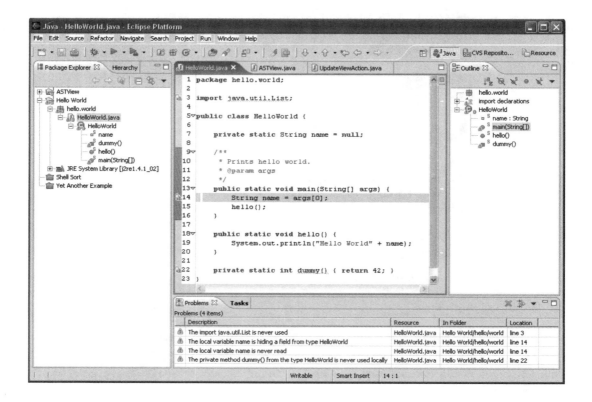

Figure 20.2
The ECLIPSE workbench.

ever, only one is visible because multiple editors are displayed in a *stacked* manner.

20.2.2   Views

Views

In contrast to editors, *views* focus on the presentation of information on an item. It is possible to change the item, but the changes take effect immediately. ECLIPSE provides many predefined views (the list is not complete):

❑ The *Bookmarks View* contains all bookmarks.

❑ The *Navigator View* simplifies navigation through the workspace.

❑ The *Outline View* shows the structure of files.

❑ The *Problems View* displays warnings and errors.

❑ The *Properties View* contains properties of files, for example, the size.

❏ The *Search View* lists results of a search.

❏ The *Tasks View* collects tasks for the user.

In Figure 20.2, several views are opened: the Outline View, the Tasks View (concealed), and the Problems View. Furthermore, two JAVA views are displayed: the *Package Explorer* and the *Hierarchy View* (concealed). The Package Explorer simplifies – like the Navigator View – the navigation, but its main focus is on JAVA projects. The Hierarchy View visualizes inheritance hierarchies and will be discussed in detail in Section 20.5.1.

20.2.3 Perspectives

The selection and arrangement of editors and views depends heavily on the task of the user. For instance, during development, a programmer needs other views than during debugging. In order to enable a fast shift between tasks, ECLIPSE groups editors and views to *perspectives*. A perspective controls the arrangement and visibility of editors and views (*task orientation*). Furthermore, perspectives can restrict the visibility of resources and actions (*information filtering*). Several perspectives can be opened at a particular time, but only one perspective is visible. In practice, perspectives are defined and customized by the user. However, ECLIPSE provides many predefined perspectives:

Perspectives

Task orientation and information filtering

❏ For exploring the workspace: *Resource*.

❏ For working with CVS: *Repository Exploring*, *Team Synchronizing*.

❏ For tracking bugs: *Debug*.

❏ For JAVA programming: *Java, Java Browsing, Java Type Hierarchy*.

❏ For developing ECLIPSE plug-ins: *Plug-in Development*.

In Figure 20.2, the JAVA perspective is opened. By the use of the horizontal tool bar on the top right, we can shift to other perspectives very fast, like to the CVS Repository Exploring or the Resource perspective.

20.3 Working in teams

In practice, a team works in several locations simultaneously, and each developer has an own workspace that needs to be synchronized with the other ones (for concepts of version control, see Chapter 3 and 4). ECLIPSE supports teamwork by a special team environment that simplifies management, sharing, and synchronization of resources. The version archive is called

Repository provider   *repository* by ECLIPSE and is accessed with plug-ins called *repository providers*. ECLIPSE supports optimistic as well as pessimistic cooperation strategies.

Local history   In order to prevent an accidental loss of resources, ECLIPSE maintains a built-in *local history*. This history stores complete copies and not only differences like RCS. Besides recovery, the history is valuable for comparing two different versions of a file. The history is limited by maximum size and maximum age thresholds.

ECLIPSE supports CVS by default. However, other SCM products can be integrated with additional plug-ins. Such plug-ins exist for CLEARCASE, PERFORCE, PVCS, SOURCE INTEGRITY, SUBVERSION, VISUAL SOURCE SAFE, and many others.

Integration of a repository provider   Although the functionality is the same for all SCM systems, the workflow is always different. In order to allow developers to easily use familiar tools in ECLIPSE, repository providers have very much freedom in their realization. The integration in ECLIPSE takes place in two levels:

Integration into the workspace. In some cases, a repository provider has to intervene or even prevent actions that change resources, for example, modification of a locked file. For this purpose, ECLIPSE provides two *hooks*: Before moving or deleting a resource, ECLIPSE calls the *resource move/delete hook*, and before a file is opened or saved, it calls the *file modification validator*.

Hooks

Integration into the workbench. The integration into the user interface is passive, too. ECLIPSE defines placeholders for actions, preferences, and properties, but it is up to the repository provider to define concrete UI elements.

Synchronize View   In ECLIPSE, the central view for version control with CVS is the *Synchronize View* (Figure 20.3), which is opened from the context menu by *Team → Synchronize with Repository*. This view compares the workspace with the repository, and shows differences that are classified in *incoming* and *outgoing changes*. For incoming changes, the file in the CVS archive has been modified, and for outgoing changes, the file in the workspace. Files that need to be integrated have incoming and outgoing changes, and are emphasized – like in Figure 20.3 the file `HelloWorld.java`. The directory `images` and the file `HelloWorldGUI.java` have been added to the repository and are incoming changes. ECLIPSE can sort changes by *change sets* that are changes grouped logically by comment, author, and date.

Incoming and outgoing changes

Change sets

If changes need to be integrated, ECLIPSE provides, besides automatic integration, a graphical *diff/merge* tool. Like SDIFF (Section 2.4), this tool compares both files vis-a-vis in two columns (see Figure 20.3 in the bottom

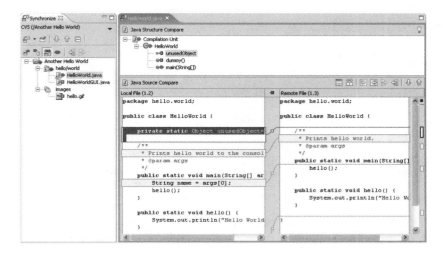

Figure 20.3
The Synchronize
View.

right). Differences are highlighted and can be accessed easily. During integration, the developer decides for every difference, whether to use the version of the first or second file.

In addition to the line-based comparison of DIFF (Chapter 2), this tool compares hierarchical structures (*structure-based comparison*). In the top right of Figure 20.3, the structure of the file HelloWorld.java is compared. The tool recognizes that the method dummy() and the field unusedObject have been deleted. Furthermore, it finds a conflict in the method main because it has been changed in both versions. On source code level of main, we notice that a local variable called name has been removed and the comment of main has been adjusted. The compare tool works on arbitrary files and can even use the local history as a source for version comparisons.

Structure-based comparison

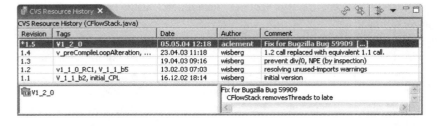

Figure 20.4
The CVS Resource History.

The *Resource History View* is important for version control because it visualizes the course of versioning. Figure 20.4 shows the Resource History for the file CFlowStack.java of ASPECTJ. For every revision, it contains the tags, date, author, and comment. By performing a double-click on the revision number, the revision can be viewed without overriding the

Resource History View

working copy. Furthermore, arbitrary revisions can be compared with each other.

20.4 The JAVA editor of ECLIPSE

The JAVA editor of ECLIPSE supports developers in many ways. It

❑ improves presentation of and navigation through source code,

❑ reduces annoying type work,

❑ checks for errors and *code smells* during editing, and

❑ presents fixes for frequent programming errors.

The *syntax highlighting* of the editor improves the readability of source code. If the mouse pointer hovers above an element, additional information (such as JAVADOC comments) fades in. ECLIPSE can collapse complete methods or classes to a single line, thus increasing the clarity of large source files. Remarkable are the *quick diffs*, which highlight changes since the last saving or commit to the version archive. The *hyperlink mode* simplifies navigation by making all JAVA elements clickable. For instance, clicking on `Object` opens the source code of the class `Object`. This mode is enabled by holding down the *Ctrl* key.

Quick diffs

Hyperlink mode

Figure 20.5
The content assist
functionality.

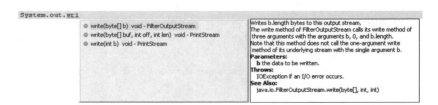

Content assist

By using the *content assist* features, developers can reduce annoying type work. For instance, it is sufficient to type the beginning of a class or function name, and then select one of the recommended names (see Figure 20.5). ECLIPSE also takes care of necessary import statements in this scenario. In a similar way, ECLIPSE creates skeletons for JAVADOC comments or loops. For instance, a `/**` and a line break produce a JAVADOC comment, and a `for` makes a `for` loop. Furthermore, ECLIPSE can create getters and setters for fields. Content assist features simplify not only development but also avoid programming mistakes.

Checks for errors
and code smells

ECLIPSE checks for errors and *code smells* during programming. In the menu *Windows* → *Preferences* → *Compiler* a multitude of checks can be activated (have a look at the topics *Style*, *Advanced*, *Unused Code*, and *Javadoc*). It is highly recommended to activate most of these checks to recognize potential defects early. Figure 20.2 shows some examples of such warnings in the Problems View. Usually, variables and methods, that are never read or used, are candidates for superfluous code (like dummy() in our example). However, in many cases, they are indicators for programming errors and undesired effects. The same holds for local variables that hide fields. In our example, the variable name of the method main() hides the field name of the class HelloWorld. Thus, the field name remains null and our program print "Hello World, null" in any case. Such errors are avoided by taking warnings seriously.

Additional plug-ins extend the Problems View with more messages. For instance, the CHECKSTYLE plug-in checks for further code smells, including user-defined ones (see also Chapter 17), and displays the results in the Problems View.

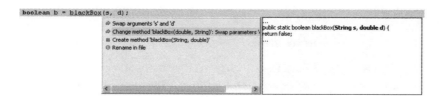

Figure 20.6
Sample quick fixes.

A special feature of ECLIPSE are the so-called *quick fixes*, which fix an error at the touch of a button. Instances for such quick fixes are add a type cast, catch an exception, add missing imports, or change the order of parameters in method calls or declarations (see Figure 20.6).

Quick fix

20.5   Program comprehension with JDT

Software engineering separates between *forward* and *reverse engineering*:

Forward Engineering is the *proceeding* development of software: from the requirements specification to the design, and from the design to the finished product.

Reverse Engineering is the process of *identifying* and *displaying* structures and relations in a finished or unfinished product.

Reverse engineering is not only important during maintenance but also during earlier phases, for instance, if one has to work in unfamiliar code. The main problem is a *lack of locality*: if you look at an element (e.g., a function, method, class, or a variable) in unfamiliar software, the dependencies and effects of these elements are spread across the entire software. You must therefore try to restore locality by abstraction: important elements are made visible, unimportant elements are not displayed.

Locality

For analyzing and understanding large software, command line tools are not well suited because they are text-based. For example, GREP can restore locality, since only the lines containing the text pattern are shown. However, GREP takes no other dependencies into account. In order to detect connections and structures better, we finally have to abstract from the source code, since a textual representation gets confusing even for small

Graphical browser

programs. *Graphical browsers* use icons and annotations to provide various levels of abstraction, which make intuitive comprehension and navigation easier.

The JAVA standard library consists of several thousand files and classes – a size that is almost impossible to handle with traditional tools

Java Development Tools, JDT

and editors. The *Java Development Tools (JDT)* of ECLIPSE on the other hand, support us in many ways: If we want to understand what a Button is in this library, not only does JDT provide many special views and perspectives but also a powerful search engine for JAVA.

20.5.1   The Hierarchy View

Hierarchy View

The *Java Type Hierarchy View* is displayed in the workbench by *Window → Show View → Other → Java → Hierarchy*. The symbol to be shown is selected with *Focus on* from the view, or with *Open Type Hierarchy* of its context menu.

Figure 20.7
The Hierarchy View.

The Hierarchy View in Figure 20.7 shows the elements of the class Button. In the upper area of the view, we find the inheritance hierarchy of the class Button. It contains all classes and interfaces from which

`Button` inherits methods or fields. We recognize that `Button` extends the classes `Component` and `Object`. Furthermore, we notice that `Button` implements the interface `Accessible` itself, and for the other interfaces, it inherits the implementation of `Component`.

The lower area of the view displays the methods and variables defined by `Button`. With *Show all Inherited Members*, we extend this list to all methods and variables that are visible for `Button`. Different icons and colors are used to emphasize the kind, the visibility, and the inheritance of methods. For instance, we recognize that the method `toString()` is inherited from the class `Component`, where the original implementation of the class `Object` was overridden.

20.5.2 The Java browsing perspective

Another abstraction of the class `Button` is the *Java Browsing Perspective* (see Figure 20.8, *Window → Open Perspective → Other → Java Browsing*). In contrast to the Package Explorer, the projects, packages, types, and members are displayed in separate views, which can be filtered using certain criteria. Thus, the developer can switch to other program parts faster. Like every perspective, the Java Browsing Perspective can be extended by additional views, for example, by the Hierarchy View that has been described in the previous section.

Java Browsing Perspective

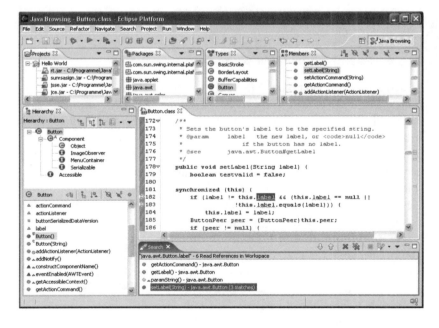

Figure 20.8
The Java Browsing Perspective.

20.5.3   The call hierarchy

Call Hierarchy

The *Call Hierarchy* is another important abstraction for program comprehension. The Call Hierarchy shows for a given method

❏ by which methods it is called (*caller hierarchy*), and

❏ which methods it calls itself (*callee hierarchy*).

The Call Hierarchy is opened from the context menu of a method by selecting *Open Call Hierarchy*. Figure 20.9 shows the Caller Hierarchy for the method wait(long) of the class Object. All methods that call wait(long) are displayed in a tree: wait(long) is called by the method remove(long), which is only called by remove().

Figure 20.9
The Call Hierarchy.

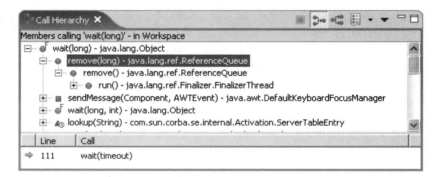

20.5.4   Searching in JAVA source code

Syntax-based search

In addition to a traditional *text-based search* (including regular expressions), ECLIPSE allows a *syntax-based search* for JAVA elements (see Figure 20.10, *Search* → *Java*). It is possible to search for types, constructors, fields, and packages; the search can be restricted to declarations, references, implementations, read accesses, or write accesses. For instance, this syntax-based search can find all locations that read the variable label of Button. The results of this query are listed in the *Search View* and marked with arrows in the source code (see Figure 20.8). In our example, there are six read references distributed across four methods: getActionCommand, getLabel, paramString, and setLabel. The occurrence of setLabel may be surprising, but is reasonable because setLabel checks that label actually changed, before assigning a new value and notifying its observers.

     Search is not limited to single files; if desired, it takes place in the entire workspace or the system libraries. However, for a quick search, the command *Occurrences in File* exists in the context menus. This command only searches for any occurrence of the selection in the currently active editor.

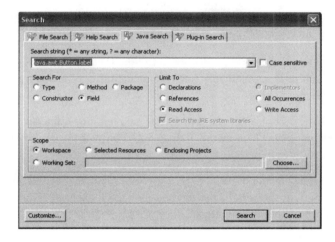

Figure 20.10
The JAVA search in ECLIPSE.

In contrast to a text-based search, a syntax-based search is more precise and returns no incorrect results. For that reason, syntax-based search is superior to text-based search in most situations. Exceptions are makefiles or text files, in which a syntax-based search is not available or impossible. In some situations, inaccuracy is desired like for the search in comments.

However, a *semantic-based search* is even more powerful than a syntax-based search. For instance, it finds references across method calls (variables are passed as parameters and referenced inside the called method). Such a search needs a *data flow analysis*, as described in Chapter 18 and 19.

20.6 Refactoring

A *refactoring* is a semantic preserving code transformation, which improves the structure and quality of programs. Like design patterns, there is no general approach, rather a catalog of approaches. Refactorings can be applied during the design, the implementation, and the maintenance phases of the software development process. In practice, refactoring is not always semantic-preserving and is therefore risky to some degree. For that reason, refactoring should be performed exclusively with tool support and never manually. Furthermore, a test suite for regression tests is recommended to guarantee semantic-preservation, and a version control to restore previous versions, in case the refactoring fails.

ECLIPSE and JDT support refactoring actively (see menu *Refactor*): on the one hand, ECLIPSE integrates CVS and JUNIT, and on the other hand, JDT provides automatic refactoring procedures. A selection of such procedures is presented below.

Move/Rename classes, methods, and fields. This refactoring adjusts packages and file names, as well as uses of the element to the new name. Even references in comments are handled and for fields the names of getters and setters are changed.

Extract Method converts a selection into a new method. The signature is determined automatically, and the selection is replaced by a call to the new method.

Extract Interface supports the process of creating a new interface from an existing class. The methods that should be part of the new interface are selected in a dialog.

Change Signature modifies the signature of a method. For this, the refactoring adjusts calls to the method and inserts user-specified dummy values for new parameters.

Local Rename is not a pure refactoring because it works only on the opened file and not on the whole project. Local Rename is invoked like a quick fix and is very helpful when it comes to renaming local variables of a method.

Organize Imports is not a pure refactoring, either. Organize Imports optimizes import statements: superfluous imports are removed and wildcards such as * are resolved.

The refactorings of ECLIPSE do not guarantee that the semantic of a program is preserved. Therefore, ECLIPSE displays a preview, which lists all changes that will be performed by a refactoring (Figure 20.11). Developers can select desired changes from this list or cancel the refactoring completely.

20.7 Debugging with ECLIPSE

With the JAVA debugger of ECLIPSE, we can control the execution of programs and examine and change program states (for concepts of debugging, see Chapter 15). The debugger supports *hot fix*, which means that modifications on source code affect the running program immediately. Furthermore, it not only supports *local debugging* on the developer's computer but also *remote debugging* over networks.

Debug Perspective   For debugging of programs, the developer can access the *Debug Perspective* (see Figure 20.12, *Window → Open Perspective → Other → Debug*), which provides many additional views:

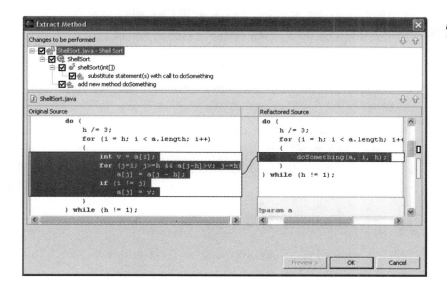

Figure 20.11
The refactoring
"Extract Method".

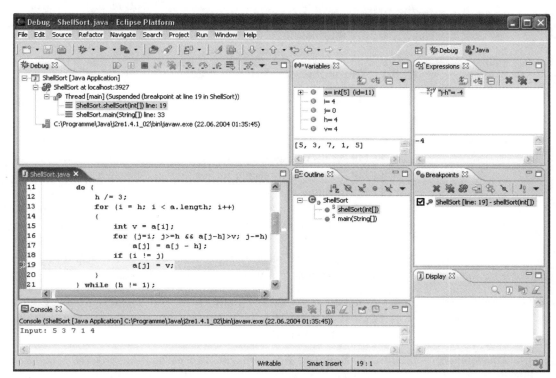

Figure 20.12
The Debug
Perspective.

❏ The *Debug View* contains processes, threads, and call stacks.

❏ The *Variables View* shows values of visible variables.

❏ The *Breakpoints View* lists all breakpoints.

❏ The *Expressions View* evaluates expressions and manages watch-points.

❏ In the *Displays View*, we can define displays that are refreshed at every program stop.

❏ The *Threads and Monitors View* shows which threads hold locks and which threads wait for the release of locks.

20.8   The design of ECLIPSE

ECLIPSE is an open and extensible platform for development tools. This requires a mechanism that allows tool developers to integrate their tools into ECLIPSE without loss of independence. ECLIPSE realizes this idea by its plug-in architecture. At the time of this writing, more than 500 plug-ins exist for ECLIPSE.

20.8.1   The architecture of ECLIPSE

Figure 20.13 shows the architecture of ECLIPSE. The *Software Development Kit* (SDK) of ECLIPSE consists of three parts:

Eclipse Platform   **Eclipse Platform.** The *Eclipse Platform* provides the basic functionality of ECLIPSE. It consists of the *Platform Runtime*, which is the core of ECLIPSE and is responsible for loading and managing plug-ins. The Platform Runtime is the only part of ECLIPSE that is not realized as a plug-in; all other components are integrated via the plug-in mechanism. The *Workspace* manages resources (see also Section 20.1) and the *Workbench* realizes the graphical user interface (see also Section 20.2). All other components, such as *Team*, *Help*, or *Debug*, are built on both, the Workspace and the Workbench.

Java Development   **Java Development Tools (JDT).** The *Java Development Tools* extend
Tools, JDT   ECLIPSE in order to provide functionality specific to JAVA, like the views described in Section 20.5.

Plug-in Development   **Plug-in Development Environment (PDE).** The *Plug-in Development En-*
Environment, PDE   *vironment* extends ECLIPSE to provide functionality specific for plug-in development. As plug-ins are developed in JAVA, PDE not only extends the Eclipse Platform but also JDT.

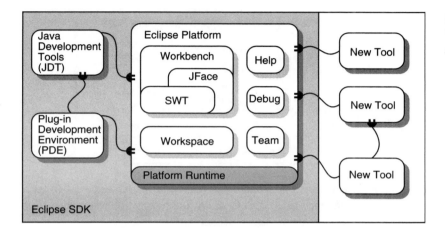

Figure 20.13
The ECLIPSE
architecture.

20.8.2 The plug-in mechanism

A *plug-in* is the smallest possible unit that extends ECLIPSE with a new functionality. A plug-in must contribute to at least one *extension point*, which means that it provides an implementation for it. In other words, extension points are a mechanism to connect two plug-ins with each other. ECLIPSE defines many extension points itself, but third-party plug-ins can also define extension points. A plug-in consists of two parts:

Extension point

Declaration. The *declaration* of a plug-in is the *manifest* file called `plugin.xml`. This XML file describes which extension points are implemented (at least one) and what new extension points are defined (optional). Furthermore, this file contains dependencies to other plug-ins. Example 20.1 shows a complete manifest file that is described in detail in Section 20.9.

Declaration of a plug-in

Implementation. The *implementation* of a plug-in is written in JAVA. However, some plug-ins do not need any JAVA implementation; an example is the help of ECLIPSE that is also realized with the plug-in mechanism.

Implementation of a plug-in

Figure 20.14 illustrates the plug-in concept for two plug-ins. The plug-in `Foo` defines a new extension point `P` and an interface `I`. In order to use this new extension point, the plug-in `Bar` has to implement interface `I` with an own class `C`. This class is contributed to the extension point via the manifest file. Finally, the plug-in `Foo` can query for extensions, and use located classes, like in our example `C`.

Interaction of plug-ins

Simple tools consist of only one plug-in; however, complex tools have multiple plug-ins. Therefore, ECLIPSE allows the combination of several

Figure 20.14
The plug-in concept.

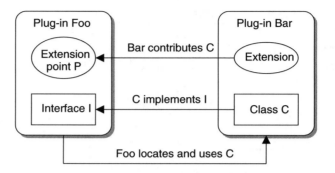

Feature   plug-ins into a *feature*. A feature has additional information, such as a license and a reference to an update site in the Internet. These updates are installed with the *update manager* of ECLIPSE.

During the start-up of ECLIPSE, the Platform Runtime reads all manifest files and creates the *plug-in registry*. The plug-in registry contains dependencies between plug-ins, and manages contributions to extension points. Plug-ins are not loaded until that moment, where their functionality is requested by the user for the first time (*lazy loading*). This approach speeds up the start-up of ECLIPSE enormously. The activation of a plug-in may cause the activation of other plug-ins on which the activated plug-in depends.

Plug-in registry

Lazy loading

20.8.3   Resource changes and building programs

Resource change listener   The different views of ECLIPSE have to be updated if resources change. For this, ECLIPSE uses the concept of *resource change listeners* that are notified at changes.

Resources are organized hierarchically. Thus, changes do not affect only the resource itself, but also resources that are in the hierarchy above the changed resource. For instance, ECLIPSE highlights erroneous files and directories with *label decorations*. A directory is erroneous if one of the contained files or subdirectories is erroneous. In case the developer fixes an erroneous file, ECLIPSE possibly has to refresh the label decorations of all enclosing directories. Therefore, ECLIPSE does not just notify resource *Resource delta tree* listeners, but provides them with a *resource delta tree*. A resource delta tree contains all resources affected by a change in a tree. Figure 20.15 shows an example for such a tree: the directory C, including all of its files, has been deleted (-); the file b has been added (+) to the directory B; and the file a2 has been modified (*). We recognize that a change on a file always affects the enclosing directories and that unchanged files, such as a1, are not contained in a resource delta tree.

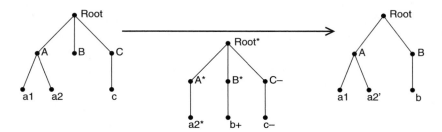

Figure 20.15
Resource delta tree.

Resource delta trees are not only important for resource listeners but also for *project builders*. A project builder gets a resource delta tree and provides several kinds of program construction:

Project builder

❏ For an *incremental build* (see Section 8.2), the project builder uses the resource delta tree to determine the resources that need to be rebuilt. Afterward, it rebuilds only these resources. For instance, a JAVA project builder might recompile only modified JAVA files.

Incremental build

❏ A special case of incremental build is *auto build*, which automatically performs an incremental build after every resource change.

Auto build

❏ After some changes, an incremental build is not possible anymore (e.g., changes on compiler settings), and a *full build* is necessary.

Full build

Both resource listeners and project builders react to resource changes – what are the differences? A resource listener watches a single resource, while a project builder always watches a complete project. Therefore, a resource listener registers with the resource; a project builder, in contrast, registers with ECLIPSE and is assigned to projects that have a specific *project nature*. They also differ in the cost of implementation: Project builders are much more complicated than resource listeners, which are rather lightweight.

Resource listener versus builder

Project natures

20.8.4 Integration of tools in ECLIPSE

The complete integration of a tool into ECLIPSE can be very expensive. Therefore, several *levels of integration* exist.

Levels of integration in ECLIPSE

No integration. An integration into ECLIPSE is not always necessary, for instance, if the tool has a comfortable user interface and does not exchange data with other tools.

Integration by call. This kind of integration starts the tool in an own process and window. The tool is responsible for the management of resources, and profits of some ECLIPSE components like the version control.

Data integration. The integration of tools is possible with *data sharing*. Tools that follow this approach need an access method, an exchange protocol, and a transformation procedure. ECLIPSE supports data integration by many open standards, such as WebDAV, XMI, and XSLT. The risks of data sharing are loss of integrity and the danger of high coupling between tools.

Integration by an API. In this case, a tool provides access to its functionality by an API. However, the user interface of the tool should be separated from its core.

Integration by GUI. This level integrates the tool directly into the ECLIPSE user interface by extending menus, tool bars, views, and perspectives.

20.9 A sample plug-in: the ASTView

In this section, we present a sample plug-in. The plug-in shows the abstract syntax tree (AST) of a JAVA file in a view (Figure 20.16). Internally, ECLIPSE represents JAVA files with such trees. However, they are a mixture between a pure abstract syntax tree and a parse tree because ECLIPSE includes brackets and comments.

Figure 20.16
The ASTView.

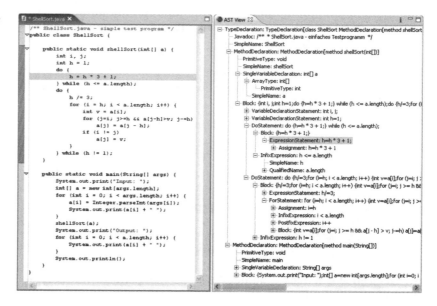

The plug-in provides the following functionality:

❏ Select a JAVA file from its context menu.

❏ Show the AST for this file in a view.

❏ Open vertices in an editor at a double-click.

We are now going to explain snippets of the plug-in. The complete source code is printed on pages 365–370. For trying the plug-in yourself, please consider the notes in the practice section on page 363.

Declare the Plug-in

The file `plugin.xml` (see Example 20.1) contains the declaration of a plug-in. Besides general information and a reference to the code archive (`ASTView.jar`), the file contains dependencies to other plug-ins:

- ❑ `org.eclipse.core.resources` for access to resources,

- ❑ `org.eclipse.ui` for the user interface,

- ❑ `org.eclipse.jdt.core` for JAVA-specific functionality, and

- ❑ `org.eclipse.jdt.ui` for the JAVA editor.

In order to extend ECLIPSE with a new view, we use the extension point `org.eclipse.ui.views`:

```
<extension
     point="org.eclipse.ui.views">
  <category
       name="Wiley"
       id="astview.category.wiley">
  </category>
  <view
       name="AST View"
       icon="icons/sample.gif"
       category="astview.category.wiley"
       class="astview.views.ASTView"
       id="astview.views.ASTView">
  </view>
</extension>
```

By the use of `category`, we extend the dialog *Windows* → *Show View* → *Other* with a new category named "Wiley" (name). Using `view`, we insert a new view in this category. The view is called "AST View" and realized in the class "astview.views.ASTView" (`class`). Our view is identified throughout ECLIPSE by the value in `id`.

Furthermore, we want to extend all context menus for JAVA files. The respective extension point is `org.eclipse.ui.popupMenus`:

```
<extension
     point="org.eclipse.ui.popupMenus">
  <objectContribution
```

```
objectClass=
    "org.eclipse.jdt.core.ICompilationUnit"
    id="astview.ICompilationUnit">
    <action
        label="Update AST View"
        class="astview.actions.UpdateViewAction"
        enablesFor="1"
        id="astview.actions.UpdateView">
    </action>
    </objectContribution>
</extension>
```

To show our entry only for JAVA files, we define an `object Contribution` that shows entries only for elements of type `objectClass`. We select `ICompilationUnit` as type because this class represents JAVA files in ECLIPSE. The action will be called "Update AST View" (`label`), and is enabled for exactly one selected element (`enablesFor`). In case the user selects our action, ECLIPSE calls the class "astview.actions.UpdateViewAction" (`class`).

Create the AST

In ECLIPSE, the creation of an AST from a JAVA file is simple:

```
ICompilationUnit unit = ...;
ASTParser parser = ASTParser.newParser(AST.JLS2);
parser.setSource(unit);
CompilationUnit root =
    (CompilationUnit) parser.createAST(null);
```

The variable `unit` represents the JAVA file of interest and is determined by selection of the context menu (see below).

Display the AST

TreeViewer   We display the AST in a view by the use of a *TreeViewer*. A TreeViewer consists of four parts:

Input. The *input data* will be displayed by the TreeViewer. For our plug-in, the input data is the root of the AST, because it can be used to access the complete AST.

ContentProvider. A *ContentProvider* maps the input to the structure of the viewer. In our example, the structure is a tree, and we have to implement methods to access the parents (`getParent()`) and children of a node (`getChildren()` and `hasChildren()`). The parent is stored in nodes, but for determining the children we have to traverse the AST with an implementation of an *ASTVisitor*.

LabelProvider. A *LabelProvider* defines the format of tree elements. The text is determined by getText() and an optional icon by getImage(). For our example, we simply use the class name of a node and its toString-representation.

Sorter. A *Sorter* sorts the displayed input. For our example, we need no Sorter.

Update the view

Whenever the user selects the action *Update AST View* in a context menu, the method run() of the class UpdateViewAction is called. This method performs the following steps:

❑ Determine the selected JAVA file: We take the first and only element of the selection (selection) of the context menu.

```
Object obj = ((IStructuredSelection)
    selection).getFirstElement();
ICompilationUnit unit = (ICompilationUnit) obj;
```

❑ Find the ASTView: Before updating the view, we have to find it. For that purpose, we use the workbench and the identifier of the view, to determine the IViewPart that represents our ASTView.

```
IWorkbenchPage page = workbenchPart.getSite().
    getWorkbenchWindow().getActivePage();
IViewPart vp =
    page.findView("astview.views.ASTView");
```

Open elements in an editor

In order to open elements in an editor, we define an action called doubleClickAction. The run() method of this action determines the element, on which the user double-clicked (node), and opens this element in an editor:

```
IJavaElement elem =
    unit.getElementAt(node.getStartPosition());
IEditorPart javaEditor = JavaUI.openInEditor(elem);
JavaUI.revealInEditor(javaEditor, elem);
```

The action has to be added to the TreeViewer with a call to the method addDoubleClickListener().

20.10   Automation and intuition

In the previous sections, we showed how the requirements for integrated environments, such as *intuitive operation*, *interoperability*, *abstraction*, and *functionality* are met by ECLIPSE. Compared to traditional command line tools, ECLIPSE has clear advantages in the area of abstraction and intuitive operation.

But what about the last requirement, that of *automation*? Command line tools can be automated without any major problems by the use of shell scripts. Usually, integrated environments have large deficits here, because an operation is only possible via the graphical user interface; unfortunately, this holds for ECLIPSE as well. However, most tools integrated by ECLIPSE, such as JUNIT, ANT, and CVS, are available as command line tools as well. Therefore, the lack of automation does not matter very much.

For ECLIPSE, a more important issue is the growing number of plug-ins. Every day, more plug-ins are published that are not mature enough. Furthermore, the support for other programming languages lags behind the support of JAVA. However, the ECLIPSE boom has just begun, and we do not know its future yet.

Concepts

❑ *Integrated environments* provide various tools in a shared, unified, and intuitively operational environment.

❑ *Open environments* allow the integration of external tools. *Access interfaces* to the data and functions of the environment are useful (like the ECLIPSE API).

❑ *High integration* provides programmers with a uniform user interface, *modularity* allows the individual further development of external tools, and *interoperability* enables the cooperation and exchange between integrated tools.

❑ A user interface divides into *editors*, *views*, and *perspectives*. *Graphical browsers* provide different views with various levels of abstraction.

❑ *Refactorings* improve the structure of programs.

❑ *Incremental builder* enables editing of source code *on-the-fly* by efficient compiling techniques.

❑ *Plug-ins* allow the flexible extension of ECLIPSE.

❏ *Extension points* are potential locations for extensions. All contributed extensions are managed in the *plug-in registry*.

Review exercises

1. Discuss the advantages and the potential risks of an open development environment, like ECLIPSE, for industrial software development.

2. We have introduced different views on JAVA source code. What views are reasonable for other programming languages, such as C, C++, PYTHON, PERL, and PHP?

3. Not all tools presented in this book are integrated in ECLIPSE. Is an integration of the following tools reasonable, and if yes how can it look like?

   (a) AUTOCONF (Chapter 9)

   (b) DEJAGNU (Chapter 12)

   (c) BUGZILLA (Chapter 14)

   (d) GPROF and GCOV (Chapter 16)

   (e) LINT (Chapter 18)

   (f) UNRAVEL (Chapter 19)

   If an integration is not reasonable, is it possible to integrate some of the tool's concepts?

4. Why does ECLIPSE use its own widget toolkit (JFACE and SWT) and not the default JAVA toolkits (AWT and SWING)? Research on the Internet.

5. Your company develops an editor that is based on AWT and SWING. Your boss likes ECLIPSE and wants to integrate it into ECLIPSE. Compare the costs and benefits of the different kinds of integration to each other, and plan the integration. Research on the Internet, whether a direct integration of AWT and SWING components is possible.

6. We only considered integration from the user's and developer's perspective. What other perspectives can you think of?

7. There exist more than 500 plug-ins. What are the disadvantages of such a huge number? Figure out a reasonable categorization for plug-ins. Are there plug-in catalogs on the Internet?

8. Research on the ECLIPSE *Rich Client Platform*. Make up the future of ECLIPSE on the *dark side of the moon*. What about a *Sun*?

Further reading

The first integrated development environment was SMALLTALK, in which the graphical programming environment was part of the system and was described in Goldberg (1983). SMALLTALK was developed together with graphical workstations.

Earlier software development environments were strongly *syntax oriented*: The source code was input for a *syntax controlled* editor, and the program always was kept in a compiled state. These include PSG from Bahlke and Snelting (1986) and the *Synthesizer Generator* from Reps and Teitelbaum (1988).

The term *source code engineering*, describes the activities taken on by many development environments. In the meantime, the research has broken loose from its source code orientation and now looks at *software engineering environments*, which are oriented to the entire software development process.

Object Technology International (2003) describes the architecture of ECLIPSE. The operation of ECLIPSE is topic of Daum (2004), as well as of Shavor et al. (2003). In contrast, Beck and Gamma (2003) focus on the development of plug-ins. You can find recent information on ECLIPSE at:

$$\texttt{http://www.eclipse.org/}$$

Other programming environments

Most commercial compilers come in as an *integrated development environment (IDE)*. However, apart from integrated GUI builders, they rarely support more than the *edit-compile-debug cycle*. Typical programming environments, such as CODEWARRIOR, NETBEANS, the *Visual* series of *Microsoft*, or the *VisualAge* series of IBM, have the problem that many visualization tools are only available for sources that have been compiled *without any errors*.

There are only a few cross-platform environments that support several programming languages, version control systems, and external tools:

- ❏ SNiFF+ by *Wind River* is an open environment that supports several programming languages and operating systems. External tools are integrated by *adapters*. SNiFF+ provides graphical browsers that are similar to those of ECLIPSE. However, the focus of SNiFF+ is on code analysis.

- ❏ SOURCE NAVIGATOR is very similar to SNiFF+, and also focuses on code analysis. It supports the integration of external tools, and is the only *open* environment, besides ECLIPSE and SNiFF+.

❏ C-FORGE by *Code Forge* supports more than 30 programming languages and several version control systems. Like ECLIPSE, it provides searches and browsers for source code, as well as debugging tools.

❏ CODEBEAMER by *Intland* is a web-based development environment, that supports program comprehension and communication between developers. A web-interface accesses version control systems, and examines source code with several tools. CODEBEAMER is a enhancement for existing development environments; consequently, there is a CODEBEAMER plug-in for ECLIPSE.

❏ TOGETHER by *Borland* contains an integrated UML editor and provides many skeletons for design patterns. Another highlight is the numerous software metrics. TOGETHER also exists as a plug-in for ECLIPSE.

Sometimes, ECLIPSE is called the "EMACS of the 21. century". The EMACS editor, or the "grandmother" of all editors, is famous since ever. It can be extended by LISP , and many external programming tools are supported. This even goes to real programming environments, such as JDE for JAVA. Besides programming, with EMACS one can write emails, surf in the Internet – or write books like this one . . .

Exercises VII

In this exercise, you create the *Rational* example of Chapter 13 in ECLIPSE. Furthermore, you develop your own plug-in: the *ASTView* presented in Chapter 20.

Introduction to ECLIPSE

1. Download and install ECLIPSE.

2. Create a new JAVA project named `Rational` (use *File → New → Project*).

3. Create a class `Rational` that contains methods for comparison (`equals`, `compareTo`), and for the four basic arithmetics (`add`, `subtract`, `multiply`, `divide`).

4. Create a tester named `RationalTest` as described in Chapter 13 (for methods `equals`, `compareTo`). Use the dialog *File → New → Other → Java → JUnit → Test Case*.

5. Execute `RationalTest` with *Run → Run As → JUnit Test*, and check whether `Rational` passes all test cases.

6. Now create a `RationalArithTest` class that contains test cases for the basic arithmetics (`add`, `subtract`, `multiply`, `divide`).

7. Create a test suite named `AllRationalTests` that combines the tests of `RationalTest` and `RationalArithTest`. Use the dialog *File → New → Other → Java → JUnit → Test Suite*. Check with this test suite whether your `Rational` class passes all tests.

8. Compare the current version of the class `Rational` with a previous version from the local history (in the context menu *Compare with → Local History*).

9. Reconstruct the version history of an arbitrary open-source project with the tools of ECLIPSE. (You will find some open-source projects on `www.sourceforge.net`).

10. Explore the JAVA standard library (`rt.jar`) with ECLIPSE. Start with the *Java Browsing* Perspective or with the *hyperlink mode* (press *Ctrl* key). Possibly, you have to add the JAVA source code as a *source attachment*. You will find the source in the archive `src.zip` in the main directory of your JAVA installation.

Plug-in development in ECLIPSE

1. Create a *Hello World* plug-in before trying out the *ASTView* plug-in. You will find instructions on the Internet, for example, in the article "Your First Plug-in" on `www.eclipse.org`.

2. Make yourself familiar with the ECLIPSE help (*Help* → *Help Contents*). Use it to research on:

   ❑ abstract syntax trees (AST)

   ❑ actions

   ❑ viewers, particularly, the TreeViewer

   ❑ the extension point `org.eclipse.ui.views`

   ❑ the extension point `org.eclipse.ui.popupMenus`.

3. Create a new plug-in project named `ASTView`. In the *New File* dialog, use the wizard *Plug-in Project* and name the class that controls the plug-in life cycle `astview.ASTViewPlugin` (case-sensitive). ECLIPSE should automatically import the correct libraries.

4. Open the *manifest editor* for the file `plug-in.xml`, and create the plug-in description (see Example 20.1). You can enter the source code in the page *plugin.xml* or use the input fields on the other pages of the editor.

5. Call the command *PDE Tools* → *Update Classpath* in the context menu of `plugin.xml`, to refresh the list of libraries that will be imported by ECLIPSE.

6. Now you can test the declaration of our *ASTView*: Start the plug-in test environment with *Run* → *Run As* → *Runtime Workbench*. A second workbench opens; check whether the dialog *Windows* → *Show View* → *Other* contains the entry "Wiley". Close the test workbench afterward.

7. Use the Resource Perspective to create a directory called `icons` and insert an arbitrary image named `sample.gif`. This image will be the logo of the *ASTView*.

8. In order to finish the plug-in, implement the remaining classes `ASTView` and `UpdateViewAction` (see Examples 20.2 and 20.3). If you are unfamiliar with an operation, look it up in the ECLIPSE help.

```xml
1   <?xml version="1.0" encoding="UTF-8"?>
2   <?eclipse version="3.0"?>
3   <plugin
4       id="ASTView"
5       name="ASTView Plug-in"
6       version="1.0.0"
7       provider-name=""
8       class="astview.ASTViewPlugin">
9
10      <runtime>
11          <library name="astview.jar"/>
12      </runtime>
13      <requires>
14          <import plugin="org.eclipse.core.runtime.compatibility"/>
15          <import plugin="org.eclipse.ui.ide"/>
16          <import plugin="org.eclipse.ui.views"/>
17          <import plugin="org.eclipse.jface.text"/>
18          <import plugin="org.eclipse.ui.workbench.texteditor"/>
19          <import plugin="org.eclipse.ui.editors"/>
20          <import plugin="org.eclipse.core.resources"/>
21          <import plugin="org.eclipse.ui"/>
22          <import plugin="org.eclipse.jdt.core"/>
23          <import plugin="org.eclipse.jdt.ui"/>
24      </requires>
25
26      <extension
27          point="org.eclipse.ui.views">
28          <category
29              name="Wiley"
30              id="astview.category.wiley">
31          </category>
32          <view
33              name="AST View"
34              icon="icons/sample.gif"
35              category="astview.category.wiley"
36              class="astview.views.ASTView"
37              id="astview.views.ASTView">
38          </view>
39      </extension>
40
41      <extension
42          point="org.eclipse.ui.perspectiveExtensions">
43          <perspectiveExtension
44              targetID="org.eclipse.jdt.ui.JavaPerspective">
45              <view
46                  relative="org.eclipse.ui.views.ContentOutline"
47                  relationship="stack"
48                  id="astview.views.ASTView">
49              </view>
50          </perspectiveExtension>
51      </extension>
52
53      <extension
54          point="org.eclipse.ui.popupMenus">
```

Example 20.1

Plug-in description

`plugin.xml`

```
55          <objectContribution
56                objectClass="org.eclipse.jdt.core.ICompilationUnit"
57                id="astview.ICompilationUnit">
58            <action
59                label="Update AST View"
60                class="astview.actions.UpdateViewAction"
61                enablesFor="1"
62                id="astview.actions.UpdateView">
63            </action>
64          </objectContribution>
65        </extension>
66
67    </plugin>
```

Example 20.2

Class ASTView

```
1     package astview.views;
2
3     import java.util.ArrayList;
4
5     import org.eclipse.core.resources.ResourcesPlugin;
6     import org.eclipse.jdt.core.ICompilationUnit;
7     import org.eclipse.jdt.core.IJavaElement;
8     import org.eclipse.jdt.core.JavaModelException;
9     import org.eclipse.jdt.core.dom.AST;
10    import org.eclipse.jdt.core.dom.ASTNode;
11    import org.eclipse.jdt.core.dom.ASTParser;
12    import org.eclipse.jdt.core.dom.ASTVisitor;
13    import org.eclipse.jdt.core.dom.CompilationUnit;
14    import org.eclipse.jdt.ui.JavaUI;
15    import org.eclipse.jface.action.Action;
16    import org.eclipse.jface.dialogs.MessageDialog;
17    import org.eclipse.jface.viewers.DoubleClickEvent;
18    import org.eclipse.jface.viewers.IDoubleClickListener;
19    import org.eclipse.jface.viewers.IStructuredSelection;
20    import org.eclipse.jface.viewers.ITreeContentProvider;
21    import org.eclipse.jface.viewers.LabelProvider;
22    import org.eclipse.jface.viewers.TreeViewer;
23    import org.eclipse.jface.viewers.Viewer;
24    import org.eclipse.swt.SWT;
25    import org.eclipse.swt.graphics.Image;
26    import org.eclipse.swt.widgets.Composite;
27    import org.eclipse.swt.widgets.Display;
28    import org.eclipse.swt.widgets.Shell;
29    import org.eclipse.ui.IActionBars;
30    import org.eclipse.ui.IEditorPart;
31    import org.eclipse.ui.ISharedImages;
32    import org.eclipse.ui.PartInitException;
33    import org.eclipse.ui.PlatformUI;
34    import org.eclipse.ui.part.ViewPart;
35
36
37    /**
38     * Class OurVisitor
39     */
40    class OurVisitor extends ASTVisitor {
41
42        private int currentDepth;
43        private int maxDepth;
44        private ArrayList children;
45
```

```
46    public OurVisitor(int depth) {
47       this.currentDepth = 0;
48       this.maxDepth = depth;
49       children = new ArrayList();
50    }
51
52    public void postVisit(ASTNode node) {
53       currentDepth--;
54    }
55
56    public void preVisit(ASTNode node) {
57       if (currentDepth > 0 && currentDepth <= maxDepth) {
58          children.add(node);
59       }
60       currentDepth++;
61    }
62
63    public Object[] getChildren() {
64       return children.toArray();
65    }
66 }
67
68
69 /**
70  * Class ASTView
71  */
72 public class ASTView extends ViewPart {
73
74    private TreeViewer viewer;
75    private Action sampleAction;
76    private Action doubleClickAction;
77    private ICompilationUnit unit;
78
79    /**
80     * Inner Class ViewContentProvider
81     */
82    class ViewContentProvider implements ITreeContentProvider {
83
84       public void inputChanged
85          (Viewer v, Object oldInput, Object newInput) {
86       }
87
88       public void dispose() {
89       }
90
91       public Object[] getElements(Object parent) {
92          return getChildren(parent);
93       }
94
95       public Object getParent(Object child) {
96          if (child instanceof ASTNode) {
97             return ((ASTNode)child).getParent();
98          }
99          return null;
100      }
101
102      public Object [] getChildren(Object parent) {
103         if (parent instanceof ASTNode) {
104            OurVisitor myVisitor = new OurVisitor(1);
105            ((ASTNode) parent).accept(myVisitor);
106            return myVisitor.getChildren();
107         }
108         return new Object[0];
```

```
109          }
110
111          public boolean hasChildren(Object parent) {
112              if (parent instanceof ASTNode) {
113                  OurVisitor myVisitor = new OurVisitor(1);
114                  ((ASTNode) parent).accept(myVisitor);
115                  return myVisitor.getChildren().length>0;
116              }
117              return false;
118          }
119      }
120
121
122      /**
123       * Inner Class ViewLabelProvider
124       */
125      class ViewLabelProvider extends LabelProvider {
126
127          public String getText(Object obj) {
128              String[] className =
129                  obj.getClass().getName().split("\\.");
130              return className[className.length - 1]
131                  + ": " + obj.toString();
132          }
133          public Image getImage(Object obj) {
134              return null;
135          }
136      }
137
138
139      /**
140       * Source code of ASTView
141       */
142      public ASTView() {}
143
144
145      public void createPartControl(Composite parent) {
146          viewer = new TreeViewer
147              (parent, SWT.MULTI | SWT.H_SCROLL | SWT.V_SCROLL);
148          viewer.setContentProvider(new ViewContentProvider());
149          viewer.setLabelProvider(new ViewLabelProvider());
150          viewer.setSorter(null);
151          viewer.setInput(ResourcesPlugin.getWorkspace());
152
153          makeActions();
154          hookDoubleClickAction();
155          contributeToActionBars();
156      }
157
158
159      private void makeActions() {
160
161          sampleAction = new Action() {
162              public void run() {
163                  Shell shell = Display.getDefault().getActiveShell();
164                  MessageDialog.openInformation
165                      (shell, "Sample Action", "A message dialog.");
166              }
167          };
168          sampleAction.setImageDescriptor
169              (PlatformUI.getWorkbench().getSharedImages().
170              getImageDescriptor(ISharedImages.IMG_OBJS_INFO_TSK));
171
```

```
172            doubleClickAction = new Action() {
173               public void run() {
174                  IStructuredSelection selection =
175                     (IStructuredSelection) viewer.getSelection();
176                  ASTNode node = (ASTNode) selection.getFirstElement();
177                  try {
178                     IJavaElement elem =
179                        unit.getElementAt(node.getStartPosition());
180                     IEditorPart javaEditor = JavaUI.openInEditor(elem);
181                     JavaUI.revealInEditor(javaEditor, elem);
182                  } catch (JavaModelException e) {
183                     e.printStackTrace();
184                  } catch (PartInitException e) {
185                     e.printStackTrace();
186                  }
187               }
188            };
189         }
190
191
192         private void hookDoubleClickAction() {
193            viewer.addDoubleClickListener(new IDoubleClickListener() {
194               public void doubleClick(DoubleClickEvent event) {
195                  doubleClickAction.run();
196               }
197            });
198         }
199
200
201         private void contributeToActionBars() {
202            IActionBars bars = getViewSite().getActionBars();
203            bars.getToolBarManager().add(sampleAction);
204         }
205
206
207         public void setFocus() {
208            viewer.getControl().setFocus();
209         }
210
211
212         public void setInput(ICompilationUnit unit) {
213            this.unit = unit;
214            ASTParser c = ASTParser.newParser(AST.JLS2);
215            c.setSource(unit);
216            c.setResolveBindings(false);
217            CompilationUnit root =
218               (CompilationUnit) c.createAST(null);
219            viewer.setInput(root);
220         }
221      }
```

```
1    package astview.actions;
2
3    import org.eclipse.jdt.core.ICompilationUnit;
4    import org.eclipse.jface.action.IAction;
5    import org.eclipse.jface.viewers.ISelection;
6    import org.eclipse.jface.viewers.IStructuredSelection;
7    import org.eclipse.ui.IObjectActionDelegate;
8    import org.eclipse.ui.IViewPart;
```

Example 20.3

Class

UpdateViewAction

```
 9   import org.eclipse.ui.IWorkbenchPage;
10   import org.eclipse.ui.IWorkbenchPart;
11
12   import astview.views.ASTView;
13
14
15   public class UpdateViewAction implements IObjectActionDelegate {
16
17      private IWorkbenchPart workbenchPart;
18      private ISelection selection;
19
20      public void setActivePart(IAction action,
21                                IWorkbenchPart targetPart)
22      {
23         workbenchPart = targetPart;
24      }
25
26      public void run(IAction action) {
27         Object obj =
28            ((IStructuredSelection) selection).getFirstElement();
29         ICompilationUnit unit = (ICompilationUnit) obj;
30
31         IWorkbenchPage page =
32            workbenchPart.getSite().getWorkbenchWindow().
33            getActivePage();
34
35         IViewPart vp = page.findView("astview.views.ASTView");
36
37         if (vp instanceof ASTView) {
38            ((ASTView) vp).setInput(unit);
39         }
40
41      }
42
43      public void selectionChanged(IAction action,
44                                   ISelection selection)
45      {
46         this.selection = selection;
47      }
48   }
```

Bibliography

ADAMS, P. AND SOLOMON, M. 1995. An overview of the CAPITL software development environment. In *Software Configuration Management: Selected Papers / ICSE SCM-4 and SCM-5 Workshops*, J. Estublier, Ed. Lecture Notes in Computer Science, Vol. 1005. Springer-Verlag, Seattle, Washington, 1–34.

AHO, A. V. 1980. Pattern matching in strings. In *Formal Language Theory: Perspectives and Open Problems*, R. Book, Ed. Academic Press, London, UK, 325–347.

AHO, A. V., HOPCROFT, J. E., AND ULLMAN, J. D. 1983. *Data Structures and Algorithms*. Addison-Wesley, Reading, Massachusetts.

AHO, A. V., SETHI, R., AND ULLMAN, J. D. 1986. *Compilers*. Addison-Wesley.

AHO, A. V., SETHI, R., AND ULLMAN, J. D. 1988. *Compilerbau*. Addison-Wesley, Bonn, Germany.

ARNOLD, R. S. 1993. *Software Reengineering*. IEEE, Los Alamitos, California.

ATKINSON, D. C. AND GRISWOLD, W. G. 2001. Implementation techniques for efficient data-flow analysis of large programs. In *Proceedings of the International Conference on Software Maintenance (ICSM 2001)*, Florence, Italy. 52–61.

BABICH, W. A. 1986. *Software Configuration Management*. Addison Wesley, Reading, Massachusetts.

BAHLKE, R. AND SNELTING, G. 1986. The PSG system: From formal language definitions to interactive programming environments. *ACM Transactions on Programming Languages and Systems 8*, 4 (Oct.), 547–576.

BALZERT, H. 1996. *Lehrbuch der Software-Technik*, Vol. 1. Spektrum-Verlag, Heidelberg, Germany.

BALZERT, H. 1997. *Lehrbuch der Software-Technik*, Vol. 2. Spektrum-Verlag, Heidelberg, Germany.

BECK, K. AND GAMMA, E. 2003. *Contributing to Eclipse: Principles, Patterns, and Plugins*. Addison-Wesley.

BENTLEY, J. L. 1982. *Writing Efficient Programs*. Prentice Hall, Englewood Cliffs, New Jersey.

BERLINER, B. 1990. CVS II: Parallelizing software development. In *Proceedings of the 1990 Winter USENIX Conference*. Washington, DC.

BERZINS, V. 1994. Software merge: Semantics of combining changes to programs. *ACM Transactions on Software Engineering and Methodology 16*, 6 (Nov.), 1875–1903.

BERZINS, V. 1995. *Software Merging and Slicing*. IEEE Computer Society Press, Los Alamitos, California.

BINKLEY, D. AND GALLAGHER, K. 1996. Program slicing. *Advances in Computers 43*, 1–50.

BINKLEY, D., HORWITZ, S., AND REPS, T. 1995. Program integration for languages with procedure calls. *ACM Transactions on Software Engineering and Methodology 4*, 1 (Jan.), 3–35.

CHRISTIANSEN, T. AND TORKINGTON, N. 1998. *Perl Cookbook*, 1st ed. O'REILLY, Sebastopol, California.

CIMITILE, A. AND MÜLLER, H. A., Eds. 1996. *4th Workshop on Program Comprehension*. IEEE Computer Science Press, Los Alamitos, California.

CLEMM, G. M. 1988. The Odin specification language. In *Proc. of the International Workshop on Software Version and Configuration Control*, J. F. H. Winkler, Ed. Teubner Verlag, Stuttgart, Grassau, 145–158.

CONRADI, R., Ed. 1997. *Proceedings of the 7th International Workshop on Software Configuration Management*. Lecture Notes in Computer Science, Vol. 1235. Springer-Verlag, Boston, Massachusetts.

CONRADI, R. AND WESTFECHTEL, B. 1996. Version models for software configuration management. Tech. Rep. AIB 96-10, RWTH Aachen. Oct.

COURINGTON, W. 1989. The network software environment. Tech. Rep. FE 197-0, Sun Microsystems, Inc. Feb.

DAUM, B. 2004. *Beginning Eclipse 3 for Java Developers*. John Wiley & Sons.

DETLEFS, D. L., RUSTAN, K., LEINO, M., NELSON, G., AND SAXE, J. B. 1998. Extended static checking. Tech. Rep. Research Report 159, Compaq Systems Research Center.

DONNELLY, C. AND STALLMAN, R. 1995. *Bison – The YACC-compatible Parser Generator*, 1.25 ed. Free Software Foundation, Inc. Distributed with Bison.

DUBY, C. K., MEYERS, S., AND REISS, S. P. 1992. CCEL: A metalanguage for C++. In *Proceedings: USENIX C++ Technical Conference*. Portland, Oregon, August 10–13, 1992; USENIX Association, Ed. USENIX, Berkeley, California, 99–115.

EMMERICH, W., SCHÄFER, W., AND WELSH, J. 1993. Databases for software engineering environments – the goal has not yet been attained. In *Proceedings of the 4th European Software Engineering Conference*, I. Sommerville and M. Paul, Eds. Lecture Notes in Computer Science, Vol. 717. Springer-Verlag, Garmisch-Partenkirchen, 145–162.

ESTUBLIER, J., Ed. 1995. *Software Configuration Management: Selected Papers / ICSE SCM-4 and SCM-5 Workshops*. Lecture Notes in Computer Science, Vol. 1005. Springer-Verlag, Seattle, Washington.

ESTUBLIER, J., Ed. 1999. *Proceedings of the 9th Symposium on System Configuration Management*. Lecture Notes in Computer Science, Vol. 1675. Springer-Verlag, Toulouse, France.

ESTUBLIER, J. AND CASALLAS, R. 1994. The Adele configuration manager. In *Configuration Management*. W. F. Tichy, Ed. Trends in Software, Vol. 2. John Wiley & Sons, Chichester, UK, Chapter 4, 99–133.

EVANS, D. 1996. Static detection of dynamic memory errors. In *Proceedings of the ACM SIGPLAN Conference on Programming Language Design and Implementation*. ACM Press, New York, 44–53.

EVANS, D. AND LAROCHELLE, D. 2002a. Improving security using extensible lightweight static analysis. *IEEE Software* 19(1): 42–51.

EVANS, D. AND LAROCHELLE, D. 2002b. *Splint Manual*. Secure Programming Group, University of Virginia.

FEILER, P. H., Ed. 1991. *Proceedings of the 3rd International Workshop on Software Configuration Management*. ACM Press, Trondheim, Norway.

FELDMAN, S. I. 1979. Make – A program for maintaining computer programs. *Software – Practice and Experience 9*, 255–265.

FENLASON, J. AND STALLMAN, R. 1997. *GNU gprof – The GNU Profiler.* Free Software Foundation, Inc. Distributed with GNU gprof.

FOSDICK, L. D. AND OSTERWEIL, L. J. 1976. Data flow analysis in software reliability. *ACM Computing Surveys 8,* 3 (Sept.), 305–330.

FOWLER, G., KORN, D., AND RAO, H. 1994. *n*-DFS: The multiple dimensional file system. In *Configuration Management.* W. F. Tichy, Ed. Trends in Software, Vol. 2. John Wiley & Sons, Chichester, UK, Chapter 5, 135–154.

FRIENDLY, L. 1995. The design of distributed hyperlinked programming documentation. In *Proceedings of the International Workshop on Hypermedia Design (IWHD'95).* Montpellier, France, June 1-2, 1995. Springer-Verlag, 151–173.

GAMMA, E., HELM, R., JOHNSON, R., AND VLISSIDES, J. 1994. *Design Patterns: Elements of Reusable Object-Oriented Software.* Addison-Wesley, Reading, Massachusetts.

GHEZZI, C., JAZAYERI, M., AND MANDRIOLI, D. 1991. *Fundamentals of Software Engineering.* Prentice Hall.

GOLDBERG, A. 1983. *Smalltalk 80: The Interactive Programming Environment.* Addison-Wesley.

GRAHAM, S., KESSLER, P., AND MCKUSICK, M. 1982. gprof: A call graph execution profiler. In *Proceedings of the SIGPLAN '82 Symposium on Compiler Construction.* ACM SIGPLAN Notices, Vol. 17(6). ACM, 120–126.

GRAHAM, S., KESSLER, P., AND MCKUSICK, M. 1983. An execution profiler for modular programs. *Software – Practice and Experience 13,* 671–685.

GULLA, B., KARLSSON, E.-A., AND YEH, D. 1991. Change-oriented version descriptions in EPOS. *Software Engineering Journal 6,* 6 (Nov.), 378–386.

GUNTER, C. A. 1996. Abstracting dependencies between software configuration items. In *Proceedings of the 4th ACM SIGSOFT Symposium on the Foundations of Software Engineering,* D. Garlan, Ed. ACM Software Engineering Notes, Vol. 21 (6). ACM Press, San Francisco, California, 167–178.

HIMSTEDT, T. AND MÄTZEL, K. 1999. *Mit Python Programmieren.* dpunkt.verlag, Heidelberg, Germany.

HOFFNER, T., KAMKAR, M., AND FRITZSON, P. 1996. Evaluation of program slicing tools. In *2nd International Workshop on Automated and Algorithmic Debugging (AADEBUG)*, Saint Malo, France, 51–69.

HOPCROFT, J. E., MOTWANI, R., AND ULLMAN, J. D. 2000. *Introduction to Automata Theory, Languages, and Computation*, 2nd ed. Pearson Addison Wesley.

HOPPER, G. M. 1981. The first bug. *Annals of the History of Computing 3,* 3 (July), 285–286.

HORWITZ, S., PRINS, J., AND REPS, T. 1989. Integrating noninterfering versions of programs. *ACM Transactions on Programming Languages and Systems 11,* 3 (July), 345–387.

HUNT, J. J., VO, K.-P., AND TICHY, W. F. 1996. An empirical study of delta algorithms. In *Proceedings of the 6th International Workshop on Software Configuration Management*, I. Sommerville, Ed. Lecture Notes in Computer Science, Vol. 1167. Springer-Verlag, Berlin, Germany, 49–66.

HUNT, J. W. AND McILROY, M. D. 1976. An algorithm for differential file comparison. Computing Science Technical Report 41, AT&T Bell Laboratories, Murray Hill, New Jersey. June.

IEEE 1988. *IEEE Guide to Software Configuration Management*. IEEE, New York. ANSI/IEEE Standard 1042-1987.

IEEE 1990. *IEEE Guide to Software Configuration Management Plans*. IEEE, New York. ANSI/IEEE Standard 828-1990.

JEFFREY, E. F. F. 2002. *Mastering Regular Expressions*, 2nd ed. O'Reilly & Associates.

JOHNSON, S. C. 1977. *Lint, a C Program Checker*. Computer Science Technical Report 65, Bell Laboratories, Murray Hill, New Jersey.

KERNIGHAN, B. W. AND PIKE, R. 1999. *The Practice of Programming*. Addison-Wesley, Reading, Massachusetts.

KERNIGHAN, B. W. AND PLAUGER, P. J. 1974. *The Elements of Programming Style*. Bell Telephone Laboratories, Murray Hill, New Jersey.

KIFER, M. 1996. *Ediff User's Manual*. Free Software Foundation, Inc. Distributed with Emacs.

KLEENE, S. C. 1956. Representation of events in nerve nets and finite automata. In *Automata Studies, Annals of Math. Studies 34*, C. Shannon and J. McCarthy, Eds. Princeton University Press, Princeton, New Jersey, 3–40.

KOLAWA, A. 2002. Using bug-tracking systems as idea repositories. *stickyminds.com*.

LEBLANG, D. B. 1994. The CM challenge: Configuration management that works. In *Configuration Management*, W. F. Tichy, Ed. Trends in Software, Vol. 2. John Wiley & Sons, Chichester, UK, Chapter 1, 1–37.

LEVINE, J. R., MASON, T., AND BROWN, D. 1992. *Lex & Yacc*, 2nd ed. O'Reilly & Associates.

LIBES, D. 1990. Expect: Curing those uncontrollable fits of interaction. In *Proceedings of the Summer 1990 USENIX Conference*. Anaheim, California. Distributed with DejaGnu.

LIBES, D. 1992. Regression testing and conformance testing interactive programs. In *Proceedings of the Summer 1992 USENIX Conference*. San Antonio, Texas. Distributed with DejaGnu.

LIBES, D. 1994. *Exploring Expect*. O'Reilly, Sebastopol, California.

LIEBERMAN, H. 1997. The debugging scandal and what to do about it. *Communications of the ACM 40*, 4 (Apr.), 26–29.

LIGGESMEYER, P. 1990. *Modultest und Modulverifikation: State of the Art*. Angewandte Informatik. BI-Wissenschafts Verlag, Mannheim, Berlin, Zürich.

LINK, J. 2002. *Unit Tests mit Java: der Test-first-Ansatz*. dpunkt.verlag, Heidelberg, Germany. Unter Mitarbeit von Peter Fröhlich.

LYLE, J. R., WALLACE, D. R., GRAHAM, J. R., GALLAGHER, K. B., POOLE, J. P., AND BINKLEY, D. W. 1995. Unravel: A case tool to assist evaluation of high integrity software. Tech. Rep. 5691, National Institute of Standards and Technology, Gaithersburg, Madison. Aug.

MACKENZIE, D., EGGERT, P., AND STALLMAN, R. 1993. *Comparing and Merging Files*. Free Software Foundation, Inc. Distributed with GNU diffutils.

MACKENZIE, D., MCGRATH, R., AND FRIEDMAN, N. 1994. *Autoconf – Creating Automatic Configuration Scripts*. Free Software Foundation, Inc. Distributed with GNU autoconf.

MAGNUSSON, B., Ed. 1998. *Proceedings of the 8th Symposium on System Configuration Management*. Lecture Notes in Computer Science, Vol. 1439. Springer-Verlag, Brussels, Belgium.

MAHLER, A. 1994. Variants: Keeping things together and telling them apart. In *Configuration Management*, W. F. Tichy, Ed. Trends in Software, Vol. 2. John Wiley & Sons, Chichester, UK, Chapter 3, 39–69.

MAHLER, A. AND LAMPEN, A. 1988. An integrated toolset for engineering software configurations. In *Proceedings of the 2nd SDE*, P. Henderson, Ed. Boston, Massachusetts, 191–200. Appeared as *ACM SIGSOFT Software Engineering Notes* 13(5) or *ACM SIGPLAN Notices* 24(2).

MCCONNELL, S. 1993. *Code Complete – A Practical Handbook of Software Construction*. Microsoft Press.

MENAPACE, J., KINGDON, J., AND MACKENZIE, D. 1998. *The "stabs" Debug Format*. Cygnus Support. Distributed with GDB.

MEYER, B. 1992. Applying "design by contract". *Computer 25,* 10 (Oct.), 40–51.

MEYERS, S. 1997. *Effective C++*, 2nd ed. Addison-Wesley, Reading, Massachusetts.

MILLER, P. 1997. Recursive make considered harmful. Available via http://www.canb.auug.org.au/~millerp/.

MILLER, W. AND MYERS, E. 1985. A file comparison program. *Software – Practice and Experience 15,* 11 (Nov.), 1025–1040.

MIRRER, B. 2000. Organize your problem tracking system: cleaning up your bug database can be as easy as organizing your sock drawer. *Software Testing Quality Engineering Sept./Oct.*, 34–39.

NAGL, M., Ed. 1996. *Building Tightly Integrated Software Development Environments: The IPSEN Approach*. Lecture Notes in Computer Science, Vol. 1170. Springer-Verlag.

OBJECT TECHNOLOGY INTERNATIONAL. 2003. Eclipse platform technical overview. White Paper. Available online at www.eclipse.org.

OLENDER, K. M. AND OSTERWEIL, L. J. 1992. Interprocedural static analysis of sequencing constraints. *ACM Transactions on Software Engineering and Methodology 1,* 1 (Jan.), 21–52.

ONOMA, A. K., TSAI, W.-T., POONAWALA, M. H., AND SUGANUMA, H. 1998. Regression testing in an industrial environment. *Communications of the ACM 41,* 5 (May), 81–86.

OSTERWEIL, L. J. AND FOSDICK, L. D. 1976. DAVE – a validation, error detection and documentation system for Fortran programs. *Software – Practice and Experience 6,* 4, 832–838.

OTTENSTEIN, K. J. AND OTTENSTEIN, L. M. 1984. The program dependence graph in a software development environment. In *Proceedings of the ACM SIGSOFT/SIGPLAN Software Engineering Symposium on Practical Software Development Environments*. 177–184. ACM SIGPLAN Notices 19(5).

OUSTERHOUT, J. K. 1994. *Tcl and the Tk Toolkit.* Addison-Wesley, Reading, Massachusetts.

PERRY, D. E. 1989. The Inscape environment. In *Proceedings of the 11th International Conference on Software Engineering*. Pittsburgh, Pennsylvania, 2–12.

REICHENBERGER, C. 1989. Orthogonal version management. In *Proceedings of the 2nd International Workshop on Software Configuration Management*, W. F. Tichy, Ed. ACM Press, Princeton, New Jersey, 137–140.

REPS, T. W. AND TEITELBAUM, T. 1988. *The Synthesizer Generator: A System for Constructing Language–Based Editors.* Springer-Verlag.

RICH, A. AND SOLOMON, M. 1991. A logic-based approach to system modelling. In *Proceedings of the 3rd International Workshop on Software Configuration Management*, P. H. Feiler, Ed. ACM Press, Trondheim, Norway, 84–93.

RITCHIE, D. M. 1993. The development of the C language. In ACM SIGPLAN HOPL-II. 2nd ACM SIGPLAN History of Programming Languages Conference (Preprints), ACM, Ed. *ACM SIGPLAN Notices 28*, 3, 201–208.

ROCHKIND, M. J. 1975. The source code control system. *IEEE Transactions on Software Engineering SE-1,* 4 (Dec.), 364–370.

ROSENBERG, J. B. 1996. *How Debuggers Work.* John Wiley & Sons.

SAVOYE, R. 1996. *The DejaGnu Testing Framework.* Free Software Foundation, Inc. Distributed with DejaGnu.

SCHMERL, B. D. AND MARLIN, C. D. 1995. Designing configuration management facilities for dynamically bound systems. In *Software Configuration Management: Selected Papers / ICSE SCM-4 and SCM-5 Workshops*, J. Estublier, Ed. Lecture Notes in Computer Science, Vol. 1005. Springer-Verlag, Seattle, Washington, 88–100.

SCHWANKE, R. W. AND KAISER, G. E. 1988. Smarter recompilation. *ACM Transactions on Programming Languages and Systems 10,* 4 (Oct.), 627–632.

SEIWALD, C. 1996. Inter-file branching – a practical method for representing variants. In *Proceedings of the 6th International Workshop on Software Configuration Management*, I. Sommerville, Ed. Lecture Notes in Computer Science, Vol. 1167. Springer-Verlag, Berlin, Germany, 67–75.

SEWELL, W. 1989. *Weaving a Program.* Van Nostrand Reinhold.

SHAO, Z. AND APPEL, A. W. 1993. Smartest recompilation. In *Proceedings of the 20th Annual ACM Symposium on Principles of Programming Languages*, S. L. Graham, Ed. ACM Press, Charleston, South Carolina, 439–450.

SHAVOR, S., D'ANJOU, J., FAIRBROTHER, S., KEHN, D., KELLERMAN, J., AND McCARTHY, P. 2003. *The Java Developer's Guide to Eclipse.* Addison-Wesley, Reading, Massachusetts.

SOMMERVILLE, I., Ed. 1996a. *Proceedings of the 6th International Workshop on Software Configuration Management.* Lecture Notes in Computer Science, Vol. 1167. Springer-Verlag, Berlin, Germany.

SOMMERVILLE, I. 1996b. *Software Engineering*, 5th ed. Addison-Wesley.

STALLMAN, R. 1988a. *GNU Emacs Manual*, 6th ed. Free Software Foundation, Inc. Distributed with Emacs.

STALLMAN, R. 1998b. *Using and Porting GNU CC.* Free Software Foundation, Inc. Distributed with GNU CC.

STALLMAN, R. AND McGRATH, R. 1995. *GNU Make – A Program for Directing Recompilation*, 0.48 ed. Free Software Foundation, Inc. Distributed with GNU Make.

STALLMAN, R. M. AND PESCH, R. H. 1998. *Debugging with GDB*, 5th ed. Free Software Foundation, Inc. Distributed with GDB 4.17.

STROUSTRUP, B. 1997. *The C++ Programming Language*, 3rd ed. Addison-Wesley.

Sun Microsystems, Inc. 2000. *How to Write Doc Comments for the Javadoc Tool.* Sun Microsystems, Inc.

Sun Microsystems, Inc. 2002. *javadoc – The Java API Documentation Generator.* Sun Microsystems, Inc.

TICHY, W. F. 1984. The string-to-string correction problem with block moves. *ACM Transactions on Computer Systems 2,* 4 (Nov.), 309–321.

TICHY, W. F. 1985. RCS – A system for version control. *Software – Practice and Experience 15,* 7 (July), 637–654.

TICHY, W. F. 1986. Smart recompilation. *ACM Transactions on Software Engineering and Methodology 8,* 3 (July), 273–291.

TICHY, W. F., Ed. 1989. *Proceedings of the 2nd International Workshop on Software Configuration Management.* ACM Press, Princeton, New Jersey.

TICHY, W. F., Ed. 1994. *Configuration Management.* Trends in Software, Vol. 2. John Wiley & Sons, Chichester, UK.

TICHY, W. F. 1995. Software-Konfigurationsmanagement: Wie, wann, was, warum? In *Proceedings of the Softwaretechnik 95.* Softwaretechnik-Trends, Vol. 15(3). GI, Braunschweig, 17–23.

TIP, F. 1995. A survey of program slicing techniques. *Journal of Programming Languages 3,* 3 (Sept.), 121–189.

VAN ROSSUM, G. 1999. *Python Tutorial*, 1.5.2 ed. www.python.org.

WALL, L. 1988. *PATCH –Apply a DIFF File to an Original.* Free Software Foundation, Inc. Distributed with GNU patch.

WALL, L., CHRISTIANSEN, T., AND SCHWARTZ, R. L. 1996. *Programming Perl*, 2nd ed. O'Reilly & Associates, Inc., Sebastopol, California.

WARREN, I. AND SOMMERVILLE, I. 1995. Dynamic configuration abstraction. In *Proceedings of the 5th European Software Engineering Conference,* W. Schäfer and P. Botella, Eds. Lecture Notes in Computer Science, Vol. 989. Springer-Verlag, Sitges, Spain, 173–190.

WEISER, M. 1982. Programmers use slices when debugging. *Communications of the ACM 25,* 7, 446–452.

WESTFECHTEL, B. 1991. Structure-oriented merging of revisions of software documents. In *Proceedings of the 3rd International Workshop on Software Configuration Management*, P. H. Feiler, Ed. ACM Press, Trondheim, Norway, 86–79.

WHITGIFT, D. 1991. *Methods and Tools for Software Configuration Management.* John Wiley & Sons, Chichester, UK.

WILSON, C. AND OSTERWEIL, L. J. 1985. Omega – A data flow analysis tool for the C programming language. *IEEE Transactions on Software Engineering 11,* 9, 832–838.

WINKLER, J. F. H., Ed. 1988. *Proc. of the International Workshop on Software Version and Configuration Control.* Teubner Verlag, Stuttgart, Grassau.

WU, S. AND MANBER, U. 1992. agrep – A fast approximate pattern-matching tool. In *Proceedings of the Winter 1992 USENIX Conference*. San Francisco, California, January 20 – January 24, 1992,; USENIX Association, Ed. USENIX, Berkeley, California, 153–162.

YANG, W., HORWITZ, S., AND REPS, T. 1992. A program integration algorithm that accommodates semantics-preserving transformations. *ACM Transactions on Software Engineering and Methodology 1*, 3 (July), 310–354.

ZELLER, A. 1998. Versioning system models through description logic. In *Proceedings of the 8th Symposium on System Configuration Management*, B. Magnusson, Ed. Lecture Notes in Computer Science, Vol. 1439. Springer-Verlag, Brussels, Belgium, 127–132.

ZELLER, A. 1999. Yesterday, my program worked. Today, it does not. Why? In *Proceedings of the ESEC/FSE'99 –7th European Software Engineering Conference / 7th ACM SIGSOFT Symposium on the Foundations of Software Engineering*. Lecture Notes in Computer Science, Vol. 1687. Springer-Verlag, Toulouse, France, 253–267.

ZELLER, A. 2000. *Debugging with DDD*, 1st ed. Universität Passau. Distributed with DDD.

ZELLER, A. AND LÜTKEHAUS, D. 1996. DDD – A free graphical front-end for UNIX debuggers. *ACM SIGPLAN Notices 31*, 1 (Jan.), 22–27.

ZELLER, A. AND SNELTING, G. 1997. Unified versioning through feature logic. *ACM Transactions on Software Engineering and Methodology 6*, 4 (Oct.), 398–441.

Index

abstract data type, 311–312
abstraction barrier, 311
abstract syntax tree, 20, 354
aclocal, 154
action
    in YACC, 91
ADA, 233
    grammar for ANTLR,
       118
ADELE, 40, 42
AEGIS, 61
AGREP, 83
alias detection
    in DDD, 272
ANT, 139, 174
    and ECLIPSE, 358
antithesis, 250
ANTLR, 107–120, 174
    Specification, 108
antlr.Tool, 109
Apache
    as version server, 58
arithmetic
    in Tcl, 180
    in YACC, 86–95
ASPECTJ, 341
assert, 222, *see also* assertion
assertion
    and specification, 308–310
    for debugging, 252
    in tests, 221–223
AST, *see* abstract syntax tree
autoconf, 153
AUTOCONF, 150–155,
       173–174
    and MAKE, 151
autoheader, 153
AUTOMAKE, 155
automation
    and intuition, 358

automaton
    finite ∼, 68, *see also* NFA
autoscan, 154
auxiliary functions
    in YACC, 91–93

backward slicing, 318
basic block, 305
bc, 205, 209
binary pool, 136–137
BISON, 97, *see also* YACC, 105
BITKEEPER, 58
BOUNDSCHECKER, 278
box
    for data representation, 271
branch, 30, 50
branch coverage, 291
branching, 31, 33, 37, 155
break, 260, 266
breakpoint, 260
    conditional ∼, 266
    ∼ instructions, 269
    ∼ register, 269
buffer overflows, 310–311
bug report, *see* problem report
bug tracking, *see* problem tracking
BUGZILLA, 238–247
build.xml, 174
buildfile, 137–138
building, *see* construction
buttons
    in Tk, 185–186

C preprocessor, *see* CPP
C++
    assertion, 222
    free store, 272
    grammar for ANTLR, 118
C++TEST, 300
C-FORGE, 360
call stack, 263

CAPITL, 142
Capture/Replay, 218
cat, 74
change
    determine ~s in ECLIPSE, 340
change, 10
    apply, 21
    as extensions, 30
    as fixes, 30
    coordinate, 27
    determine, 24
        in RCS, 37
    effects, 205, *see also* regression
        test
    failure-inducing ~, 256
    in binary files, 14
    reconstruction after ~, *see*
        construction
    applying
        in RCS, 37
change context, 17
integrate
    change, *see* integration
change log, 33–35, 37
change time
    in MAKE, 127
determine
    changes, 10
using
    changes, 13
characters
    concrete, 71
character strings
    in Tcl, 180
check in, 28
check out, 28, 29
    in CVS, 48, 51
    in MAKE, 130
    in RCS, 29–30
        with lock, 32
CHECKSTYLE, 296–299
    and ECLIPSE, 343
chop, 325
ci, 32, 33, 48
CLEARCASE, 39, 42, 57, 61, 340
    determining dependencies,
        135–136, 141
clear, 262
CLOVER, 294
co, 29–30
    in MAKE, 130

with -l, 32
with -r, 47
CODEBEAMER, 361
code smells, 297, 299
CODESURFER, 327
CODEWARRIOR, 360
CODEWIZARD, 300
command
    in DIFF, 10
    in Tcl, 179
comments, 160–162
comparison
    structure-based ~, 341
component, 45–46
    dependent ~, 124
    derived ~, 123
component test, 221–233
configuration, 27
    dynamic ~, 61
    identify, 27
    name, *see* configuration tag
    reconstruct, 27, 31
    reconstruction, 137
    threaded representation, 46
configuration file
    read in, 67
    reading, 85
configuration management, 9, *see also*
        software ~
configuration name
    in problem reports, 237
configuration script, 150
    creation, 152–154
    use, 150–152
configuration tag
    in CVS, 49–50
    in RCS, 46–47
configure, 150, *see also*
        configuration script
conflict
    between changes, 27
    between modifications, 55
    between parser actions,
        97–101
    in LEX, 77
    reduce/reduce ~, 99–100
    shift/reduce ~, 97–99
consistency
    of configurations, 45
construction, 123–142
    incremental, 125

program ~, *see* construction
    script, 124
cont, 264
context
    of changes, 17
context-format
    in DIFF, 17
CONTINUUS/CM, 61
control dependence, 320–321
control flow, 305
control flow graph
    in LINT, 305
control flow graph, 288, 305
    in UNRAVEL, 320
cooperation strategy, 53, 56
    in ECLIPSE, 340
coordination
    of changes, 27
core, 267, 309
coverage, 288–290
CPP, 146–147
    and debugging instructions, 252
    Macros, 146–147
CPPUNIT, 223, 228, 232, 279
cvs add, 50
CVS archive, 48–57
cvs checkout, 48, 61
cvs commit, 48–50, 62
CVS, 47–58, 61–63, 119, 237, 238
cvs diff, 62
cvs edit, 55–56
cvs import, 61
cvs init, 61
cvs release, 50–51
cvs remove, 52–53
cvs tag, 49–50
cvs update, 54
cvs watch, 56
    and ECLIPSE, 339–342, 347, 358
    and RCS, 47–48
    check out, 48, 51
    cooperation strategy, 53, 56
    integrating modifications, 55
    mode of operation, 51–53
    parallel program development,
        53–56
    user interface, 57
    watching, 55–56
.cvsignore, 63
CVSROOT, 56–57
CYGWIN, 3

data
    representing graphically, 271–272
database
    in SCM, 40
data dependence, 320–322
data display debugger, *see* DDD
data flow analysis, 305, 347
    in LINT, 304–308
    in UNRAVEL, 319
data flow equations, 306
data flow problems, 317
data flow set, 305, 321
DDD, 256–265, 294
    internals, 271–272
DEBUG, 252
debugger, 256–272
    in ECLIPSE, 348
debugging, 249–274
    with ECLIPSE, 348–350
debugging information, 258, 269–270
debugging instructions, 252
DEJAGNU, 212–218, 279
    initialization script, 213
    test output, 212
    test script, 214
déja vu, 212
delta, 37, *see also* change
delta debugging, 219
dependence
    of components, 124
dependency
    automatically determining,
        133–135
    of components used, 133
    of construction tools, 133
dependency graph, 123
    extended, 134
derived components, 123
design documents, 159
design patterns, 143
development environment, 335, 335, *see
        also* ECLIPSE
dialog
    programmed, 207
dice, 325
DIFF, 9–26, 62
    algorithm, 21–24
    and AGREP, 83
    context-format, 17
    in RCS, 37
    optimization, 23–24

diff, 11–13, 17
    with -r, 12
distance
    for character strings, 21
distance matrix, 22
DocCheck, 164
doclet, 164, 170
DocLint, 164
documentation, 159–171
down, 263
DOXYGEN, 166–168, 170, 174
dynamic analysis, 301

ECLIPSE, 335–358
    architecture, 350
    CHECKSTYLE in ~, 343
    CVS in ~, 340–342
    editors, 337–338
    hooks, 340
    integration of tools, 353–354
    JAVA editor, 342–343
    markers, 337
    perspectives, 339
    plug-ins, *see* plug-in
    program comprehension, 343–347
    projects, 336–337
    refactoring, 347–348
    resources, 337
    version control, 339–342
    views, 338–339
    workbench, 337–339, 350
    workspace, 336–337, 350
EDIFF, 16, 26
editor
    in ECLIPSE, 337–338
EGREP, 71
ELECTRIC FENCE, 273
EMACS, 16, 57, 197, 361
enableassertions, 223, 255
EPOS, 60
expect action, 207
expect, 207, 208
EXPECT, 207–218
    and FTP, 207–209
    in regression tests, 209–212
extension point, 351
Extreme programming, 231

facet
    variant ~, 144
FAIL, 212, 250

fail, 210
Fibonacci function, 304
file system
    virtual ~, 39
finish, 263
finite automaton, 68, *see also* NFA
fix, 249
fix point iteration, 307
fixture
    test ~, 227–228
flexibility
    of configurations, 45
FORTRAN, 79, 111, 112, 315
forward engineering, 343
forward slicing, 318
FTP, 207–209
function
    in Tcl, 181

GCC, 128, 151, 219, 288, 303
    Variables, 149
GCOV, 288–292, 329
    internals, 290–291
    testing with ~, 291–292
GDB, 219, 256–267
    internals, 268–270
GIMP, 197
GLR parser, 101–103, 105
GNU
    C compiler, *see* GCC
    debugger, *see* GDB
GPROF, 284–288, 290–292
    flat profile, 285–286
    internals, 290–291
    setting up, 285
    structured profile, 287–288
    testing with ~, 291–292
grammar, 77, 85–88
    context free, 86, 113
graphical data representation, 271
GREP, 71
GUI builder, 189
GUILE, 197

hashcode
    in DIFF, 21
HASKELL, 197
heap
    faults, 272–274
Hello, 61–63
history, *see* revision tree

HTML, 75
hypotheses, 249–251
    refining, 250
    testing, 249
hypothesis
    choice, 251

ICE, 60
ident, 35
identifying versions and
            components, 27
IMAKE, 150
implementation, 45
instrumented code, 290
INSURE++, 278, 294
integrating
    in CVS, 55
integration, 14–21
    automatic ∼, 16–21
    manual, 14–16
    of changes in ECLIPSE, 340
    of tools in ECLIPSE, 353–354
    semantic ∼, 20–21
    syntactical ∼, 19–20
    three-way ∼, 15–21
    two-way ∼, 15
interact, 208
interface, 45, 143
interfile branching, 61
invariants
    and assertions, 253
IPSEN, 26

javac, 137–139, 141
JAVADOC, 162–166, 170, 174
    and ANT, 137
    and CHECKSTYLE, 296
JAVA
    assertion, 222
    code conventions, 295, 296, 299
    creating interfaces
        with SpecTcl, 189
    Development Tools, see JDT
JCOVERAGE, 294
JDT, 342–350
jikes, 141
JTEST, 300
jump, 267
JUNIT, 223–229, 279
    and ECLIPSE, 347, 358
    und ANT, 137

keyword
    in RCS, 34
Kleen closure, 70

LALR parser, 105
LATEX, 35
LCS, see longest common subsequence
lex, 74
LEX, 72–81, 105, 119–120,
            173
    and AUTOCONF, 173
    and MAKE, 173–174
    and YACC, 93–95
    as scanner generator, 81
    conflict, 77
    context, 77–80
    limitations, 85–86
    overlapping rules, 80
    specification, 73–81
    states, see start states
life cycle
    of a problem, 241–244
LINT, 301–308
    control flow graph, 305
    data flow analysis, 304–308
    type checking, 301–303
LINUX
    and programming tools, 3
LISP, 197, 361
Literate Programming, 168–170
LL parser, 105, 113
lock
    in RCS, 31–32
        avoid, 33
longest common subsequence, 21
lookahead, 96
LR parser, 95, 105

M4, 145–146
    in AUTOCONF, 153
    in autoheader, 153
MacOS
    script ability, 218
macro
    in CPP, 146–147
    in M4, 145
main function
    in Tcl, 184, 201
main path, 30, see also branching
maintenance
    and revisions, 27

maintenance phase, 205
Makefile, 125–133
    created by AUTOCONF, 151
    template, 145
MAKE, 125–137, 173–174
    and AUTOCONF, 151
    change time, 127
    determining dependency, 133–135
    files, *see* Makefile
    implicit rule, 129
    implicit variable, 129
    recursion, 131–133
    rule, 125
    targets, 125
    variables, 128
MAKE variable, 132–133
MALLOC_CHECK, 273
memory leak, 274
memory management, 312–314
METACONFIG, 150
minimum coverage, 291
MODULA-2, 82, 193, 311
modularization, 205

NDEBUG, 255
n-DFS, 40, 42
NETBEANS, 360
NFA
    algorithms, 69
NFA, 68–69
nonterminals, 86
notification
    in BUGZILLA, 240
notifying
    during modification, 55
NSE, 60

object file, 123
object-oriented programming, 205
ODIN, 135, 141
off by one errors, 311
option
    in Tk, 186–187
OTI, 335

parser, 85, 86
PASS, 210, 212, 250
PATCH, 13–14, 16–19, 26
    in RCS, 37
patch, 13
pattern rule, 130

pcl-cvs, 57
PDG, 320
    calculation, 320–323
    slicing, 323–324
PERFORCE, 39, 61, 340
PERL, 72, 150, 191
permanent variants $\sim$
    in CVS and RCS, 155
perspective
    in ECLIPSE, 339
plug-in, 351–352
porting
    and variants, 28
postmortem debugging, 267
precedence declarations, 100–101
print, 260, 261, 263
problem database, *see* BUGZILLA
problem list, 238
problem management
    classification, 238–240
problem report, 236–238
problem tracking, 235–247
    and tests, 246–247
    life cycle, 241–244
    managing $\sim$, 244–246
/proc file system, 268
production, 86, *see also* rule
profiling, 283–294
program analysis, *see* profiling, static
        analysis
program comprehension
    with ECLIPSE, 343–347
program construction, *see* construction
program dependency graphs, 21
program documentation, 159–171
program generator, 85
programming guidelines, 295–297
program profile, 284–288
    flat, 285–286
    structured, 287–288
program slicing, 317–326
program state
    access via debugger, 268–270
    after crash, 267
    change, 256
    changing, 255
    changing
        in the debugger, 263–265
    printing
        in the debugger, 260–262
    representing graphically, 271–272

validating ∼
  in the debugger, 266–267
  with assertions, 252–255
  with tools, 272–274
  watching, 266–267
program status
  outputting
    with instructions, 252
projects
  in ECLIPSE, 336–337
PROLOG, 197
prototype, 177–191
  horizontal ∼, 178, 189
  vertical ∼, 178
pseudo target, 131
PSG, 360
ptrace, 268–269
PURECOVERAGE, 294
PURIFY, 278
PVCS, 61, 340
PYTHON, 72, 193

QUANTIFY, 294

RAZOR, 61
RCS archive, 28, see also RCS file
RCS directory, 28
RCS file, 28, 35–38
  in CVS, 51
  in MAKE, 130
RCS, 28–41, 119, 340
  and CVS, 47–48
  and DIFF, 37
  and PATCH, 37
  branches, 30–31
  check out, 29–30
  determining changes, 37
  file format, 35–38
  keyword, 34
  lock, 31–32
    avoid, 33
  log, 33–35
  saving versions, 28–30
  tagging configurations, 47
  applying changes, 37
  variants, 30–31
rcs, 47
reconstruction
  of configurations, 27, 31,
    137
recursive descent, 113

reduce, 95
  ∼/∼ conflict, 99–100
  shift/∼-conflict, 97–99
reducing, 95
refactoring, 347–348
  in ECLIPSE, 347–348
  requirements, 347
reference manual, 160
registry, 150
regression test, 205–218, 229
regular expression
  in EXPECT, 219
  in Tcl, 182
regular expressions, 70, see also LEX,
    69–72
removal of functionality, 255
  in the debugger, 267
report
  in BUGZILLA, 235
repository, see version archive
return, 267
reuse, 178
reverse engineering, 343
revision, 27–42, 45–62
  archive, see version archive
  tag ∼, 46
revision chain, 29, see also revision tree,
    30, 37
revision number, 28
revision tree, 29
revision history, see revisions tree
rlog, 34
rule
  in Makefile, 125
  in MAKE
    implicit, 129
  in YACC, 86, 90–91
run, 260, 265
runtest, 212
runtime, 283–284

sample.c, 256
scanner, 81, see also LEX
SCCB
  see software change control board,
    246
SCCS-file, 38–39
SCCS, 38–39, 41
  file format, 38–39
SCHEME, 197
scientific method, 250

script
>   for program construction, 124, 133
script languages, 178
scrollbars
>   in Tk, 185
SDIFF, 15–16, 340
sdiff, 16
search
>   semantic-based ∼, 347
>   syntax-based ∼, 346
>   text-based ∼, 346
SED, 72, 145
>   in AUTOCONF, 152
semantic predicates, 111
send action, 207
send, 208
SHAPE, 142, 157
shift, 95
>   ∼/reduce-conflict, 97–99
shifting, 95
shortest sequence, 21
showstopper, 239
signal, 269
SILKTEST, 220
SCM, *see* SCM
sleep, 210
slice, 21, 317
>   backbone-∼, 325
>   backward-∼, 324
>   executable ∼, 318
>   forward-∼, 323
>   intersection, 325
>   set operations, 324–326
>   union, 325
slicing criterion, 318
slicing, *see* program slicing
SMALLTALK, 197, 360
smart recompilation, 141
SNiFF+, 360
software change control board, 246
software configuration management,
>   9–10
>   in ECLIPSE, 340
>   tool, 27
software crisis, 177
software design, 177
software engineering, 177
software system, 45
source components, 123
SOURCE INTEGRITY, 340
SOURCE NAVIGATOR, 360

spawn, 208
specification, 308–314
>   and assertion, 309–310
>   with test cases, 229–231
SpecTcl, 189
spelling
>   American, 10
>   British, 10
SPLINT, 308–314
>   abstract data type, 311–312
>   Buffer overflows, 310–311
>   memory management, 312–314
SQABasic, 220
SQL, 105
>   grammar for ANTLR, 118
STABS format, 269–270
start states, 79–80
start symbol, 86
statement coverage, 291
static analysis, 301
statistic
>   in DEJAGNU, 215
statistical analysis, 316
step, 262
stop conditions
>   in GDB, 260
subpath, 30, *see also* branching
SUBVERSION, 58, 340
SUNIT, 232
SWT, 336
symbolic expressions
>   reading, 85
symbols
>   abstract, 70
syntactic predicates, 111
syntax, 67
syntax tree, 297
synthesizer generator, 360
system model, 125, *see also* Makefile
>   in ANT, *see* buildfile

taglet, 165–166, 170
tags, 163–166
TANGLE, 168
target
>   in Makefile, 125
task
>   in ANT, 137
>   in ANT, *see* task
Tcl, 72, 179–191, 194–195, 199–201
>   and LEX, 199–201

arithmetic, 180
as a prototype language, 189–191
character strings, 180
command substitution, 180
extending, 183–185
functions, 181
in EXPECT, 207
interpreter, 179
Parser, 179
user interface, *see* Tk
variables, 180
tclsh, 179, 184
TEAMTEST, 220
template
for creating variants, 144
temporary variants ∼, 155
terminal, 86
virtual ∼, 207
test, *see* system test, component test,
coverage
test case, 205
in JUNIT, 223
test coverage, *see* coverage
TEST DIRECTOR, 220
test-first approach, 230–231
tests
and problem tracking, 246–247
Testsuite, 228
TESTSUITE, 220
text window
in Tk, 185, 187–189
thread, 46
TIME, 283–284
Tk, 185–191, 199–201
buttons, 185–186
options, 186–187
regression tests, 215–218
text window, 187–189
variable, 186
tkcvs, 57
TOGETHER, 361
token, 81, 86
reading, *see* yylex
Tomita style parser, *see* GLR parser
transaction
long ∼, 60
tree structure
reading, 85, 87
tuning, 283, *see also* profiling
tutorial, 160
type

abstract ∼
in SPLINT, 311
type checking
in LINT, 301–303

UNIX
and programming tools, 3
UNRAVEL, 318–326, 329–332
control dependences, 320–321
control flow graph, 320
data dependences, 321–322
data flow analysis, 319
PDG construction, 322–323
program dependence
graph, 323
set operations, 324–326
slicing, 323–324
UNRESOLVED, 212, 250
UNSUPPORTED, 212
UNTESTED, 212
up, 263 s

VALGRIND, 273–274
validation functions, 254, 255
in the debugger, 266
variable
in MAKE
implicit, 129
in offers MAKE, 128
in Tcl, 180
in Tk, 186
variant, 27
in CLEARCASE, 39
permanent ∼, 28, 143–144
temporary ∼, 28, 30–31
variant properties
extrinsic, 149
intrinsic, 149
version, 10, 27
version archive, 28
in CVS, *see* CVS archive
in RCS, *see* RCS archive
version control
in ECLIPSE, 339–342
of problem lists, 238
of released products, 237
with BITKEEPER, 58
with CVS, 47–58
with RCS, 28, 40
with SUBVERSION, 58
versioning

extensional ∼, 60
    intensional ∼, 60
view
    in ECLIPSE, 338–339
VISUAL BASIC, 197, 220
VISUAL SOURCE SAFE, 62, 340
VISUAL TEST, 220

watch, 266
watching, 55–56
watching
    program state, 266
WEAVE, 168
WEB, 168
WebDAV, 58, 354
widget, 185
WINDOWS
    and programming tools, 3
    script ability, 218
WINRUNNER, 220
wish, 185
work space
    in CLEARCASE, 58
    in CVS, 48, 50, 53–56
    in NSE, 60
    in RCS, 28

XLOAD, 148
XMI, 354

XML
    as buildfile format, 138
XRUNNER, 220
XSLT, 233, 354
X Window System, 40, 148,
    150

YACC specification, 88–93
YACC, 85–103, 105, 119–120,
    173
    actions, 91
    and AUTOCONF, 173
    and LEX, 93–95
    and MAKE, 173–174
    auxiliary functions, 91–93
    C declarations, 89
    conflicts, 97–101
    grammar, 86–88
    mode of operation, 95–101
    precedence declarations, 100–101
    rule, 86, 90–91
    value, 91
    YACC declarations, 89
yyerror, 92
yyleng, 76
yylex, 75, 81, 92, 94–95
yylineno, 76
yyparse, 93
yytext, 76